THE ART OF REFORM IN ELEVENTH-CENTURY FLANDERS

STUDIES IN THE HISTORY OF CHRISTIAN TRADITIONS

FOUNDED BY HEIKO A. OBERMAN †

VOLUME CXXVIII

D.J. REILLY

THE ART OF REFORM IN ELEVENTH-CENTURY FLANDERS

THE ART OF REFORM IN ELEVENTH-CENTURY FLANDERS

GERARD OF CAMBRAI, RICHARD OF SAINT-VANNE AND THE SAINT-VAAST BIBLE

BY

DIANE J. REILLY

BRILL

LEIDEN · BOSTON

2006

On the cover: Arras BM MS 559 (435), vol. II, fol. 144, Saint-Vaast Bible, Wisdom

This book is printed on acid-free paper.

Library of Congress Cataloging-in-Publication Data

Reilly, Diane J.
    The art of reform in eleventh-century Flanders : Gerard of Cambrai, Richard of
Saint-Vanne, and the Saint-Vaast Bible / by Diane J. Reilly.
        p. cm. — (Studies in the history of Christian traditions, ISSN 1573-5664 ; v. 128)
    Includes bibliographical references and index.
    ISBN 90-04-15097-8 (hardback : alk. paper)
        1. Saint-Vaast Bible. 2. Illumination of books and manuscripts—Flanders. 3.
Illumination of books and manuscripts, Romanesque—Flanders. 4. Monasticism and
religious orders—Flanders—History—Middle Ages, 600-1500. I. Title. II. Series.

ND3355.5.S32R45 2006
741.6'7094428—dc22

                                                                                    2005058251

ISSN   1573-5664
ISBN-13: 978-90-04-15097-3
ISBN-10: 90-04-15097-8

PRINTED IN THE NETHERLANDS

For Ian

CONTENTS

LIST OF PLATES

LIST OF FIGURES

ACKNOWLEDGEMENTS

This project grew out of my dissertation, completed at the University of Toronto under the direction of Robert Deshman, and after his untimely death in 1995, Luba Eleen. I am eternally grateful to both of them for the grounding they gave me in research and academic writing. Elizabeth MacLachlan, my first professor of Medieval Art at Rutgers University and the supervisor of my undergraduate thesis on a manuscript in the Princeton University collection, instilled in me an enduring fascination with the life of medieval manuscripts.

This research was undertaken in part during the term of a Social Sciences and Humanities Research Council of Canada Doctoral Fellowship. A Neil Ker Memorial Fellowship from the British Academy allowed a trip to France and England in the summer of 2000 to explore related issues, as did a Heckman Stipend to the Hill Monastic Manuscript Library at St. John's University in 1999. A Summer Faculty Fellowship from Indiana University funded a further period of writing. The final revisions of the manuscript were completed during the term of an Andrew W. Mellon Foundation Post-Doctoral Fellowship at the Pontifical Institute of Mediaeval Studies in Toronto, during the academic year 2004–2005. A Grant-in-Aid of Research and Scholarly Activity from Indiana University funded the final preparation of the typescript, photographs and index and provided a subvention for the color plates. I am grateful to all of these institutions.

During this time I have consulted the resources of more libraries than I could count, and taxed the patience and strength of numerous librarians and archivists. I would like to thank especially Mme. Normand-Chanteloup and M. Pascal Rideau of the Mediathèque d'Arras for their constant help over the course of four summers. In North America, I am particularly grateful to Father James Farge, Director of the Pontifical Institute Library, and his assistant, Caroline Suma, B. J. Irvine, Director of the Fine Art Library at Indiana University, Adelaide Bennett and the Index of Christian Art at Princeton University, and Celestina Wroth, Area Librarian for Medieval Studies at the Herman B. Wells Library at Indiana University.

Plates I–X, and figures 1–26, 29–36, photographed by the author, are reproduced courtesy of the Mediathèque d'Arras (Plates I–X,

figures 1–25, 29, 35 and 36), the Bibliothèque municipale de Boulogne (figure 26, 30, 33 and 34), and the Bibliothèque municipale de Douai (figures 31 and 32). Figures 27 and 43 are reproduced with the permission of the British Library. Figures 28, 37–39, 42 and 44 are reproduced with the permission of the Bibliothèque nationale de France. Figure 40 is reproduced with the permission of Aachen Cathedral, while figure 41 is reproduced with the permission of Pierre-Alain Mariaux. Finally, figure 46 is reproduced with the permission of the Biblioteca Apostolica Vaticana.

A series of colleagues have listened to many incarnations of various arguments in this book, read smaller component studies with unflagging good humor, and offered welcome critiques and advice. These include Susan Boynton, Isabelle Cochelin, Adam Cohen, Richard Gameson, Jeffrey Hamburger, Frank Henderson, Daniel Hobbins, Ethan Matt Kavaler, Carolyn Malone, Vasileios Marinis, Lawrence Nees, Glenn Peers, Karine Ugé and Yolanta Zaluska. John Ott and Herbert Kessler read large portions of the manuscript and offered invaluable criticism. Peter Sutton skillfully refined many of the Latin translations and Daniel Hobbins offered invaluable help with others.

Holly Silvers copy-edited the entire manuscript and compiled the index, both thankless and exacting tasks that she completed admirably. I have also benefited from the constant support of several colleagues at Indiana University, including my departmental chairs at the Hope School of Fine Art, first Bruce Cole and then Janet Kennedy, faculty mentor Leah Shopkow, and departmental colleagues Deborah Deliyannis, Michelle Facos, Gene Kleinbauer and Julie Van Voorhis.

Finally, I must thank my husband, Giles Knox, also a departmental colleague, who read almost every word of both this book and the dissertation that preceded it, sometimes more than once, and still managed to offer constructive advice and support at every step. This book would not have been completed without his help.

LIST OF ABBREVIATIONS

BAV	Biblioteca Apostolica Vaticana
BL	British Library
BM	Bibliothèque Municipale
BnF	Bibliothèque nationale de France
Catalogue général	*Catalogue général des manuscrits des bibliothèques publiques des départements*, in 4° (Paris, 1849–1885), 7 vols., continued as *Catalogue général des manuscrits des bibliothèques publiques de France*, Départements, in 8° (Paris, 1885–1904), 62 vols.
CCM	Kassius Hallinger, ed., *Corpus consuetudinum monasticarum*, 14 vols. (Siegburg, 1963–1996).
CSEL	*Corpus scriptorum ecclesiasticorum Latinorum*
MGH	Monumenta Germaniae Historica
Epist.	Epistolae
SS	Scriptores
Les ordines romani	Michel Andrieu, *Les ordines romani du haut moyen âge*, Spicilegium sacrum Lovaniense; Études et documents, fasc. 11, 23–24, 28–29 (Louvain, 1931–1961).
PL	*Patrologiae cursus completus, sive biblioteca universalis, integra, uniformis, commoda, oeconomica, omnium ss. patrum* . . . (Series Latina), ed. J. P. Migne, 221 vols. (Paris, 1844–1904).
SSCISAM	*Settimane di studio del centro italiano di studi sull'alto medioevo*, Centro italiano di studi sull'alto medioevo (Spoleto, 1953+)

Biblical quotations in English are taken from the Douay-Rheims translation of the Latin Vulgate, with the exception that names of persons and places have been changed to accord with the Revised Standard Version of 1952.

INTRODUCTION

It may come as a surprise to scholars of Romanesque manuscripts that the early eleventh-century Saint-Vaast Bible, today preserved in the Bibliothèque municipale in Arras, has never before been the subject of a book-length study. Included in all surveys of French or Romanesque manuscripts, and many other more general books besides, the Bible is famous for its quirky illustrations of books such as the Song of Songs and Ecclesiasticus. Writers frequently repeat the same few observations about it: that the Bible is the earliest surviving illustrated Giant Bible produced in Northern Europe, and that several of its initials introduce themes that would appear hundreds of times thereafter in Bibles. Nonetheless, the illustrative program of the Bible, its context, and its patronage have never been studied as a whole. The Saint-Vaast Bible has fallen victim to a series of prejudices among historians and art historians that have discouraged scholars from exploring its wealth of decoration and setting it within its historical, social, and religious context.

Firstly, the Bible was produced not in the heart of Capetian France or Ottonian Germany but instead on the borderland between these two realms, near the Scheldt River in what was then the County of Flanders. Thus it cannot easily be termed either "French" or "German," and, despite the overwhelmingly political nature of its imagery, cannot automatically be assigned to the patrimony of either of these then nascent countries. Secondly, art historians have generally dismissed the art of early eleventh-century northwestern Europe as suffering from the lingering effects of the Norman invasions. The royally patronized abbeys of the Ottonians were producing lavishly painted and gilded manuscripts that broadcast the close ties between the emperors and their Church. Anglo-Saxon monasteries across the Channel were perfecting the exuberant "Winchester" style in manuscript art, ornamenting newly reformed liturgical books. The early eleventh century in southern Europe is universally acknowledged as an era of architectural ferment, when towering churches sporting innovative forms of vaulting sprang up across the landscape of southern France, northern Italy and Spain. Northern monasteries so recently assaulted by marauding tribes, on the other hand, had little energy

to devote to elaborate artwork, much less architecture to rival the churches of Lombardy and the Pyrenees. The Saint-Vaast Bible and its contemporaries thus represent a period of early growth, rather than a later flowering. Finally, both phenomena have contributed not only to the neglect of the few strikingly sumptuous artworks that were created, like the Saint-Vaast Bible, but to the tendency to label those that do survive as awkward, provincial, and derivative.

I believe, on the contrary, that the abbey of Saint-Vaast's location on the periphery of two kingdoms made it a flashpoint for confrontations between leaders and clerics attempting to defend their realms and their ideologies. As has already been demonstrated for other eras and places, art was one of the most powerful tools in medieval campaigns to enhance the prestige of office and office-holders. The Arras Bible should be seen as the preeminent tool of its creators in the construction of the political and theological identity of the monastery of Saint-Vaast and the diocese of Arras-Cambrai. In addition, the Bible was created to answer the needs of a newly reformed monastic environment. Saint-Vaast, in the County of Flanders, became the nexus between an enormous web of reformed monasteries that reached deep into Lotharingia, France, and Ottonian Germany. The leaders of the monastery and the diocese wielded a well-recognized influence over the inhabitants of the entire region. The success of this particular reform speaks volumes about the political problems and beliefs of the clerics who dominated this boundary area.

Finally, the Bible's style, which borrows both from the art of the, by then, defunct Carolingian dynasty, and from the contemporary Anglo-Saxons across the Channel, does not demonstrate that the monks of Arras inhabited an artistic vacuum. Rather it shows that the artists of the Bible knowingly absorbed the aesthetic vocabulary identified with rulers whom they regarded as models, and incorporated these motifs into a new product meant to advertise the aspirations and beliefs of the Bible's patrons. Adding to this potent mixture of iconography from Carolingian and Ottonian artworks, the artists were able to craft a message that would have been easily understood by educated contemporary viewers.

These factors make the Saint-Vaast Bible an ideal candidate for a dedicated study. As the most lavish manuscript produced in early eleventh-century Flanders, and one, as will be shown below, that would have been handled and seen every day in the most prominent

monastery of the region, the Arras Bible's picture program had the ability to make a powerful and far-reaching statement. Although it is one of the few artworks to survive from early eleventh-century Flanders, we can already hypothesize that even when it was copied and decorated it would have been the single most important artistic undertaking in the region at that time. Additionally, the manuscript's manufacture can be framed by a stunning collection of documents. The records of a contemporary trial of heretics in Arras conducted by the local bishop, the chronicle and correspondence of that same bishop compiled over many years, and the cathedral's Pontifical, copied at Saint-Vaast, all survive. This is an almost unprecedented richness of historical material for the period, giving us access not just to the events that took place in early eleventh-century Arras, but also to the statements of prominent personalities and the spiritual life of the diocese.

I will begin by tracing the hands of the artists employed in the early eleventh-century Saint-Vaast scriptorium and their stylistic inspirations. A group of at least three different artists working at the same time all contributed to the Bible's program, sometimes even cooperating to draft a particularly complex composition. The artists began their project with a group of artistic models at their disposal, and selectively mined them according to their personal tastes and the demands of the text they chose to illustrate. They produced an eclectic and rather uneven series of miniatures that nonetheless presents a coherent message that must have been designed by and for specific clergymen.

I will then explore two themes in particular. I am especially interested in the ways in which art was used as an instrument employed by the elite, especially royal families and their image-makers in the Church, to shape the perceptions of contemporaries. The Saint-Vaast Bible is a rich source for this type of exploration, as it appeared between two well-known flowerings of political art, the Carolingian and later Capetian eras, and contemporary with the wealth of art commissioned for and from the Church by Anglo-Saxon and Ottonian rulers. My second theme will revolve around the relationship between the Saint-Vaast Bible and its reform context, which itself was intimately connected with the power structure that dominated Arras and Flanders. Following in the footsteps of their Carolingian ancestors, the leaders of early eleventh-century Northern Europe bound their fortunes to those of powerful monastic reformers such as Odilo

of Cluny and Richard of Saint-Vanne, choosing to patronize reforms
and reformers that complemented their own interests.

Recently we have witnessed a flurry of writing about the function
of art in the construction of European monarchical power, either of
a dynasty or of a single ruler. In England and France especially,
where monarchies grew strong in the thirteenth and fourteenth centuries, the rulers and their church were equally invested in the type
of office that developed. Although any artistic, or even architectural,
medium could transmit the ideology of the State, manuscripts were
among the most frequently chosen objects for this end. The works
of seven art historians have set the stage for my study. Herbert
Kessler and Paul Dutton, Daniel Weiss, Paul Binski, and Peter Burke
have explored how medieval and early modern art contributed to
broader campaigns to shape the popular view of leaders and leadership. Adam Cohen and Robert Deshman have investigated the
role of lavish manuscripts in the reforms that remade the monasteries that produced them. Studying either single monuments or
groups of artworks commissioned over the course of years, they have
shown that these techniques were well known centuries before artists
put pen to parchment in Arras, and continued to be employed in
the centuries that followed.

In the Middle Ages, when the vast majority of artworks were
Christian in iconography and intended to be used in a religious context, they nonetheless could contain powerful political messages. Paul
Dutton and Herbert Kessler, *The Poetry and Politics of the First Bible of
Charles the Bald* (Ann Arbor, 1997) used the visual and written program of a single Bible to explore how an artwork could express the
patrons' interpretation of the Carolingian emperor's role and responsibilities to the Church and to the clerical bureaucrats on whom they
relied.[1] This Bible, commissioned for King Charles and produced by
the scriptorium of Saint Martin at Tours, was presented to the king
as a didactic tool and display volume composed by Audradus Modicus,
a canon of the monastery who recorded his political visions in his
Book of Revelations.[2] Thus already in the ninth century, artists in a
monastic scriptorium participated in a campaign to imagine the role

---

[1] Paul Dutton and Herbert Kessler, *The Poetry and Politics of the First Bible of Charles
the Bald* (Ann Arbor, 1997), 91.
[2] Dutton and Kessler, 11–19.

of the king in Christian society by depicting it in an artwork addressed both to him and to the members of his court.

The same techniques were used many centuries later in both England and France. Paul Binski, in *Westminster Abbey and the Plantagenets. Kingship and the Representation of Power 1200–1400* (New Haven, 1995), examined a patron, Henry III, and his involvement with one monument, Westminster Abbey, in his attempt to link it with the hopes and self-imaging of a family. In his words, "At work in the patronage of Westminster Abbey was, I believe, a somewhat deeper and more specialized process in the formation of the English royal state: the process whereby the state, the government, and the persona and mythology of the king, obtained a location."[3] Absolutely essential to this process was the cooperation of the Benedictines of the abbey, who acted as bureaucrats for the dynasty and contributed to this image-making.

A very similar chain of events occurred under the thirteenth-century Capetian king Louis IX. Daniel Weiss, in *Art and Crusade in the Age of Saint Louis* (Cambridge, 1998), combined examinations of two important Capetian monuments, the Sainte-Chapelle in Paris and the Arsenal Old Testament, copied and illustrated in the Holy Land scriptorium of Saint-Jean d'Acre. He showed that from the capital of the Capetian kingdom to its farthest reaches, the art of the Church was used to construct what has been called 'the religion of monarchy.'[4] In Weiss's words, art was used as part of a campaign to build the royal persona, wherein the "Christian populace is united under the authority of a divinely chosen secular and religious ruler . . . Religious symbolism, revitalized by new objectives and expressive opportunities, was being placed squarely within the political sphere."[5]

This tactic was not abandoned with the death of Saint Louis and the waning of the Capetian empire. Peter Burke, in *The Fabrication of Louis XIV* (New Haven, 1992), studied the construction of the king's image as the Sun King by both the king himself and his

---

[3] Paul Binski, *Westminster Abbey and the Plantagenets. Kingship and the Representation of Power 1200–1400* (New Haven, 1995), 4.

[4] Daniel Weiss, *Art and Crusade in the Age of Saint Louis* (Cambridge, 1998), 7, after Joseph Strayer, "France: The Holy Land, the Chosen People, and the most Christian King," in *Medieval Statecraft and the Perspectives of History* (Princeton, 1971), 300–314.

[5] Weiss, *Art and Crusade*, 7.

advisors, among whom were numbered prominent churchmen. Propagandists used all media to transmit an impression of glory and magnificence intended to impress subjects and foreigners alike. In Louis's case, although the king's rule was still, by nature, Christian, the iconography employed by his image-builders had ceased to be overtly Christian in its content. The stray Christian image does survive, however, such as a painting of Louis XIV as the Good Shepherd, possibly by Pierre Paul Sevin.[6]

Because records of Louis XIV's court ceremonial, artistic commissions, correspondence and the artworks themselves all survive, it is much easier to document how Louis and his contemporaries orchestrated every aspect of the king's day to day life in order to awe his observers, than it is to undertake a similar task for a medieval leader. In addition, the program to illustrate the Saint-Vaast Bible was initiated in a time and place where no single ruler clearly dominated. The picture we can paint of the loyalties displayed in its miniature cycle is murkier. One dynasty, the Carolingians, had recently and with great controversy been supplanted. The successors, the Capetians, were just beginning to stand firmly on their own feet, and had only the loosest grasp on the County of Flanders. A third dynasty, the Ottonians, at this time saw their power in the region waning. All three of these dynasties, however, relied heavily on the Church for bureaucracy and support, and especially as proponents and designers of the royal image. Not only were these rulers pictured with their clerical supporters, the monks and bishops themselves composed the propaganda, in both words and images, that elevated the rulers on whom they relied for the defense of the rights and goods of the Church.

The Saint-Vaast Bible, although it draws on the artistic heritage of these dynasties, differs from their artworks because its illustrations do not elevate an individual ruler, King Robert the Pious or Emperor Henry II. Instead it contains a visual panegyric to two powerful offices, that of the King and the Bishop. As I will demonstrate below, the artists borrowed from Carolingian, Ottonian and Anglo-Saxon art the iconography of the divine origin of both offices, crafting a defense of their authority in the face of the threat posed by Count Baldwin IV of Flanders and minor nobles in his employ. Although

---

[6] Peter Burke, *The Fabrication of Louis XIV* (New Haven, 1992), 29, fig. 11.

the artists did not portray any historical rulers, they did depict biblical prototypes for kings and bishops that could themselves serve as
models for contemporary secular and ecclesiastical leaders. This more
generic program also strongly transmits the ideology of its context,
the newly reformed house of Saint-Vaast.

Adam Cohen, in *The Uta Codex: Art, Philosophy and Reform in Eleventh-
Century Germany* (Penn State Press, 2000), has already revealed how
the illustrative program of a manuscript can make manifest a reform
then taking over the monastery that produced it. He suggested that
the ideology of the monastery's leader, abbess Uta of Niedermünster,
and her theological advisor, the monk Hartwic of St. Emmeram,
was expressed in the pictorial program of a seemingly standard text,
the Gospel lectionary. Like the reform that was visited upon Saint-
Vaast, Uta's reform of Niedermünster was in part forwarded by the
cooperative efforts of the local secular ruler, in this case Duke Henry
of Bavaria, and the bishop, Wolfgang of Regensburg.[7] Another study,
Robert Deshman's *The Benedictional of Aethelwold* (Princeton, 1995),
pursued the same end in that it examined a manuscript of a standard genre, a benedictional, with an extraordinarily rich cycle of
images, and in the process identified the hand of a single reforming
mind. This benedictional was drafted to accompany the Anglo-Saxon
reform of the monastic liturgy initiated with Aethelwold's *Regularis
Concordia*, again, a reform that was dependent on royal support.[8] Both
the late tenth-century Benedictional of Aethelwold and the early
eleventh-century Uta Codex are nearly contemporary with the Saint-
Vaast Bible and produced in very similar contexts. The artists of the
Uta Codex and the Benedictional of Aethelwold, like those of the
Saint-Vaast Bible, drew on sources from previous and contemporary
dynasties during their inventive process.

One of the most challenging questions for students of manuscripts
of the central Middle Ages addresses the issue of audience. The manuscripts surveyed above, including the Uta Codex, the Benedictional
of Aethelwold, and the First Bible of Charles the Bald are all easily
identifiable types of books: a Gospel lectionary, a benedictional, a
Bible. Yet the messages encoded in their imagery could be addressed

---

[7] Adam S. Cohen, *The Uta Codex: Art, Philosophy and Reform in Eleventh-Century
Germany* (Penn State Press, 2000), 17.
[8] Robert Deshman, *The Benedictional of Aethelwold*, Studies in Manuscript Illumination
IX (Princeton, 1995), 252.

both to those who would use these books in a liturgical service and those who were given the books or even would have seen them only occasionally. Both Cohen and Richard Gameson have explored this point. As Gameson stated, "The fact that certain images in late Anglo-Saxon manuscripts can be shown to correspond to practices and beliefs that are articulated in the literature of the monastic church by no means excludes the nobility from the possession of such volumes and the contemplation of such pictures. Nor, incidentally, does it prove all monks to have used them in the way in question."[9] Cohen, as well, investigates how the images within a manuscript can be seen and understood by a variety of diverse audiences. Simply because a manuscript was copied primarily to serve as a tool for liturgy or the monastic office does not prevent it containing a message intended for a wider clientele. The most lavish manuscript of any foundation was undoubtedly displayed to all the important visitors who passed through its gates. A book that took over a generation to copy and illustrate must have included a program that was not simply copied by rote but rather composed by the more important thinkers of the monastery with a great deal of consideration. The Saint-Vaast Bible was this type of manuscript.

Like the other dynastic monuments that have recently grabbed the scholarly spotlight, the Saint-Vaast Bible expresses its environment as much as it does the beliefs of a single secular or religious leader. The city of Arras was one of the cultural and religious capitals of Southern Flanders at the beginning of the eleventh century, while the County of Flanders was constantly exposed to outside influences because it lay on the most commonly used route between England and Italy. Between the mid-tenth century and the end of the twelfth century, the port of Wissant on the north-west coast was the chief embarkation point for journeys to and from England. From there the main road south passed through St. Omer, Arras and Cambrai and led eventually to Rome.[10]

In addition, the diocese of Arras-Cambrai was at that time led by one of the most powerful bishops in the archdiocese of Reims, a man who held sway in not one, but two royal courts. Because of

---

[9] Richard Gameson, *The Role of Art in the Late Anglo-Saxon Church* (Oxford, 1995), 252.

[10] Philip Grierson, "The Relations between England and France before the Norman Conquest," *Transactions of the Royal Historical Society* XXIII (1941), 80–81.

the division of his diocese between two realms, Gerard of Cambrai (c. 980–1051), Bishop of Arras-Cambrai from 1012 to 1051, was put in the unusual and delicate position of being subject to both the Holy Roman Emperor and the Capetian King of France. The Treaty of Verdun in 843 had established the frontier at the Scheldt, or Escaut, river between what later became the County of Flanders, under French domination, and the realm of Lotharingia, which fell under the Holy Roman Empire. This river runs through Cambrai, and on its west bank began the County of Flanders, in which Arras was situated. Until 1094, when Arras was again consecrated an independent bishopric, the diocese of Arras-Cambrai therefore bridged two realms, the city of Arras lying in Capetian Flanders, and the city of Cambrai in Ottonian Lotharingia.

Gerard of Cambrai managed to maintain good relations with both Robert II the Pious, the Capetian king of France, and Emperor Henry II, and even acted as a negotiator between them, yet he remained a vassal of the Empire as the Count of Cambrai. The political ideology developed by Gerard to cope with his unusual and highly sensitive situation must have inspired the program focusing on secular and ecclesiastical rulership in the Saint-Vaast Bible. Its series of narrative images of Old Testament kings, patriarchs and prophets sets up a typology of Christological kingship by emphasizing the divine origin of kingship as an institution, and the virtues of the successful king. In addition, the Bible's miniature cycle underlines that the division between ecclesiastical and secular rule originated in the Old Testament, where church and state leaders cooperated to lead the Chosen People. In the New Testament, Christ founded the Christian church and transferred the role of religious leader to the bishops, who, like kings, ruled in his image. Faced with the twin threats of a weakened royal dynasty that allowed powerful nobles and churchmen to trespass on the divine right of kings, and a surge in monastic reform movements that removed moral and administrative authority from the bishops, the author of this program hoped to shore up the traditional powers of both.

Another closely related series of images in the Saint-Vaast Bible was intended to set out an image of ideal queenship. Again using a series of Old Testament prototypes, the illustrators attempted to explain appropriate queenly behavior while stressing that the role of the queen was subsidiary to that of her husband, the king. The Bible's program restricts the functions of the queen to intercessor for

the Church, educator of royal heirs, and virtuous ornament and consort to her husband.

Furthermore, yet another historical event contemporary with the reemergence of the scriptorium at Arras may have affected the Bible's program of illustration. In 1025, Arras was shaken by one of the most famous incidents of heresy in the early eleventh century. A description of the synod convened by Bishop Gerard to deal with the heresy has been preserved, and gives evidence not only of the beliefs of the heretics, but also of Gerard's own attitudes toward ecclesiastical office. Seizing the opportunity to defend orthodoxy, Gerard accused the heretics of having rejected the hierarchy of the church, as well as the sacraments and the greater part of the Bible.[11] The memories of this heresy may have caused a Saint-Vaast artist to return to the Bible at a later stage to add the elaborate miniature prefacing Ecclesiasticus to the Saint-Vaast Bible's program.

Finally, the codicology of the Bible and the contents of its pictorial program make it a particularly important specimen for understanding the genesis of Romanesque Bible production. Scholars have long recognized the originality of the giant luxury Romanesque Bibles. Full Bibles were seldom produced in the pre-Romanesque era because they were too big to copy and carry around the monastery conveniently. Instead, scribes tended to copy only single books of the Bible or small groups of books, such as the Pentateuch, the Psalter, the Gospels, the Apocalypse or the Wisdom books. Nonetheless, many older monasteries still possessed Bibles made in the only earlier flowering of large-format Bible production, which coincided with the reforms of Charlemagne and the correction of the biblical text undertaken by Alcuin.[12] The most famous Bibles from this period, the ninth-century Tours Bibles, such as the Grandval Bible (London BL

---

[11] For a brief discussion of this heresy, see Robert I. Moore, *The Birth of Popular Heresy* (London, 1975), 15–20, or Jeffrey Burton Russel, *Dissent and Reform in the Early Middle Ages* (Los Angeles, 1965), 21–26. Peter Brieger has already drawn a connection between heresy and the Saint-Vaast Bible ("Bible Illustration and Gregorian Reform," in *Studies in Church History* II [1965], 154–164).

[12] For the most recent bibliography, see David Ganz, "Mass Production of Early Medieval Manuscripts: The Carolingian Bibles from Tours," in *The Early Medieval Bible: Its production, decoration and use*, ed. Richard Gameson (Cambridge, 1994), 53–62, and Rosamund McKitterick, "Carolingian Bible Production: The Tours Anomaly," in *The Early Medieval Bible*, 63–77. Also Dutton and Kessler, *The Poetry and Painting of the First Bible of Charles the Bald*.

Add 10546) and the First Bible of Charles the Bald (Paris BnF MS lat. 1), are well known to scholars for their cycles of whole-page scenes and a few historiated initials.

Despite the examples of older Bibles that still existed, and the expense and inconvenience involved in copying such big manuscripts, for reasons that have never been fully explained, in the eleventh and twelfth centuries monastic scriptoria renewed the practice of producing large-scale illustrated Bibles. Although the later Romanesque boom in Bible production has been associated, especially in the work of Peter Brieger, with the reform of the Church undertaken by Pope Gregory VII in the late eleventh century, the Saint-Vaast Bible was produced as much as fifty years before this reform. Walter Cahn and Larry Ayers have suggested that monastic reform movements preceding the broader church movement of Gregory could have provided the inspiration for the production of such Bibles.[13] Thus, although a Church-wide push to produce such Bibles may have occurred in the late eleventh-century, the Saint-Vaast Bible and Bibles close to it furnish some of our best proof that at least fifty years earlier the copying of Bibles was a standard component of monastic reform programs.

Richard of Saint-Vanne (d. 1046) dominated religious life in the diocese of Arras-Cambrai in the early eleventh century. Called to the diocese as abbot of Saint-Vaast in 1008 from his home abbey in Verdun by Bishop Gerard of Cambrai's predecessor, Erluinus, Richard reformed the abbey of Saint-Vaast, and then, in cooperation with Gerard, used Saint-Vaast as a base to reform monasteries throughout the diocese.[14] His disciples Leduinus and Poppo of Stavelot carried this reform even further afield, so that it dominated northern France and Flanders until the advent of the Cluniac reform in the region at the end of the eleventh century. The Saint-Vaast Bible was copied and decorated there during the abbacy of Leduinus. This reform movement's model of cooperation between episcopal and

---

[13] Brieger, 161–164, and doubts expressed by François Masai in his review of Brieger's article in "Bulletin codicologique," *Scriptorium* XXI (1968), 102–103. Walter Cahn, *Romanesque Bible Illustration* (Ithaca, 1982), 95–102.

[14] Only one monograph on Richard of Saint-Vanne has been published: Hubert Dauphin, *Le bienheureux Richard, abbé de Saint-Vanne de Verdun, 1046* (Louvain, 1946). Richard's reform has been analyzed in other contexts, particularly in studies of Cluniac monasticism of the eleventh century. See chapter two, note 49.

abbatial authority helped to mold the Saint-Vaast Bible's pictorial program.

Also, although significant damage to the Saint-Vaast Bible immediately after the French Revolution makes a detailed codicological survey of the manuscript difficult, it is clear that the Bible never included either the books of the Gospels or the Psalter (Appendix).[15] This is also true of several other Giant Bibles copied and illustrated either at monasteries reformed by Richard of Saint-Vanne and his followers or at a cathedral under his strong influence. These and other codicological characteristics of the Saint-Vaast Bible make it a member of a recognizable group of Flemish Bibles, and reveal the intended function of these Bibles as tools for daily refectory and choir reading within the reformed monasteries where they were produced.

The Saint-Vaast Bible's decorative style and iconography provide an invaluable window into life inside a newly reformed eleventh-century monastery and a vibrant document of the political outlook of its leaders. A first step to unlocking the meaning of the Saint-Vaast Bible's program will be to survey the history of Arras and examine the decorative vocabulary used by its artists, in chapter 1.

---

[15] See Appendix 1, note 1, for a discussion of the damage to the manuscript.

CHAPTER ONE

THE SAINT-VAAST BIBLE AND MEDIEVAL ARRAS

The Saint-Vaast Bible, Arras BM MS 559 (435), has perplexed scholars because there is no precedent for a work of this intricacy and
lavishness surviving from the earlier Carolingian scriptorium of Saint-
Vaast, and no contemporary Bible from northern Europe offers as
complex a program. The Saint-Vaast Bible stands alone in its period
and its region. When the monastery of Saint-Vaast produced this
enormous three-volume Bible during the first half of the eleventh
century, Arras, in the County of Flanders, was still recovering from
its recent nadir during the Norman invasions. Nonetheless, the monks
of the Saint-Vaast scriptorium aspired to ornament it with a series
of full-page frames enclosing decorative initials, and an elaborate
program of twenty-four figural scenes illustrating many parts of the
Old and New Testaments.

Just as confusing is the Bible's unorthodox collection of imagery
and inharmonious jumble of styles. A quick glance over both could
leave the viewer with the impression that the artists, faced with a
dearth of illustrated manuscripts from which to copy, adapted what
few resources they had and created an amalgam of decorative motifs
and figural scenes that reflected the poverty of their workshop rather
than the choices made by a guiding director.

The general type of decoration found in the Saint-Vaast Bible is
far from unique. Like some of the Carolingian Bibles of the previous era and the Romanesque Bibles to follow, the Saint-Vaast Bible
is illuminated with a combination of narrative scenes and author
portraits prefacing the individual books of the Bible (Appendix). If
the genres of illustration found here are relatively standard for a
Carolingian or Romanesque illustrated Bible, however, the selection
of books with figural imagery is in many cases unusual and surprising. Narrative scenes are found before the Books of Deuteronomy,
Joshua, III Kings, IV Kings, II Chronicles, Jeremiah, Ezekiel, Nahum,
the Song of Solomon, Ecclesiasticus, Ezra, Esther, II Maccabees, the
Passion of the Maccabees, Paul's Epistle to the Colossians, I Peter,
the Epistle of John, and Acts. Author portraits appear before Habbakuk,

Wisdom, Tobit, Paul's Epistle to Philemon, and II Peter.[1] Not only
are books which had received narrative imagery in the earlier
Carolingian Bibles now bare of figural illustration,[2] but also opening books of sets, such as the First Book of Kings, go without illustrations while subsequent books in the series are embellished with
elaborate narrative scenes.[3] For instance, the Books of Genesis and
Exodus, favored with illustrations by the Carolingian artists of the
Tours Bibles and San Paolo Bible, are in the Saint-Vaast Bible introduced only with framed full-page initials. Instead, the first extensive
figural illustrations of the Bible crown the two folios opening the
Book of Deuteronomy, vol. I, fols. 53v–54 (figs. 2 and 3). Similarly,
the opening folio of I Chronicles, vol. I, fol. 158, lacks figural decoration, while that of II Chronicles, fol. 170 (fig. 7 and pl. III), features a quatrefoil frame enclosing a two-tier narrative scene. In the
same vein, while the beginning of the First Book of Maccabees, vol.
III, fol. 52v, is decorated with only a framed double initial, the
Second Book of Maccabees and the pseudepigraphical Passion of the
Maccabees are both graced with full-page figural images, fols. 70v
and 81v (fig. 17 and pl. IX).

It is tempting to attribute the seemingly scattered and inconsistent
nature of this collection of images to either lack of planning or later
damage to the manuscript. The repeated absence of 'first' book illustrations could suggest that a knowledgeable thief excised the most
common and saleable miniatures, leaving behind those that would
have been less recognizable, and therefore less valuable, to the layper-
son. A careful examination of the Bible quickly reveals that this cannot be the case. In only a handful of instances have the first folios
of a biblical book been lost, indicating that the introductory deco-

---

[1] Narrative illustrations and author portraits have been reproduced in the figures
in the order in which they would have been encountered by a viewer paging through
the manuscripts from beginning to end.

[2] Carolingian Bibles, including the Grandval Bible, London BL MS Add. 10546,
the Vivian Bible, Paris BnF MS lat. 1, the Bamberg Bible, Staatsbibliothek Misc.
class. Bibl. 1, and the San Paolo Bible, Rome, San Paolo fuori le mura, were illustrated with a varying selection of narrative images, which could include illuminations prefacing the books of Genesis, Exodus, and Psalms, the Pauline Epistles, and
the Apocalypse, among others.

[3] I Kings, vol. I, fol. 97v, marked only by a framed initial and two crouching
atlas figures, is followed by a two-register illustration before III Kings, fol. 128v,
and a second two-register image before IV Kings, fol. 144v.

ration of almost all the books is as complete today as when the Bible was originally illustrated.[4]

My investigation of the content and meaning of the images has revealed that the choice of books embellished with narrative paintings was guided not by happenstance, but by a programmer intent on elaborating a complex political agenda within the illuminations of the Bible. The artists did not attempt to illustrate every book of the Saint-Vaast Bible, or to conform to the choices made within its closest models, the Carolingian Tours Bibles. Instead, the programmer selected books for illustration based on their ability to transmit the concept of the divine authority of ecclesiastical and secular rulership as it was set out in the text of the Old Testament. The desire to depict virtuous kings, queens, and clergy and the biblical precedents for the cooperation between Church and State guided the construction of the picture cycle. Using decorative motifs, iconography and narrative techniques inspired by Carolingian, Anglo-Saxon, Ottonian and even Byzantine art, the artists at Saint-Vaast in Arras expressed political and reform ideas pictorially within the, according to Carolingian tradition, authoritative setting of a Bible.

Medieval Arras

The city of Arras today retains not even a shadow of its former importance from the high Middle Ages and Renaissance. To a modern visitor, it is hard to imagine how this environment could have elicited the powerful statement of political and reform ideology displayed in the Saint-Vaast Bible. From the Roman period onward, however, the city's geographical location near a busy waterway and on the road between the English Channel and Rome made it an important strategic and mercantile center. In the Middle Ages Arras became a spiritual destination as well. Finally, in the Renaissance its manufacture of textiles was so well known that the term 'arras' was used to refer to tapestries. By the early twentieth century, however, Arras had begun to shrink. The depredations of World War I, when

---

[4] The introductory initial of the following books seems to have been lost: Numbers, Judges, Ruth, Isaiah, Job, the Epistle of Jacob and the Apocalypse. See the Appendix, a catalogue of the Saint-Vaast Bible.

it was heavily shelled, reduced the city to a quiet provincial town. Today it is visited only occasionally by tourists coming either to see its two striking seventeenth-century scroll-gabled market squares, or to visit the World War I battle sites and cemeteries that dot the surrounding countryside.

Nemetacum, as the Romans called Arras, existed as a city by the second century A.D., when it was cited in Ptolemy's *Geography*.[5] Situated on a broad plain south of the Scarpe river, the city has always straddled the minor, and now mostly covered, Crinchon river, with the population's center of gravity shifting back and forth across the river according to which spiritual or governmental institutions were in ascendancy. In the Roman era, when Arras was one of the principal cities of Northern Gaul,[6] settlement was centered west of the Crinchon, a section later called la Cité and dominated by the now destroyed cathedral, Notre Dame.[7] Already by the late imperial period the water supplied by the Crinchon had allowed Arras to become a center of commerce, known throughout the Roman world for its production of textiles, called in antique texts *atrebates birri*.[8] At the end of the fourth century A.D., *Nemetacum* was renamed *Atrebates*, after the Belgic tribe that predominated in the area.[9] Finally, the Salian Franks arrived in the region between 445 and 451, effectively ending Roman domination.[10]

---

[5] Alain Jacques et al., *Histoire d'Arras*, ed. Pierre Bougard, Yves-Marie Hilaire and Alain Nolibos (Arras, 1988), 16.

[6] Jacques, *Histoire*, 12–13. Caesar describes in the *Gallic Wars* his confrontation with the *Atrebates* in 57 B.C., a Belgic tribe that had invaded the Scarpe river valley between the fourth and second centuries B.C. *Libri IV de bello Gallico*, ed. Renatus Du Pontet (Oxford, 1900), book II:4. Pierre Pierrard, *Histoire du Nord: Flandre-Artois-Hainaut-Picardie* (Paris, 1978), 26. Also, Janine Desmulliez and Ludo Milis, *Histoire des provinces Françaises du Nord; 1. De la préhistoire à l'an mil*, Westhoek-Editions (1988), 34–45. In his efforts to conquer this area, Caesar settled troops at *Nemetocenna* in c. 51 (*De Bello Gallico*, book VIII:46, 52). This encampment may have been set up at the joining of the routes to Amiens, Therouanne and Cambrai, where Arras is today, at a hypothetical Celtic settlement called by the Romans *Nemetacum*.

[7] Desmulliz and Milis, 55 and 60–61, and Alain Jacques, "Arras gallo-romaine," *Archeologia* CCXIII (1986), 58–63. Jean Lestocquoy, "Les étapes du développement urbain d'Arras," *Revue belge de philologie et d'histoire* XXIII (1944), reprinted in *Études d'histoire urbaine: Villes et abbayes Arras au moyen-âge* (Arras, 1966), 122–137. *Les cultes à Arras au bas empire*, Exh. 26 April–17 September, 1990, Musée des Beaux Arts (Arras, 1990), 10–15.

[8] Jacques, *Histoire*, 23. Texts listed in Desmulliez and Milis, 113. Diocletian also lists something called *lanae atrebaticae* in his edict on prices 25:13, of c. 301, Marta Giacchero, *Edictum Diocletiani et collegarum de pretiis rerum venalium* (Genoa, 1974), I, 184.

[9] Jacques, *Histoire*, 24.

[10] Jacques, *Histoire*, 25.

In the Carolingian period the city's center shifted to the east of the Crinchon as its fortunes became closely aligned with those of the local abbey, Saint-Vaast.[11] Named after Vedastus, the baptizer of the sixth-century Merovingian king Clovis and reputed apostle to northern Gaul, the abbey was, according to tradition, founded in the seventh century under the auspices of another Merovingian king, Thierry III. This was the beginning of a long tradition of association between the abbey and the ruling houses of kings and lesser nobles. The abbey had obviously gained prominence by the time of Charlemagne, because in 790 he chose Rado, his own chancellor, to be its abbot.[12] In 843 Lothar received the abbey as part of the

---

[11] A good summary of the history of the abbey and a survey of the relevant sources is provided by Eugène F. J. Tailliar, "Recherches pour servir à l'histoire de l'abbaye de St. Vaast d'Arras, jusqu'à la fin du XIIe siècle," *Mémoires de l'academie des sciences, lettres et arts d'Arras* XXXI (1859), 171–501. Much of the early history of the Abbey of Saint-Vaast is contained in a now lost cartulary copied by Guiman, a monk at the abbey in the later twelfth century. On this cartulary, see G. Besnier, "Le Cartulaire de Guiman d'Arras, ses transcriptions. Les autres cartulaires de Saint-Vaast," *Moyen-âge* LXII (1956), 453–478 and Jean F. Lemarignier, "L'exemption monastique et les origines de la réforme grégorienne," in *À Cluny. Congrès scientifique* (Dijon, 1950), 288–340, reprinted in *Recueil d'articles rassemblés par ses disciples* (Paris, 1995, Appendix 1, 332–337. The sixteenth- and seventeenth-century transcriptions of the cartulary were published many times before they were destroyed in World War I. The most accessible is E. Van Drival, *Cartulaire de l'abbaye de Saint-Vaast rédigé au XIIIe siècle par le moine Guiman* (Arras, 1875). This edition combines the later copies of the cartulary, but provides little criticism of its reliability (pp. vii–xxx). Tailliar, 210 note 1, speculates that the pre-tenth-century parts of the cartulary are probably fabrications, based on anachronisms within the texts, and the fact that much of the library of the monks of Saint-Vaast was supposedly lost in a fire in 886. Parts of the cartulary were also included as the *Libro de possessionibus Sancti Vedasti* in MGH SS XIII, ed. Georg Waitz (Hanover, 1881), 710–715, and in an appendix to Tailliar. The other main source for the early history of Saint-Vaast is the chronicle of the abbey up to 899. The *Chronicon Vedastinum*, MGH SS XIII:674–709, was transcribed from an early eleventh-century manuscript, Douai BM MS 753, which incorporates paraphrases of other sources from early Christian times to 899. Chrétien Dehaisnes edited parts of both that manuscript and Brussels, Bibliothèque Royale MS 15835, and published a more complete chronicle for the years 874–900 in *Les annales de Saint-Bertin et de Saint-Vaast* (Paris, 1871), hereafter *Annales Bertiniani* and *Annales Vedastini*. He notes, p. ix, that certain allusions to events of the early eleventh century imply that the chronicle was actually compiled then. Parts of the Chronicle of Saint-Vaast for 874–900 were also transcribed from Brussels, Bibliothèque Royale MS 6439–6451 as the *Annales Vedastini* in MGH SS II, ed. George Pertz (Hanover, 1829), 196–209.

[12] Details of the missionary work of Saint Vedastus are included in the abbey chronicle, MGH SS XIII:683–685. Two privileges reputed to describe the foundation of the abbey are found in Guiman's cartulary, Van Drival, 17–19, *Privilegium Theodorici regis de prima fundatione monasterii sancti Vedasti Atrebatensis* and *Privilegium sancti Vendiciani episcopi de libertati monasterii et castri*. On the appointment of Rado, MGH SS XIII:705. See also Jacques, *Histoire*, 32 and Tailliar, 197 and 203.

Treaty of Verdun and in 866 it was ceded to Charles the Bald by
Lothar's son, Lothar II.[13]

Under Abbot Rado, the scriptorium of the abbey of Saint-Vaast
flowered. In the second half of the ninth century a group of North
French schools, including Saint-Vaast, Saint-Bertin and Saint-Amand,
excelled in the Franco-Saxon style of decoration, favoring insular
motifs such as interlace and animal heads over the Mediterranean-
style foliage used in other Carolingian workshops.[14] Although Franco-
Saxon manuscripts are commonly said to be almost entirely aniconic,
at least one manuscript with figures survives from each of these
Franco-Saxon scriptoria.[15] Two manuscripts from Saint-Vaast include
either small figures incorporated into the decoration or larger narrative scenes painted in a style that recalls the manuscripts of
Carolingian Reims. Several manuscripts produced in Saint-Vaast's
skilled Franco-Saxon style are preserved, and clearly these and others
that no longer survive provided the foundation for the scriptorium's
eleventh-century decorative style. The most famous of these manuscripts is the Franco-Saxon lectionary still found in the municipal
library of Arras, MS 1045 (233) (fig. 25).[16] Ornamented throughout

---

[13] Deshaines, *Annales Bertiniani*, 55–56, and 156. See also Jacques, *Histoire*, 32 and
Tailliar, 233–239. Another privilege in Guiman's cartulary is alleged to be that of
Charles the Bald, reconfirming the original donation of Thierry III, Van Drival
38–40, *Privilegium Karoli regis et imperatoris confirmantis subdata et collata a Theodorico augen-
tisque munera.*

[14] André Boutemy, "Le style franco-saxon, style de Saint-Amand," *Scriptorium* III
(1949), 260–264 and Florentine Mütherich and Joachim E. Gaehde, *Carolingian
Painting* (New York, 1976), 17, 66.

[15] The Gospels of Francis II (Paris BnF lat. 257), which is illustrated with full-
page evangelist portraits, survives from Saint-Amand. Carl Nordenfalk, *Early Medieval
Book Illumination* (Geneva, 1988), 72. Florentine Mütherich and Joachim E. Gaehde,
Carolingian Painting (New York, 1976), 93, pl. 30, 31, suggest that these paintings
are so different from the local style they must have been carried out by a visiting
artist. Also from Saint-Amand is the Gospelbook, Valenciennes BM MS 69, with
miniatures inside the frame medallions. The heavily-illustrated Valenciennes Apocalypse,
Valenciennes BM MS 99, may also have been carried out at Saint-Amand. At
Saint-Bertin, the Life of Saint Wandrille, Saint-Omer BM MS 764, was decorated
with illustrations (André Boutemy, "Un trésor injustement oublié: les manuscrits
enluminés du nord de la France [période pré-gothique]," *Scriptorium* III [1949] 114).

[16] First published extensively by Leopold Delisle, *L'evangéliaire de Saint-Vaast d'Arras
et la calligraphie franco-saxonne du IXe siècle* (Paris, 1888), it is also included in Amédée
Boinet, *La miniature carolingienne* (Paris, 1913), pls. xciii–xciv, and Carl Nordenfalk,
"Ein karolingisches Sakramentar aus Echternach und seine Vorläufer," *Acta Archaeologica*
II (1931), 234–235. More recently, André Boutemy, "La miniature," in *Histoire de
l'église en Belgique des origines aux débuts du XIIe siècle*, ed. Edouard de Moreau (1940),

with elaborate interlace initials set into complex geometric frames that in one case hold tiny writing evangelists, it was consulted assiduously by the eleventh-century artists of the Arras Bible. Another Gospel book sometimes localized to Saint-Vaast, now Prague, Knihovna Metropolitní Kapituly, Cim. 2, includes both full-page decorative initials, and full-page narrative scenes depicting the calling of each evangelist as a preface to each Gospel.[17]

It is remarkable that even this paltry number of Franco-Saxon manuscripts survived to inspire later artists given events in late Carolingian Arras. With the advent of the Norse incursions in the ninth century, production at the scriptorium of Saint-Vaast must have virtually ceased.[18] In November, 880, Arras was burned by attacking Vikings. The monks of Saint-Vaast fled to Beauvais with the body of their patron saint, their treasure, and their library, to remain there for the next twelve years. Disaster struck Arras again on the Monday before Easter, 892, when the entire city burned a second time in an accidental fire.[19] In addition, while the monks were still in Beauvais in September of 886 that city was attacked and burned by Vikings, consuming more of their treasures and books.[20]

The declining years of the Carolingian Empire also saw the abbey handed back and forth as a pawn between warring successors to Charlemagne and the increasingly powerful counts of Flanders, all

---

311–361 and *L'art du moyen âge en Artois* (Arras, 1951), 52–53. C. R. Dodwell, *The Pictorial Arts of the West, 800–1200* (New Haven, 1993), 74, maintained that this manuscript was a gift to Saint-Vaast from Charles the Bald's wife, Irmintrude.

[17] Mütherich and Gaehde, 17–18, 27, XVIII pls. 39–41 and Rainer Kahsnitz, "'*Matheus ex ore Christi scripsit*': Zum Bild der Berufung und Inspiration der Evangelisten," in *Byzantine East, Latin West. Art Historical Studies in Honor of Kurt Weitzmann*, eds. Christopher Moss and Katherine Kiefer (Princeton, 1995), 173–176. Nordenfalk, *Early Medieval Book Illumination*, 75, localized the illuminated of this manuscript to Saxony, although he did not explain the basis for this reattribution. Mütherich and Gaehde (p. 18) believed that the manuscript was carried east with monks fleeing before the Norman invasions, and heavily impacted the art of Saxony once there.

[18] See Janet L. Nelson, however, for a reassessment of the impact of "Viking" invasions on ninth century Arras, "England and the Continent in the Ninth Century: II, the Vikings and Others," *Transactions of the Royal Historical Society* XIII (2003), 9–10.

[19] On the flight to Beauvais, see the chronicle, MGH SS XIII:709 and Dehaisnes, *Annales Vedastini*, 306–307. For the fire that destroyed Arras, Dehaisnes, *Annales Vedastini*, 343. See also Jacques, *Histoire*, 34 and Tailliar, 260.

[20] Dehaisnes, *Annales Vedastini*, 326. *His diebus, id est 15 kal. octobris, Bellovagus civitas ex parte crematur; in quo incendio omnis ornatus monasterii sancti Vedasti, in thesauro et sacris vestibus et libris et kartis, deperiit.* Also Tailliar, 252.

of whom sought to control the monastery's considerable landed wealth.[21] With the rise of Hugh Capet in 987, however, the abbey was finally given over to Count Baldwin IV of Flanders (988–1035) as part of marriage negotiations for Robert the Pious's first wife, Suzanne. It remained one of the most prized possessions of the counts of Flanders for the remainder of the tenth and eleventh centuries, including the time period in which the Saint-Vaast Bible was copied and decorated.[22]

In the tenth century the scriptorium may have made a few tentative forays into manuscript illumination. Two manuscripts possibly from Saint-Vaast survive, the Leofric Missal and the Anhalt-Morgan Gospels, both of which signaled the scriptorium's continuing attachment to its traditional style. At the same time, some novel transformations to these manuscripts acted as harbingers of the future. The Leofric Missal, Oxford, Bodleian Library MS Bod. 579, has frequently been localized to Saint-Vaast, although its place of origin is far from certain. Ornamented in the late-ninth or early-tenth century with a small series of rather rigid and minimalist Franco-Saxon initials and framed pages, it left the continent almost immediately for England. Artists at Glastonbury then added a collection of colorful line drawings and computational charts some time between 969 and 979. This and other Franco-Saxon manuscripts profoundly affected the development of the 'Winchester style' of decoration, which was imported to Glastonbury by its abbots along with the monastic reform then being so assiduously supported by King Edgar.[23] The Anhalt-Morgan Gospels, New York, Pierpont Morgan MS M 827, may also have been copied at Arras in the late tenth century,

---

[21] See the treatment of this period in Guiman's cartulary, *Quod usque ad tempora Karoli regis abbatia Sancti Vedasti in manu regum semper fuerit* . . . MGH SS XIII:711 and in the chronicle, Dehaisnes, *Annales Vedastini*, 342–345, 348–352, 358–359, and Tailliar, 260–266. Most recently these issues have been dealt with by David C. Van Meter, "Count Baldwin IV, Richard of Saint Vanne and the Inception of Monastic Reform in Eleventh-Century Flanders," *Revue bénédictine* CVII (1997), 130–148.

[22] Jacques, *Histoire*, 36 and Tailliar, 271.

[23] Nicholas Orchard, ed., *The Leofric Missal*, Henry Bradshaw Society CXIII–CXIV (London, 2002) and Robert Deshman, "The Leofric Missal and tenth-century English art," *Anglo-Saxon England* VI (1977), 145–176. The Franco-Saxon sections of the manuscript are fols. iv, 1–37v, and much of 60–378v. An Anglo-Saxon initial was added to the manuscript in the first half of the ninth century, signaling that by then the missal was already in England (Deshman, "The Leofric Missal," 147–148).

when it was decorated with a whittled-down version of Franco-Saxon interlace and a few human and animal marginalia, much in the tradition of Carolingian Saint-Vaast. Very soon afterwards, an Anglo-Saxon artist added a series of evangelist portraits inside the pre-existing frames. Like the Leofric Missal, the Anhalt-Morgan Gospels were quickly exported. The manuscript was in Saxony by the early-eleventh century, when a different artist embellished many of the frames and initials with a multi-colored patchwork of ornament.[24] The modern-day appearance of both of these manuscripts forecasts Saint-Vaast's later close relationship with Anglo-Saxon manuscript art, even though the codices themselves were not at Saint-Vaast in the early-eleventh century, when the scriptorium's most striking changes in style occurred.

In the era of peace and prosperity after the cessation of the Norse raids, Arras grew and again became a mercantile center. A cartulary of Saint-Vaast written in the twelfth century by a monk called Guiman records the tithes collected by the abbey in 1036, and reveals that the inhabitants of Arras were wealthy enough to engage in international commerce in such materials as iron, fabric, and even foodstuffs.[25] By this time the newly prosperous town of Arras was firmly centered not around the old Cité and cathedral, but in the area known as La Ville, situated east of the Crinchon, around the monastery of Saint-Vaast.[26] This shift in gravity towards the monastery probably reflects, in part, the fact that Arras had not been an autonomous bishopric since c. 545, five years after Vedastus's death, when the *cathedra* was transferred to Cambrai, and the dioceses of Arras and Cambrai were combined.[27] In the absence of a residential bishop, the inhabitants of Arras sought the safety and trade provided within the monastery's walled enclosure.

---

[24] On this manuscript, Hans Swarzenski, "The Anhalt Morgan Gospels," *Art Bulletin* XXXI (1949), 77–83.

[25] The privilege recording the tithes is transcribed in Van Drival, 170–175, *Privilegium Leduini abbatis de terminis et consuetudinibus census et thelonei*. See also Jacques, *Histoire*, 38–39.

[26] Lestocquoy, 125–131, 136–137. Even in the twelfth century, the inhabitants recognized this migration away from the old Roman center marked by ruins, then known as Baudimont, as described in Guiman's cartulary, MGH SS XIII:710. *Nec super hoc quisquam ambiguitatis scrupulus subrepat, quod hic locus tunc extra civitatem ad orientalem plagam fuisse, nunc autem in medio civitatis esse probatur, quia, sicut in veteribus chronicis legimus, hec civitas antiquitus in monte qui Baldui-mons dicitur sedit, sicut ruinarium vestigia et vallorum aggeres, qui contra Iulium Cesarem et Romanos constructi sunt.*

[27] Henry Gruy, *Histoire d'Arras* (Arras, 1967), 34.

The Saint-Vaast Scriptorium in the Eleventh Century

By the beginning of the eleventh century, the monastery had recovered sufficiently to invest in its scriptorium, which began once again to decorate luxuriously books intended for use inside its own walls. The eleventh-century scriptorium of Saint-Vaast has been the subject of three general studies, which have competently localized a series of manuscripts to the abbey and devised a workable chronology while leaving aside, for the most part, any investigation of their iconography. Boutemy drew attention to the products of the scriptorium as a group in his 1949 article "Un Trésor injustement oublié: les manuscrits enluminés du nord de la France (période pré-gothique)."[28] In 1954, Sigrid Schulten completed her extensive study of the manuscripts of Saint-Vaast, and in 1956 published the results in an article.[29] Her work has rightly formed the basis of all subsequent studies of the scriptorium. Denis Escudier incorporated a survey of Saint-Vaast manuscripts into his 1970 study of musical notation in Arras.[30] More recently, a brief overview of the scriptorium was included in a general survey of the arts of the region, *Nord roman*.[31] Out of all the manuscripts produced in the eleventh century at Saint-Vaast, only the Saint-Vaast Bible has received any detailed attention, and that mostly in the context of studies of Bibles in general. Not since Boutemy's 1950 article examining the codicology of the manuscript has the Bible been the exclusive subject of a study.[32]

Despite the late ninth-century misadventures of the monks and their collection, by the twelfth century Saint-Vaast owned a considerable number of codices in addition to the illuminated manuscripts copied in the eleventh-century scriptorium. Between the library cat-

---

[28] *Scriptorium* III (1949), 111–122.

[29] "Die Buchmalerei im Kloster St. Vaast in Arras im 11 Jahrhundert," Ph.D Dissertation, Ludwig-Maximilians-Universität, Munich, 1954, and idem, "Die Buchmalerei im Kloster St. Vaast in Arras," *Münchner Jahrbuch der bildenden Kunst* VII (1956), 49–90.

[30] "Le scriptorium de Saint-Vaast d'Arras des origines au XIIe siècle: contribution à l'étude des notations neumatiques du Nord de la France," Thèse, Paris, École nat. Chartes, 1970, 3 vols. Idem, "Le scriptorium de Saint-Vaast d'Arras des origines au XIIe siècle," *Positions des thèses de l'École des Chartes* (1970), 75–82.

[31] Hervé Oursel, Colette Deramble-Moubès and Jacques Thiébaut, *Nord roman*, La nuit de temps LXXXII (Saint-Léger-Vauban, 1994), 260–267.

[32] "La Bible enluminée de Saint-Vaast à Arras (Ms. 559)," *Scriptorium* IV (1950), 67–81.

alogues and the several hundred surviving manuscripts demonstrably owned by Saint-Vaast, a stunning amount of information can be accumulated about the literary environment of the scriptorium when the Arras Bible was created. A twelfth-century catalogue copied into a manuscript of the *Registrum Gregorii*, Arras BM MS 323, fol. 71v, lists 229 manuscripts belonging to the library, and another late-eleventh-century list describes the thirty-three books given to the monastery in 1074 by Abbot Seiwold of Bath on his way to Flanders (Arras BM MS 849, fol. 159).[33] Many of the books from both lists have been identified, a task made easier by the labeling of most manuscripts belonging to Saint-Vaast in 1628 with the ownership mark *Bibliothecae monasterii sancti Vedasti Atrebatensis* 1628.[34] In 1790 the monastery's collection was handed over to the state, and in part dispersed to other regional libraries. Fortunately, 598 manuscripts from the Saint-Vaast library are still preserved in Arras, in the seventeenth-century buildings that formerly belonged to the monastery.[35] In addition, thirty-two manuscripts were sent to the municipal library in nearby Boulogne-sur-Mer. Altogether, the monastery's eleventh-century corpus of Biblical, liturgical, exegetical and scholarly manuscripts can be reconstructed with a gratifying degree of accuracy.

Of all the manuscripts it owned, the Saint-Vaast Bible was probably the monastery's greatest treasure and showpiece when it was created. Although the Bible was not listed with the collection in the twelfth-century library catalogue, Schulten succinctly argued that this does not disprove its Saint-Vaast origin. Like other highly decorated Saint-Vaast manuscripts that were not catalogued, the Bible may have been kept in the treasury of the monastery rather than in the library.[36] Alternatively, because, as I will show below, this Bible was used several times a day, it was likely to be found at any given

---

[33] Philip Grierson, "La bibliothèque de Saint-Vaast d'Arras au XIIᵉ siècle," *Revue bénédictine* LII (1940), 117–140 and idem, "Les livres de l'abbé Seiwold de Bath," *Revue bénédictine* LII (1940), 96–116.

[34] This inscription is found in all three volumes of the Saint-Vaast Bible, on fol. 2 of vol. I, fol. 1 of vol. II, and fol. 2 of vol. III.

[35] These holdings have been catalogued several times, and therefore bear several sets of catalogue numbers. The most often used are those of the *Catalogue général* IV, Arras, and Zephir François Cicéron Caron, *Catalogue des manuscrits de la bibliothèque de la ville d'Arras* (Arras, 1860). I will use the numeration found in Caron, which is the system presently in use at the Bibliothèque municipale in Arras.

[36] Schulten, *Münchner Jahrbuch*, 50 and Grierson, "La bibliothèque de Saint-Vaast," 119. This was a common occurrence with medieval liturgical books.

moment either in the choir or the refectory. In fact, not a single
book of the Bible, whether Gospels, Psalter, Apocalypse or Epistelary,
is included in the twelfth-century list, even though clearly the monastery
must have possessed several. This omission suggests that the monastery's
biblical books may have been listed on a now missing subsequent
folio, as the list breaks off mid-word at the bottom of the right hand
column, or perhaps included in a separate list.

Furthermore, although there is no direct internal evidence for
either the dating or localization of the Bible, its strong stylistic similarity to several other manuscripts irrefutably connected to Saint-
Vaast places it in the heart of the scriptorium's early eleventh-century
revival.[37] Two of the artist's hands that Schulten identified in the
Bible she also found in other, securely localized Saint-Vaast manuscripts.[38] She identified the hand that produced the Esther illustration in volume three, fol. 44 (pl. VIII), with its flat and opaque dark
paint covered with harsh black lines delineating diagonal and horizontal folds, with that of the artist responsible for the similarly flatly
opaque and clumsily outlined miniatures in Boulogne BM MS 9
(fol. 1, fig. 26). This Gospel Book can be localized to Saint-Vaast
because of its dedication page illustration, where a donor presents
the manuscript to a figure labeled *SCS VEDASTUS*.[39] The most
accomplished initials in a breviary from Arras, BM MS 860, according to Schulten, were drawn by an artist she termed the 'präzisen
Ornamentzeichner,' the same artist who produced six small initials
in volume two of the Bible.[40] And indeed in both manuscripts, this
artist's work is easily identified through its energetic and tightly packed
striated white tendrils, with many little twisting leaf ends that cup
around crossing stems. MS 860 contains an ownership inscription
by the original scribe localizing it to Saint-Vaast.[41]

---

[37] Arras BM MSS 616, 860, and 903, which belong stylistically to the same family as the Arras Bible, all invoke Saint Vedastus in their colophons. In addition,
ownership inscriptions in the hand of the scribe of each manuscript are found in
Arras BM MSS 60 and 826, both of which are also decorated with Saint-Vaast-
style ornament. Finally, Cambrai BM MS 75, a Gradual decorated with Saint-Vaast
type tendril interlace, has a calendar and a litany which both feature Saint Vedastus.
Schulten, *Münchner Jahrbuch*, 62.
[38] Schulten, *Münchner Jahrbuch*, 51.
[39] Schulten, *Münchner Jahrbuch*, 61. Boulogne BM MS 9, fol. 1.
[40] Schulten, *Münchner Jahrbuch*, 63. She identified this artist as Albertus, the scribe
whose elaborately painted colophon *Albertus scripsit* decorates fol. 6 of Arras BM MS
734, a *Liber miraculorum et officii Sancti Vedasti* (p. 72).
[41] For localization, see note 32, above.

None of the Saint-Vaast manuscripts are internally datable, and yet a combination of evidence provided by the manuscripts, the evolution of their style, and the events at Saint-Vaast establish both a reasonable chronology for the manuscripts and bracket dates for the eleventh century output of the school. Schulten proposed a date for the Saint-Vaast Bible of between c. 1025 and c. 1050, based on a convincing analysis of its style developed in her 1954 dissertation on the scriptorium and in her subsequent 1956 article. The scriptorium's figure style, especially, changed markedly over a period of fifty to seventy-five years. The first artists worked in a rather clumsily-executed, Anglo-Saxon influenced, line-drawing technique with color-washes and some touches of flat, opaque over-painting, as seen in the Saint-Vaast Bible. Later manuscripts were decorated with an illusionistic and colorfully elaborate painted style unique to Saint-Vaast. This was paralleled by a change in the school's script. The script used in the scriptorium developed from a rounded late-Carolingian minuscule found in the Saint-Vaast Bible and other early manuscripts, to a slightly more upright and angular proto-Gothic script.

A *terminus ante quem* for this stylistic development is provided by the scriptorium's supposed latest product, a Psalter today in Dijon, BM MS 30, which must have been finished when it was presented to Robert of Molesme during his visit to Saint-Vaast in 1094 or 1095, as recorded in an inscription on fol. 10.[42] Schulten quite reasonably localized the Psalter to Saint-Vaast because it is stylistically related to the later manuscripts of the Saint-Vaast school, and Saint Vedastus features prominently in both its calendar and litany.[43] Its tendril ornament can also be compared with that found in a manuscript from nearby Saint-Amand dated ca. 1087, suggesting that the Saint-Vaast manuscript now in Dijon was produced around this time.[44]

A beginning point for the school's development is more difficult to pin down. Schulten attempted to generate a date for initial work on the Bible in particular by comparing its figure style to surviving Anglo-Saxon manuscripts. She posited that the different hands at

---

[42] Schulten, *Münchner Jahrbuch*, 85 and 90, note 75. Visits between Bishop Lambert of Arras and Robert of Molesme are recorded in the Cartulary of Molesme for 1094 and 1095.
[43] Schulten, *Münchner Jahrbuch*, 74–75.
[44] Schulten, *Münchner Jahrbuch*, 76.

work in the Bible assimilated consecutive styles of English line drawing as work progressed from the first volume through the third. Thus,
in her view the style of the Bible developed over time, with the
artists of successive volumes continually exposed to later English
influences.[45]

Schulten's chronology for the arrival of models at the workshop
is too rigid for several reasons. First, the artworks of the different
hands in the Bible cannot be very far apart in date. Instead, it
appears that three identifiable artists were working either contem-
poraneously, or serially, but with their tenure in the scriptorium at
times overlapping. Occasionally two artists even worked on the same
miniature. Second, the harmony she saw between the progression of
work in the Bible and the regular arrival at the scriptorium of new
manuscripts from England that were immediately absorbed and regur-
gitated by the artists denies them any originality. Instead, they may
have had a selection of manuscripts of various vintages at their disposal in the scriptorium, and borrowed from them eclectically. Schulten
convincingly demonstrated, however, that Saint-Vaast artists were
quite familiar with manuscripts produced across the Channel before
about 1030, and were eager to adapt these new influences. Their
knowledge of the style popular in England around 1030, such as
that demonstrated in the New Minster *Liber Vitae* (London BL MS
Stowe 966), shows that the Bible, and the other manuscripts they
illustrated, could have been begun no earlier than the first quarter
of the eleventh century. One can also suggest a *terminus post quem*
using contemporary events. It is unlikely that a project as lavish and
complex as the production of a heavily illustrated three-volume Bible
was undertaken before the reform of the monastery by Richard
of Saint-Vanne and Leduinus around 1018, as will be discussed in
chapter two.

The Saint-Vaast Style

As the first large-scale project of a newly reorganized scriptorium,
the Saint-Vaast Bible is a unique record of the monks' search for a
workshop method and style. Even a cursory examination of the Bible

---

[45] Schulten, *Münchner Jahrbuch*, 76.

reveals the scriptorium's program of work, which progressed from the beginning to the end of the Bible in linear order. In the first folios of the manuscript, the artists copied frames and initials from Saint-Vaast manuscripts that survived from earlier centuries and then crudely squeezed figures into the margins in whatever space was left. By the final volume, the artists were able to create compositions of striking harmony, incorporating figures, initials, frames and text. The competence of the artists to integrate their figural images into the decorative framework around the text pages clearly increased as work unfolded. Because different artists appear to have been responsible for frames, initials or figural images, one cannot attribute this change to a switch from one artist to another. Rather, the entire workshop gradually refined its vision and its ability to cooperate. Thus, although the hands of different artists remained identifiable, by the end of the project they were able to work together as a coherent group. All the same, the decoration of the Saint-Vaast Bible can be characterized as a derivative pastiche.

The stylistic vocabulary of the manuscript is very revealing. Although their scriptorium had been virtually moribund for over a century, in the few manuscripts that may have been created there in the tenth century, such as the Leofric Missal and the Anhalt-Morgan Gospels, the artists still clung to the monastery's ancient Franco-Saxon style exclusively. In the Anhalt-Morgan Gospels, an artist at some point inserted into the pre-existing Franco-Saxon frames evangelist portraits that were so authentically Anglo-Saxon that they seem to have been painted by an artist trained in England, possibly at Winchester.[46] Yet the Anglo-Saxon additions remained completely discreet from their Franco-Saxon framework. By the early-eleventh century, the Saint-Vaast monks who had created these tenth-century manuscripts may still have been alive, but the artists were no longer content simply to mine the manuscripts of their Franco-Saxon past for stylistic inspiration. This time they enhanced their frames, initials and figures with Anglo-Saxon-derived decorative motifs, using both schools of ornament to create a new synthesis. All the while, they effectively ignored the styles then most popular with nearby Ottonian scriptoria such as Echternach and Cologne.

---

[46] El'zbieta Temple, *Anglo-Saxon Manuscripts 900–1066* (London, 1976), 66–67.

The artists may have been consciously referencing the monastery's past grandeur, former royal patrons, and the authority of their own manuscript tradition when they chose to preserve the Franco-Saxon interlace and framed decorative pages of the scriptorium's Carolingian flowering as the basis of their new style. After all, not only was the celebrated 'Second Bible of Charles the Bald,' a late-ninth-century Franco-Saxon manuscript from nearby Saint-Amand, created for Charles and inscribed with dedicatory verses that referenced the emperor's close connection to the monastery,[47] but Charles' wife, Queen Ermentrude, also made a gift of three Franco-Saxon Gospel-books to Saint-Vaast, including the ninth-century Boulogne Gospels, BM MS 12.[48] Later generations of Flemish artists could reasonably have associated this style with their Imperial age.

The eleventh-century artists often borrowed very closely from their models, as Schulten documented in her study through comparisons to the Saint-Vaast Lectionary, the Leofric Missal or the Boulogne Gospels, which probably was in Arras during the eleventh-century rejuvenation of the scriptorium.[49] Many of the folios introducing books of the Saint-Vaast Bible are set off with frames of a variety of shapes constructed of solid bands filled with pen-drawn interlace and accented with rectangular or circular medallions set in the corners and mid-frame. Inside these frames are giant interlace initials, which often bristle with animal heads and bodies. Even a superficial comparison with manuscripts that may have originated at Saint-Vaast in the Carolingian era shows how diligently the Bible's artists mimicked their Franco-Saxon models. The frame around the incipit to the prologue *Frater Ambrosius* on folio 2, vol. I (fig. 1 and pl. I), even includes seated writing evangelists in the corner medallions, just like an unusual framed incipit with figure paintings in the Saint-Vaast Lectionary (fig. 29).[50] So indebted is the Saint-Vaast Bible to its Carolingian decorative heritage that it was once suggested that it was simply a replica of an older Franco-Saxon Bible, rather than a new creation.[51]

---

[47] Paris BnF MS lat. 2, Boutemy, "La style franco-saxon," 262–264.
[48] J. Hubert, J. Porcher and W. F. Volbach, *L'empire carolingien* (Paris, 1968), 163.
[49] Schulten, "Die Buchmalerei," 104–108. Boutemy, "Un trésor injustement oublié," 113, gave Boulogne BM MS 12 a Saint-Vaast provenance.
[50] Arras BM MS 1045 (233), fol. 8.
[51] Nordenfalk, "Ein karolingisches Sakramentar," 235 n. 54.

The Romanesque artists of Saint-Vaast were not content, however, simply to copy the work of their predecessors wholesale. As Schulten and Richard Gameson have both demonstrated, they also borrowed ornamental details from a variety of different Anglo-Saxon manuscript schools and incorporated them into their Franco-Saxon framework.[52] In one case, one of the Bible's artists even seems to have copied directly from an Anglo-Saxon manuscript. As Gameson recently pointed out, a late-tenth-century manuscript of Boethius's *De consolatione philosophiae* copied at Christ Church, Canterbury, must have been in the possession of the scriptorium while the Bible was being decorated. One of the initials in the Saint-Vaast Bible is virtually identical to an initial in the Boethius manuscript.[53] Most of the time, however, the artists were much more imaginative in their adaptation of Anglo-Saxon decorative motifs, fusing details from several different insular schools with their own Franco-Saxon visual heritage. At least some of the artists at Saint-Vaast seem to have been drawn not just to Anglo-Saxon motifs but also to that country's line-drawing method of book illustration. While the abbey's decorated Carolingian manuscripts were brightly painted, the framed initial pages of the Saint-Vaast Bible were drawn almost entirely in brown and orange inks, with other colors restricted to pale washes of green, orange, ochre and blue. Even more striking, although earlier Saint-Vaast manuscripts, such as the Gospel Lectionary Arras BM MS 1045 (233), could have provided the necessary model for a painted figural style, the artists instead turned again for inspiration to the art of Anglo-Saxon England, where they found a pen-drawn figure style on which they modeled their own compositions.

Saint-Vaast was one of a number of Flemish and Norman scriptoria that were exposed to art from across the Channel and incorporated these foreign elements into their own manuscripts. In fact, the impact of Anglo-Saxon manuscript style in monasteries near the coast is so pervasive that one may be left with the impression that it invaded nearby workshops like a virus infecting its host, inevitably changing the existing house style. Continental artists routinely adapted

---

[52] Richard Gameson, "La Bible de Saint-Vaast d'Arras et un manuscrit anglo-saxon de Boèce," *Scriptorium* LII (1998), 319.
[53] Gameson, "La Bible de Saint-Vaast," 319.

their new motifs and techniques in novel and inventive ways, however, so that the artworks of each house retained a distinctive appearance. Anglo-Saxon influence is demonstrated around the turn of the
millennium at the abbey of Saint-Bertin at St. Omer, for instance,
where a visiting Anglo-Saxon artist illustrated a late tenth-century
Gospel book, Boulogne BM MS 11 (fol. 56, fig. 30), and added marginal drawings to the well-known Odbert Psalter, Boulogne BM MS
20.[54] In the wake of this artist's visit to Saint-Bertin, the scriptorium's
principle miniaturist, Abbot Odbert, adapted his style to create a
composite of Franco-Saxon and Anglo-Saxon motifs, such as fluttering
drapery tips and echoes of Anglo-Saxon iconography executed using
the technique of tinted line drawing. Nonetheless, the artworks retained
much of their characteristic 'Odbert' style. The same Anglo-Saxon
artist may have moved on to Arras to enrich the Anhalt-Morgan
Gospels with its evangelist portraits. Could the manuscripts of Saint-
Bertin, rather than influences coming directly from England, have
inspired the stylistic shift seen several decades later at Saint-Vaast?
This is very unlikely. Not only does the Saint Vaast Bible reflect the
style of English manuscripts crafted after Saint-Bertin had ceased to
be an artistic center, but artists at both schools found different ways
to integrate Anglo-Saxon influences into their homegrown style,
achieving markedly different results. Saint-Vaast manuscripts look
almost nothing like those from Saint-Bertin.

The Anhalt-Morgan Gospels with their Anglo-Saxon additions were
already in Saxony by the early-eleventh century and could not have
inspired the Saint-Vaast artists when the Bible was decorated.[55] By
this time, however, Saint-Vaast had cultivated enough of a relationship with Anglo-Saxon clerics that they regularly stopped at the
monastery on their way to Rome or when in exile, leaving manuscripts there in the process, as happened later in the century when
Abbot Seiwold fled England and deposited his library at Arras.[56]
Nevertheless, the artists in Arras did not just opportunistically adopt

---

[54] See *The Golden Age of Anglo-Saxon Art 966–1066*, ed. Janet Backhouse, D. H.
Turner, and Leslie Webster (London, 1984), 60–65 and Claire Kelleher, "Illumination
at Saint-Bertin at Saint-Omer under the Abbacy of Odbert," Ph.D. Dissertation,
University of London, 1968, 53.

[55] Swarzenski, 81–82.

[56] See above on Seiwold of Bath's gifts to Saint-Vaast, and V. Ortenberg,
"Archbishop Sigeric's Journey to Rome," *Anglo-Saxon England* XIX (1990), 197–246.

Anglo-Saxon decorative style because it was easily available and new. Their conscious adaptation of the accompanying iconography argues otherwise. As I will show below, they appear to have understood the highly developed iconography of divine rulership seen in such manuscripts as the New Minster Charter, London BL MS Cotton Vespasian A. VIII, and the New Minster *Liber Vitae*, London BL MS Stowe 944 (fig. 27) and borrowed it knowledgeably.

They may also have associated the Anglo-Saxon styles that they copied with the English monastic reform that had by then so firmly taken root in insular abbeys. The 'Winchester style' itself may have been an outgrowth of reform when it was developed in conjunction with Archbishop Aethelwold's overhaul of the abbey. The style that had been practiced at Winchester before his arrival was quickly subsumed into a new, more international style that echoed continental manuscripts, including the Leofric Missal, originally from Arras.[57] Much like the hybrid style created in early-eleventh-century Saint-Vaast, the composite style created at Winchester may have been intended to recall both ancient insular monasticism and contemporary continental reformed houses that had inspired the new reform then making its way through England. The Saint-Vaast monks' frequent exposure not just to Anglo-Saxon manuscripts but also to their patrons, English abbots and bishops who traveled through their gates, signals that they may have admired not only the art but also the reform philosophy of the English. Perhaps they reversed the practice of the reformed monks at Winchester, cultivating their own, ancient continental style and combining it with an imported insular style they associated with reformed monasticism, even though the reform that arrived at Saint-Vaast came instead from Lotharingia.[58]

The First Campaign

Not surprisingly given the scope of the project, the Bible's twenty-four figural illustrations show evidence of several different hands, and of two significant campaigns of illustration. Schulten, lamenting that a true division by hands was impossible for a manuscript of such

---

[57] Robert Deshman, *The Benedictional of Aethelwold* (Princeton, 1995), 252.
[58] See chapter 2.

variability and low quality, divided the work of the first campaign between two 'workshop groups,' based on details in composition, framing and tendril ornament, and similarity to a few examples of Anglo-Saxon manuscripts.[59] On the contrary, I believe that identifying the work of individual artists is possible if one restricts the field to the figural imagery, rather than considering all aspects of the decoration. Furthermore, it is essential to pin down which artists carried out which figures in order to show that the scriptorium as a whole participated in the crafting of the sophisticated political program contained in the Bible's figural imagery.

The bulk of the first campaign of figural illustration seems to have been divided between two easily identifiable artists, both of whom were obviously influenced by Anglo-Saxon techniques of pen drawing and had attempted to assimilate them.[60] The first of these artists can be called the Ezra Master for the sake of convenience. Schulten connected many of his figures with her 'first workshop group,' and compared his style to the Sherborne Pontifical, Paris BnF MS lat. 943 (fig. 28), a late-tenth-century liturgical manuscript made at Christ Church, Canterbury, for Dunstan.[61] The Anglo-Saxon artist or artists who decorated the Sherborne Pontifical favored large-headed, short-waisted figures with narrow, rounded shoulders, long upper arms attached to abbreviated forearms, broad hips and drooping, outlined bellies and thighs. These artists employed the same fluttering drapery tips common to many Anglo-Saxon scriptoria, but rather than being energetically windblown, the draperies hang in rigid, symmetrical folds with carefully curved upper edges. The artists outlined both the folds and the edges of wings and haloes with heavy, evenly delineated double-lined tubes. The facial expressions of all of the figures could be characterized as somber, with small, tight frowns below dipping noses.

The Ezra Master's work is found in all three volumes of the Bible, but disappears abruptly after fol. 29 of volume III. His work is first encountered near the beginning of volume I, in the Bible's first exten-

---

[59] Schulten, "Die Buchmalerei," 22–42 and 115–117.

[60] The first campaign includes the illustrations for Deuteronomy, Joshua, III Kings, IV Kings, II Chronicles, Jeremiah, Ezekiel, the Song of Solomon, Wisdom, Ezra, Esther, II Maccabees, the *Passio Machabeorum*, Paul's Epistle to Philemon, I and II Peter, I John, and Acts.

[61] Schulten, "Die Buchmalerei," 41–42, 115–117. On the Sherborne Pontifical, Temple, 60–61.

sive figural illustration, a pair of framed pages introducing the Mosaic book of Deuteronomy. Although the Ezra Master's figures echo the style found in English manuscripts such as the Sherborne Pontifical, they display none of the Anglo-Saxon artists' sureness of hand. As in the Sherborne Pontifical, Moses and God, who sit atop the bowed frame on fol. 53v (fig. 2), possess sloping shoulders and regularized, tube-like, double-line drapery. Whether sitting or standing, their prominent bellies hang between their hips, often accented with a curled drapery fold. Frequently, their shoulders swell inwards into a curved lobe. In addition, the Ezra Master's figures have joints that are rounded and rubbery, as if boneless. The artist endowed some figures with extraordinarily long and multiple-jointed arms. The drawing is conspicuously heavy and labored, and in several instances the artist appears to have unevenly and heavily inked certain lines.

On the facing page, where Moses addresses a group of bowing Israelites (fig. 3), the figures display short-waisted proportions similar to those in the Sherborne Pontifical, and their poses and gestures are restrained. Their faces are frequently characterized by continuous eyebrows that hover over rounded noses, connected to their mouths by a single short, straight line. The next figural image in the book, for Joshua (fol. 72, fig. 4), contains figures with many of the same traits. Joshua himself, for instance, who sits in the right-hand roundel, possesses the same long, skinny arms accented with alternating, rippled folds on the forearm as the standing trumpeter on fol. 53v. He has the same recessive, rounded chin, round nose, straight mouth and short line that connects them as the Lord, on fol. 53v and Moses on fol. 54. His right arm has the same multiple-jointed effect as the figures in Deuteronomy. His drapery has been heavily outlined with brown pen.

As one pages through volume I, the same type of figure is encountered again and again. III Kings (fol. 128v, pl. II) is prefaced, for instance, with a double-register image populated by the same heavy-hipped figures with swelling bellies and rippling sleeves clinging to long, curving arms. Their faces share the same familial resemblance, with rounded noses connected to tiny mouths by short lines, rounded chins and low foreheads. Once again, the draperies and other motifs often have been heavily outlined with uneven, brown penwork. Unlike the miniatures that precede it, however, the painting prefacing III Kings demonstrates the artists' increased competence in combining their frames with their figural compositions.

The miniature that introduces the second book of Chronicles (vol. I, fol. 170, pl. III) was clearly the product of the same figural artist. We encounter, once again, the figures from the same low-foreheaded, receding chinned family. The enthroned Christ-Logos shares with Solomon, enthroned in profile below, even longer, more rubbery limbs than in previous miniatures by the Ezra master. While Christ-Logos' right arm appears to have two elbows, Solomon's left leg has at least two knees. Despite these infelicities, however, one can again observe the increased sophistication with which the frame and initials have been used to construct the composition, the letter C forming a canopy above Solomon's head and the upper frame lobe enclosing Christ and his angelic host.

The miniature for Jeremiah, in volume II (fol. 15, pl. IV), was a joint production between the Ezra Master and his colleague, the Acts Master. The Ezra Master was responsible for the figure of the Prophet, who shares with Solomon, David, and Joshua from previous folios the bulging, rounded nose joined to his small mouth by a short line, the arms wrapped in rippled sleeves, and the heavily-outlined drapery folds. The Ezra Master also contributed to the second volume the illustrations for Ezekiel (fol. 42v, fig. 9) the Song of Solomon (fol. 141, pl. V) and Wisdom (fol. 144, pl. VI). Note, for instance, the long, double-elbowed right arm of the seated Christ-Logos of the Song of Solomon miniature, the tell-tale line linking his nose and mouth, his sagging belly, sloping shoulders and his heavily outlined drapery folds, all of which (except for the multiple elbows) he shares with his companion to the left, Ecclesia. Wisdom's Solomon mimics the Song of Solomon's Christ-Logos, even down to the double-elbowed right arm, except for the addition of long sleeves, a crown, scepter and beard. Finally, in volume III, the Ezra Master was responsible for providing the tiny head of Tobit at the bottom of the framed incipit page for that book, and the miniature for Ezra (fol. 29, pl. VII). The scribe Ezra and his companion, in the roundel at the far left, both exhibit the same drooping bellies outlined by drapery, and the same small-mouthed, rounded-chinned visages with which we are now very familiar. King Artaxerxes, to the right, shares these attributes as well as displaying the excessively long right arm with tight, wrinkled sleeves seen on Joshua and Wisdom's Solomon, and the curl over the belly seen in the miniatures for Deuteronomy.

This artist thus produced the figures prefacing Deuteronomy, Joshua, III Kings, II Chronicles, parts of the Jeremiah illumination,

Ezekiel, the Song of Solomon, Wisdom, Tobit, and Ezra.[62] At least six of these miniatures (Deuteronomy, III Kings, II Chronicles, Jeremiah, Wisdom, and Ezra) play a part in the miniature cycle's royal and episcopal program, as will be discussed below, and one (Song of Solomon) finds a place in the smaller program addressing queenship. Generally, his drawing style echoes that used by the late-tenth-century Anglo-Saxon Sherborne Pontifical artists, but he departs from any Anglo-Saxon model to which he had access both in the lack of fluidity with which he wielded his pen, and in details of faces and draperies.

The most technically accomplished figural artist in the first campaign, the Acts Master, may have preferred the line-drawing style of early-eleventh-century New Minster, Winchester. Characterized by recessive, pointy chins, broad noses, large hands, and quick, excited gestures, his figures reveal a much more fluid pen with a surer handling of drapery and anatomy than that of the Ezra Master. As Schulten pointed out, the figure style of this artist, which she assigned to her 'second workshop group,' resembles that found in such Anglo-Saxon manuscripts as the early-eleventh-century New Minster *Liber Vitae*, London BL MS Stowe 944 (fig. 27), from Winchester, implying that the Acts Master may have been copying the style of a relatively recent model.[63] The Acts Master's work shares many details with contemporary Winchester illuminations, including the forward thrust of the heads, frequent long torsos, oversized hands and crinkly ridges outlining tubes of drapery.

Shulten suggested that the Acts Master's debt to early-eleventh-century Winchester illumination implied a pause of several decades in workshop production, or that the artists came from different generations. Yet, the Acts Master provided one miniature in each of the first two volumes of the Bible, and there is nothing, either in their codicological context, their relationship to the text, or the materials and techniques used, to suggest that they weren't part of the same campaign of work as the Ezra Master's contributions. The Ezra Master and the Acts Master appear to have been working in the Saint-Vaast scriptorium at the same time and their pen drawing

---

[62] Deuteronomy, vol. I, fols. 53v–54, Joshua, 72, III Kings, 128v, and II Chronicles, 170, Jeremiah, vol. II, fols. 15, Ezechiel, 42v, Song of Solomon, 141v, and Wisdom, 144, and Tobit, vol. III, fol. 17 and Ezra, 29.

[63] Schulten, "Die Buchmalerei," 40–41, 115–117.

styles take the same sorts of Anglo-Saxon sources as their inspiration. Nonetheless, the artwork of the Acts Master can be separated
from that of the Ezra Master by comparing a few telling details.

If one were to read the Bible from beginning to end, the first
miniature by the Acts Master that one would encounter would be
to IV Kings (vol. I, fol. 144v, fig. 6), added in the blank space left
underneath four lines of text, the explicit for III Kings, and the
incipit for IV Kings. Here one sees three registers of figures who
vigorously gesture toward one another. Whereas in III Kings (pl. II)
the Ezra Master's figures have small, curved noses constructed of a
curled line, the Acts Master's noses are large and aquiline. His noses
are most often not connected to the figures' mouths by a short line,
and those mouths are broader and more active than those of the
Ezra Master. The Acts Master's eyebrows are more wing-like, and
his chins come to a noticeable point, although one would still not
term them prominent, and his foreheads are still low. The facial
expressions of his figures are noticeably more cheerful and animated
than those of the Ezra Master, and in their gestures they appear to
react more to the people and events around them. The figures lack
the drooping bellies, prominent inwardly bulging shoulders and multiple-jointed limbs so common to the Ezra Master's figures.

Most recognizable, however, are the Acts Master's draperies. While
the Ezra Master's draperies for III Kings are typically thick, and
cling to their wearers, or hang in stiffly starched folds with deeply
shadowed pockets, the Acts Master's draperies in IV Kings flutter
in the breeze (fig. 6). Both artists employed the double-line fold to
articulate surfaces, but the Ezra Master's double-line folds either skirt
the edges of objects and garments, or lie, ladder-like, in regular rows
across the surface. The Acts Master instead drew folds across his
figures in irregular corrugations, with double-line folds that project
outwards from the surface.

While the Ezra Master drew the prophet Jeremiah in the illustration for that book (vol. II, fol. 15, pl. IV), the Acts Master seems
to have drawn the flanking choir of angels, the Apocalyptic Lamb,
and the hand of God, above. The angels sport the same facial
features already encountered in the drawings for IV Kings, and the
same crinkled drapery. While the Ezra Master typically depicted
fur and feathers as scales or carefully-set swirls that lie tightly on
the surface of the beast, for instance in the two illustrations for

Deuteronomy (vol. I, fols. 53v–54, figs. 2–3), the wool of the Acts Master's lamb springs away from its body in loose curls.

The Acts Master also illustrated the miniatures prefacing II Maccabees and the *Passio Machabeorum* (vol. III, fols. 70v and 81v, fig. 17 and pl. IX). In both illustrations the figures have the same broad, aquiline noses, wing-like eyebrows, pointy chins, long torsos, and corrugated draperies. The profile lions that form the throne in the *Passio Machabeorum* have the same springy curls as the Apocalyptic Lamb from Jeremiah. This artist provided the bulk of the figural illustration for the New Testament section of the third volume. His work can be found before Paul's Epistle to Philemon (fol. 126, fig. 20), the two Petrine Epistles (fols. 133v and 135v, figs. 21–22), and Acts (fol. 141, pl. X). In the illustration for Paul's Epistle to Philemon, for instance, one may observe the Acts Master's characteristic lively, fluttering drapery and broad, hooked nose. In the First Epistle of Peter, one encounters the same detailed drapery with wind-whipped ends on the bust-length Peter, above, while a crowd of men and women standing below gesticulates. As is typical for the Acts Master, their broad-nosed, pointy-chinned faces are thrust forwards, as if listening attentively to their companions.

This miniature and the single standing figure prefacing II Peter provide almost the only renditions of full-face figures in the corpus of the Acts Master. He shows Peter tonsured, in typical Anglo-Saxon fashion, with high, arched eyebrows, a pointy, outlined nose, tightly smiling mouth below dotted cheeks, and a semi-circular jaw. In II Peter, the portrait is identical except that the dots are missing from his cheeks. The only other full-face figure drawn by the Acts Master is found in the illustration for Acts itself (vol. III, fol. 141, pl. X). Here, a frontally seated Christ addresses the Apostles who are clustered on benches to either side of him. Christ's elongated torso, broad, outlined nose, arched eyebrows, slightly grinning mouth, and crinkled drapery all belong to the Acts Master's signature style.

As in the work of the Ezra Master, one can recognize that as the Acts Master worked through the manuscript, his compositions became more sophisticated, and more smoothly integrated into the framework of each page. In his first miniature, for IV Kings (fig. 6), he scattered two-dozen figures in four loose registers across what would otherwise have been wasted space. Behind one register he, or an assistant, shaded the background with a mauve wash, but otherwise the page

lacks any framing devices. By the third volume of the Bible, he had mastered the art of combining frames, initials, and figures. In the illustrations for II Maccabees (fig. 17), Peter's first epistle (fig. 21) and Acts (pl. X), the figures perch above and below the bars and bows of the initials, which have been used to create a setting or to divide separate vignettes of the story from each other.

This artist was thus responsible for the figural illustrations prefacing IV Kings, parts of Jeremiah, II Maccabees, the *Passio Machabeorum*, Paul's Epistle to Philemon, I and II Peter, Acts, and perhaps the under-drawing of the First Epistle of John (fol. 136v, fig. 23), in which one may be able to pick out his characteristic broadly outlined noses and crinkling drapery. Out of all these images, only two are found in the first two volumes of the Bible, and the first of these appears to be an ad hoc addition. Therefore, although he contributed to the illustration of all three volumes of the Bible, the Acts Master was probably not the first artist to work on the project, but rather joined the effort some time after it was initiated. Nonetheless, the Acts Master contributed at least two images that belong within the royal and episcopal program (Jeremiah and Acts, pls. IV and X) and one that belongs within the program addressed to queens (*Passio Machabeorum*, pl. IX). In addition, the Ezra Master and the Acts Master both participated in the composition of the Jeremiah miniature. In this illumination, all of the figures were added either while or after the frame and initial were drawn, and none overlap in a way that suggests one artist's work preceded the other. Both artists also worked in volume III, suggesting that their tenure in the Saint-Vaast workshop overlapped.[64]

A third artist may have been responsible for the two illustrations of the first campaign that were painted, rather than drawn. The illustrations for Esther (vol. III, fol. 44, pl. VIII) and John (vol. III, fol. 136v, fig. 23), both found in volume III, show an awkward mixture of matte patches of under-painting, and surfaces that have been articulated by black or brown pen drawing. The figures in the Esther miniature display the high-waisted proportions characteristic of the Ezra Master, the same heavily outlined, prominent hips with bellies

---

[64] A close examination of the Jeremiah miniature reveals that, in keeping with the practice in the rest of the Bible, the initial and frame were drawn first, and the figural composition added later.

drooping in between, long arms with misunderstood joints, the familiar small heads, the small noses painted with a single small curve,
and tiny straight-line mouths. Yet, although this may be the work
of the Ezra Master, the difference in medium succeeds in disguising
most similarities to his pen drawings. The same can be said about
the drawing for the Epistle of John. The still-visible under-drawing
of the face of Christ, to the left, has the broad nose with outlined
nostrils of the Acts Master's figures. Yet the drapery has been indicated on top of the paint wash with hard, tubular folds of cloth that
heavily blanket the arms, shoulders, and legs of the figure, who also
has a hint of the Ezra Master's inwardly bulging shoulders. It is
therefore prudent to assume that these illuminations were produced
by a third artist who favored painting over pen drawing, identified
by Schulten as Master A.[65]

All three artists of the earlier campaign, the Acts Master, the Ezra
Master, and Master A, working either simultaneously or only a few
years apart, carried out components of the programs of kingship,
queenship and episcopal governance which make up the underlying
theme of the Bible's cycle of illustrations. This amount of cooperation indicates that a programmer of some sort, either one of the
artists or an educated member of the clergy, must have dedicated
considerable attention over the course of years to the content and
composition of the images, as well as possibly to their accompanying inscriptions.

The Second Campaign

Sometime between twenty-five and fifty years after the original nine-
teen figural illustrations were produced, a monk at Saint-Vaast added
five painted miniatures, at least one in each volume of the Bible.[66]

---

[65] Although Master A played only a small role in the illustration of the Saint-
Vaast Bible, his contribution to the artistic output of the scriptorium was considerable. He was largely responsible for the illumination of several other manuscripts,
including the Arras Gospels, Boulogne BM MS 9, and a collection of Jerome and
Cassiodorus texts, Arras BM MS 732, illustrated with a prefatory image of the
Assumption of Mary (Schulten, "Die Buchmalerei," 52 and 87). Schulten compared
his painting style to the late tenth-century Prudentius manuscript, Cambridge, Corpus
Christi College MS 23 ("Die Buchmalerei," 115–117).
[66] Schulten, "Die Buchmalerei," 77–83.

This artist, who for convenience we will call the 'Colossians Master,' used a much more sophisticated painting technique than that employed many decades earlier by Master A, who had simply modified the local line-drawing technique by adding an under-layer of opaque color.[67] His technique contrasts strongly with the color washes and excited linear effects sought by the Arras artists of the early-eleventh century. The later style accords with that found in other manuscripts executed in the Saint-Vaast scriptorium beginning in the middle of the eleventh century, a group that Sigrid Schulten, in her study of Saint-Vaast manuscripts, termed the 'Spätstufe,' and dated ca. 1040–1090.[68] In particular, the figures added to the Saint-Vaast Bible, with their ringed eyes, heavily outlined chins and noses, black hair, and spidery white highlights, can be compared to those in a Sacramentary today found in Paris, BnF MS lat. 9436.[69] Once localized to Saint-Denis because of its illustration of Saint Dionysius taking communion, Schulten convincingly argued based both on the manuscript's calendar of feasts and its style that the Paris Sacramentary originated in the Saint-Vaast scriptorium, perhaps as a gift for the abbey of Saint-Denis.[70] Although neither the Sacramentary nor the additions to the Bible are internally dateable, Schulten speculated that the Sacramentary could have been produced to coincide with the opening of the shrine of Saint-Denis in 1050, a date that accords well with the stylistic development observed in other Saint-Vaast manuscripts.[71]

In the illustration for *Frater Ambrosius*, the Colossians Master continued the scriptorium's early-eleventh-century practice of drawing heavily on its Franco-Saxon heritage. The frame on the incipit page of *Frater Ambrosius* (vol. I, fol. 2, pl. I), contains four corner medal-

---

[67] Schulten, "Die Buchmalerei," 22 and 77–83 on the characteristics of the Colossians Master.

[68] Schulten, "Die Buchmalerei," 64–77.

[69] Fol. 15v, God in a mandorla flanked by cherubim and twelve angels, fol. 71v, the stoning of Saint Stephen, fol. 106v, the communion of Saint Dionysius and his followers, and fol. 129, Mary with angels.

[70] "Die Buchmalerei," 66–70. The calendar contains a number of feasts for Saint Vedastus, and has the saint's name written in gold not only in the calendar, but in the saint's day mass. Autbertus and Vindicianus, two other local saints, also appear. Despite Schulten's localization, Dodwell, *The Pictorial Arts of the West*, 211, favors an origin at St. Denis.

[71] Schulten, "Die Buchmalerei," 77.

lions, each ornamented with a seated or crouching author. Scholars have long noted that the artist seems to have copied this composition directly from the same Franco-Saxon manuscript illuminated at Saint-Vaast in the Carolingian era that had inspired so much of the Bible's earlier decorative vocabulary.[72] The decoration of this manuscript, the Saint-Vaast Lectionary, Arras BM MS 1045 (233), begins on fol. 8 with a framed text page (fig. 29). The interlace frame is ornamented with four corner squares containing tiny depictions of evangelists writing at lecterns. The interlace frame and medallions for the Saint-Vaast Bible's *Frater Ambrosius* Incipit were probably the product of the early-eleventh-century campaign. In the middle of the eleventh century, the Colossians Master copied the four evangelists into the medallions, probably using the Saint-Vaast Lectionary as inspiration, but he neglected to include the evangelists' lecterns, thus leaving the lower left-hand figure oddly contorted.

The next two illuminations, found within initials prefacing the Books of Nahum and Habakkuk (vol. II, fols. 106v and 108, figs. 10 and 11), herald the development at Saint-Vaast of a full-blown Romanesque tradition. The vast majority of the figural illustrations from the earlier campaign spill out around the initials to fill the frames of the pages, and sometimes even beyond. The initials themselves are connected to and surrounded with an extensive decorative framework, an aesthetic inspired by the scriptorium's Franco-Saxon heritage. The illuminations to Nahum and Habakkuk, added in the second campaign, are instead self-contained and confined to the space within the initial or its immediate border.[73] No longer does a network of tendril or interlace spring from the ends and midpoints of the initial to work its way around the text. Rather, the initial is a

---

[72] André Boutemy, "La Bible enluminée de Saint-Vaast à Arras (Ms. 559)," *Scriptorium* IV (1950), 71, *L'art du moyen âge en Artois* (Arras, 1951), 53, and Schulten, "Die Buchmalerei," 51.

[73] Interestingly, the nearby scriptorium of St. Bertin in St. Omer had already begun to make extensive use of this type of historiated initial at the turn of the century under Abbot Odbert. See Claire Kelleher, "Illumination at Saint-Bertin at Saint-Omer under the Abbacy of Odbert," Ph.D. Dissertation, University of London, 1968, 199–210, and Francis Wormald, "The Development of English Illumination in the Twelfth Century," *Journal of the British Archaeological Association*, 3rd ser., VIII (1943), 31–49, reprinted in *Collected Writings*, 2 vols., ed. J. J. G. Alexander, T. J. Brown and Joan Gibbs (London, 1988), II, 21–42, on a parallel development in English manuscript illumination.

discreet unit and the figural illustration is, in both cases, completely contained within the loop of the initial, the method of illustration that would dominate Romanesque manuscript workshops in the eleventh and twelfth centuries.

As in the *Frater Ambrosius* medallions, the figural style also breaks with that practiced earlier in the century. In the historiated initial prefacing Nahum (vol. II, fol. 106v, fig. 10), the proportions of the standing Christ-Logos, his lively gestures made with large hands, the oversized feet, the sloping shoulders, and firmly outlined hips and thighs with a drooping belly hanging in between, all recall the drawings of the Ezra Master. If one compares Christ-Logos with the standing woman who listens to Moses in the second Deuteronomy miniature (vol. I, fol. 54, fig. 3) for instance, one can see similar proportions and drapery outlines. The Colossians Master, however, modeled his figures three-dimensionally with white highlights and dark shadows, used white cross-hatching to define draperies, and greenish-gray modeling for the skin-tones. Sodden folds of blue cloth cling heavily to Christ-Logos's legs, articulated with brown, white, and black lines and patches, and a black line runs almost continuously around the figure as well as around his eyes, nose, and mouth. His face has a yellow-brown tinge, while his ears are set very high on the sides of his head, and his neck and brow are shadowed with lines.

The same motifs are evident in the historiated initial for Habakkuk (vol. II, fol. 108, fig. 11). Here the prophet stands in a pose almost identical to that of the Christ-Logos illustrating Nahum, except that he grasps a rotulus in his left hand rather than a sword in his right. His drapery is also thick and clingy, but this time the artist has added white cross-hatching over his shins. Finally, this artist also added to the top lobes of the now badly damaged framed Incipit for Paul's Epistle to the Colossians (vol. III, fol. 114, fig. 19) a crowd of six bust-length figures and a cluster of architectural elements. The heavily-lined, almost haggard faces of figures with black hair, darkly shadowed draperies, and hands muscled with green and brown lines, peer down towards the hole where once some other pictorial element, perhaps a standing figure of Paul, must have stood to the left of the initial 'P.'

Because in the cases of the *Frater Ambrosius* Incipit and Paul's Epistle to the Colossians, the artist inserted his figures into frames or initials rendered earlier in the eleventh-century by Saint-Vaast artists,

it would be tempting to assume that in all cases the Colossians Master merely painted over drawings that were already part of the Bible's program. A thorough examination of the illuminations both with the naked eye and using raking light as well as light shone through the folio from behind reveals that the illuminations do not cover earlier images, nor is there any evidence that previous illustrations have been scraped off.

For the miniature for Ecclesiasticus (vol. III, fol. 1, fig. 14) the Colossians Master once again combined some aspects of Saint-Vaast tradition with his new opaque painting style. The artist echoed the page arrangement from the Song of Solomon, where the framing of the miniature with a large circle repeats the beginning of the text, with its smaller initial O. He then surrounded the frame with ranks of seated personifications and evangelists encased in a fantastical arcade, with details that recall the architecture of the heavenly Jerusalem behind Christ-Logos in the Song of Solomon. The architecture, decorated with colorful checks, stripes, and variegated marble patterns, also recalls the tower with a cupola inserted into the right lobe of Paul's Epistle to the Colossians. The artist has employed his signature color palette of dark mauve, orange, dark green, pink, ashy blue, and mint, all accented with white highlights and cross-hatching. The figures have the same greenish-brown hued skin, sunken neck folds, lined foreheads, high-set ears, and heavily muscled hands and feet as in other work by the Colossians Master. Although these paintings are later than the Bible's initial program, one of them nevertheless fits into its overall ideological scheme, as will be discussed below.[74]

Thus by the middle of the eleventh century the Saint-Vaast Bible contained a full complement of decorative frames and initials, and an extensive cycle of narrative miniatures, most of which were completely unprecedented. The artists at Saint-Vaast, scrambling to revive their scriptorium in the wake of at least a century of neglect, harvested motifs and styles both from their own tradition and from some, but not all, of their neighbors. Only the powerful pull of some kind of political or religious necessity could have compelled the monks to spend so much time and effort creating this lavish monument when the scriptorium was still so poorly equipped, both artistically

---

[74] See chapter six.

and materially. In fact, both the liturgical needs of the monastery
following the reform of Richard of Saint-Vanne, and the opportunity
to broadcast an important political message seem to have drawn the
monks into this giant project, as we will see in chapters 2 and 3.

CHAPTER TWO

THE LECTERN BIBLE AND ELEVENTH-CENTURY
MONASTIC REFORM

Just as the artists of eleventh-century Saint-Vaast drew on the motifs
and styles used by their ancestors and neighbors when building their
decorative vocabulary, the Arras Bible's program addressed to kings,
queens, and bishops mirrors that found in several of the Carolingian
Touronian Bibles, establishing that the monks of Saint-Vaast intended
to build on the foundations provided by their Carolingian predecessors.
As I will show in Chapter 4, they recognized, probably inspired by
the Carolingians, the power of the Bible as a setting for a message
intended to elevate the holders of political and ecclesiastical office.
The roots of the Arras Bible's iconographic program lie in the miniature cycles of the Carolingian Tours Bibles. At the same time, the
Saint-Vaast and Carolingian Bible programs were composed with
similar goals in mind. This suggests that the designers of the
Romanesque Bible were well aware of the intended audience of the
Touronian Bibles and the messages encoded within the picture cycles
and text.

First, however, an examination of the contexts that inspired the
Carolingian Bibles and the Saint-Vaast Bible, and their codicology,
will show that the Arras monks drew on more than one of the Tours
Bibles' functions for their new creation. They must have been familiar with the workaday use of Carolingian Bibles as vehicles for choir
reading in both monasteries and houses of canons. As we will see,
even though the primary audience for the royal program imbedded
in some of these Bibles was the nobility, most Carolingian Bibles
were to be read, not cherished as showpieces. The Saint-Vaast Bible,
like the Carolingian Bibles, was able to satisfy many needs. Encompassing both a lavish royal message and intended to be used for the
reform-oriented monastic Bible reading becoming ever more established in the eleventh and twelfth centuries, the Saint-Vaast Bible
bridges the gap between the Carolingian and Romanesque flowerings
of Bible creation.

Evidence for the function of single or multi-volume large-format Bibles is frustratingly thin on the ground. Monastic customaries and other liturgical books detail instructions for the reading of the Old and New Testaments, but they don't dictate the type of volume intended to provide that text. Thus the history of the use of these large-scale Bibles has to be written as a detective story, with tangential evidence used to construct a workable scenario. Nonetheless, I will show that from at least the Carolingian era onwards, large-format Bibles were developed for the same function and by the same types of workshops. A survey of instructions found in early monastic customaries as well as evidence from church reform documents and the codicology of the Bibles themselves will reveal that the custom of reading the Bible as part of the Night Office in both monasteries and chapters of canons was already well established by the end of the Carolingian era. Touronian and other Carolingian Bibles were developed with the intent that they be read out loud in an ecclesiastical setting. This emphasis on Nocturn Bible reading coincides with the state-sponsored ecclesiastical reforms of Charlemagne and his descendents.

An examination of evidence within several centuries of large-format Bibles will show that from one generation to the next, the adjustments made to the Bible manuscripts became ever more specific. At the same time, the instructions for the reading of the Bible became more and more detailed. Many of the Carolingian Bibles seem to have been used for several hundred years, repaired and adjusted, until the wave of reforms of the late-tenth and eleventh centuries. Then, slowly, these Bibles were copied and supplemented by the elaborately illustrated Bibles of the eleventh and twelfth centuries. Romanesque monastic customaries provided increasingly elaborate instructions for the reading of the Bible, not just in the choir during the Night Office, but in the refectory as well. Thus it will become clear that one goal of both the Carolingian and Romanesque Bible copyists was to create a large and legible Bible meant to be read out loud by a lector.

The Carolingian Bible

The intended use of the Carolingian Bibles that began to be produced in the late-eighth century has been very difficult to pin down.

Most scholars attempting to define the Bibles' function have focused on the Touronian Bibles from Saint-Martin at Tours, with their Alcuinian revision of the Vulgate text and, occasionally, lavish synthetic picture cycles. Recently, for instance, Christopher De Hamel surveyed the development of Bible manuscripts in his far-reaching study *The Book. A History of the Bible.*[1] De Hamel identified three main campaigns of Carolingian Bible production, and connected all of them with Charlemagne's project to reform the Latin Vulgate text. About the Carolingian Tours Bibles, he stated that the initial purpose of the Tours Bibles was "political and strategic." In other words, the volumes were intended primarily as gifts from the canons of Tours or their patrons to other institutions or powerful laypeople in expectation of favors in return. A by-product of their wide distribution was that a standardized, corrected, Latin Vulgate text, called the 'Alcuin' text after its principal redactor, Charlemagne's advisor Alcuin of York, was dispersed throughout Europe and later copied.

This assessment was supported by Lawrence Nees in his study "Problems of Form and Function in Early Medieval Illustrated Bibles from Northwest Europe."[2] Nees states that the ninth-century Tours Bibles could not have been used for liturgical reading, because "only a small portion of the Bible is read in the mass or the liturgical hours, except from the Gospels, Psalms and Epistles." He suggests that whatever brief texts were needed could have been provided by an Epistolary. Instead, he sees Tours Bibles primarily as gift manuscripts or votive offerings, intended to elicit the reward of eternal life from God and signify the recipient's spiritual orthodoxy. He identifies the less luxurious Bibles of the Carolingian era as reference works and epitomes of the Bible's scriptural unity.[3]

As both of these scholars observed, Bibles were produced all over the Carolingian Empire in monasteries and cathedral chapters of every description. Yet the fact that several of the most lavish Carolingian Bibles were copied as gifts to and from royalty and high placed clergymen has obscured the reality that most of them, including those manufactured at Tours following the instructions of Alcuin,

---

[1] Christopher De Hamel, *The Book. A History of the Bible* (New York, 2001), 37–38.
[2] Lawrence Nees, "Problems of Form and Function in Early Medieval Illustrated Bibles from Northwest Europe," in *Imaging the Early Medieval Bible*, ed. John Williams (University Park, PA, 1999), 121–177.
[3] Nees, "Problems of Form and Function," 131–134.

were designed to be used on a daily basis for the recitation of the Divine Office.

There is evidence that Charlemagne and his advisors saw revision of the whole Bible as an integral part of the campaign to improve scriptural and liturgical texts. While Charlemagne's *Admonitio generalis* of 789 mentions only that Gospelbooks, Psalters and missals must be corrected in order to be used in churches and schools,[4] the *Epistola generalis* of Charlemagne, written between 786 and 801, is much more specific in condemning the texts of the Old and New Testaments in current use and calling for their correction. "Inter quae iam pridem universos veteris ac novi instrumenti libros, librariorum imperitia depravatos, deo nos in omnibus adiuvante, examussim correximus."[5] The *Libri Carolini*, possibly written by Theodulph of Orléans, also called for the whole of the Bible's text to be made uncorrupt, in order that theological questions could be answered correctly.[6] In 800, Alcuin wrote that he was occupied with the correction of the Old and New Testaments at the request of the king, to the point where he couldn't undertake other projects.[7]

The extent of Alcuin's revisions is probably less vast than originally believed, unlike those undertaken by Theodulph.[8] In addition, no one has been able to conclusively prove that there was an officially sanctioned and mandated version of the Bible within the Carolingian realm, even though the Tours text seems to have achieved a wide distribution because it was produced in quantity for export. Charlemagne's *Admonitio generalis*, seeking to supply the *scholae cantorum* founded under his father, directed that the Scriptures must be copied carefully in house, not that entirely new copies of the Bible be sought

---

[4] *Admonitio generalis*, ed. Alfred Boretius, MGH Leges II: Capitularia regum Francorum I (Hanover, 1883), 52–62, at 60, 2–7.

[5] *Epistola generalis*, MGH Leges II: Capitularia regum Francorum I, 80, 25–30. Bonifatius Fischer, "Bibeltext und Bibelreform unter Karl dem Grossen," in *Karl der Grosse. Lebenswerk und Nachleben II: Das geistige Leben*, ed. B. Bischoff (Dusseldorf, 1965), 156.

[6] *Opus Caroli regis contra synodum (Libri Carolini)*, ed. Ann Freeman, MGH Concilia II, supp. I (Hanover, 1998), 165–166. See Ann Freeman, "Theodulf of Orleans and the *Libri Carolini*," *Speculum* XXXII (1957), 663–705.

[7] Alcuin, *Epistola* 195, in *Epistolae karolini aevi* II, ed. Ernst Dümmler, MGH Epist. IV (Berlin, 1895), 323:5–8.

[8] Fischer, "Bibeltext und Bibelreform," 159–160 and Rosamund McKitterick, "Carolingian Bible production: the Tours anomaly," in *The Early Medieval Bible: Its production, decoration and use*, ed. Richard Gameson (Cambridge, 1994), 67.

from a central distributor.[9] While his later *Epistola Generalis* suggests that the revised Vulgate he had requested and that Alcuin seemingly provided was part of a grander scheme, the surviving manuscripts provide no evidence that the court took over the management of Bible production.[10] As Rosamund McKitterick has pointed out, we have concrete evidence that many Bible text reform projects were begun at the same time Alcuin began his in Tours. Even with Alcuin's and Theodulph's newly corrected versions of the Vulgate in circulation, many scriptoria seem to have preferred their own local versions of the texts.[11] Scribes laboriously assembled the different parts of the Bible together from their own or nearby collections, and undertook to copy a coherent and corrected Bible text for their own use.[12]

Several tantalizing clues hint that these Carolingian houses, in the midst of a manuscript project that could consume many years, incorporated devices that would allow for the anticipated functioning of these mammoth texts in the choir and refectory. David Ganz has noted that a series of Tours Bibles, including the famous, illustrated Moutier-Grandval Bible, had the Gospels and Psalter copied in a small Caroline minuscule used otherwise only for copying chapter lists, instead of the large script used for the rest of the Bible.[13] As Ganz suggests, this was probably because these manuscripts were intended for church reading, where a separate Gospel book and

---

[9] F. L. Ganshof, "La revision de la Bible par Alcuin," in *Bibliothèque d'humanisme et renaissance* IX (1947), 7–20, reprinted "Alcuin's revision of the Bible," *The Carolingians and the Frankish Monarchy, Studies in Carolingian History*, trans. Janet Sondheimer (Ithaca, 1971), 28–40 at 29. *Admonitio generalis*, MGH Leges II: Capitularia regum Francorum I: 52–62, at 60, 2–7, *Et ut scolae legentium puerorum fiant. Psalmos, notas, cantus, compotum, grammaticam per singula monasteria vel episcopia, et libros catholicos bene emendate, quia saepe, dum bene aliqui Deum rogare cupiunt, sed per inemendatos libros male rogant. Et pueros vestros non sinite eos legendo vel scribendo corrumpere. Et si opus est evangelium, psalterium et missale scribere, perfectae aetatis homines scribant cum omni diligentia.*

[10] Ganshof, 29–30, *Epistola generalis*, MGH Leges II: Capitularia regum Francorum I, 80, 25–30, Bonifatius Fischer, *Die Alkuin-Bibel* (Freiburg, 1949), 6.

[11] McKitterick, "Carolingian Bible production," 69–70.

[12] McKitterick, "Carolingian Bible production," 67–69, and Fischer, "Bibeltext und Bibelreform," 156–216.

[13] David Ganz, "Mass production of early medieval manuscripts: the Carolingian Bibles from Tours," in *The Early Medieval Bible*, 59. The Bibles surveyed by Ganz which include small text Gospels and Psalters are Zürich, Zentralbibliothek MS Car C.1, London BL MS Harley 2805 (first half of a Bible), the Moutier Grandval Bible, London BL MS Add. 10546, Munich, Bayerische Staatsbibliothek MS Clm 12741, Trier, Bistumsarchiv MS 95 1/2 (a fragment of the Psalter), and Paris BnF MS lat. 47 (missing Psalter and Wisdom books).

Psalter would have been available.[14] The multi-volume Bible produced under the direction of Abbot Maurdramnus (772–781) at
Corbie in the late-eighth century, possibly the earliest Bible to have
been copied to accommodate the Carolingian monastic reform, may
have lacked the Gospels and the Psalter altogether, though this is
difficult to prove in its current fragmentary condition.[15] A series of
Carolingian Bibles may also have been organized in a variant order
that accords with the *lectio continua* of the Nocturns, which will be
described below. Brussels, Bibliothèque royale MS II 1052, f. 137–140,
a fragmentary late-eighth-century Bible perhaps written at Echternach
in an Anglo-Saxon influenced script, may have been arranged in
reading order,[16] as was possibly the fragmentary mid-ninth-century
Douai BM MS 14.[17] A series of Bibles from Italy also followed this
unusual ordering. Monza, Biblioteca Capitolare della Basilica di San
Giovanni Battista MS $^{i\text{-}2}/_9$, from the second half of ninth century,
is the remnant of a Bible in reading order,[18] while two other late
Carolingian Bibles from Northern Italy, the Bobbio Bible[19] and the
Biasca Bible[20] both lacked the Gospels and Psalter and were in read-

---

[14] Ganz, "Mass production," 59 and 56.

[15] McKitterick, "Carolingian Bible production," 67, Fischer, "Bibeltext und
Bibelreform," 186. Amiens BM MSS 6, 7, 9, 11 and 12, and Paris BnF MS lat.
13174, fols. 136 and 138. An inscription in the Maurdramnus Bible explains "Ego
Maur dramnus abb. propter Dei amorem et propter conpendium legentium hoc
volumen fieri jussi. Quicumque hunc librum legerit Domini misericordiam pro me
exoret." Amiens BM MS 11, fol. 96. Larry Ayres, "Le Bibbie atlantiche. Dalla
Riforma alla diffusione in Europa," in *Le Bibbie atlantiche. Il libro delle Scritture tra monumentalità e rappresentazione* (Rome, 2000), 28 and Samuel Berger, *Histoire de la Vulgate
pendant les premiers siècles du moyen âge* (Paris, 1893, reprinted New York, 1958), 102.

[16] Fischer, "Bibeltext und Bibelreform," 196.

[17] Fischer, "Bibeltext und Bibelreform," 191. Unlike many other Carolingian
Bibles, however, this was a small-format volume, only 260 by 220 mm. Its even-
tual home was the abbey of Marchiennes, where on fol. 158v a scribe added an
Ordo librorum catholicorum quos in Ecclesiis Romani ponunt ad legendum. Catalogue général VI,
Douai, 11.

[18] Fischer, "Bibeltext und Bibelreform," 212.

[19] Milan, Bibliotheca Ambrosiana MS E.26 inf. Fischer, "Bibeltext und Bibelreform,"
213–214, and Berger, *Histoire de la Vulgate*, 394, both believed it to date from the
second quarter of the ninth century. Antonio Ceruti, *Inventorio Ceruti dei manoscritti
della biblioteca ambrosiana* (Milan, 1973), 712, on the other hand, assigned it to the
tenth century under the abbacy of Lunibertus, as did P. Callura, *La precarolina e la
carolina a Bobbio* (Florence, 1965), 146–150, who believed it was begun earlier, under
Audericus. Renata Cipriani, *Codici miniati dell'Ambrosiana*, Fontes Ambrosiani XL
(Milan, 1968), 235, assigned it to the early eleventh century. The manuscript mea-
sures 44.5 by 29.5 cm and has 307 folios written in two columns of 42–44 lines.

[20] Milan, Bibliotheca Ambrosiana MS E.53 inf. Again, Fischer, "Bibeltext und

ing order. Specifically, in this type of Bible, the biblical books are not arranged in roughly the order in which they were written, with the Octateuch preceding the Books of Kings and Chronicles, and the Old Testament placed before and separated from the New Testament, as they were in most Bibles, including the Flemish Bibles lacking the Psalter and Gospels. Rather, in these liturgically-ordered Bibles the biblical books are arranged in the order in which they were meant to be read in the *lectio continua*, with the books of the Old and New Testament interspersed.[21]

These are only the first of several clues, however, that Carolingian Bibles were intended to be read aloud as part of an ecclesiastical observance. Ganz has translated the prefatory poems that Alcuin designed for the Bibles produced at St. Martin's.[22] As Ganz pointed out, included in these poems are references to the Touronian Bibles' workaday life.

> It should be in the church for the readers, and whosoever reads the sweetest words of the Lord, let him remember the author who ordered it to be written. Farewell to you who are reading I pray you take care of the reading, so that you resound the heavenly words of God with the right meaning and the great reward of Christ will remain for you.[23]

Even more specific is another poem.

> Whosoever as a reader in church reads in the sacred body of this book the high words of God distinguishing the meanings, titles, cola and commata with his voice, let him say with his mouth as he knows the accent sounds.[24]

Bibelreform," 212 and Berger, *Histoire de la Vulgate*, 394, believed this manuscript to date from the ninth century, but Ceruti, *Inventorio Ceruti*, 726, instead dated it to the tenth century, as did Cipriani, *Codici miniati*, 238. The Biasca Bible is 48.5 by 38 cm, and is written in two columns of 49 to 51 lines. Fischer pointed out that the text of the Biasca Bible can be localized to the diocese of Milan, and that none of these Italian Bibles share a copy relationship.

[21] Berger, *Histoire de la Vulgate*, 305–306, and Appendix I, section VII, 338–339. The order in which the books are found varies slightly from Bible to Bible, and begins at different points in different manuscripts. Roughly, however, it can be summarized thus: Isaiah, Pauline Epistles, Octateuch, Jeremiah, Acts, Apocalypse, Catholic Epistles, Kings, Chronicles, Wisdom Books, Job, Tobit, Judith, Esther, Ezra, Maccabees, Ezechiel, Daniel, and the Minor Prophets. Certain Bibles begin instead with the Octateuch, in which case Isaiah and the Pauline Epistles follow the Minor Prophets.

[22] Ganz, "Mass production," 55–56.

[23] Ganz's translation, 55–56, of MGH, *Poetae Latini aevi Karolini*, ed. Ernst Dümmler (Berlin, 1881) I, 285.

[24] Ganz's translaton, 56, of MGH, *Poetae Latini aevi Karolini* I, 288–292.

Clearly, Alcuin envisioned that Bibles would be kept in the church and carefully read out loud on a regular basis. In addition, acknowledging the hazards of liturgical reading in a darkened choir, the Touronian scribes equipped these Bibles to make reading aloud as easy and mistake-free as possible. The manuscripts feature a limited number of lines on each folio, usually fifty to fifty-two, running titles guide the reader through the book, the Caroline minuscule is even, and there is a hierarchy of scripts intended to distinguish different parts of the Bible text and prologues, and orderly capitula. All are details that tailor these volumes for vocal performance.[25] Tours was not the only scriptorium to produce such an eminently readable and accessible text. The Franco-Saxon monastery of Saint-Amand also produced a Bible that uses all of these aids, including running titles, prologues and a hierarchy of scripts, as did other contemporary scriptoria.[26]

Furthermore, the differences between Carolingian Bibles designed to accommodate Office reading and those destined primarily for private study are pronounced. The six surviving Theodulph Bibles, for instance, were all written in a tiny script in two or three columns, with few rubrics, no running titles, and no distinctive scripts intended to set off the beginnings of books. Margaret Gibson characterizes the script as "a minute hand such as would normally be used for gloss rather than text."[27] Their text was complicated by an internal apparatus intended to inform the reader of the source of the reading of each word, and explained by supplements that clearly were not meant to be read out loud.[28] Such a manuscript would have constituted a veritable minefield for reading during the Divine Office, but instead was perfect as a study Bible used to write correct biblical commentaries, as most likely envisioned by Theodulph.[29] Also inappropriate for reading aloud were the Spanish Bibles that are similar to the Theodulph Bibles, such as the three-column mid-ninth-

---

[25] McKitterick, "Carolingian Bible production," 75.

[26] McKitterick, "Carolingian Bible production," 75, Paris BnF MS lat. 2.

[27] Margaret T. Gibson, *The Bible in the Latin West*. The Medieval Book, I (Notre Dame, 1993), 32 and Fischer, "Bibeltext und Bibelreform," 176–178.

[28] McKitterick, "Carolingian Bible production," 74, Freeman, 693, and John Contreni, "Carolingian Bible Studies," in *Carolingian Essays*. Andrew W. Mellon Lectures in Early Christian Studies, ed. Uta-Renate Blumenthal (Washington, D.C., 1983), 77–79.

[29] Fischer, "Bibeltext und Bibelreform," 177–178.

century Cava Bible,[30] or the Spanish half-uncial Bible, Leon Cathedral
MS 15, with 72 lines squeezed onto each page.[31]

Significantly, monastic customaries and other liturgical manuscripts
from this era began to include specific directions for Bible reading
during the Night Office on the model of Rome. This type of instruction, typically termed an *ordo librorum*, served as an index of which
Biblical books were to provide the lections in the Nocturns, the series
of readings and responsories imbedded into the Night Office. Each
monastery or house of canons that observed the Night Office would
have needed a copy of the *ordo librorum*, because instead of reading
through the Bible from beginning to end in the order in which most
Bibles were compiled, a Nocturn reading cycle instead skipped back
and forth within the Bible. The *ordines librorum* worked hand in hand
with the multi-volume Bibles and pandects of the Carolingian period
to provide the means for the *lectio continua*, the structured reading of
the entire Bible over the course of the monastic year.

The *lectio continua* was a simple and yet very demanding devotion.
During the Night Office, now known as Matins, monks and canons
read a series of prayers, psalms, biblical readings and responsories,
called Nocturns.[32] While in houses of secular canons the adherents
might read only three Nocturns, or three passages from the Bible
or another spiritual text, in the more demanding Benedictine houses
on the Matins of a feast day or Sunday, they were compelled to
read as many as twelve lections, with their accompanying responsories. Although a single lection might be no longer than one column
of a manuscript's text, reading a cycle of nine or twelve paired with
responsories could consume much of the night. The bulk of these
readings routinely came from the Bible, thus a large, legible, and
corrected text of the Old and New Testaments would be kept in
the choir for this nightly program of readings. An *ordo librorum ad
legendum* would have told the lector which book of the Bible to read,

---

[30] McKitterick, "Carolingian Bible production," 74, La Cava dei Tirreni, Biblioteca
della Badia, MS Memb. I.

[31] Ganz, "Mass production," 55.

[32] For a useful introduction to the Divine Office, see Jonathan Black, "The Divine
Office and Private Devotion in the Latin West," in *The Liturgy of the Medieval Church*,
eds. Thomas J. Heffernan and E. Ann Matter (Kalamazoo, M.I., 2001), 45–71. On
the Night Office, see Stephen Joseph Peter van Dijk, "The Bible in Liturgical Use,"
in *The Cambridge History of the Bible* II: *The West from the Fathers to the Reformation*, ed.
Geoffrey William Hugo Lampe (Cambridge, 1969), 231.

and on what day he should begin reading each book or set of books. He would then read the entire book or series, be it Ezekiel, the Wisdom books, or the Pauline Epistles, from beginning to end. The only guide needed on a daily basis was one that suggested how long each reading should be, perhaps a simple I, II or III, or an L and F scribbled in the margin of the manuscript that provided the reading.

The Bible was read during the night from very early in the history of the western Church. The fourth-century *Canons of Hippolytus* explained that all were to gather each day to "perform the prayer, the psalms and the reading of Scripture and the prayers, according to the precept of the Apostle who said 'Apply yourself to the reading until I come.'" Meanwhile, the devoted were to dedicate themselves to reading the Bible outside of church as well.[33] Jerome, writing in the late-fourth century, advised that Christians rise two or three times in the night to read the Bible, while in Rome by the fifth century Biblical lessons were a standard part of the night vigil.[34] Early monastic rules stayed mum on the subject of Biblical reading outside of the Gospels and the Psalms. For example, the late-fourth-century rule of Saint Augustine, the sixth-century *Regula monachorum* of Cesarius of Arles, the seventh-century *Regula* of Isidore of Seville, and the seventh-century rule of Saint Columban, among a host of others, make no mention of regular reading from the Old and New Testaments.[35] Benedict was the first to prescribe the reading of the Old and New Testaments in the monastery during the Night Office. "Both the Old and New Testaments are read at Mattins (Nocturns) along with commentaries by famous and orthodox Catholic fathers."[36] Yet even though he set up a program of Psalter readings to ensure

---

[33] *The Canons of Hippolytus*, ed. Paul F. Bradshaw, trans. Carol Bebawi (Bramcote, 1987), 26–29.

[34] Paul Bradshaw, *Daily Prayer in the Early Church. A Study of the Origin and Development of the Divine Office* (New York, 1982), 134–136.

[35] *The Rule of Saint Augustine. Masculine and Feminine Versions*, Cistercian Studies CXXXVIII, trans. Raymond Canning, commentary Tarsicius J. Bavel (Kalamazoo, 1996), Cesarius of Arles, *Oeuvres monastiques* II: Oeuvres pour les moines, Sources chrétiennes CCCXCVIII, eds. Joël Courreau and Adalbert de Vogüé (Paris, 1994), 204–227, San Leandro, San Isidoro, San Fructuoso. Reglas monásticas de la España visigoda. Los res libros de las 'Sentencias'. Santos Padres Españoles II (Madrid, 1971), 90–125 and *Sancti Columbani opera*, Scriptores Latini Hiberniae II, ed. G. S. M. Walker (Dublin, 1957).

[36] *Regula monasteriorum* VIII, CSEL LXXV, ed. Rudolphus Hanslik (Vienna, 1960), 55. Translation, *The Rule of St. Benedict*, trans. by Anthony C. Meisel and M. L. del Mastro (New York, 1975), 62, chapter 10.

that all Psalms were read within a certain time, he never provided such a schedule for the reading of the rest of the Bible.

The first hint that the Bible was to be read on a set schedule appeared in the seventh century in Rome, when the *scholae cantorum*, foundations to educate boys in the reading and chanting of the Office attached to the grand basilicas of St. John Lateran and St. Peter's, began to develop *ordines librorum ad legendum*.[37] The seventh-century ordo allegedly used at Saint Peter's in Rome is known in its modern edition as Ordo XIV.[38] The list of Old and New Testament readings developed at St. John Lateran between 700 and 750, today commonly known as Ordo XIIIA within the *Ordines Romani*, was adopted by southern European monasteries, but also soon made its way north.[39]

According to Ordo XIIIA, the earliest surviving *ordo librorum* to be used in Carolingian houses, the reader was to read the Heptateuch starting in Septuagesima and up to the beginning of Holy Week. Holy Week was filled with the reading of Jeremiah, followed until the octave of Pentecost by Acts, the Canonical Epistles and the Apocalypse. From the octave of Pentecost until the first Sunday of August, Kings and Chronicles were read, followed, in the month of August itself, by the books of Wisdom. From the first Sunday in September the books of Job, Tobit, Judith, Esther, and Ezra were read, so that by the first Sunday in October the reader had reached the Books of Maccabees, which were read until November. Finally,

---

[37] Pierre Batiffol, *History of the Roman Breviary* (London, 1912), 41 and Aimé-Georges Martimort, *Les lectures liturgiques et leurs livres*. Typologie des sources du moyen âge occidental LXIV (Turnhout, 1992), 72. These were probably associated in some way with the monasteries founded in the sixth through eighth centuries to furnish the choir service at Roman churches. On the basilical monasteries associated with St. Peter's and St. John Lateran, see Guy Ferrari, *Early Roman Monasteries. Notes for the History of the Monasteries and Convents at Rome from the V through the X Century*, Studi di antichità cristiana XXIII (Vatican City, 1957), 365–375, and 235 note 12 on the *scholae cantorum*.

[38] Michel Andrieu, *Les ordines romani du haut moyen age*, Spicilegium sacrum lovaniense; études et documents, fasc. 11, 23–24, 28–29, 5 vols. (Louvain, 1931–1961), II, 476 and III, 25–35, 39–41. Eric Palazzo, *A History of Liturgical Books from the Beginning to the Thirteenth Century*, trans. Madeleine Beaumont (Collegeville, MN, 1973), 150, suggests in a note that Ordo XIV could date from the sixth century, but does not provide a reason.

[39] *Les ordines romani* II, 469–526, on the origins, date, and many versions of Ordo XIII. Also Christopher A. Jones, *Aelfric's Letter to the Monks of Eynsham* (Cambridge, 1998), 217–218.

in November the lector read Ezekiel, Daniel, and the Minor Prophets. The reader finished up the annual round in the season of Advent with Isaiah.

Several clues hint that a renewed rigor in the observance of the Night Office with its grueling cycle of Nocturns, both in Carolingian Benedictine monasteries and reformed houses of canons, might have motivated the copying of single and several-volume Bibles. From the time of Pepin, through the reign of Charlemagne and again under Louis the Pious, prominent Church writers and reformers encouraged the reading of the Bible aloud during the Night Office according to a set program. Pepin, according to both Charlemagne and Walahfrid Strabo, fostered the chanting of the Office, and apparently both founded Roman-style *scholae cantorum*, where students were taught by masters brought from Rome, and imported books of instructions.[40] Both initiatives provided the channels for *ordines librorum* and the practice of reading the Bible during the Nocturns to become established in northern Europe well before the advent of the more famous Carolingian pandects. This devotion would have been followed by monks and secular clergy alike, as a standardized Office of Roman origin began to be imposed on reformed colleges of secular canons under Chrodegang, Bishop of Metz (742–766).[41] A later follower of

[40] Rosamund McKitterick, *The Frankish Church and the Carolingian Reforms, 789–895*, (London, 1977), 122–123, 122, note 5. Charlemagne, *Admonitio generalis*, MGH Leges II: Capitularia regum Francorum I, 61, *Omni clero ut cantum Romanum plenitur discant et ordinabiliter per nocturnale vel gradale officium peragatur secundum quod beatae memoriae genitor noster Pippinus rex decertavit ut fieret, quando Gallicanum tulit ob unanimitatem apostolicae sedis et sanctae Dei aecclesiae pacificam concordiam*, and Walahfrid Strabo, *Libellus de exordiis et incrementis quarundam in observationibus ecclesiasticus rerum*, c. 26, ed. Alice L. Harting-Correa (Leiden, 1996), 169, "In fact, when Pope Stephen came into Francia to Pippin, Emperor Charles the Great's father, to seek justice for St. Peter against the Lombards, his clergy brought the more perfect knowledge of plainchant, which almost all Francia now loves, to Pippin at his request." Also Cyrille Vogel, "La réforme liturgique sous Charlemagne," in *Karl der Grosse. Lebenswerk und Nachleben II: Das geistige Leben*, ed. Bernard Bischoff (Dusseldorf, 1965), 217–232, esp. 222, note 31 on Pepin's *scholae cantorum*. See also Pope Paul I's letters to Pepin about the *scholae*, Epistola 41, MGH Epist. III, Epistolae Merovingici et Karolini aevi I, 553–554, and about a gift of books, Epistola 24, MGH Epist. III, 529. Vogel also recalls a pastoral instruction issued by Arno of Salzburg in the wake of the council of Rispach in 798 (MGH Leges Sectio III, Concilia II, Concilia aevi Karolini I [Hanover, 1906], ed. Albert Werminghoff, 199, chapter VIII), *Episcopus autem unusquisque in civitate sua scolam constituat et sapientem doctorem qui secundum traditionem Romanorum possit instruere et lectionibus vacare et inde debitum discere ut per canonicas horas cursus in ecclesia debet canere unicuique secundum congruum tempus vel dispositas festivitates.*

[41] Black, "The Divine Office," 61. On Chrodegang, most recently, Martin A.

Chrodegang, in chapters fourteen through sixteen of the "Aachen version" of his *Regula canonicorum*, used a variety of scriptural quotations to defend at length the importance of the night vigil and its accompanying Nocturn reading, even referring to the same scriptural passages as had the *Canons of Hippolytus*.[42] Books for the Nocturn readings were also thought essential to the household of a priest, according to chapter seventy-nine.[43] This version of Chrodegang's rule was distributed to canons after the Aachen synod of 816, and was the standard canonical rule used in Europe until the eleventh century.[44] Near the same time, Amalarius of Metz, in his *Liber de ordine antiphonarii*, defended the practice of extensive lection reading during the Nocturns by equating the clerics at their night vigil to soldiers guarding a *castrum*.[45]

Furthermore, the process of importing *ordines librorum* seems to have been well under way even before the Aachen synod of 816–817, when the Benedictine Rule and the much-expanded "Aachen version" of Chrodegang's *Regula canonicorum* were mandated as the uniform rules of Carolingian houses. Manuscript copies of *ordines librorum* were transcribed starting in the eighth century, as northern monastic houses were just beginning to use the Benedictine Rule exclusively.[46] At first

Claussen, *The Reform of the Frankish Church: Chrodegang of Metz and the* Regula canonicorum *in the Eighth Century* (Cambridge, 2004).

[42] *Regula canonicorum*, PL 89:1066–1067, Otto Hannemann, *Die Kanonikerregeln Chrodegangs von Metz und der Aachener Synode von 816, und das Verhältnis Gregors VII dazu* (Greifswald, 1914), 27–29 and Gaston Hocquard, "La règle de Saint Chrodegang. État de quelques questions," in *Saint Chrodegang. Communications préséntées au colloque tenu à Metz à l'occasion du douzième centenaire de sa mort* (Metz, 1967), 61. Hocquard, 79, claims that Chrodegang himself must have been exposed to either Ordo XIIIA or Ordo XIV, but provides no textual evidence. Chrodegang's interlocuter referenced the teachings of Isaiah, David, Matthew, Luke, and Paul in defending the practice of reading, singing psalms, and praying throughout the night.

[43] *Regula canonicorum*, PL 89:1090. Claussen, 71, has noted that in chapter eight of the earlier version of Chrodegang's rule, he had already transformed the daily Chapter into a forum for "common reading," which was meant as much to educate the canons as to enhance their sense of unity by creating a textual community. See also Hocquard, 86–87 on the importance of the *lectio divina* in Chrodegang's original rule.

[44] Claussen, 8–9. PL 89:1057–1096 and *Concilium Aquisgranense* (816), MGH Leges sectio III, Concilia II, Concilia aevi Karolini I, 307–421.

[45] *Amalarii episcopi opera liturgica omnia*, ed. Jean-Michel Hanssens, III (Vatican City, 1970), IV, 25.

[46] Gérard Moyse, "Monachisme et réglementation monastique en Gaule avant Benoît d'Aniane," in *Sous la règle de saint Benoit. Structures monastiques et sociétés en France du moyen âge à l'époque moderne*. Centre de recherches d'histoire et de philologie V, Hautes études médiévales et modernes XLVII (Geneva, 1982), 8–9.

they circulated independently before being compiled with other *ordines* and then adapted to Frankish usage.[47] By the middle of the eighth century, these *ordines librorum* were popular enough north of the Alps that a series of different versions had been developed.[48] In fact, by the tenth century at least seven identifiable versions existed and survive in at least thirty-three different manuscripts, many of which can be localized to the most famous houses of Carolingian monks and canons. Because instructions for church life are typically copied for the benefit of those who need to learn them, rather than those who already conform to these rules, this sudden wealth of ordines suggests that a new discipline was being imposed. The variety of different northern *ordines librorum* are the result of repeated attempts to tweak them to make them conform more to developing practice, and to augment them with feast days popular in the Gallican tradition.[49]

The correct practice of the *lectio continua* was also the subject of discussion among highly placed clergy and laity. In the late-eighth century, Theodomar, abbot of Montecassino, wrote to Theodoric, probably a northern count and acquaintance of Charlemagne's, describing the practices in his house that supplemented the Benedictine rule.[50] At Montecassino, he said, according to Roman custom they read "veteris ac novi testamenti per ordinem libris . . ." implying a specific order of reading, rather than whatever non-standardized reading order might have been suggested by the Bible manuscript at hand.

> After Pentecost and through the whole summer we in the monastery of our Savior read, following Saint Benedict, three readings on ordinary days, until the Kalends of October, one being from the Old Testament. Because it was not yet the custom of the Romans to read on ordinary days in the summer time in the books, as we suppose our saintly father taught that we not read in the book, but recite by heart; but afterwards it was instituted [either by blessed Pope Gregory, or as others affirm] by Pope Honorius, when he taught that the whole scrip-

---

[47] *Les ordines romani* II, 471, *Initia consuetudines Benedictinae: Consuetudines saeculi octavi et noni*, ed. Kassius Hallinger, CCM I (Siegburg, 1963), 5, note 24 and Cyril Vogel, "Les échanges liturgiques entre Rome et les pays francs jusqu'à l'epoque de Charlemagne," in *Le chiese nei regni dell'Europa occidentale e i loro rapporti con Roma sino all'800*, SSCISAM VII (Spoleto, 1960), 218–257.

[48] Andrieu's Ordines XIII B–D. Christopher A. Jones, *Aelfric's Letter to the Monks of Eynsham* (Cambridge, 1998), 217 and Vogel, "Les échanges liturgiques," 229–237.

[49] Vogel, "Les échanges liturgiques," 246–250.

[50] *Epistola ad Theodoricum*, CCM 1, 128.

ture was supposed to be read in the church. Whence also, because we believe it to be more pleasing to our venerable father, we follow the Roman custom in reading the books of the Old and New Testaments in order.[51]

He may have reiterated his claim about the papal institution of Bible reading in a disputed letter to Charlemagne himself.[52] The impetus to correct their directions for the Night Office went hand in hand with efforts of reformers to codify some of the other lesson readings. Charlemagne invited Paul the Deacon to compose a Homiliary to be distributed throughout his realm so that churches could satisfy the requirement for lessons of patristic homilies from a standardized source.[53] Amalarius of Metz's *Liber de ordine antiphonarii* was another volume reformed in this program to standardize the Office readings, this time dealing directly with the program for the Night Office.[54] In 831 Amalarius journeyed to Rome at the request of King Louis the Pious to visit Pope Gregory IV.[55] Near the end of his life he recorded in the prologue to his *Liber de ordine antiphonarii*, an addendum to his much-revised *Liber officialis* which augmented the material used during the Church Offices, that while in Rome he asked the Archdeacon Theodore what responses were used in the Office.[56] The nature of the question indicates that Amalarius was already familiar with the idea of reading the biblical lessons as part of the Night Office. Furthermore, the rest of his prologue reveals that he

---

[51] Martimort, *Les lectures liturgiques*, 72, note 10, based on *Epistula ad Theodoricum*, in CCM 1, 131–132. *Post Pentecosten vero per totam aestatem legimus apud sanctum Benedictum quotidianis diebus tres lectiones, in monasterio autem Domini Salvatoris usque ad octobris calendas de testamento veteri unam. Quam ideo sanctus pater noster, ut putamus, non in codice legi, sed ex corde recitari praecepit, eo quod necdum aestatis tempore mos esset Romanis quotidianis diebus in volumine legere; sed postea [sive a beato Gregorio papa, sive, alii affirmant] ab Honorio papa hoc institutum, quando et totam scripturam in ecclesia legi praecepit. Unde et nos, quia et id potius arbitramur venerabili patri nostri esse gratius, Romanum in legendis veteris ac novi testamenti per ordinem libris consuetudinem sequimur.*

[52] *Theodomari epistula ad Karolum regem*, CCM I, 160–161. On the authorship of this letter, 152–154.

[53] Martimort, *Les lectures liturgiques*, 87–89. Vogel, "Les échanges liturgiques," 289–292, and note 302.

[54] Vogel, "Les échanges liturgiques," 292–293.

[55] Jones, *Aelfric's Letter*, 61.

[56] The *ordo librorum* was not included in the *Liber officialis* itself, *Amalarii episcopi opera liturgica omnia*, ed. Hanssens, II. The last few chapters of the *Liber de ordine antiphonarii* (LXXI–LXXVI, 100–107) include an extensive explanation of the responsories from Kings, the Solomonic books, Job, Tobit, Judith, Esther, Ezra, the Maccabees and the Prophets, and reiterate the Roman origin of the practice.

was very concerned about how greatly the northern *ordines librorum* differed from the Roman version. Amalarius was clearly intent on reproducing the Roman practice of Nocturns north of the Alps.

> I asked the aforesaid deacon in what order the responsories are sung after the Octave of Pentecost up until Advent, [and] he responded: In the Octave of Pentecost we begin to read the book of Kings. In the first week of that same [month] we sing responsories from the Psalms; in the following weeks up until the month of August from the history of Kings. In the first week of August we read Solomon, and we sing responsories from Psalms. In the following [weeks] up until the month of September [we read] from Solomon. In the first week of September we read Job, and sing responsories from Psalms. In the two following [weeks we read] from Job; in the last week of the above-mentioned month, from Tobias; in the first two weeks of the month of October, [we read] from Judith and from Esther and Ezra; in the last two weeks of the aforesaid month from Maccabees; in the first week of the month of November we read from Prophets, and sing responses from Psalms. In the rest following up until Advent [we read] from Prophets.[57]

The list that Amalarius copied was supposedly that used in the daily rituals of the secular clerics, for he asked Theodore for information about practices in the generic "Romana ecclesia."[58] Already in the late-eighth century, however, these lists had made a transition from their original clientele of canons to a new one: monks. At the same time, they began to be included in a different genre of manuscript, highlighting that in the Carolingian period reformers saw fostering the correct reading of the Nocturns as a vital component of monastic reform. *Ordines librorum* had sometimes been included in collections of liturgical ordines and pontificals, service books that were also then in the process of being corrected according to Roman models. But because the *ordo librorum* was so different in character from the

---

[57] Amalarius, *Liber de ordine antiphonarii, Prologus*, 13. *Interrogavi memoratum archidiaconum quo ordine responsorios cantarent post octavas Pentecostes usque ad Adventum Domini responsum est: In octavis Pentecostes incipimus legere librum Regum; in eadem prima hebdomada cantamus responsorios de psalmis; in sequentibus hebdomadis usque in Augustum mensem de historia Regum. In prima hebdomada Augusti legimus Salomonem, et responsorios cantamus de Psalmis. In sequentibus usque in Septembrem mensem de Salomone. In prima hebdomada Septembris legimus Job, et cantamus responsorios de Psalmis; in duabus sequentibus de Job; in novissima hebdomada mensis memorati, de Tobia; in primis duabus hebdomadis mensis Octobris, de Judith et de Esther et Esdra; in duabus novissimis mensis suprascripti de Machabaeis; In prima hebdomada mensis Novembris legimus de Prophetis, responsorios cantamus de Psalmis. In caeteris sequentibus usque in Adventum Domini de Prophetis.*
[58] Amalarius, *Liber de ordine antiphonarii*, 13.

other ordines, scribes copying other liturgical directions often left it out. After all, an *ordo librorum* was not a series of instructions for a discrete service from beginning to end, like the other ordines that had developed by that time, but rather a list that dealt primarily with the readings from the Bible. Presumably, it quickly became so well known to the regular inhabitants of a monastery that it was referred to only occasionally throughout the year. Instead, *ordines librorum* were soon appended to instructions for life inside the monastic cloister or to the manuscripts that would have provided other yearly readings, such as lives of the saints, homilies, didactic works and *florilegia*, as well as seemingly unrelated works like grammars.[59] Benedict of Aniane, who could be considered the inventor of the monastic customary, did not include one in his description of monastic life, the *Concordia regularum*.[60] Nonetheless, three monastic manuscripts from the eighth century include *ordines librorum ad legendum* that state in their first passage that they were designed to accommodate the cycle of offices required by the Benedictine Rule. The best known of these, Saint Gall, Stiftsbibliothek MS 349, preserves eighth-century monastic practice in the monasteries of the Rhine valley and Alemannia.[61]

The first part of this manuscript is the remaining section of an eighth-century book of prayers to be read during Vespers, the Night Office, and on the principle feasts, taken from the Gregorian and Gelasian sacramentaries. This has been combined with a contemporary liturgical collection written in a pre-Caroline minuscule, probably at Saint Gall some time before the year 800. It includes decretals of Pope Innocent I, a list of the chapters of the Old and New Testaments, prayers for Vespers and Matins, and a series of instructions for those leading the monastic life, including two different versions of the *ordo librorum ad legendum*. The first, designated by Michel Andrieu Ordo XIV, is a fairly direct copy of the seventh-century rite as practiced at St. Peter's in Rome.[62] It is followed by Ordo XV, a very elaborate series of instructions to all types of clergy for celebrations throughout the church year, which is found in several

---

[59] *Les ordines romani* II, 471, Ordines XIIIA–D.
[60] *Benedicti Anianensis concordia regularum*, ed. Pierre Bonnerue (Turnhout, 1999).
[61] *Les ordines romani* I, 330–333 on Saint Gall 349. The monastery of Saint Gall already possessed a copy of Ordo XIIIA in the eighth century, in a patristic collection (Saint Gall, Stiftsbibliothek MS 225).
[62] *Les ordines romani* III, 39–41, Ordo XIV.

other manuscripts.[63] The second *ordo librorum*, Ordo XVI, is unique to this manuscript, though a variant version was soon included in two other monastic manuscripts, one from north-eastern France or Cologne, the other from Alsace.[64] Combining elements of ordines XIV and XV, the *incipit* indicates that this version, unlike the others, was intended specifically for monks.

> . . . arrangement of the ecclesiastical orders, in what way are to be faithfully celebrated in the monastery serving the Lord, as much according to the catholic and apostolic authority of the Roman Church as according to the disposition and rule of Saint Benedict, the solemnities of the mass or the birthdays of the saints or the Divine Office of the year day and night, God willing . . .[65]

The author has adjusted much of the text accordingly. In this case, the *ordo librorum* not only has been introduced as a text for the instruction of monks, it is also found in the context of other monastic directives.

I believe that the Carolingian large-format Bibles produced at Tours, with their highly legible script and handy reference format, other Bibles with similar characteristics such as the Saint-Amand Bible and the smaller, multi-volume Maurdramnus Bible, and the Bibles reordered to follow the *lectio continua* such as the Brussels Bible fragments, the Douai, Monza, Bobbio and Biasca Bibles,[66] were developed in part to accommodate the reading cycle of the *ordo librorum ad legendum* as it was increasingly observed both in monasteries and houses of canons. The elaborate decorations found in some Tours

---

[63] *Les ordines romani* III, 95–125, Ordo XV.

[64] *Les ordines romani* III, 149–154, Ordo XVI. The revised version is Ordo XVII, *Les ordines romani* III, 175–193. It combines elements from ordines XV and XVI. Rome BAV cod. Vat. Palat. lat. 574, from late-eighth or early-ninth-century north-eastern France or the Cologne region and Gotha, Forschungsbibliothek Cod. Membr. I.85, from Alsace, early ninth century (CCM I, 27–44, *Les ordines romani* III, 175–193, Renate Schipke, *Die Maugérard-Handschriften der Forschungsbibliothek Gotha*, Veröffentlichungen der Forschungsbibliothek Gotha XV [Gotha, 1972], 54–57).

[65] *Les ordines romani* III, 147, Saint Gall, Stiftsbibliothek MS 349 p. 54. . . . *instruccio ecclesiastici ordinis, qualiter in coenubiis fideliter domino servientes tam iuxta auctoritatem catholice atque apostolice romane ecclesie quam iuxta dispositione et regulam sancti Benedicti missarum solemniis vel nataliciis sanctorum seu et officiis divinis anni circoli die noctuque, auxiliante domino, debeant celebrare* . . .

[66] Paris BnF MS lat. 2, Amiens BM MSS 6,7,9,11 and 12 and Paris BnF MS lat. 13174, fols. 136 and 138, Brussels, Bibliothèque royale MS II, 1052 f. 137–140, Douai BM MS 14, Monza $^{i\text{-}2}/_9$, Milan, Bibliotheca Ambrosiana MSS E.26 inf and E.53 inf.

Bibles may lead one to assume these volumes to have been objects of veneration, set on the altar or kept in a treasury for occasional display. An examination of the entire corpus of Carolingian Bibles, taking into account especially the format of the text, on the other hand, tells a different story. Above all, these were designed as working manuscripts, expected to provide the means for regular Biblical reading according to the demands of Alcuin and the other reformers, in addition to their utility as corrected textual exempla.

As copies and variant versions of the *ordo librorum* were multiplying, these same monasteries and houses of canons began to compile and correct Bibles for their own use. Saint Gall, the home of the newly invented late eighth-century Ordo XVI, acquired one of the earliest surviving Tours Bibles some time in the ninth century, Saint Gall, Stiftsbibliothek MS 75, but may have copied its own two-volume Bible already, Fulda, Landesbibliothek MS Aa 10–11.[67] Metz, where Bishop Chrodegang imposed the *Regula canonicorum* on his canons in the mid-eighth century, and where Amalarius worked so diligently to reform the Office and correct the *lectio continua* according to Roman tradition, received the oldest surviving (until its destruction in 1944) large-format pandect, in the late-eighth or early-ninth century.[68] Its patron may have been Angilramn, Bishop of Metz and archchaplain at Charlemagne's court before his death in 791.[69] Other monasteries received or copied a Bible even earlier. Fulda, Landesbibliothek MS Aa 10–11 was given to Constance in the early-ninth century, but that house may have copied its own Bible already in the late-eighth century.[70] Corbie possessed a copy of the Lateran *ordo librorum* (Ordo XIIIA) in a ninth- or tenth-century manuscript,

---

[67] McKitterick, "Carolingian Bible production," 64 and 71, and Fischer, "Bibeltext und Bibelreform," 162, 170, 202 and 206 and idem, "Bibelausgaben des frühen Mittelalters," *La bibbia nell'alto medioevo*, Settimane di studio del centro Italiano di studi sull'alto medioevo X (Spoleto, 1963), 597.

[68] Metz BM MS 7. McKitterick, "Carolingian Bible production," 67–68, Fischer, "Bibelausgaben," 590–591, and idem, "Bibeltext und Bibelreform," 191–192. Written in two columns of 40 lines, and measuring 45 by 35 cm, this manuscript was as large as the later Tours Bibles and similar in format.

[69] This, of course, depends on its still disputed date. Nees, "Problems of Form and Function," 138, and Fischer, "Bibeltext und Bibelreform," 191.

[70] Fischer, "Bibeltext und Bibelreform," 202 and idem, "Bibelausgaben," 597. The earlier Bible is Stuttgart, Württembergische Landesbibliothek, Cod. HB. II, 35. Today only the end of Proverbs, the remaining Wisdom books, and Job, Tobias, Judith, Esther and Ezra survive.

of which parts are today in Saint Petersburg, Cod. Q.V.II n. 5, fols. 53v-56, and a slightly different one (Ordo XIIIB) in a ninth-century compilation written at Corbie, Paris BnF MS lat. 14088, fols. 100–102. Even earlier, a scribe associated with Corbie had copied the St. Peter's ordo (Ordo XIV) into an eighth-century volume of ecclesiastical canons, Paris BnF MS lat. 3836, fols. 103v–104.[71] The late-eighth-century Maurdramnus Bible from Corbie is perhaps the oldest surviving multi-volume Bible copied in response to the Carolingian textual reform, as discussed above.[72] Salzburg produced a multi-volume Bible similar to the Maurdramnus Bible in the late-eighth century under Bishop Arn.[73] Würzburg, where an innovative version of the *ordo librorum* would later be produced in a Cluniac customary for St. Stephen's abbey, acquired a multi-volume Bible from its bishop in the early-ninth century.[74] In combination with the Carolingian Bibles discussed above that are either ordered to accommodate the *lectio continua*, have the Psalter and Gospels in miniature script, or lack those books altogether, the number of Carolingian Bibles that can demonstrate some connection to the practice of Nocturn reading is suggestive.

Although many of these Bibles were relatively plain, if carefully executed, some of them were lavishly decorated with elaborate schemes of didactic miniatures tailored for their royal recipients. An example is the First Bible of Charles the Bald, Paris BnF MS lat. 1, copied and illustrated by the canons at Saint-Martin at Tours under

---

[71] *Les ordines romani* I, 271–272, 276–279, 348–350 and McKitterick, *The Frankish Church*, 32.

[72] McKitterick, "Carolingian Bible production," 67, and Fischer, "Bibeltext und Bibelreform," 186. Amiens BM MSS 6, 7, 9, 11 and 12, and Paris BnF MS lat. 13174, fols. 136 and 138. An inscription in the Maurdramnus Bible explains "Ego Maur dramnus abb. propter Dei amorem et propter conpendium legentium hoc volumen fieri jussi. Quicumque hunc librum legerit Domini misericordiam pro me exoret." Amiens BM MS 11, fol. 96r. Ayres, "Le bibbie atlantiche," 28 and Berger, *Histoire de la Vulgate*, 102 and 374. The Bible varies in format, from two columns of 24 lines, to one column of 20 lines. Although it perhaps couldn't be termed a lectern Bible, the dimensions of the Maurdramnus Bible vary from 35 by 25 cm, to 30 by 19.5 cm, so it is rather large.

[73] Mattsee, Stiftsbibliothek MS 46 and Kremsmünster, Stiftsbibliothek MS frg. I/1, and perhaps Salzburg, St. Peter MS a.IX.16. Fischer, "Bibeltext und Bibelreform," 209 and idem, "Bibelausgaben," 587–588.

[74] Ganz, "Mass production," 54–55, and Fischer, "Bibeltext und Bibelreform," 200. Today fragmentary, Oxford, Bodleian MS Laud lat. 92, Würzburg, Universitätsbibliothek MSS M.p.th.f. 18, 14 and 147, and M.p.th.f. 5 and 77, probably once all belonged to a single Bible, produced under Bishop Hunbert (832–842).

the patronage of Count Vivian as a gift for the Emperor Charles the Bald. As Herbert Kessler and Paul Dutton have shown, the programmer of the Bible incorporated an interlocking series of poems and images intended to instruct the king in his duty to absorb the message of the Bible and with it to promote Christianity within his realm.[75] While most of the Carolingian Bibles were probably intended to be used in the houses where they were produced, the Tours Bibles were manufactured for export to other monasteries and cathedrals, and were frequently given as gifts or commissioned by wealthy clergy or the nobility. Lawrence Nees suggested that "The very few luxuriously decorated Bibles were extraordinary gifts, impressive but fundamentally useless except as gift to all but a few great scholars like Bede, except in the different but nonetheless important sense of a representation in physical form of the unity of the scriptural corpus."[76] All the same, while some of these high-end manuscripts may have retained the status of relics,[77] set on the altar and admired rather than used, their format facilitates public reading and instruction as well as private study. It is also significant that while many were commissioned *by* prominent clerics and laypeople, as Rosamund McKitterick has pointed out, almost always they were given *to* ecclesiastical foundations. For instance, two of the most elaborate Tours Bibles were given to monasteries: the Rorigo Bible (Paris BnF MS lat. 3) was given to Glanfeuil by Count Rorigo of Maine, and the Moutier-Grandval Bible (London BL MS Add. 10546) was given to the abbey of Moutier-Grandval in the Jura, a foundation well known to Saint Gall.[78] The Cologne Bible was given to the cathedral chapter by Bishop Heriman, although well after it was redacted.[79] Even the First Bible of Charles the Bald may have been given to the Cathedral of Metz by Charles.[80] Surely not all of these houses were simply in need of a text reference or a symbolic showpiece.

---

[75] Paul Edward Dutton and Herbert L. Kessler, *The Poetry and Painting of the First Bible of Charles the Bald* (Ann Arbor, 1997), conclusion.

[76] Nees, "Problems of Form and Function," 174.

[77] McKitterick, "Carolingian Bible production," 72.

[78] McKitterick, "Carolingian Bible production," 71–72 and Berger, *Histoire de la Vulgate*, 211.

[79] Cologne, Erzbischöfliche Diözesan Dombibliothek, Dom MS 1, Berger, *Histoire de la Vulgate*, 212.

[80] Paris BnF MS lat. 1. Berger, *Histoire de la Vulgate*, 219.

Romanesque Giant Bibles

The Saint-Vaast Bible, in addition to resurrecting the function of several Tours Bibles as vehicles for political messages, also heralded the Romanesque revival of the large-format Bible as an Office reading tool. As in the Carolingian era that preceded it, once again in the Romanesque period a distinct class of large-format Bibles arose. The Saint-Vaast Bible and the lavishly ornamented and illustrated Bibles that followed have long been set apart as a distinct type of manuscript, under the title "Giant Bible." Although the name seems to have been applied first to the Bibles produced in Italian scriptoria, it can be used as an umbrella term describing eleventh- and twelfth-century lectern Bibles in general; the Italian Romanesque Bibles are not significantly larger than their contemporary northern counterparts. Produced in the monasteries of northern Europe, Spain and Italy beginning in the eleventh century, these large, often multivolume Bibles share many characteristics. For instance, they are remarkably consistent in their overall dimensions, usually measuring between 45 and 60 centimeters tall, and between 30 and 40 centimeters wide when closed.[81] The most typical form of decoration for these manuscripts is the historiated initial, although many of the Bibles also include illustrated frontispieces before the more important books of the Bible, such as the Book of Genesis. They are also usually written with a large and very legible late Caroline minuscule script.

The Saint-Vaast Bible and the other Romanesque Giant Bibles, it seems, merely built on and refined the preexisting Carolingian tradition. The large dimensions they share with the Carolingian pandects, in many cases their decoration, which was at times directly copied from Carolingian models, and the tenth-, eleventh- and twelfth-century monastic customaries that accompanied them, all point to the continued use of the large-format Bible as a tool for reading

---

[81] Walter Cahn, *Romanesque Bible Illumination* (Ithaca, 1982), 101, Knut Berg, *Studies in Tuscan Twelfth-Century Illumination* (Oslo-Bergen-Tromsö, 1968), and Edward B. Garrison, *Studies in the History of Medieval Italian Painting*, 4 vols. (Florence, 1953–1962). See Larry Ayres, "The Italian Giant Bibles: aspects of their Touronian ancestry and early history," in *The Early Medieval Bible*, 125 n. 3, on the origin of the term. For a survey of manuscript dimensions, see the catalogue of Bibles in Cahn, *Romanesque Bible Illumination*, 251–293.

during the Night Office. The Romanesque reformers left no equivalent to Charlemagne's *Epistola generalis* or Theodulph's *Libri Carolini*
demanding the revision of the Bible. Nonetheless, the Romanesque
copyists and their supervisors were most likely aware of the traditions of their Carolingian predecessors, and may even have called
on their authority when they chose Carolingian Bibles as their models, in the wake of a new set of monastic reforms in the tenth,
eleventh and twelfth centuries. Larry Ayres has suggested that the
Roman Bibles, copied in the orbit of the reform papacy, consciously
used models such as the Carolingian San Paolo Bible to help recre-
ate the cultural atmosphere associated with the Carolingian Empire.[82]
Although the Roman Bibles are the most obvious examples of this
revival, the renewal of Carolingian Bibles and their subsequent replacement by Romanesque volumes happened all over Europe in the
same era.

Striking parallels between the Carolingian large-format Bible movement and that of the Romanesque period can also be found in their
places of manufacture and their patterns of distribution. Both periods
share an interesting combination of methods. In some cases single
Bibles seem to have been manufactured by the monasteries or houses
of canons that intended to use them, while in others, a workshop
produced Bibles in quantity for export. In the Carolingian period,
this second phenomenon was best exemplified, of course, by the
workshop originally set up by Alcuin at Tours in the late-eighth
century. Theodulph of Orléans' workshop, possibly at St. Mesmin
de Micy, may be another example.[83] In the Romanesque period, the
as yet unlocalized scriptorium that provided the Atlantic or "Roman"
Bibles, a group of eleventh-century Bibles that overlap in iconography, codicology and paleography, is the closest comparison.[84] In both
the Carolingian and the Romanesque eras, a central authority, either
the Imperial household or the Pope, seems to have instigated or at

---

[82] Ayres, "The Italian Giant Bibles," 129.

[83] McKitterick, "Carolingian Bible production," 65, 67 and Fischer, "Bibeltext
und Bibelreform," 176.

[84] Ayres, "The Italian Giant Bibles," 127, makes the comparison between scriptoria that produced the Italian Romanesque Bibles and St. Martin at Tours, the
workshop of the Touronian Bibles, explicit. Guy Lobrichon, "Riforma ecclesiastica
e testo della Bibbia," in *Le Bibbie atlantiche*, 15–26 and Ayres, "Le Bibbie atlantiche,"
33–34.

least encouraged the copying of the Bible and its distribution across the leaders' sphere of influence.

Observers have long remarked on the links between the Carolingian Bibles, especially those from Tours, and their successors, the Romanesque Giant Bibles. For instance, the Italian "Atlantic" Bibles draw heavily on their Carolingian predecessors for their structure, including their use of hierarchy of text, layout of canon tables, and *tituli*, and the version of Psalms chosen by the compiler.[85] Unlike other Romanesque Bibles, the Italian Bibles are also typically pandects, or single-volume Bibles like the Touronian Bibles. Some artists went even further, copying the yellow, frame initial style of the Carolingian Bibles explicitly.[86] The Italian artists and scribes may have been consciously imitating as many aspects of the Touronian Bibles as possible.[87] Other artists copied entire compositions or full-page layouts.[88]

Such copying was not restricted to Italy, however. Northern Bibles also took advantage of Carolingian models. The artists of both the Stavelot and Lobbes Bibles, working in northern scriptoria under the direction of the same artist and scribe, Goderannus, seem to have copied Old and New Testament miniatures from Carolingian Bibles similar to the San Paolo Bible as well.[89] As we will see in chapter 4, the Saint-Vaast illustrators also echoed the miniature programs of Carolingian Bibles. Despite the limited number of illustrated Carolingian Bibles that survive today, in the eleventh and twelfth centuries many

---

[85] Ayres, "The Italian Giant Bibles," 128–129 and Ayres, "Le Bibbie atlantiche," 28–35.

[86] See, for instance, Munich, Bayerische Staatsbibliothek, Clm 13001, fol. 88, the initial for Judith. Ayres, "The Italian Giant Bibles," 130–133. See, however, Virginia Brown for an important exception to this practice and its implications, "Contenuti, funzione e origine della 'Bibbia di San Vincenzo al Volturno' (Roma, Biblioteca Vallicelliana, D 8)," *Nuovi annali della scuola speciale per archivisti e bibliotecari* XVIII (2004), 37–60.

[87] Berg, 17.

[88] In the case of the Pantheon Bible's Genesis illustration, they must have used as their source of inspiration the Genesis illustrations of the Touronian Bibles. Rome BAV cod. Vat. lat. 12958, fol. 4v. Cahn, *Romanesque Bible Illumination*, 100.

[89] St. Peter of Lobbes (Tournai, Bibliothèque du Séminaire, MS 1), includes at least three historiated initials with iconography likely condensed from a model similar to the San Paolo Bible: II Kings, fol. 132v's illustration of the death of the Amalekite, Leviticus's scene of animal sacrifice, fol. 46v, and Deuteronomy, fol. 77's image of Moses and Aaron before the Ark of the Covenant. Don Denny, "Historiated Initials of the Lobbes Bible," *Revue belge d'archéologie et d'histoire de l'art* XIV–XV (1976), 4–8 and Cahn, *Romanesque Bible Illumination*, 126–130.

a European monastery must have had a more or less decorated version in its library or choir that was still in use. These versions served as models to a new generation of scribes and illuminators seeking to accomplish the same goal: the revival of monastic Bible reading.[90]

De Hamel, in his recent survey of the history of Bible manuscripts, expressed his belief that the primary purpose of a Romanesque Giant Bible was symbolic. Many of them can be documented as gifts from high clergy to their dependent foundations. The assumption that the representative value of the books outweighed their day-to-day function as texts, De Hamel points out, explains their often luxurious appearance. "A gift from a major patron," he states, "had to present an appearance appropriate to the donor's status."[91] Because De Hamel believes that their Carolingian models functioned as lavish gifts as well, he rejects the possibility that the Romanesque Giant Bibles were destined for a practical use. Although he acknowledges that they were intended to be placed on display, and that they show several other hallmarks of public reading, he doubts that these manuscripts were intended to be read out loud. Instead, he suggests that they served primarily as master copies of the Bible, used to double-check the text editions found in other monastic manuscripts, particularly liturgical books.[92]

Because the Carolingian predecessors of the Romanesque Giant Bibles were inspired by the textual and liturgical reforms spearheaded by Charlemagne and his advisors, however, one can logically connect the Romanesque versions with subsequent Church reforms that sponsored the revival of Bible reading as well. Not surprisingly, the *ordo librorum* once again is our key to tracing the life of a Bible inside the monastic setting. The *ordo librorum* never became universal in monastic customaries. Customaries and monastic instructions produced by some of the most famous reforming monasteries of the tenth and eleventh centuries, such as the *Consuetudines Floriacenses antiquiore*, the *Regularis concordia* of Dunstan, and the admittedly fragmentary customary of Saint-Vanne of Verdun, include no *ordo librorum*.[93]

---

[90] Diane Reilly, "French Romanesque Giant Bibles and their English Relatives: Blood Relatives or Adopted Children?" *Scriptorium* LVI (2002), 294–311.

[91] De Hamel, 73.

[92] De Hamel, 73–76. He later contradicts this statement by suggesting that many monasteries eventually required a second giant, luxuriously decorated Bible to be read in the choir and refectory (p. 81).

[93] *Consuetudinum saeculi X/XI/XII monumenta non-Cluniacensia*, ed. Kassius Hallinger,

Nonetheless, it proliferated in the eleventh and twelfth centuries and is found in examples of customaries from most orders and reform movements. In addition, the customaries record several other clues to the ever-increasing importance of Biblical reading in the monastery.

While the Carolingians typically included the *ordo librorum ad legendum* as a more or less straightforward list in their manuscripts, late-tenth-century Cluniac reformers took the lead in adapting this *ordo* into their monastic directives, subdividing it and interspersing it throughout the customaries in the course of the late-tenth and eleventh centuries.[94] The contrast between different customaries produced by the same order reveals a variety of approaches. In two redactions of the *Cluniacensium antiquiorum*, for instance, the schedule has been integrated into instructions for the rest of the church year.[95] In the mid-eleventh-century Cluniac customary of Bernard, the *ordo librorum* is both integrated into the text and appended to the end of the customary.[96] Other Cluniac customaries, such as the *Redactio Burgundica-Mellicensis-Moriana*, the *Redactio Vallumbrosana* and the *Constitutiones* of William of Hirsau include only part of the *ordo librorum* or none of it at all.[97] The eleventh-century *Liber tramitis* of Odilo takes up the practice of the *Cluniacensium antiquiorum* and integrates the instructions on Bible reading.[98] English and Norman monasteries show an equally varied approach. Aelfric's early-eleventh-century letter to the monks of Eynsham, a sort of customary in itself, records the list, interrupted by a few other instructions and responses.[99] After the Norman

---

CCM VII/3, (Siegburg, 1984), for Fleury, 7–60, for the *Regularis concordia*, 70–147, and for the *Redactio Virdunensis*, 381–426.

[94] Diane Reilly, "The Cluniac Giant Bible and the *Ordo librorum ad legendum*: a reassessment of monastic Bible reading and Cluniac customary instructions," in *From Dead of Night to End of Day: The Medieval Cluniac Customs/Du cour de la nuit à la fin du jour: les coutumes clunisiennes au Moyen Age*, eds. Susan Boynton and Isabelle Cochelin, Disciplina monastica I (Turnhout: Brepols, 2005), 163–189.

[95] *Cluniacensium antiquiorum redactiones principales*, and *Redactio Wirzeburgensis*, in *Consuetudines Cluniacensium antiquiores cum redactionibus derivatis*, ed. Kassius Hallinger, CCM VII/2, (Siegburg, 1983), 9–150 and 271–308.

[96] Rule, in Marquard Herrgott, *Vetus disciplina monastica: seu collectis auctorum ordinis s. Benedicti maximam partem ineditorum . . .* (Paris, 1726), 283–364.

[97] CCM VII/2, 315–379, 385–408 and for the *Constitutiones Hirsaugiensis* PL 150:923ff.

[98] *Liber tramitis aevi Odilonis abbatis*, ed. Peter Dinter, CCM X (Siegburg, 1980), 47–188.

[99] CCM VII/3, 181–185, Christopher A. Jones, *Aelfric's Letter to the Monks of Eynsham* (Cambridge, 1998), 3, 36 and M. McC. Gatch, "The Office in Late Anglo-Saxon Monasticism," in *Learning and Literature in Late Anglo-Saxon England*, eds. Michael

Conquest, a new version found its way across the channel in the form of Lanfranc of Bec's late-eleventh-century *ordo*, which includes integrated Biblical reading instructions.[100] Clearly, in these customaries the *ordo librorum* was not simply being copied by rote but was being analyzed and incorporated by scribes who used it on a day-to-day basis. Although because of the spotty survival of both Giant Bibles and Romanesque customaries only a general parallel between the growth of the *ordo librorum* and the blossoming of Bible production can be observed, enough examples of both survive to demonstrate that this was an almost universal component of Romanesque monastic reform.

Still, the main difference between Carolingian and Romanesque practice of the *lectio continua* in practical terms was one of extent. By the Romanesque era monastic reading of the Bible had expanded from its traditional domain of Nocturns read in the choir to include lections read in the refectory during meals.[101] References to the reading of the Bible in the refectory multiplied in the eleventh and twelfth centuries, as did telltale suggestions that the monks were reading from a Giant Bible. The Würzburg redaction of the *Cluniacensium antiquiores* instructs that although the reading of the Heptateuch began in the church during the Nocturns, it continued in both the church and the refectory, "simul et in aecclesia et in refectorio," until all the books were finished.[102] Udalric of Cluny agreed that the Bible was to be read "et in ecclesia, et in refectorio," as did the author of Odilo of Cluny's *Liber tramitis* when describing the reading of the books of Solomon.[103] Aelfric explained in his epistle under the heading *De ordine lectionum per anni circulum* that because the entire Bible

---

Lapidge and Helmut Gneuss (Cambridge, 1985), 352–362. Equally significant is the fact that Aelfric specified in several letters which books a parish priest ought to own, and did not include the Bible. The reading of the Bible as a whole was obviously, in his view, a specifically monastic undertaking. Richard Gameson, *The Role of Art in the Late Anglo-Saxon Church* (Oxford, 1995), 242 and note 44.

[100] *Decreta Lanfranci monachis Cantuariensibus transmissa*, ed. David Knowles, CCM III (Siegburg, 1967).

[101] Heinrich Fichtenau, "Neues zum Problem der italienischen 'Riesenbibeln'," *Institut für Österreichische Geschichtsforschung: Mitteilungen* LVIII (1950), 59–61. Also Ayres, "The Italian Giant Bibles," 126, Cahn, *Romanesque Bible Illumination*, 95–96 and Peter Brieger, "Bible Illustration and Gregorian Reform," in *Studies in Church History* II (1965), 161.

[102] CCM VII/2, 293.

[103] Udalric of Cluny, *Antiquiores consuetudines Cluniacensis monasterii*, PL 149:643 and CCM X, 145.

must be read in the course of the year, what was omitted in the choir should be read in the refectory.[104]

This may have engendered a few problems: the enormous pandects designed for choir reading in the Carolingian era could be left on a lectern, or at least in the church, from one service to the next. As David Ganz has observed, they were never portable.[105] De Hamel noted that the 60-centimeter tall Italian Pandect that Bishop Frederick gave to Geneva Cathedral in the later-eleventh century weighed almost fifty pounds.[106] Once refectory reading was included in the reading cycle, the cumbersome book had to be carried back and forth between the different reading locations. This problem was addressed by a monk named William in his eleventh-century customary for Hirsau, when he instructed that the person responsible for reading to the servants was to carry the book back into the refectory, with the help of the weekly reader, if necessary.[107] This is one possible explanation for the division of the majority of Romanesque Bibles into several, albeit very large, volumes. Nonetheless, the Romanesque scribes seem to have been committed to the production of large-format Bibles despite the problems inherent in having to transport them regularly from one part of the monastery to another. Most likely this was due both to their adherence to the authoritative model provided by the Carolingian pandects, and to the function of the Bibles themselves. Choir and refectory reading required a large and legible text of the type exemplified by the new Romanesque Bibles.

Monastic customaries are not the only sources to contain more frequent references to the reading of the Bible in the refectory. The twelfth-century Sawalo Bible from Saint-Amand, Valenciennes BM MS 1–5, contains written instructions after Kings, Chronicles and

---

[104] CCM VII/3, 184.

[105] Ganz, "Mass production," 61, note 29.

[106] De Hamel, 68. Geneva, Bibliothèque publique et universitaire MS lat. 1.

[107] Fichtenau, 60 and Brieger, 161 n. 3, point out that when the customary of Hirsau mentions only one 'librum' which must be carried back and forth between the church and the refectory, sometimes by two people, just such a lectern Bible is probably being discussed. PL 150:1028 *Librum in quo legendum est, in refectorium portat et reportat is qui legit ad servitores, adjuvante eum ipso, si opus est, mensae lectore: qui et mox cum eum deposuerit, quod legendum est invenit.* See also Laura Light, "Versions et révisions du texte biblique," in *Le moyen âge et la Bible,* ed. Pierre Riché and Guy Lobrichon, Bible de tous les temps IV (Paris, 1984), 71, for evidence of reading from the Bible in the refectory in England.

the Song of Songs about where to find the next book to be read 'ad mensam.'[108] The *ordo librorum* was copied into many Italian Giant Bibles so that it would always be at the disposal of the monks who were closing the manuscript and transporting it through the monastery as often as twice a day.[109] Although no eleventh-century customaries with an *ordo librorum* survive from Saint-Vaast or any of the associated monasteries that subsequently produced Bibles, the practice of monastic reading of the Bible according to the *ordo librorum* was certainly known in the region of Saint-Vaast. Saint-Omer BM MS 2, an early-twelfth-century volume containing the Octateuch and Job, was once part of a Bible, as an inscription on fol. 1, "Biblia Sacra Bibliothecae sancti Audomavi," testifies.[110] An *ordo librorum ad legendum* was written on fol. 1 in the same era that the Flemish Bibles we will now examine were produced.

An Idiosyncratic Group of Flemish Bibles

The Saint-Vaast Bible conforms to the definition of a Romanesque Giant, or lectern, Bible in its size, its decoration and script, and in its division into several volumes. As one of the very first Romanesque Giant Bibles to be produced, and one of the more elaborate, in some ways it serves as a benchmark for the hundreds of Bibles that would follow. Even in this early example of a Giant Bible, many of the genre's standard features had already been established. Several striking characteristics, however, set the Saint-Vaast Bible apart. First, it is in fact not a complete Bible, but lacks both the Psalter from the Old Testament, and the Gospels from the New Testament.[111] Although it is tempting to assume that these lacunae represent losses sustained by the manuscript when it was mutilated in the early-nineteenth century, a careful examination of the codicology proves that

---

[108] Vol. II, fol. 78v, vol. III, fol. 139v and vol. IV, 43v.

[109] Ayres, "Le Bibbie atlantiche," 28. Ayres points out, however, that these ordines may have been added to the Bibles as late as the thirteenth century.

[110] Henri Michelant, *Catalogue général* III, St. Omer, 11–12. Michelant, surprisingly, did not transcribe either the inscription of ownership or the instructions for reading.

[111] André Boutemy was the first to recognize that these lacunae were original, although he did not provide a detailed explanation for his opinion ("La Bible enluminée de Saint-Vaast à Arras," *Scriptorium* IV [1950], 70).

these books were never included in the Bible (Appendix). Second, the Saint-Vaast Bible includes an unusual pseudepigraphical addition, the text of the *Passio Machabeorum*. Rather than separating this Bible from the class, the details that may seem anomalous instead reveal yet more important information about the function of this Bible in particular and Romanesque large-format Bibles in general.

Romanesque Giant Bibles display amazing variety in their contents and structure. The modern predilection to regard the Bible as a set series of books conditions most viewers to believe that a Bible is not 'correct' unless it includes a certain number of books in a standard order. For instance, an English reader will expect it to have at least all the books found in more modern printed versions, such as the Church of England's King James, and no more books than are found in the Roman Catholic Douay-Rheims, and in something similar to the order found in these Bibles. In reality, the order of the books in a Bible when copied as a unit was not standardized before the thirteenth century, when the so-called Paris Bibles were first mass-produced. The books that were included in earlier Bibles varied according to regional tradition, the models available to the scriptorium, and the function envisioned for the Bible. Nonetheless, it is still possible to suggest where the Gospels and Psalter might have fallen in an eleventh-century Bible, as well as to establish the continuity of the text in the Arras Bible around these areas, proving that the Saint-Vaast Bible, with all its present-day lacunae, is almost as complete as when it was first copied and bound.[112] In all the North French Romanesque Bibles the prefatory material of the subsequent book usually followed on the same folio, or even in the same column, the ending and *explicit* of the previous book, making it easy to ensure that the text of any given section is in the same state as when the original scribe finally lifted his pen from the page. Because the Saint-Vaast Bible, like its companions, was designed to serve monks following the demands of the Office in a newly reformed setting, it will be very revealing to pin down how the scribes who created the Bible adjusted it to serve this purpose.

The Touronian Bibles and several Bibles contemporary with them all placed the Psalter between the Book of Job and the Wisdom books.[113] This practice was taken up by many of the surviving tenth-

---

[112] See chap. 1, on the loss of individual pages from the manuscript.

[113] Touronian Bibles are the Grandval Bible, London BL MS Add. 10546, the

and eleventh-century Bibles, such as the León Bible of 960, the Stavelot Bible, and the First Bible of Saint-Martial.[114] Thus in Romanesque Bibles, as in Carolingian Bibles before them, the Psalter is almost always found before the Wisdom books: Proverbs, Ecclesiastes, the Song of Solomon, Wisdom, and Ecclesiasticus. In the Arras Bible, as in the Touronian Bibles and the later First Bible of Saint-Martial, the Book of Job follows the Prophets in the Bible. However, in the Arras Bible Job ends on fol. 132 of vol. II, and immediately there-after the *incipit* to the first of the Wisdom Books, Proverbs, begins. There is no break between the two books, and therefore the Psalter was never there.

A different order is found in two other Bibles, the ninth-century Hincmar Bible and the eleventh-century Moissac Bible.[115] In these, the Psalter is placed after the Prophets, rather than after Job, and before the Wisdom books. Once again, however, there is no gap in the Arras Bible either before the Wisdom books, or at the end of the Prophets on fol. 119v of vol. II that would provide evidence of the removal of an entire biblical book. In addition, in 1628 an inscrip-tion of ownership was added on fol. 1 of vol. II of the Bible, and at that time the same scribe listed the biblical books then found in that volume. This table of contents, added long before the large-scale destruction of the post-revolutionary period, lists all the books found in the volume in the correct order, but makes no mention of the Psalter.[116] While it is impossible to prove that the Saint-Vaast Bible never contained a Psalter, the evidence certainly argues against it.

The same dilemma occurs when one hunts for the hypothetical home of a missing set of Gospel books. Again, a table of contents was added to fol. 2 of vol. III in the early-seventeenth century. This list makes no mention of the Gospels, but lists the rest of the surviving

---

Vivian Bible, Paris BnF MS lat. 1, the Rorigo Bible, Paris BnF MS lat. 3, and contemporary Bibles, the San Paolo Bible and the Second Bible of Charles the Bald, Paris BnF MS lat. 2 For the order of books in several hundred different Bibles, see the confusing but exhaustive index in Berger, *Histoire de la Vulgate*, Appendix I, 331–339. See Ganz, 53–62, on the amount of standardization among Tours Bibles.

[114] León, Colegiata de San Isidoro, Cod. 2, London BL MS Add. 28106–7, and Paris BnF MS lat. 5, Berger, *Histoire de la Vulgate*, Appendix I, numbers 20, 27 and 50.

[115] Reims BM MS 1 and Paris BnF MS lat. 7, Berger, *Histoire de la Vulgate*, Appendix I, numbers 40 and 42.

[116] See the Appendix.

books in the correct order.[117] In earlier and contemporary Bibles the
placement of the Gospels varied. They could be found at the beginning of the New Testament, followed by Acts, as in the Touronian
Bibles. Sometimes the book of Acts and the Pauline Epistles were
switched, and Acts was instead found before the Apocalypse at the
end of the New Testament, as it was in the Arras Bible, in which
case one should find the Gospels before the Pauline Epistles.[118] There
is no gap in the Arras Bible where one would expect to find the
Gospels, between the end of the Old Testament, here with the *Passio
Machabeorum*, and the beginning of the Pauline Epistles. Rather, both
fall on fol. 85v of vol. III. In fact, there is no sign of a series of
folio stubs large enough to show that more than two or three folios
were removed in a group anywhere in the Bible. It is therefore
almost impossible to maintain that the Psalter and Gospels have been
removed from the manuscript at some point in its history. In addition, the manuscript is otherwise complete, with no large sections of
text left unfinished.

It appears that at least four other Giant Bibles later produced in
the same region of Northern France and under the aegis of a single monastic reformer also never possessed a Psalter, although the
evidence is complicated because, like the Saint-Vaast Bible, several
of these Flemish Bibles were later mutilated. Three of these manuscripts, and a fourth from one of the same scriptoria, can be shown
never to have included the Gospels. Cataloguers of these Bibles have
occasionally tried to explain the absence of these seemingly crucial
books by complicated hypotheses about damage to the manuscripts.
When they are examined as a group, however, it becomes obvious
that these Bibles were never intended to be 'complete' in the commonly accepted modern sense. Like the Carolingian Maurdramnus
Bible from Corbie, and the late Carolingian Bobbio and Biasca
Bibles,[119] the Flemish Bibles were designed within a milieu where
the text of Psalter and the Gospels would have been superfluous to
their function.

---

[117] See the Appendix.
[118] The Gospels are followed by Acts in the Hincmar Bible, the Stavelot Bible
and the Moissac Bible, and by the Pauline Epistles in the Leon Bible of 960, where
Acts is placed before Apocalypse.
[119] Amiens BM MSS 6, 7, 9, 11 and 12, and Paris BnF MS lat. 13174, fols. 136
and 138, Milan, Bibliotheca Ambrosiana MS E.26 inf, and Milan, Bibliotheca
Ambrosiana MS E.53 inf.

The least damaged of this series, Douai BM MS 1, is a two-volume Giant Bible written and decorated at the abbey of Saint-Rictrude in Marchiennes in the early-twelfth century.[120] In vol. I, which contains the first half of the Old Testament, one might expect to find the beginning of a Psalter before the first of the Wisdom books, and at the end of Chronicles. Instead, the *explicit* of II Chronicles on fol. CCIv is followed immediately on the same folio by the *incipit* for Proverbs, signaling that there has never been a Psalter between these two books. In the second volume, the New Testament begins with the Acts of the Apostles, on fol. CLXVIIv, the verso of the folio on which the last of the minor prophets, Malachi, is found. There are no significant gaps or missing sections in the manuscript. Douai BM MS 1 therefore never included either the Psalter or the Gospels.

The situation for the other surviving Bibles from Douai is more complicated. Douai BM MS 3, also from Marchiennes, is a later compilation made when the surviving parts of two twelfth-century Giant Bibles were sandwiched together.[121] In Douai BM MS 3a, which contains the Wisdom books and some historical books, one would expect to find the Psalter before Proverbs, at the end of the Book of Job. There is no break, however, between the end of Job on fol. 18 and the beginning of Proverbs, signaling that the Psalter was probably never included. Douai BM MS 3b, the second Bible remnant of the compilation, begins in the midst of the Book of Proverbs on fol. 148. It is, therefore, impossible to tell now if it ever had a Psalter. The New Testament section of this Giant Bible, however, does survive. As in the Saint-Vaast Bible, there is no interruption between the *Passio Machabeorum* and the Pauline Epistles, where the Gospels would usually belong, both of which occur on fol. 238. The remainder of the New Testament follows without a

---

[120] Cahn, *Romanesque Bible Illumination*, 271, and *Catalogue général* VI, Douai, 3–4. Vol. I contains the Octateuch, the Books of Kings and Chronicles, as well as the Wisdom books. Vol. II contains the historical books of Job, Tobias, Judith, Esther, Ezra, and the Maccabees, the Major and Minor Prophets, and the New Testament.

[121] *Catalogue général*, VI, Douai, 4–5. Douai BM MS 3a, the remnant of the first Bible, begins with the Book of Job, followed by the Wisdom books, Tobias, Judith, Ezra, Esther and the Maccabees, and ends with the *Passio Machabeorum*. Douai BM MS 3b contains the Wisdom books, Tobias, Judith, Ezra, Esther, the Maccabees, the *Passio Machabeorum*, the Pauline Epistles, the Canonical Epistles, Acts, and the Apocalypse.

gap. It is thus very unlikely that this manuscript ever contained the Gospels.

The first Bible of Saint-Amand, Valenciennes BM MSS 9–11, sometimes known as the Alardus Bible, was written and illustrated in the late-eleventh or early-twelfth century at the monastery of Saint-Amand.[122] It has suffered some damage, but enough of the original manuscript survives that it is possible to assess that, once again, it was created without a Gospels or Psalter. In MS 10 there is no break between II Chronicles and the Book of Proverbs, where one might expect to find the Psalter. In MS 11 the last of the minor Prophets, Malachi, and the beginning of the Acts of the Apostles are found on the same folio, 60v. No gaps exist in the text of the New Testament, and thus no Gospels were ever included.

This codicological evidence is reinforced by that provided in a mid-twelfth-century catalogue of the monastery of Saint-Amand, the *Index maior*, Paris BnF MS lat. 1850, which lists 315 manuscripts from the library.[123] The second item on the list is described as *Duo magna volumina in quibus separatim vetus et novum testamentum continetur, praeter evangelium et psalterium.—Alardus*. André Boutemy was able to identify this as Valenciennes BM MSS 9–11, and speculated that the mid-twelfth-century author of the list was describing the losses that the volume had already suffered.[124] It seems surprising, however, that this indexer would not have noted the other books now missing from the Bible, such as the prophets Ezekiel and Jeremiah, and the historical books of Tobias, Judith, Ezra, Esther and the Maccabees. Furthermore, MSS 9 and 10 were originally one volume, as can be deduced from the sudden break mid-sentence in the text of I Kings on fol. 122v of MS 9. I Kings continues at the beginning of MS 10, with the missing text sentences supplied in Gothic

---

[122] *Catalogue général* XXV, Poitiers-Valenciennes, 195–196, and André Boutemy, "Les enluminures de l'abbaye de Saint-Amand," *Revue belge d'archéologie et d'histoire de l'art* XII (1942), 135–141, and Cahn, *Romanesque Bible Illumination*, 283. MSS 9 and 10, originally one volume, contain the Octateuch, the Books of Kings and Chronicles, and the Wisdom books. MS 11 begins with the Books of Ezekiel and Daniel, continues with the minor Prophets, and ends with the New Testament.

[123] Léopold Delisle, *Le cabinet des manuscrits de la Bibliothèque nationale*, 3 vols. (Paris, 1868–1881), II, 448–458.

[124] Boutemy, "Les enluminures de l'abbaye de Saint-Amand," 136–137. He appears subsequently to have revised his opinion, for he later compared the Alardus Bible to the Saint-Vaast Bible in its Gospel- and Psalterless design (idem, "La Bible enluminée de Saint-Vaast à Arras [Ms. 559]," *Scriptorium* IV [1950], 70, n. 1).

script. If the loss of the Gospels and Psalter had taken place already in the mid-twelfth century, it is striking that it was not rectified when the losses to I Kings, suffered through the division of the first volume, were replaced by the scribe writing in Gothic script. Given the existence of other contemporary Bibles with similar lacunae, it seems more likely that the compiler of the list instead intended to describe the original extent of the Bible in its twelfth-century form: two large volumes containing the Old and New Testaments, except for the Psalter and the Gospels.

The final Bible of this series was not produced for a monastery, but for a college of cathedral canons. Cambrai BM MSS 278–280 from the late-eleventh or early-twelfth century, originated at Notre-Dame de Cambrai, the cathedral church of the diocese which before 1093 had been Arras-Cambrai.[125] Once a four-volume Giant Bible, the first volume, containing the Octateuch, is now lost. The three surviving volumes have been numbered out of sequence.

In MS 279, the New Testament begins with the Acts of the Apostles on fol. 91v, after the *explicit* for Job. The rest of the New Testament, the Catholic Epistles, the Apocalypse, and the Pauline Epistles follow without a break. It is, therefore, clear that the manuscript never contained the Gospels, for the New Testament runs without interruption, and ends in a blank verso, signaling that no subsequent folios have been lost. The status of the Psalter is more difficult to determine. It is very unlikely that it was lost with the Octateuch volume, since the Psalter was at that time not usually included there. A more likely location for it would have been after Ezra in MS 280, or before Proverbs in MS 279. Nonetheless, neither the end of MS 280 nor the beginning of MS 279 show any evidence that they are missing folios. In fact, the last folio of MS 280, fol. 112v, is blank beneath the *explicit* for Ezra. It is probable, therefore, that the Cambrai Bible was also originally planned without a Psalter.

Even if a codicological examination of each one of these manuscripts cannot conclusively prove that it never contained either the

---

[125] Cahn, *Romanesque Bible Illumination*, 269, and Auguste Molinier, *Catalogue général* XVII, Cambrai, 108. MS 280 contains the Books of Kings and Chronicles, as well as Ezra. MS 278 begins with Wisdom books, then includes the Books of Tobias, Judith, Esther, and the Maccabees, and finally the prophets Isaiah, Jeremiah, and the incipit for Ezekiel. This volume appears to have been split from MS 279, where the chapter list for Ezechiel picks up midstream. Daniel, the Minor Prophets, Job and the New Testament follow.

Gospels or Psalter, it seems hard to believe that all the Giant Bibles surviving from the eleventh- and early-twelfth-century Arras region would have suffered exactly the same damage. Taken together, the evidence leads to the almost inevitable conclusion that Bibles in this milieu were planned to exclude these books. In addition, these Bibles share another very unusual codicological characteristic.

The final thread connecting these Bibles is that all include the *Passio Machabeorum*, a pseudepigraphical addition to the two books of Maccabees that describes the gruesome martyrdoms of the seven Maccabean brothers and their mother under the reign of Antioch. This was not a canonical part of the Western Bible, but occasionally appeared in manuscripts of the Bible and the Lives of the Saints.[126] In the first Marchiennes Bible, Douai BM MS 1, the *Passio* is the very last book of the Bible, beginning on fol. CCXXXIX of vol. II. The two Bible fragments from Marchiennes making up Douai BM MS 3 each include a copy of the *Passio*, Douai 3a beginning on fol. 146v, and Douai 3b beginning on fol. 234v. The Alardus Bible from Saint-Amand, Valenciennes BM MSS 9–11, is missing the section where this book might have been found. In the Cambrai Bible, Cambrai BM MS 278–280, the *Passio* begins on fol. 103 of MS 278. The *Passio Machabeorum* is found in four of these Bibles and the fifth cannot be shown *not* to have included it.

Despite the similarities that help us identify them as a group, however, these Flemish Bibles otherwise show a striking lack of conformity in the order of their books, the choice of prologues and *capitula* prefacing the various books, and even the *incipits* used to introduce them.[127] Disparities among the Bibles demonstrate that the similarities

---

[126] See the manuscripts listed in Donatien DeBruyne, *Les anciennes traductions latines des Machabées*, Anecdota Maredsolana IV (Maredsous, 1932), Friedrich Stegmüller, *Repertorium biblicum medii aevi*, 11 vols. (Madrid, 1950–1961), I, 70–71 and *Vetus Latina; die Reste der altlateinischen Bibel*, ed. Bonifatius Fischer et al. (Freiburg, 1949–), I, 23–24. It survives in fewer than fifty medieval manuscripts.

[127] For example, Douai BM MS 1 from Marchiennes, Cambrai BM MS 278–280 from the Cathedral chapter of Cambrai, and Valenciennes BM MS 9–11 from St. Amand all differ from Arras BM MS 559 in placing the Wisdom books before rather than after the Major and Minor Prophets. Cambrai BM MS 278–280 and Valenciennes BM MS 9–11 order the New Testament books in this way: Acts, Catholic Epistles, Apocalypse, Pauline Epistles. Douai BM MS 3b, also from Marchiennes, on the other hand, follows the order found in Arras BM MS 559: Pauline Epistles, Catholic Epistles, Acts, and then Apocalypse. The number and variety of prologues also steadily increases in the later Bibles. Cambrai BM MS 278–280 has a selection of prologues very close to that in the Arras Bible, but

they do share are not merely the result of their all being copies of
a single earlier manuscript, either the Saint-Vaast Bible, or its textual
model. Rather, these Bibles were copied or compiled from diverse
sources. Their similarities must be the result of conscious choices
made to answer a need dictated by their environment. As in the
Carolingian period, the entire process of planning and producing a
single- or multi-volume Bible for use in a local monastery or cathedral, from finding the model manuscripts, to assessing the needs of
its future home, to obeying any dictates of the local religious authority, seems to have led to the almost infinite variability obvious in
Romanesque Bibles.[128]

The same holds true for the programs of decoration found in these
Bibles. Although the later Flemish Bibles in some cases may reflect
the influence of the images developed at Arras for the Saint-Vaast
Bible, they did not adapt the complex pictorial program of the Bible
or its underlying meaning. Rather, the images found in these manuscripts are more typical of later Romanesque Bibles, particularly in
their emphasis on the Book of Genesis, and their use of historiated
initials instead of full- or half-page framed illustrations like those in
the Arras Bible.[129] In a few cases, however, the Bibles may have
copied selected images from the Saint-Vaast Bible.

For instance, the artists of all three of the Bibles from Marchiennes
adapted the Arras Bible's Ecclesiasticus illustration (fig. 14). Douai
BM MS 1's Ecclesiasticus is similar to, although much less elaborate
than, that in the Saint-Vaast Bible. Christ sits enthroned holding a

---

includes in addition for Chronicles *Quomodo Graecoruum historias* (Samuel Berger, "Les
Préfaces jointes aux livres de la Bible dans les manuscrits de la Vulgate," *Mémoires
présentés par divers savants à l'Académie des inscriptions et belles-lettres*, 1st ser., XI/2 [Paris,
1902], 37, #37) and for I Maccabees *Machabeorum libri duo prenotant* (Donatien De
Bruyne, *Préfaces de la Bible latine* [Namur, 1920], 151) as well as a different prologue
for Apocalypse, *Apocalypsi Iohannis tot habet sacra* (DeBruyne, *Préfaces*, 261). Douai BM
MS 1 includes these first two prologues, in addition to the Arras Bible prologues,
but favors the Arras Bible's Apocalypse prologue over that found in the Cambrai
Bible. Like the prologues, the number of *capitula* also seems to increase over time.
The later Bibles include *capitula* for the Books of Numbers, Judges, Kings, Chronicles
and Acts, none of which are found in the Arras Bible. In addition, Douai BM MS
1 and Valenciennes BM MS 9–11 include different *capitula* for Exodus, Leviticus,
Deuteronomy, and Joshua than those found in the Arras Bible. Such minor differences
abound in these Bibles.

[128] Reilly, "French Romanesque Giant Bibles," 302–311.
[129] Cambrai BM MS 278–280, from the cathedral chapter of Cambrai, contains
very few decorations.

book and blessing, while two flanking angels hold cross-staffs (fol. CCXXV, fig. 31).[130] In Douai BM MS 3a Ecclesiasticus is illustrated with an historiated initial of Christ enthroned with his arms outstretched (fol. 50v, fig. 32). An illustration in Douai BM MS 3b complements those found in part 3a. The Book of Ecclesiasticus is again prefaced with a portrait of Christ, who this time blesses with his right hand and holds a book with his left.[131] In Valenciennes BM MS 10, fol. 113, from Saint-Amand, the illustration for Ecclesiasticus might recall its predecessor at Arras. In an historiated initial 'O' Christ sits enthroned on a heavenly arc while holding a book and a sheaf of wheat.

The Saint-Vaast illustration for the Song of Songs also had its imitators (pl. V). In Valenciennes BM MS 10, fol. 123, from Saint-Amand, before the Song of Solomon one finds an historiated initial 'O' filled with an embracing Christ and Ecclesia, an illustration which carries the iconography of the Saint-Vaast Bible's *Sponsus-Sponsa* image into a more intimate realm. In Douai BM MS 3b, fol. 159v, on the other hand, the Song of Songs is ornamented with a complex initial incorporating haloed men and fantastic beasts in interlocking ovals. In addition, in Douai BM MS 3a the Book of Proverbs begins with an image of Solomon enthroned holding a sword, a staff and a book, similar to the Wisdom image in the Saint-Vaast Bible. Finally, the Book of Ezra is prefaced with two medallions within an initial, one showing the scribe Ezra at work, and the other holding the portrait of a king, a combination that again recalls the Arras Bible.[132]

The problem with attempting to postulate a copy relationship between the Saint-Vaast Bible and any of these followers is that all four of these compositions became popular in Romanesque Bibles throughout Europe by the end of the eleventh century. Although the Arras Bible's versions have distinctive details that tie them into its overall program, these details were not copied in the other Flemish Bibles, none of whose illustrations are particularly close to those found in the Saint-Vaast Bible.

---

[130] Douai BM MS 1, vol. I, fol. CCXXV.
[131] Douai BM MS 3b, fol. 168v bis.
[132] Douai BM MS 3a, fols. 19v, 50v and 93v.

The Function of the Arras Bible

The preceding rather tedious recital of the similarities and differences among this series of badly battered Bibles is necessary because the peculiarities of these Bibles can provide clues to the intended function of the Giant Bible in general. The Arras Bible and its Flemish companions form a group that, from the second quarter of the eleventh century onwards, dramatically illustrates the increased importance of Bible reading in the monastic context. The codicological characteristics that make these Bibles unusual, as well as their context within the contemporary reform movement then sweeping northern France, demonstrate that they were constructed specifically to be used as tools for refectory and choir lection reading within reformed monasteries. The number of Bibles produced in this era and the similarities between them alone would suggest that they must have been made with a specific purpose in mind. And in fact, a survey of all the surviving evidence shows that the Bibles can be connected with a very particular function: the reading cycle in the monastic refectory and choir dictated by the customaries of the tenth, eleventh and twelfth centuries. Following in the footsteps of their predecessors, the inventors of the Carolingian Bibles, the Flemish Bible copyists tailored their Bibles to this function in some immediately identifiable ways, including leaving out superfluous books and keying the text with lection markings.

As already described above, in the Romanesque era many Flemish Bibles took the Touronian practice of writing the Psalter and Gospels in a smaller script one step further and left the books out entirely. Bibles lacking a Psalter were by no means uncommon in the medieval period, as a glance through Samuel Berger's concordance of the order of biblical books quickly demonstrates. Gospels were also not always included in Bible manuscripts.[133] A superficial reason for these choices is not difficult to find. Many monasteries still had in their possession in the tenth, eleventh, and twelfth centuries highly decorated luxury Gospel or Psalter manuscripts from the Carolingian era. Surviving examples of these Gospels and Psalters are much more

---

[133] Berger, *Histoire de la Vulgate*, Appendix 1, 331–339, sections I–VII, and 339–341 on the New Testament, in particular #22, 25–34, and 37. Berger lists over 30 Bibles that lack the Psalter but not the Gospels.

common than are complete Bibles. The Giant Bible they were producing was destined already to be cumbersome, and the project
absorbed much of the scriptorium's energy and resources. It would
not be surprising if, already possessing a luxury lectern Psalter or
Gospel, a monastery decided to concentrate the energies of its scriptorium on producing what it lacked: a large-format version of the
rest of the Bible, leaving out the books of which they already had
a lectern copy.

To have the Psalter *and* the Gospels missing from the same Bible
is much more unusual. In fact, aside from the Flemish manuscripts
catalogued above, almost all the pre-Gothic Bibles listed by Berger
from which both the Psalter and the Gospels are missing have been
arranged in the order of the *lectio continua*, like the Carolingian Brussels,
Douai, Monza, Bobbio and Biasca Bibles.[134] In addition to the mid-
tenth-century Einsiedeln Bible, Stiftsbibliothek MSS 5–7,[135] and a
twelfth-century Bible in Paris, Bibliothèque Mazarine MS 44–45
(3–4),[136] a cluster of four of these Bibles can be connected with Reims:

---

[134] Brussels, Bibliothèque royale II, 1052 f. 137–140, Douai BM MS 14, Monza,
Biblioteca Capitolare della Basilica di San Giovanni Battista MS i-2/9, Milan, Biblioteca
Ambrosiana, MSS E 26 inf and E 53 inf. Of the few remaining Bibles in Berger's
lists lacking both the Psalter and the Gospels which are not liturgically ordered and
do not belong to the North French group identified above, only two are pre-Gothic.
A damaged but almost complete twelfth-century Bible from the monastery of Sainte-
Colombe-lès-Sens, now Sens BM MS 1–2, appears not to have included either the
Gospels or the Psalter. See Auguste Molinier, *Catalogue général* VI, Sens, 148–149.
Despite the assessment of the cataloguer (p. 148), that these two volumes represent
the surviving halves of two different Bibles, they match so closely in contents that
they are most likely products of the same project. Surviving exempla from other
monasteries demonstrate that various volumes of a single Giant Bible do not always
have the same dimensions or style of decoration. Interestingly, the chronicle of
nearby Saint-Pierre-le-Vif records that under Abbot Arnold a four-volume Bible was
ordered in 1123 with volumes divided according to the *lectio continua*. De Hamel,
73–75. See also Cahn, *Romanesque Bible Illumination*, 281. London BL MS Add.
14788–90, from the Premonstratensian abbey of St. Mary-de-Parc near Louvain,
which contains a colophon dating it to 1148, also did not contain either book. See
Cahn, *Romanesque Bible Illumination*, 264–265, and *Catalogue of Additions to the Manuscripts
in the British Museum in the Years MDCCCXLI–MDCCCXLV* (London, 1850), Year
1844, 6.
[135] Berger, *Histoire de la Vulgate*, 132–133, 382 and *Scriptoria medii aevi Helvetica.
Denkmäler schweizerischer Schriebkunst des Mittelalters* V. Schriebschulen der Diözese
Konstanz. Stift Einsiedeln, ed. A. Bruckner (Geneva, 1943), 169. This mid-tenth-
century Bible, probably copied at Einsiedeln Abbey under its founder, Abbot Eberhard
(d. 958), was smaller in format than many. MS 5, for instance, is only 28.5 cm
tall.
[136] Auguste Molinier, *Catalogue des manuscrits de la Bibliothèque Mazarine*, 4 vols. (Paris,

Reims BM MSS 5, 16–19, 20–21, and 22–23.[137] Although the Saint-Vaast Bible is not arranged in reading order, it will be very enlightening to take a closer look at this group of Psalter- and Gospel-less Bibles.

Brieger noted that some time in the eleventh century an *ordo librorum* was inserted on fol. 104v in the first volume of the Carolingian Hincmar Bible, Reims BM MS 1–2. The ordering of the later Reims Bibles corresponds to this list.[138] The monasteries of the diocese of Reims had been reformed in the late-tenth century by Bishop Adalbero of Reims, when he replaced the secular clerks inhabiting many monasteries with more ascetic monks or celibate canons living communally and following the rule of St. Benedict.[139] Although no monastic

1885–1892), I, 16. Berger also included in his list three fragmentary Bibles from the Bibliothèque nationale, Paris BnF MS lat. 94 from the late-ninth or early-tenth century, BnF lat. 95, part of a set of four incomplete volumes of the eleventh through the thirteenth centuries from Chalons, and BnF lat. 96, part of a set of two twelfth-century volumes from Noailles. For none of these manuscripts, however, does even one book from the New Testament survive, making it nearly impossible to speculate as to their original purpose or arrangement. Philippe Lauer, *Bibliothèque nationale. Catalogue général des manuscrits latins*, 6 vols. (Paris, 1939), I, 36–37.

[137] Henri Loriquet, *Catalogue général* XXXVIII, Reims, 25–30. Also, *Trésors de la Bibliothèque municipale de Reims* (Reims, 1978), pt. 1: Manuscrits, ed. Michel De Lemps, #22–24. Cahn, *Romanesque Bible Illumination*, 280. Berger did not include MSS 22–23, the Bible of St. Thierry, on his list in *Histoire de la Vulgate*. Walter Cahn, *Romanesque Manuscripts: The Twelfth Century*, 2 vols. (London, 1996), I, 86–87, speculated that the books missing from this Bible, Isaiah, Daniel, the Minor Prophets, the Psalter, the Gospels and the Pauline Epistles, were all lost from the end of the surviving manuscript. Given the order of books in the remainder, however, and the fact that the missing books, excluding the Psalter and the Gospels, were part of a continuous series in the reading-ordered Bibles, it is more likely that the Psalter and the Gospels, as in the other Reims Bibles, MSS 5, 16–19, and 20–21, were never included here.

[138] Brieger, "Bible Illustration," 161. For a transcription of the Reims BM MS 1 list see Loriquet, *Catalogue général*, XXXVIII, Reims, 1–2. A copy of this list can be found in one of the above-mentioned Romanesque Bibles from Reims, BM MS 20, fol. 194v, where one also finds marginal notations throughout the manuscript indicating lections for choir reading, while in another of the Reims Bibles, MSS 22–23, a different list is found.

[139] Richer, *Histoire de France* (888–995), ed. R. Latouche, 2 vols. (Paris, 1937) and *Chronique ou livre de fondation du monastère de Mouzon*, ed. Michel Bur (Paris, 1989), 170. Adalbero's reform seems to have followed the model of the Lotharingian abbey of Gorze. Josef Semmler, "Das Erbe der karolingischen Klosterreform im 10 Jahrhundert," in *Monastische Reformen im 9. und 10 Jahrhundert*, ed. Raymond Kottje and Helmut Maurer (Sigmaringen, 1989), 73 and Michel Bur, "Saint-Thierry et le renouveau monastique dans le diocèse de Reims au Xe siècle," in *Saint-Thierry, une abbaye du VIe au XXe siècle, Actes du colloque international d'histoire monastique Reims-Saint-Thierry*, 11 au 14 octobre 1976, ed. Michel Bur (Saint-Thierry, 1979), 39–49.

customary survives for the churches of Reims, given the wealth of surviving copies of the *ordo librorum* it would be surprising if the reform, like other contemporary reforms, had not demanded the renewal of the *lectio continua*. After the list was inserted into the Carolingian Bible already in the possession of the cathedral of Reims, subsequent Bibles made within its jurisdiction were arranged in liturgical order, and none contained the Gospels or the Psalter, books which would have been more conveniently kept as separate codices. Given their lacunae and non-traditional arrangement, these Bibles would have been practically unusable for anything other than the reading of the Nocturns.

The misunderstanding of the Flemish Bibles is not the only case where twentieth-century prejudices about the definition of a 'Bible' led observers to the wrong conclusions about the contents of a manuscript. Just like these Romanesque Bibles, the thirteenth-century French Bibles Moralisées often seem riddled with lacunae to modern eyes. For instance, Vienna, Österreichische Nationalbibliothek MS 1179 lacks the Psalter, almost all the Prophets and the Wisdom books, and the Gospels, Epistles, and Acts.[140] This is not true of all the Bibles Moralisées, for the Oxford-Paris-London version contains abbreviated versions of almost all the books of the Bible.[141] This led scholars to assume that Vienna MS 1179 was copied with all these books, only to suffer damage later on, or that it was never finished. Instead, earlier versions of the Bibles Moralisées may have included only a few books. The composers over time expanded their innovative system of visual and textual interpretation to cover more and more of the Bible, leading to the almost full complement of biblical books in the Oxford-Paris-London volumes.[142] As with the Romanesque Bibles, though for different reasons, it seems that the makers of the Bibles Moralisées did not always believe that their Bibles had to represent the 'whole' Bible. Nonetheless, the consistency with which particular books are missing from the Flemish Bibles points to another

---

[140] John Lowden, *The Making of the Bibles Moralisées*, 2 vols. (University Park, 2000), I, 65.
[141] Oxford, Bodleian Library, MS Bod. 270B, Paris BnF MS lat. 11560 and London BL MSS Harley 1526 and 1527. Lowden, *The Making of the Bibles Moralisées*, I, 65 and A. de Laborde, *La Bible Moralisée illustrée conservée à Oxford, Paris et Londres: Reproduction intégrale du manuscrit du XIIIᵉ siècle accompagnée de planches tirées de Bibles similaires et d'une notice* (Paris, 1911–1927), 90.
[142] Lowden, *The Making of the Bibles Moralisées*, I, 65.

explanation for these lacunae. In their case, it is the manuscripts' function rather than the process by which they were created that explains the missing books.

The Arras Bible and the Flemish Bibles that followed it did not take up the practice of ordering the biblical books according to the *lectio continua*. Nonetheless, their production without the Gospels and Psalter must have answered a similar contemporary demand in the monastic and canonical context, tying them together as a group. In addition, two of the Bibles show internal evidence that they were used for liturgical and refectory reading. All of the Bibles in the Flemish group are well-thumbed volumes that were obviously heavily used, including the Saint-Vaast Bible. Although one cannot tell from simple wear and tear how a manuscript was employed, the Arras Bible and the Alardus Bible, Valenciennes BM MS 9–11, also both contain numerous lection markings in the margins of the biblical text. These markings are for the most part simply Roman numerals in groups of eight or three, starting either at the beginning of the biblical book or at some point after the beginning. They divide the text into sections roughly a chapter in length.[143] The lection marks do not run continuously through the Bibles, and were not part of their original production, although some were later rubbed out and are now only faintly visible. Occasionally the marks are prefaced with a slashed 'L' or 'Lc,' demonstrating that the marks were intended to indicate lections. Few of them are elaborated with references to the day on which they were meant to be read.[144] In the *lectio continua*, however, references to date would have been unnecessary. An

---

[143] Although at the beginning of each biblical book these markings are often easily confused with chapter divisions, particularly when more than one set of chapters has been noted, by the middle of each book it becomes obvious which numerals are intended as lection markings, for they rarely rise above VIII in number. This division into groups of three or eight corresponds to the type of instruction sometimes given in the *Liber tramitis*, such as for Holy Thursday, *Prime tres lectiones de Lamentationibus Hiaeremie legantur*, or for the Third Sunday after Pentecost, *Aliis namque diebus dominicis quae subsequuntur similiter lectiones octo ad nocturnalia obsequia legantur ex libris Regum usque ad kalendas augusti* (CCM X, 72, 121).

[144] In the Arras Bible, the marks start with the Book of Genesis, and are found throughout the Bible, although not continuously. Only in the Pauline Epistles, starting on vol. III, fol. 88v, are there any markings to indicate the reading was intended for a Sunday. In Valenciennes BM MS 9, some of the markings are more specific. In the Book of Genesis, fol. 6, the beginning of the text is marked with a somewhat confusing set of references to Sunday readings, with sets of eight lection marks finished with an F mark. The other marks in the book omit any reference to date.

entire book was read from beginning to end, starting on the day mandated in the local customary. Indeed, the first lection of a book is often not even marked. Instead, the markings pick up at 'II,' a suitable interval after the first words of the text. The only guide necessary on a daily basis was one that advised how long each reading should be, in order that the readings were not unfittingly short or tediously protracted. In fact, the Saint-Omer Bible, which is prefaced by a list instructing in what order the books are to be read, also includes a series of lection marks of the same type.

These lection markings prepared the Flemish Giant Bibles for monastic reading in reformed houses. Although they were slightly less straightforward to use for the *lectio continua* than the reordered Bibles of Reims, the legible script, hierarchy of texts, continuous titles and a nearby *ordo librorum* would have allowed the practiced monks to flip quickly to the assigned reading for the day. Carrying these heavy volumes back and forth between the choir and refectory, the monk would have been thankful that unnecessary books, namely the Gospels and Psalter, had been left out.

Romanesque Monastic Reform Movements and the Giant Bible

The adjustments made to the format and contents of these Bibles show that, as in the Carolingian era that preceded it, the reforms that suffused tenth-, eleventh- and twelfth-century ecclesiastical culture seem to have led to a Europe-wide understanding that public reading from a Giant Bible was a standard part of communal life. Peter Brieger, in his 1965 article "Bible Illustration and Gregorian Reform," saw the production of Giant Bibles as an outgrowth of the Church reform movement that culminated in the pontificate of Gregory VII (1073–1085).[145] Margaret Gibson, echoing Walter Cahn, points out that a "bishop of the Gregorian reform . . . might appropriately have given such a volume to a community that he had restored."[146] Although very few northern Romanesque Bibles come with this kind of secure pedigree, a significantly high proportion of the Italian Giant Bibles that appeared in the late-eleventh century

---

[145] See above note 101.
[146] Gibson, 9.

can be connected with an ecclesiastical donor.[147] Knut Berg and
Larry Ayres have related the production of Italian Romanesque Bibles
in the Roman sphere of influence very closely to this reform. Ayres
states of the Italian Giant Bibles: "They constitute a distinctive Vulgate
family in format, text and decoration, and they were designed as a
manifestation of the new ecclesiastical unity promoted by the Church
of Rome in the era of the Gregorian reform."[148] Both date some
examples of Italian Giant Bibles to before Gregory's arrival in Rome,
perhaps as early as the 1060s.[149] Some of the earliest Italian Bibles
may have appeared in and around Rome under Gregory's reforming predecessors, Leo IX and Alexander II.[150]

Yet the role in this renewal of monastic reformers of the late-
tenth and early-eleventh century outside Italy has frequently been
overlooked. Aside from the obvious example in this context of the
Saint-Vaast Bible, the early-eleventh-century Roda and Ripoll Bibles,
the contemporary Odilo Bible and the late-tenth or early-eleventh-
century First Bible of Saint-Martial spring immediately to mind.[151]
Some of these were highly complex projects, a fact that suggests that
they were not merely flukes, seeds of a movement that would blos-
som much later, or throwbacks to the Carolingian era.

Can the first impetus to produce these Bibles be assigned to a
particular reform movement or leader? Because most of these reforms
developed around individual charismatic and energetic leaders rather
than a single central authority, it is surprising that the revival of the
lectio continua and the provision of a Giant Bible seems to have been
a component of almost all reforms of monastic and canonical life,
whether it was led in a Cluniac cell, a Premonstratensian abbey, or
a cathedral choir. It is striking how quickly the production of Giant
Bibles seems to have spread beyond a few reform movements such
as those associated with William of Volpiano, Richard of Saint-
Vanne, Adalbero of Reims, and the Roman scriptoria that produced
the Italian Bibles, to all the major reform movements of the eleventh

---

[147] Ayres, "Le Bibbie atlantiche," 27–37.
[148] Ayres, "The Italian Giant Bibles," 129.
[149] Berg, 19 and Ayres, "The Italian Giant Bibles," 126–128.
[150] Berg, 19 and Ayres, "The Italian Giant Bibles," 151–154.
[151] The Roda Bible, Paris BnF MS lat. 6, the Ripoll Bible, Rome BAV cod. Vat.
lat. 5729, the Odilo Bible, Paris BnF MS lat. 15176, the First Bible of Saint-Martial
in Limoges, Paris BnF MS lat. 5.

and twelfth centuries. A survey encompassing only the illustrated Bibles included in Walter Cahn's corpus shows that Cluniac, Cistercian and Premonstratensian monasteries produced and used these Bibles, as did houses of Augustinian canons and cathedral chapters. Richard of Saint-Vanne's reforming efforts in French Flanders are a typical example. All of these Flemish Giant Bibles can be connected to a monastery or college of canons that was at one time under the direct influence of the reformer Richard of Saint-Vanne of Verdun, the famous early-eleventh-century abbot of Saint-Vaast. Therefore, all were probably intended to be tools in one of the reform movement's goals, to revive the practice of the daily reading of the Bible in the choir and refectory.

Brieger saw another inspiration for Bible production in the heresies that troubled Europe in the eleventh century, some of which denied the worth of the Old Testament as well as parts of the New.[152] Brieger's suggestion that the Giant Bibles were designed to counter heresy was certainly true in isolated cases. For instance, the Citeaux Bible's historiated initial for John features a monk labeled "Arrius" whose features are crushed by the claws of a hovering eagle, an explicit condemnation of heresy.[153] But this could not have been the overriding reason for the appearance of illustrated Giant Bibles. The monks who used the Bibles were rarely heretics themselves, and one wonders how such a message would have been transmitted to the often-illiterate peasantry who occasionally succumbed to heresy in the eleventh and twelfth centuries. No other miniatures in the Citeaux Bible make reference to this concern.[154]

Yet even if these heavily decorated lectern Bibles were not routinely employed in the battle against heresy, they were not simply tools for the *lectio continua*, either. The process by which hundreds of monasteries came to own lavishly illustrated Bibles shows that these manuscripts must have been considered symbols of the success of the reform. Starting in the late-tenth and eleventh centuries, many libraries seem to have renewed Bibles already in their possession in order to use them for choir and refectory reading. Embarking on

---

[152] Brieger, 159–160.
[153] Dijon BM MSS 12–15, miniature at MS 15, fol. 56v. Walter Cahn, "A defense of the Trinity in the Citeaux Bible," *Marsyas* XI (1962), 58–59.
[154] Yolanta Zaluska, *Manuscrits enluminés de Dijon*, Corpus des manuscrits enluminés des collections publiques des départements (Paris, 1991), 51–56.

the expensive and time-consuming project of copying and decorating a new Bible was thus frequently delayed by as much as a generation. In the meantime, the revision of the older Bibles signals that monasteries were already accommodating their commitment to Bible reading. For instance, at the Roman church of Santa Cecilia in Trastevere, in the middle of the eleventh century the scriptorium repaired and corrected a ninth-century Italian Bible by adding a replacement for a damaged or missing volume and correcting the text of the first volume.[155] This Bible, like its Romanesque companions, was annotated with liturgical markings and other explanations for reading out loud. This was followed by a newly copied Bible (Rome BAV cod. Vat. Barb. lat. 587) that may have arrived at the church as early as the 1060s, or a couple of decades later.[156] A similar chain of events took place in Reims, as mentioned above. In the eleventh century, soon after the late-tenth-century reform initiated by Archbishop Adalbero of Reims, someone added the *ordo librorum ad legendum* to the cathedral chapter's late Carolingian Hincmar Bible, at the same time that it was corrected.[157] A hundred years later this list was copied into the cathedral's new, liturgically-ordered, Bible, Reims BM MSS 20–21.[158] One also finds marginal notations throughout that manuscript indicating lections for choir reading. As we have already seen, two other liturgically-ordered Bibles were then produced for Saint-Remi and Saint-Thierry, both of which had been reformed by Adalbero as much as a century before.

The same cycle occurred across the Channel in the monasteries reformed by Lanfranc in the wake of the Norman Conquest. After William the Conqueror invited Lanfranc to move from Bec to England as Archbishop of Canterbury, Lanfranc quickly replaced the leadership in most English abbeys with monks he had recruited from the monasteries under his tutelage in Normandy. This wave of appointments was followed by the renewal of a late-tenth-century Bible at Christ Church, Canterbury, London BL MS Royal I.E. VII–VIII.[159]

---

[155] Ayres, "The Italian Giant Bibles," 152. The Carolingian Bible was sold at Sotheby's June 23, 1987. Christopher de Hamel, *Western Manuscripts and Miniatures*, Sotheby's Auction Catalogue, June 23, 1987 (London, 1987), 74–83, lot 72.

[156] Ayres, "The Italian Giant Bibles," 151–152 and idem, *Bibbie atlantiche*, 126–131.

[157] Reims BM MSS 1–2, MS 1, fol. 104v. *Catalogue général* XXXVIII, Reims, 1–4. See above.

[158] *Catalogue général* XXXVIII, Reims, 27–29, at MS 20, fol. 194v.

[159] Mary P. Richards, *Texts and Their Traditions in the Medieval Library of Rochester Cathedral Priory* (Philadelphia, 1988), 64.

Because the closely related monastery of Rochester, under the leadership of Gundulf of Bec, didn't have an older Bible to fall back
on, the Christ Church volume or its model was quickly copied in a
plain, serviceable two-volume manuscript, today Huntington Library
HM 62.[160] Only many decades later did Rochester receive an illustrated Bible of its own, perhaps made jointly by its own scriptorium
and that of Christ Church.[161]

This sequence was repeated throughout Europe in monastic scriptoria, including in Normandy and Flanders. Following a reform or
the arrival of a new abbot, an existing Bible, often of Carolingian
provenance, could be corrected and brought up to date for the
renewed cycle of monastic Bible reading, most likely echoing the
same Bible's original function. Alternatively, a new but very simple
large-format Bible could be copied. Within a few decades or as much
as a hundred years later, this was followed by a much more elaborate single- or multi-volume that could include a cycle of decorated
initials or a program of images. Nonetheless, usually the traditions
of an existing house or a region were accommodated to the expectations of those who ordered the new Bible. The text, format, or
even the illustrations could echo the already existing Bibles found
locally and probably still in use.[162] The Saint-Vaast Bible and its
Flemish companions differ from this paradigm only in the luxury of
the earliest surviving Bible in the series, the Saint-Vaast Bible itself.

Margaret Gibson has aptly termed the large and luxurious volumes born of this process 'Display Bibles.'[163] Presumably, any old,
tattered volume could have provided a text for choir and refectory
reading. The fact that such lavish, complete and attractively decorated manuscripts were now suddenly considered necessary within
the monastic context demonstrates that the function for which they
were intended, public reading, was considered to be fundamental to
the life of the monastery.[164] The success of the reform was 'displayed'

---

[160] C. W. Dutschke, *Guide to Medieval and Renaissance Manuscripts in the Huntington Library* (San Marino, CA, 1989), 124–130 and Richards, *Texts and their Traditions*, 61–65 and 75–76.

[161] Baltimore, Walters Art Gallery MS W. 18 and London BL MS Royal I.C.VII. Mary P. Richards, "A Decorated Vulgate Set from 12th-Century Rochester, England," *The Journal of the Walters Art Gallery* XXXIX (1981), 59–67.

[162] Reilly, "French Romanesque Giant Bibles," 294–311.

[163] Gibson, 8–9.

[164] Light, "Versions et révisions," 71.

to all who visited through the monastery's prized possession, their Giant Bible. The prominence that must have been accorded these manuscripts in the daily life of monasteries that owned them made these Bibles, including the Saint-Vaast Bible with its complex political program of illustrations, the perfect vehicles for messages designed for a variety of audiences, both among the residents and visitors.

Richard of Saint-Vanne and the Flemish Bibles

Of all of the newly copied and illustrated Bibles discussed above, the Saint-Vaast Bible is probably the earliest. Written and illustrated in the archdiocese of Reims in the second quarter of the eleventh century, it predates the major campaigns of Bible production associated with both Reims and Rome.[165] Through its connection with the prominent eleventh-century reform movement of Richard of Saint-Vanne, the Saint-Vaast Bible provides valuable evidence for the role of these manuscripts in the tenth-, eleventh- and twelfth-century reworking of monastic life. At the same time, the philosophy behind Richard's reform helps to explain the content of the Bible's pictorial program, in particular its marked support for the divine institution of the ecclesiastical and secular hierarchy.

Richard of Saint-Vanne's piety was recalled even from before the inauguration of his reforming career.[166] Educated at Reims, possibly

---

[165] For a discussion of the date of the Saint-Vaast Bible, see chapter one.

[166] The most complete sources on the life of Richard of Saint-Vanne are the *Vita Richardi Abbatis S. Vitoni Virdunensis*, ed. Wilhelm Wattenbach, MGH SS XI, ed. Georg Heinrich Pertz (Hanover, 1854), 281–290, probably written in the early twelfth century, and Hugh of Flavigny's *Chronicon*, PL 154:197–266. He is also discussed in the *Gestis episcoporum Virdunensium continuatis*, MGH SS IV, ed. Georg Pertz (Hanover, 1841), 45–51, as well as the *Gesta pontificum Cameracensium*, PL 149:9–176. Ernst Sackur, in "Richard, Abt von St. Vannes," Ph.D. Dissertation, Breslau, 1886, prepared an overview of Richard's life and reform for the study *Die Klosterreformen der Cluniacenser in Frankreich, Lotharingen, Italien und Spanien v. 910–1050*. His life has been summarized in a more hagiographic vein in Hubert Dauphin, *Le bienheureux Richard, abbé de Saint-Vanne de Verdun, 1046* (Louvain, 1946). Most recently, David C. Van Meter has explored the connections between Richard of Saint-Vanne and his contemporaries in "Count Baldwin IV, Richard of Saint Vanne and the Inception of Monastic Reform in Eleventh-Century Flanders," *Revue bénédictine* CVII (1997), 130–148 and "Apocalyptic Moments and Eschatological Rhetoric of Reform in the Early Eleventh Century: The Case of the Visionary of Saint Vaast," in *The Apocalyptic Year 1000: religious expectation and social change 950–1050* (Oxford, 2003), 311–325.

under the tutelage of the famous teacher Gerbert, Richard was apparently best known for his devotion to the Cross, and for saying the
entire Psalter daily, fifty psalms while bent over with his hands to
the ground, fifty upright, and the remaining fifty prostrate. At Reims
he also met his earliest assistant in reform, Count Frederick of
Verdun.[167] After completing their education, in 1004, Richard and
Frederick arrived at Saint-Vanne in Verdun to find that it was,
according to his biographers, in a state of decadence.[168] Seeking a
more strict observance, the pair quickly fled to Cluny, where they
sought admission to the Cluniac order while staying for several days
in the guesthouse. Abbot Odilo is alleged to have convinced them
that their true calling instead lay in reforming the house that they
had fled, Saint-Vanne.[169] They duly returned to Saint-Vanne, and
began reforming it under the reigning abbot, Fingenio the Scot, who
died only three months later.[170] Succeeding to the abbacy, Richard
was able to proceed fully with his reforms.

The process by which Richard's reform spread throughout Flanders
and Lotharingia was typical of the personality-driven monastic reforms
of the Romanesque era. Once the fame of Richard's piety began to
attract the attention of a variety of rulers and bishops, both secular
and ecclesiastical officials invited him to outside dioceses and asked
him to reform the local monasteries. The very first of these was
Saint-Vaast at Arras.[171] In 1008, Richard was called to the diocese
of Arras-Cambrai through the joint effort of Count Baldwin of
Flanders and the current bishop, Erluinus.[172] The chronicle of Hugh,
Abbot of Flavigny, explains that the ruling abbot of Saint-Vaast,
Fulrad, had sinned in allowing too great a secular influence in the
monastery, where a fortified residence had been built within the
cloister.[173] Richard soon became abbot, but instead of remaining at

[167] MGH SS XI:281–282, Hugh of Flavigny, *Chronicon* II, PL 154:199–201, and
Dauphin, *Le bienheureux Richard*, 55–56.
[168] MGH SS XI:282, PL 154:202–203 and Dauphin, *Le bienheureux Richard*, 80.
[169] MGH SS XI:282, PL 154:203–205, and *Gesta episcoporum Virdunensium*, MGH
SS IV:48.
[170] MGH SS XI:283.
[171] PL 154:214. Kassius Hallinger, *Gorze-Kluny. Studien zu den monastischen Lebensformen
und Gegensätzen im Hochmittelalter*, Studia Anselmiana XXII–XXIII (Rome, 1950).
Hallinger terms Richard's reform the 'Lotharingsiche Mischobservanz,' hereafter,
Lotharingian mixed-observance.
[172] *Gesta episcoporum Cameracensium*, PL 149:119 and Van Meter, "Count Baldwin,"
130–137.
[173] PL 154:214.

Saint-Vaast he appointed a series of priors to oversee the monastery, including the outsiders Frederick of Verdun and Poppo of Stavelot. Finally, in 1024 a local monk, Leduinus, became abbot.[174] Meanwhile, with the support and cooperation of Bishop Erluinus's successor, Gerard of Cambrai, Richard set about reforming many other monasteries in the diocese and beyond.

While Richard's reform was certainly famous among his contemporaries, today its exact nature is more difficult to pinpoint. No customary composed during Richard's lifetime survives from any of the monasteries in his reform circle. A fragment of a customary, the so-called *Consuetudines S. Vitonis Virdonunensis*, survives from the library of Saint-Vanne, but its date has always been disputed, and there is no internal evidence that it was produced either at or for Saint-Vanne.[175] Even if it did preserve some of the practices developed under Richard, it provides no information on the reading of the Bible at Saint-Vanne. Although the customary contains miscellaneous instructions for observances in the choir and refectory, its specific directions about reading refer only to the Psalter.[176]

More promising is a fourteenth-century ordinale that survives from Saint-Vaast that perhaps preserves some of the practices introduced by Richard.[177] Arras BM MS 230 (907), is localized to Saint-Vaast based on the contents of its calendar, and dated to 1307–1308.[178]

---

[174] The chronology of this series of priors, and even their status, is quite confused. The *Gesta pontificum Cameracensium* (PL 149:151), Hugh's *Chronicon*, the *Vita Richardi* (MGH SS XI:285) and the *Vita Popponis abbatis Stabulensis* (MGH SS XI:300) all give different chronologies. For one possible chronology, see Alfred Cauchie, "Richard de Saint-Vannes," in *Biographie nationale*, 44 vols. (Brussels, 1866–1986), XIX, 257.

[175] The text of the customary was once found in a manuscript cited as Verdun, Saint-Vanne Abbey Library Cod. 73, but this was later lost, probably during the French Revolution. Originally edited by Edmond Martène, *De antiquis ecclesiae ritibus*, 2nd ed., 4 vols. (Antwerp, 1737–1738), IV, 847–860. On the history of the study of this text, see Hallinger, CCM VII/1 (Siegburg, 1984), 196–205. Dated by its original editor to the tenth century, more recently Kassius Hallinger has speculated that, based on internal evidence and the reform history of the monastery, the text of the customary instead probably originated between 1060 and 1085, and certainly before 1115. Hallinger, CCM VII/1, 197–201. According to Hallinger (203–205), the linguistic usage and orthography of the customary are consistent with an origin in the region of Verdun.

[176] See the new edition in CCM VII/3, 375–426.

[177] *The Monastic Ordinale of St. Vedast's Abbey Arras*, 2 vols., Henry Bradshaw Society LXXXVI and LXXXVII, ed. Louis Brou (Bedford, 1957).

[178] *The Monastic Ordinale*, II, 14–17.

In spite of the late date, its editor suggested that because the ordinale shows similarities to early Cluniac ordinales, but lacks feasts
introduced by Cluny in the eleventh century, it must preserve remnants of the liturgy introduced to Saint-Vaast by earlier 'Cluniac-
influenced' reformers, such as Richard of Saint-Vanne.[179] There is
no evidence, however, that Richard of Saint-Vanne or an earlier
reformer such as the tenth-century Gerard of Brogne ever imposed
a Cluniac ordinale on Saint-Vaast. It is possible that Richard picked
up certain aspects of Cluniac ritual during his brief stay at Cluny,
or that he learned of them later through hearsay, and incorporated
them into his customary, along with his own practices. If this speculation were true, and the Saint-Vaast ordinale did contain remnants of Richard's customary, it could provide valuable evidence for
the use of a Giant Bible because the ordinale preserves on fols. 36r–v
an *ordo librorum*.[180] Even without the questionable evidence provided
by the fourteenth-century Arras ordinale, one can assume from the
number of Giant Bibles surviving from monasteries reformed by
Richard and his disciples that he did encourage the practice of
monastic reading.

The series of monasteries reformed by Richard or his principal
disciples, Poppo and Leduinus, spreads like a web around Saint-
Vaast. Many of these houses later produced some of the best-known
illustrated Giant Bibles. Florennes was reformed by Richard between
1010 and 1022, and Lobbes, source of the famous Lobbes Bible
(Tournai, Bibliothèque du séminaire 1) from 1084, was reformed in
1020.[181] Poppo eventually carried the reform to Stavelot, home of
the Stavelot Bible (London BL MS Add. 28106–7), copied between
1093 and 1097, and to St. Laurent in Liège, which produced a
Giant Bible in the mid-twelfth century (Brussels, Bibliothèque royale
MSS 9642–44).[182] Poppo also reformed Echternach, home of the

---

[179] *The Monastic Ordinale*, II, 19–20.
[180] *The Monastic Ordinale*, II, 50 and 184–185, where the list, entitled *HEC SUNT
QUE DEBENT LEGI AD MENSAM PER ANNI CIRCUITUM*, is reprinted.
[181] PL 149:150–152, and Hallinger, *Gorze-Kluny*, 285–286 and 289–290. On the
Lobbes Bible, see Don Denny, "The Historiated Initials of the Lobbes Bible," *Revue
belge d'archéologie et d'histoire de l'art* XIV–XV (1976), 3–26.
[182] Hallinger, *Gorze-Kluny*, 290, *Vita Popponis*, MGH SS XI:302 and the *Chronicon
sancti Laurentii Leodinensis*, MGH SS VIII, ed. Georg Heinrich Pertz (Hanover, 1848),
269–270. On the Stavelot Bible, see Wayne Dynes, *The Illuminations of the Stavelot
Bible* (New York, 1978). For the Bible from St. Laurent, Cahn, *Romanesque Bible
Illumination*, 263–264, and Joseph van den Gheyn, *Catalogue des manuscrits de la
Bibliothèque royale de Belgique*, 13 vols. (Brussels, 1901–1948), I, 17.

Giant Bible now in Luxembourg, Bibliothèque nationale MS 264, copied between 1051 and 1081.[183]

These Bibles have very little in common with the idiosyncratic Flemish Bibles without Gospels or Psalters that were produced much closer to Arras. Saint-Amand, the source of the Giant Bible now at Valenciennes, BM MS 9–11, was one of the earliest monasteries to be reformed by Richard, when he was invited to take over the monastery by Count Baldwin of Flanders between 1013 and 1018.[184] Sainte-Richtrude of Marchiennes, in the diocese of Arras-Cambrai, was reformed in 1024 by Richard's student, Leduinus of Saint-Vaast, on the advice of Gerard of Cambrai and Baldwin. The abbey welcomed a series of abbots sent from Saint-Vaast before producing the three Giant Bibles now in Douai, BM MSS 1, and 3a–3b.[185] Finally, the three-volume Bible from the cathedral of Cambrai, Cambrai BM MSS 278–280, originated outside a monastic context but nonetheless within Richard's sphere of influence. Gerard, Bishop of Arras-Cambrai, was one of Richard's most ardent supporters and undoubtedly carried some of his ideas to his own chapter of canons, where communal life was modeled after monastic practices.

Although contemporary or near-contemporary sources often detail Richard's physical improvements to a given monastery, obviously an important aspect of his reforming efforts, they say little about spiritual matters. It is clear from the surviving records that Richard considered the physical and financial well being of a monastery to be a necessary prerequisite to its spiritual health, and that Richard quickly set about meeting a monastery's material needs as a first step of his reform. The author of the twelfth-century *Vita Richardi abbatis* credited Richard and his helpmeet Frederick with building towers, a cellar and the refectory at Saint-Vanne, restoring the dormitory and donating liturgical implements for the divine rite. As to monastic practice, however, we learn only that he gave himself up to divine worship, spending day and night in praise of the Lord, seeking to

---

[183] Hallinger, *Gorze-Kluny*, 298–299, and *Vita Popponis*, MGH SS XI:305. On the Echternach Bible, see Blanche Weicherding-Goergen, *Les manuscrits à peintures de la Bibliothèque nationale de Luxembourg* (Luxembourg, 1968), 24–27.

[184] Hallinger, *Gorze-Kluny*, 287. *Catalogus abbatum Sancti Amandi Elnonensis*, MGH SS XIII, ed. Georg Waitz (Hanover, 1881), 387. See also the oblique reference in *Vita Popponis*, MGH SS XI:286–287.

[185] Hallinger, *Gorze-Kluny*, 294, *Annales Marchianensis*, MGH SS XVI, ed. Georg Heinrich Pertz (Hanover, 1859), 614 and PL 149:133.

teach his charges religious ways by example.[186] Hugh of Flavigny's
chronicle also lists many of Richard's gifts to the church, including
several service books with jeweled covers, but no Bible is mentioned.[187]
The same is true of the records of his tenure at other monasteries.
The *Vita* describes his work at Beaulieu, mentioning Richard's many
donations, but says nothing about his changes to practice.[188] Discussing
the founding of Saint-Laurent of Liège and Saint-Pierre of Châlons
around 1020, the *Vita* attests only to Richard's care for *monasticam
vitam* and *norma religionis*, while relating the story of his building activities in great detail.[189] The only instructions found for actual monastic practice are connected with his concern for the physical well
being of the monasteries under his care. According to Hugh of
Flavigny, in all the monasteries governed by Richard a calendar
listing the benefactors of the church was to be read daily in the
chapter.[190] The most specific allusion to his reforms in observance
comes from his time at St. Peter's of Corbie. Hugh of Flavigny mentions in his chronicle that the monks there were compelled to follow the Benedictine rule, and that monastic custom was reformed.[191]
Nonetheless, a desire to enrich the libraries of these monasteries with
luxuriously written and illustrated Bibles would not have been inconsistent with Richard's physical improvements and gifts. Despite the
fact that no gifts of Bibles are mentioned, and no reforms in observance requiring new Bibles are specifically described, Richard apparently gave other kinds of manuscripts to Saint-Vanne and instituted
the use of new calendars in the chapter at all the monasteries he
reformed, implying that he habitually commissioned manuscripts from
scriptoria.

   This frustrating lack of specificity about spiritual reform and its
connections to Giant Bible production in the contemporary records
adds to the confusion created by Richard's brief visit to Cluny early

---

[186] MGH SS XI:283, PL 154:206.
[187] PL 154:210. Gifts listed in this chronicle included reliquaries, fans, crosses,
votive crowns, Gospel books, an epistolary, a missal, and a collectarium.
[188] MGH SS XI:286.
[189] MGH SS XI:286–287. See also PL 154:212–213.
[190] PL 154:220.
[191] PL 154:213. *Hic ter beato patri nostro abbatiam sancti Petri Corbeiacensis regendam con-
tradidit, ut eius institutione et vigore servaretur in eo regula patris Benedicti, et rigor reformaretur
monasticae institutionis.* Although the Benedictine rule does include an injunction to
read from the Bible daily, no specific mention is made of this aspect of the rule in
the chronicle.

in his career. Scholars have speculated that Richard's reform movement is simply a northern offshoot of the Cluniac reform, and that
Richard himself was an ardent follower of Odilo from the time of
his visit to Cluny in 1004.[192] In addition, so little evidence exists
regarding the specifics of Richard's program for observance that it
is difficult to separate it from contemporary customs at Cluniac
monasteries. It would be tempting to lump Richard's reform together
with the contemporary Cluniac movement, for which so many customaries and manuscripts survive, because the Flemish Giant Bibles
connected to monasteries reformed by Richard were undoubtedly
meant to be used for the type of monastic reading outlined in Cluniac
customaries and other contemporary customaries. It is nearly impossible, however, to establish a direct link between the two movements.

Richard's alleged friendship with Odilo of Cluny might at first
suggest that he would have attempted to absorb as much of that
leader's reform philosophy as possible.[193] Yet, no one has been able
to describe the specific nature of Richard's reform, or to enumerate
any similarities between the two schools.[194] Scholars who have looked
closely at the surviving records found no evidence for any lasting
connection between the two movements.[195] In fact, in the few days
that Richard and Frederick spent in the guesthouse of Cluny, it
would have been impossible for them to learn the entirety of Cluniac
doctrine and practice. Furthermore, outside of perhaps the distant
reflections of Cluniac practice in the fourteenth-century ordinale from
Saint-Vaast, no evidence survives that they possessed a Cluniac customary after their departure from the motherhouse.[196] Also, there is
no record either that Cluniac monks were dispatched to monasteries
reformed by Richard in order to impart their customs to the newly

---

[192] See Hallinger, *Gorze-Kluny*, 493–516 for a summary of this debate.

[193] Alfred Cauchie, *La querelle des investitures dans les diocèses de Liege et de Cambrai*
(Louvain, 1890), xxxix–xlii, lxiii. See his later, altered, opinion in *Biographie nationale*,
252.

[194] Ernst Sackur, *Die Cluniacenser in ihrer kirchlichen und allgemeingeschichtlichen Wirksamkeit
bis zur Mitte des elften Jahrhunderts*, 2 vols. (Halle A.S., 1892–1894), II, 133–154, placed
Richard of Saint-Vanne's efforts under the Cluniac umbrella. Sackur did distinguish, however, between the tangential connection of Richard's reform to Cluny,
and the more straightforward connection initiated at the end of the eleventh century and beginning of the twelfth when these same monasteries accepted monks
from Cluny (p. 152).

[195] See Dauphin, *Le bienheureux Richard*, 335–345.

[196] Etienne Sabbe, "Notes sur la réforme de Richard de Saint-Vannes dans Les
Pays Bas," *Revue belge de philologie et d'histoire* VII (1928), 551.

reformed monks, or that Richard sent any of his disciples to Cluny with a similar purpose in mind.[197] At the abbey of Saint-Vanne, no Cluniacs were mentioned in the necrology of the monastery until 1047, when Milo, abbot of Moyenmoutier was added.[198] This was forty-three years after Richard's meeting with Odilo, and at least a year after his death in 1046. Also, contemporary observers carefully distinguished between the customs of the two reforms. When the Cluniac reform was finally introduced to the formerly Richardian monasteries at the end of the eleventh century and the beginning of the twelfth, it was often met with stiff resistance.[199] Chroniclers noted that the Cluniac customary finally imposed on them was different from the customary currently in use.[200]

The most convincing explanation of the connection between Richard's reform and Cluny was suggested by Kassius Hallinger in his far-reaching study *Gorze-Kluny*.[201] Richard had undoubtedly been exposed to the practices of Cluny when he visited in 1004, but he would also have been familiar with Cluny's competitor, the tenth-century reform movement that radiated outwards from the Lotharingian abbey of Gorze. Saint-Vanne had been reformed by Gorze in the tenth century, and some of its practices undoubtedly still survived when Richard arrived.[202] Richard had been educated at Reims in an era when it was still under the influence of Adalbero of Reims, himself a product of the Gorze reform.[203] Hallinger termed Richard's

---

[197] Sabbe, 555–557.

[198] Hubert Dauphin, "Monastic Reforms from the Tenth Century to the Twelfth," *The Downside Review* LXX (1952–1953), 66.

[199] Dauphin, "Monastic Reforms," 68. See also Sabbe, 560–561 and especially Hallinger, *Gorze-Kluny*, 474–492.

[200] Sabbe, 558–60. For instance, he notes that in the chronicle of Herimannus of St. Martin of Tournai, the author states explicitly that before 1080 Cluniac customs had not been observed anywhere in the Archdiocese of Reims. Herimannus, *Liber de restauratione S. Martini Tornecensis*, MGH SS XIV, ed. Georg Waitz (Hanover, 1883), 298, 313. Further, in the *Gesta abbatum Trudonensium*, the author Rudolph, who had himself introduced the Cluniac customary to St. Trond in 1107, acknowledged that it was different from the Richardian rule practiced there before. MGH SS X, ed. Georg Heinrich Pertz (Hanover, 1852), 262, 273.

[201] Hallinger, *Gorze-Kluny*, 483–484, 491–492. Although Hallinger's strict division of all contemporary reformed monasteries between these two schools is now in doubt (John Nightengale, *Monasteries and Patrons in the Gorze Reform. Lotharingia c. 850–1000* [Oxford, 2001], 2–3), his work still provides the best overview of the houses touched by Richard and his disciples.

[202] Hallinger, *Gorze-Kluny*, 280 and 474.

[203] Heinrich Sproemberg, "Gerhard I, Bischof von Cambrai," in *Mittelalter und*

reform the 'Lotharingian mixed-observance,' seeing in it a combination of the customs of the Gorze reform, with some Cluniac elements. The most striking difference administratively between the Lotharingian mixed-observance and the Cluniac reform is that the abbots appointed by Richard fostered cooperation with local ecclesiastical and secular authorities in the tradition of Gorze, rather than attempting to establish exemptions according to the Cluniac model.[204] Hallinger suggests, however, that the Richardian reform borrowed from the Cluniacs a tendency towards centralized organization, though it was less successful than Cluny in fostering an elaborate hierarchy.[205] In borrowing from two different models of monastic reform, Richard's movement was probably more typical of the paths followed by contemporary monasteries than admitted in the too-rigid monastic typology set up by Hallinger.[206]

Whether Richard intended to model his reform on certain aspects of Cluny and simply failed, or had a different program from the beginning, scholarly consensus now seems to be that Richard's reform was ultimately not formally connected to that of Cluny.[207] The Flemish Giant Bibles associated with Richard's reform were intended for a type of refectory and choir reading repeatedly prescribed and described

---

demokratische Geschichtesschreibung: Ausgewählte Abhandlungen, ed. Manfred Unger (Berlin, 1971), 106.

[204] Hallinger, *Gorze-Kluny*, 502–503. Nightengale has recently summarized the state of the question on Gorze and its interaction with lay and episcopal patrons, 1–21. On monastic exemption and Cluny, see Herbert E. J. Cowdrey, *The Cluniacs and the Gregorian Reform* (Oxford, 1970), 22–36, and the historiographical summary by Barbara H. Rosenwein, *Rhinoceros Bound: Cluny in the Tenth Century* (Philadelphia, 1982), 20–23. Also fundamental is Jean F. Lemarignier, "L'exemption monastique et les origines de la réforme grégorienne," in *Recueil d'articles rassemblés par ses disciples* (Paris, 1995), 285–337.

[205] Hallinger, *Gorze-Kluny*, 280 and 496–499. Hallinger notes that when the Cluniac rule was imposed on St. Trond, Rudolph's *Gesta abbatum Trudonensis* (MGH SS X:273) recorded that the old system of government was replaced by a priory structure from the Cluniac tradition (p. 484).

[206] Theodor Schieffer observed in his review of Hallinger's work that the Lotharingian mixed-observance most likely provides a good model for the variety of customs found in contemporary monastic houses. "Cluniazensische oder gorzische reformbewegung," *Archiv für mittelrheinische Kirchengeschichte* IV (1952), 31.

[207] In contrast to Hallinger, Dauphin believed that Richard never intended to develop a strongly centralized order, but rather accepted the previous practice of Gorze, and the original Cluniac practice, to reform an abbey, appoint a follower to lead the newly reformed monastery, and then merely hope to influence its future development. Dauphin, *Le bienheureux Richard*, 342–345, and "Monastic Reforms," 70–71. See also Sabbe, 568–569.

in Cluniac documents such as the *Cluniacensium antiquiores*, the *Liber tramitis*, which dates from only a few years after Richard's visit to Cluny, and the Udalric customary.[208] By the time the Bibles appeared, however, a revival of choir and refectory reading was so common among monastic reform movements that Richard incorporated it into his own as a matter of course.[209]

Furthermore, although the evidence is purely circumstantial, an interesting confluence of events that occurred in the archdiocese of Reims suggests that both the monasteries in and around Reims itself and the Flemish monasteries in the orbit of Gerard and Richard were motivated to manufacture Giant Bibles by the heritage of the Gorze reform. When the Gorze reform swept through Lotharingia in the ninth and tenth centuries it was carried to Reims by Archbishop Adalbero.[210] The Bibliothèque municipale of Reims includes in its collection a late-eleventh-century copy of the library catalogue of the abbey of Gorze that was transcribed by a monk from Saint-Thierry. The first two manuscripts listed in this catalogue are Bibles, one in two volumes and in 'antiquae manus. Altera novae et inunum coartata.'[211] As mentioned already, the cathedral of Reims soon updated its own Carolingian Bible, the Hincmar Bible, and then it and a series of surrounding monasteries, including Saint-Thierry and Saint-Remi, produced liturgically ordered Bibles that were clearly meant for use in the monasteries themselves. This is the very same Adalbero who, as Gerard of Cambrai's uncle, supervised his early education at the cathedral of Reims, where Gerard became a canon. Here Gerard first met his partner in reform, Richard of Saint-Vanne. Even

---

[208] See Joachim Wollasch, "Zur Verschriftlichung der klösterlichen Lebensgewohnheiten unter Abt Hugo von Cluny," *Frühmittelalterliche Studien* XXVII (1993), 317–324, on evidence for early written customaries at Cluny.

[209] Aelfric included a Cluniac-influenced reading list in his *Epistula ad monachos Egneshamnenes directa* some time after 1004, demonstrating that such reading instructions need not have reached Saint-Vaast by way of Cluny, but could also have come from England (CCM VII/3, 181–184).

[210] Nightengale, 145. Adalbero was a close friend of Adso of Montiérender, who had been a monk at Saint-Evre at Toul, and abbot at Luxeuil and Saint-Bénigne at Dijon.

[211] Anne Wagner, "Les manuscrits de la bibliothèque de Gorze. Remarques à propos du catalogue," in *Religion et culture autour de l'an mil. Royaume capétien et Lotharingie.* Actes du colloque Hugues Capet 987–1987. La France de l'an mil, Auxerre, 26 et 27 juin 1987–Metz, 11 et 12 septembre 1987 (Paris, 1990), 112–113. Edited in G. Morin, "Le catalogue des manuscrits de l'abbaye de Gorze au XIe siècle," *Revue bénédictine* XXII (1905), 3–11.

after Gerard and Richard left the city, they remained linked to it by friends and family: Gerard's brother Eilbert became a monk at Saint-Thierry, as did Poppo of Stavelot.[212] Richard and Gerard both developed a long friendship with Count Frederick of Verdun, Adalbero's nephew, who became a monk there and later served as prior at Saint-Vaast. The scriptorium of Reims Cathedral corrected and augmented the Hincmar Bible during the same time that Gerard, Richard, and possibly Eilbert, Poppo and Frederick were all in the city, but before the liturgically-ordered Bibles were produced to supercede it. Bible reading was clearly taking place in the cloisters and became a part of their daily lives before they all traveled to Arras, where the Saint-Vaast Bible was conceived, but the Reims scriptoria had not yet hit upon the idea of reordering the biblical books. Thus this particular aspect of the Giant Bible tradition did not travel to Saint-Vaast and the diocese of Arras-Cambrai along with the reformers. Although Cluniac customaries provide evidence that cannot be paralleled within the Gorze tradition for the monastic reading of the Bible within Cluniac monasteries, Giant Bible production can still be connected with the Gorze reform as it was manifest at Reims, the spiritual home of so many Flemish religious leaders.

The fact that the Richardian reform was not simply a branch of the Cluniac movement has two important implications for our understanding of the Flemish Giant Bibles in general, and the Saint-Vaast Bible in particular. First, because the monasteries reformed by Richard were not formally linked together in a centralized power structure like those of Cluny, whatever similarities one finds in their practices or in the products of their scriptoria arose from indirect influence rather than a specific mandate from the original reforming house.[213] Nonetheless, the fact that so many monastic houses that had been

---

[212] Heinrich Sproemberg, "Gérard Ier, évêque de Cambrai," *Biographie nationale*, Supplément, VII/1 (Brussels, 1969), 287–289.

[213] Warren Sanderson has documented a very similar phenomenon among the church buildings connected with Richard of Saint-Vanne's reform. While the churches serving monks he and his followers reformed display few similarities, many, including the monasteries of Saint-Bertin, Saint-Amand, Stavelot and Lobbes, eventually gained an "outer crypt" at the east end, designed to accommodate altars dedicated to a variety of saints. As with the Bibles, the church buildings were not built or renovated based on a tightly controlled plan, but rather grew over a period of many decades to accommodate accepted reforms to the liturgy, especially of Passion Week. *Monastic Reform in Lorraine and the Architecture of the Outer Crypt, 950–1100*, Transactions of the American Philosophical Society, NS LXI (Philadelphia, 1971), 14 and 26–28.

reformed by Richard and his followers subsequently produced an illuminated Bible with idiosyncratic characteristics clearly meant for internal choir and refectory reading points to a very strong influence from the reformer. Second, Richard's reform differed from the Cluniac movement in fostering cooperation between its leaders and secular and ecclesiastical authority. The Saint-Vaast Bible's pictorial program, as will be shown in the next chapter, supports a particular view of the interdependence of secular and ecclesiastical authority, specifically glorifying the role of the bishop. It is uniquely a product of Richard's milieu, and has nothing in common with the Cluniac practice of distancing their monasteries from episcopal leadership.

CHAPTER THREE

PRIESTLY PROPHETS

The interaction of two powerful religious personalities shaped the philosophy recognizable in the pictorial program illustrating the Saint-Vaast Bible. Both lived in Arras in the early-eleventh century and together they spearheaded the reform of monasteries throughout the region. Richard of Saint-Vanne was a charismatic monastic reformer who was called to Saint-Vaast in Arras as his first big reforming challenge beyond the walls of Saint-Vanne itself. He was unusually open, for his time, to episcopal involvment in the day-to-day running of houses under his direction. He may have suggested that Bishop Gerard of Cambrai, one of the most prolific and well-documented writers of the early-eleventh century, be installed as Bishop of Arras-Cambrai. Richard was the spiritual guide of Saint-Vaast in the era when the Bible was copied and illustrated, and answered to Gerard as his ecclesiastical superior. Both were in some ways throwbacks to an earlier era, with their mutually reinforcing view of the importance of cooperation between Church and State and their Augustinian political philosophy. Nonetheless, Gerard's writings and the images in the Saint-Vaast Bible effectively insert these two religious leaders into a dialogue with both written and visual components about the nature of authority that was then taking place throughout Europe.

At first glance, Arras, far from the centers of power of either the new Capetian dynasty or the waning Ottonian line, may seem an unlikely setting for the genesis of such a far-reaching statement on the nature of rule. In fact, because Arras was at the epicenter of a long-running contest over the boundaries of two realms, and the focus of patronage by the powerful Counts of Flanders, it served as a magnet that attracted some of the most active participants in eleventh-century politics. It is only by integrating Gerard's writing, Richard's actions, and the cogently combined artistic motifs of the Saint-Vaast Bible program, borrowed from Ottonian and Carolingian royal models, that this becomes clear.

Gerard's allegiance to the idea of divinely-sanctioned kingship and
the preeminence of consecrated bishops over other clerics finds its
expression in the pictorial program in the Bible. Furthermore, Gerard's
writings, with their frequent references to Old and New Testament
prototypes for proper behavior, shaped the literary and iconographic
style for the scriptoria in his circle. Gerard's language of Biblical
authority profoundly affected the appearance of the manuscripts associated with him. Two of the Bible's miniatures drawn by the same
artist, for the prophets Jeremiah and Ezra, advertise Gerard and
Richard's political philosophy by anachronistically applying the liturgical regalia of Christian priests to Old Testament prophets. Both
prophets are pictured in compositions that highlight their leadership
roles within the Church and their relationship to the secular authority, either biblical or contemporary.

Richard of Saint-Vanne and the Power of the Episcopacy

One of the most striking and complex miniatures in the Saint-Vaast
Bible demonstrates that the Bible's pictorial program expresses a fundamental underpinning of Richard's reform; his belief in the importance of cooperation with local bishops. The Ezra Master and the
Acts Master, who illustrated the Old Testament Book of Jeremiah,
vol. II, fol. 15 (pl. IV), chose not to show a dramatic narrative scene
such as Jeremiah lamenting the fate of Jerusalem, captive in the cis-
tern, or imprisoned. Instead, they crafted a highly symbolic image
designed to reference his divine calling as well as his courtly official
role. Six angels drawn by the Acts Master hover in and around an
oval interlace frame enclosing the initial V. The Acts Master also
drafted an apocalyptic Lamb who floats above, blessed by a heavenly hand within a two-layer lobed mandorla. The Ezra Master was
responsible for the figure of Jeremiah standing below. The combination of his dress, a contemporary alb and chasuble with Y-shaped
orphreys,[1] and his attributes, a crozier and a book, make it clear he

---

[1] Joseph Braun, *Die liturgische Gewandung im Occident und Orient* (Darmstadt, 1964),
213. Other similar depictions include Archbishop Stigand of York in the Bayeux
tapestry, location 30 (Herbert Norris, *Church Vestments: Their Origin and Development*
[London, 1949], 73–74), the Bishop-Saint Vedastus shown wearing a very similar
chasuble on the dedication page of the Saint-Vaast Gospel Book, Boulogne BM

is to be identified as a tonsured bishop.[2] The crozier especially was intended to signal his office, for a service for investing the bishop with his insignia redacted at Saint-Vaast in the later eleventh-century states specifically that "baculo huic quae ad pastoralis officii signum in tuo nomine dedicamus: tuae benedictionis vi copiose infunde ut eo pastor insignitus sic populum suum sollicite custodiat quatinus ab unitate aecclesiae nullatenus deviare permittat."[3] Jeremiah is enclosed in a full body mandorla, an attribute traditionally reserved for Christ, especially in the manuscripts produced at Saint-Vaast and in northern France in this era.[4]

Why would the Ezra Master have portrayed the Old Testament prophet Jeremiah as a bishop in the Saint-Vaast Bible? What could have been the motivation for a programmer in a monastic scriptorium to order the depiction of a bishop in such glorious surroundings, going so far as to make a visual parallel between the bishop and the apocalyptic lamb through their vertical alignment and enclosure in mandorlas?

On many levels Jeremiah is the perfect model for a powerful reforming bishop of the eleventh century. Prophesying in the late-seventh and early-sixth centuries B.C., Jeremiah matured under the

---

MS 9, fol. 1 (Sigrid Schulten, "Die Buchmalerei im Kloster St. Vaast in Arras," *Münchner Jahrbuch der bildenden Kunst* VII [1956]), Saints Dunstan and Aethelwold in the *Regularis Concordia*, London BL MS Cotton Tiberius A.III, fol. 2b, or the bishops throughout the Warmund Sacramentary, Ivrea, Bibl. Capitolare MS LXXXVI, Adriano Peroni, "Il ruolo della committenza vescovile alle soglie del mille: il caso di Warmundo di Ivrea," in *Il secolo di ferro: mito e realtà del secolo X*, SSCISAM XXXVIII, 2 vols. (1991), I, 243–270.

[2] Bishops in this period are sometimes shown tonsured; *Lexikon der christlichen Ikonographie*, ed. Engelbert Kirschbaum, 8 vols. (Basel, 1968–1976), I, 301–302. The wearing of the miter by cardinals and bishops was not well established until the middle of the eleventh century; see Christa C. Mayer-Thurman, *Raiment for the Lord's Service: A Thousand Years of Western Vestments* (Chicago, 1975), 33–34.

[3] Cologne, Erzbischöfliche Diözesan Dombibliothek, Dom MS 141, fol. 2. This section may have been added after the manuscript left Arras, however (Cologne, Schnütigen Museum, *Ornamenta Ecclesiae: Kunst und Künstler der Romanik. Katalog zur Ausstellung des Schnütigen-Museums in der Josef-Haubrich Kunsthalle*, ed. Anton Legner, 3 vols. [Cologne, 1985], 423).

[4] See, for instance, the Boulogne Gospels, Boulogne BM MS 9, fols. 1 and 112v, Arras BM MS 903 (549), fol. 110, (Sigrid Schulten, "Die Buchmalerei im Kloster St. Vaast in Arras im 11 Jahrhundert," Ph.D Dissertation, Ludwig-Maximilians-Universität, Munich, 1954, 53) and Boulogne BM MS 11, fols. 10, 56, and 107v, a Gospel book produced at Saint-Bertin in the late tenth century by a visiting Anglo-Saxon artist (Janet Backhouse, D. H. Turner and Leslie Webster, eds., *The Golden Age of Anglo-Saxon Art 966–1066* [London, 1984], 60–65).

leadership of King Josiah, who had piously attempted to return the
Kingdom of Judah to its covenant roots. Josiah was succeeded by
his significantly less orthodox son, Jehoiakim, who reinstated the worship of nature cults, and then by Jehoiakim's uncle, the politically
impotent Zedekiah.[5] Jeremiah railed against this lapse and began to
prophecy the coming of a vanquishing force from the north as God's
punishment on the sinful Judaeans.[6] His prophecies grew more and
more strident as the threat from Nebuchadrezzar and his Chaldaean
army increased and Zedekiah and his other advisors refused to listen
to the warnings. Finally, Jerusalem was destroyed and Jeremiah died
in exile in Egypt with the refugee Judaeans.[7]

In the Middle Ages, Jeremiah was often interpreted as a type of
Christ because of his sanctification in the womb, his experience of
being abandoned by his people, and his supposed death as a martyr.
These events are recorded in the biblical preface found before the
image in the Saint-Vaast Bible, and they provide some justification
for the choice of the Jeremiah image as a carrier of Christological
meaning (pl. IV).[8] It was his Old Testament persona, however, that
made him, for the first time in an artistic depiction, the perfect vehicle for episcopal regalia.[9] Jeremiah was a religious reformer who
preached against heresy and for a return to the ancient teachings of
the Lord. He was also an advisor to the kings of Judah, whose warn-

---

[5] Jeremiah 1:2–3.
[6] Jeremiah 1:13–16.
[7] *Dictionary of the Bible*, ed. J. Hastings (New York, 1954) 465–469.
[8] The preface to the Book of Jeremiah by Jerome, fols. 13–13v: *Sacerdos ex sacer-*
dotibus et in matris utero sanctificatus, virginitate sua evangelicum virum christi ecclesiae dedicans.
Isidore of Seville reinforces a typological interpretation of the Book of Jeremiah in
his very common preface: *Hieremias propheta, 'qui interpretatur' excelsus domini simplex in*
loquendo et ad intelligendum facilis, qui in omnibus dictis et passionibus suis redemptoris nostri
imaginem praetulit, hic postquam in typo christi regna destruxit diaboli iustitiaeque vel fidei
aedificavit imperium, iubetur prophetare super omnes gentes . . . Donatien de Bruyne, *Préfaces*
de la Bible latine (Paris, 1920), 124 and 129–130.
[9] See *Lexikon der christlichen Ikonographie*, II, 387–391. Nonetheless, the representation of Jeremiah as a prefiguration of Christ is not unknown. For instance, on the
Bury St. Edmunds Cross of c. 1180, two figures of Jeremiah surround the apocalyptic Lamb, holding text-scrolls with a quotation from Jeremiah 11:19: *Et ego quasi*
agnus mansuetus, qui portatur ad victimam . . . *et eradamus eum de terra viventium* (Elizabeth
C. Parker and Charles T. Little, *The Cloisters Cross; its Art and Meaning* [New York,
1994], 110 and 246–247). Jeremiah was shown holding a staff, but not a crozier,
along with a text scroll in the c. 900 Golden Psalter of St. Gall, St. Gall, Stiftsbibliothek
MS 22, p. 150. See Christoph Eggenberger, *Psalterium Aureum Sancti Galli; mittelalter-*
liche Psalterillustration im Kloster St. Gallen (Sigmaringen, 1987), 148 and plate 16.

ings were ignored, leading to the destruction of Jerusalem. [10] Jeremiah could act as a powerful role model to the eleventh-century bishops, who sought to increase their own power as religious reformers, to advise the divinely-sanctioned kings, and to fight against a rising tide of heresy. The significance of this new iconography in the Saint-Vaast Bible can be explained by examining the relationship between the abbots of Saint-Vaast, Richard of Saint-Vanne and Leduinus, and the local reigning bishop, Gerard of Cambrai.

The connection between Bishop Gerard of Cambrai and the reformer Richard of Saint-Vanne was deep and of long standing. Gerard had first met Richard at Reims, when both were in the course of their spiritual education at the Cathedral school. [11] As products of the same school, both men seem to have developed a respect for the importance of divinely-ordained government, both secular and ecclesiastical, and neither was later to object to limited secular involvement in the running of the religious establishments they directed. [12] Instead, the Richardian reform, like the Gorze reform on which it was, in part, modeled, relied on bishops and local lords both to invite reformers into monasteries, and then to reinforce their authority once they got there. [13] Gerard had already demonstrated his patronage of Richard around 1010, when he invited the reformer to replace the canons in a monastery founded by his family at Florennes with monks from Saint-Vanne. [14] Indeed, Richard may even have suggested Gerard to Emperor Henry II as the successor to the

---

[10] Jeremiah 36–39 especially.

[11] Gonzo of Florennes, *Ex miraculis S. Gengulfi*, ed. Oswald Holder-Egger, MGH SS XV (Hanover, 1888), 792. See Theodor Schieffer, "Ein deutscher Bischof des 11. Jahrhunderts: Gerhard I. von Cambrai (1012–1051)," *Deutsches Archiv für Erforschung des Mittelalters* I (1937), 354.

[12] Heinrich Sproemberg, "Gerhard I., Bischof von Cambrai (1012–1061)," in *Mittelalter und demokratische Geschichtsschreibung: ausgewählte Abhandlungen*, Forschungen zur mittelalterlichen Geschichte XVIII, ed. Manfred Unger (Berlin, 1971), 107, and Kassius Hallinger, *Gorze-Kluny. Studien zu den monastischen Lebensformen und Gegensätzen im Hochmittelalter*, Studia Anselmiana XXII–XXIII (Rome, 1950), 502–503.

[13] Sproemberg, *Mittelalter und demokratische Geschichtsschreibung*, 113–114 and Jean F. Lemarignier, "L'exemption monastique et les origines de la réforme grégorienne," in *À Cluny. Congrès scientifique* (Dijon, 1950), 316. On the Gorze reform, see above, chapter 2.

[14] Hallinger, *Gorze-Kluny*, 285–286, and Alfred Cauchie, "Richard de Saint-Vanne," in *Biographie nationale* (Brussels, 1907), XIX, 257. See the undated notice in the *Gesta*, PL 149:151–152, and Gonzo of Florennes, MGH SS XV:792.

bishop, Erluinus, who had first invited him to the diocese of Arras-Cambrai.[15] Richard and Gerard cooperated on more than the reformation of monasteries, for they also acted together as legates from Emperor Henry to King Robert the Pious at Compiègne in 1023.[16]

The *Gesta episcoporum Cameracensium*, most likely written for Gerard by a canon or scribe at the Cathedral of Notre Dame of Cambrai, fortunately provides us with a wealth of information about the challenges faced by Gerard of Cambrai, and in eleventh-century Arras in general.[17] The *Gesta* is composed of three books surveying the history of the diocese and its monasteries, culminating with an extensive description of the deeds of Bishop Gerard in the third book.[18] Although it was once thought that the chronicle was written between 1041 and 1043, more recently it has been suggested that much of it was written earlier, in 1024 or 1025, and that a different author added a later section, which starts at book three, chapter 50.[19] This later addition was perhaps written by an author in the employ of Gerard's successor, Lietbert, between 1051 and 1054, and at the same time examples of Gerard's correspondence from 1029–1030

---

[15] Richard was also one of the party sent to accompany the bishop to his new *cathedra*. PL 149:143. Sproemberg, *Mittelalter und demokratische Geschichtsschreibung*, 107.

[16] Jean F. Lemarignier, "Paix et réforme monastique en Flandre et en Normandie autour l'année 1023," in *Droit privé et institutions régionales: Études historiques offertes à Jean Yver* (Paris, 1976), 444–445.

[17] Early editions of the *Gesta* are Georges Colveneere, *Chronicon Cameracense et Atrebatense, sive historia utriusque ecclesiae III libris . . .* (Douai, 1615), 1–353, and André Joseph Ghislain Le Glay, *Chronique d'Arras et de Cambrai, par Balderic, chantre de Thérouane au XIᵉ siècle* (Paris, 1834), and Faverot et Petit, *Chronique d'Arras et de Cambrai, par Balderic, chantre de Thérouane au XIᵉ siècle* (Valenciennes, 1836), 25–374.

[18] C.L.C. Bethmann, in his edition of the *Gesta* for MGH SS VII, ed. Georg Heinrich Pertz (Hanover, 1846), 399–401, assembled his text from a series of incomplete manuscripts of widely varying dates, including The Hague, Koninlijke Bibliotheek MS nr. 75 F 15, an eleventh- or twelfth-century manuscript which Bethmann believed to be an autograph of the scribe, Saint-Vaast manuscript, Arras BM MS 398 (666), a fifteenth-century copy of a now lost original from the Cathedral of Arras which contains the remainder of the *Gesta* missing from the Hague manuscript, and a fourteenth-century transcription now in Paris, BnF MS lat. 5533a. Bethmann's edition was reprinted with his commentary in the more accessible PL 149:9–176, with the later interpolated letters, and book three chapters 28–32 and 34 moved to PL 142:1313–1322. Henceforth, references to the text of the chronicle will refer to the PL edition.

[19] MGH SS VII:393. See Georges Duby, "Gérard de Cambrai, la paix et les trois fonctions sociales, 1024," *Compte rendu des séances de l'Academie des inscriptions et belles-lettres* (1976), 136–146, for a thorough summary of the dating debate.

could have been inserted into the earlier text before chapter 50.[20] This earlier date for the bulk of the chronicle and the suggested later revision would explain the curious lacuna in the description of events between 1024/1025 and 1031, including possibly the best known event in Gerard's episcopate, the 1025 heretical incident in Arras. The redating means that soon after Gerard and Richard participated in some of the key political and religious events of the early-eleventh century, and not many decades later as originally thought, their roles and words were recorded. The narrative thus has more of the patina of eyewitness testimony, however biased, rather than being a formulaic rendition of distant events.

The *Gesta episcoporum Cameracensium*, written around the same time that the Saint-Vaast Bible was produced, repeatedly underlines the legitimacy of the bishop's jurisdiction over the monastery of Saint-Vaast, and praises Richard of Saint-Vanne for his willingness to submit himself and his monks to episcopal authority. According to the *Gesta*, Richard was originally invited to reform Saint-Vaast with the agreement of Gerard's predecessor, Erluinus, because the monastery had sunk to such a state of decadence that the abbot, Fulrad, no longer respected the authority of the bishop.[21] In criticizing Fulrad's leadership, the author of the *Gesta* recalls that similarly in the Carolingian era, the monastery had drifted so far from the control of the local bishop due to the incursions of the Danes that the body of Saint-Vaast was removed from the abbey.[22] In contrast, the

---

[20] Erik Van Mingroot, "Kritisch underzoek omtrent de datering van de *Gesta episcoporum Cameracensium*," *Revue belge de philologie et d'histoire* LIII (1975), 281–332.

[21] David C. Van Meter, "Count Baldwin IV, Richard of Saint-Vanne, and the Inception of Monastic Reform in Eleventh-Century Flanders," *Revue bénédictine* CVII (1997), 132–134. On Fulrad see PL 149:108–110 and 118–119. PL 149:118. *Infelix ille! qui beatum Augustinum non advertebat memoriae dicentem male illos disputare contra claves aecclesiae, qui auctoritatem aecclesiasticam, quam in episcopis constat fateri, contendunt adnullare; alioquin aecclesia quae in episcopali auctoriate habetur, potestatem ligandi atque solvendi neutiquam habere valeret.*

[22] PL 149:109. . . . *quia tantae moli impares tam arduam causam absque auctoritate episcopi attemptare formidabant, corpus sancti Vedasti quaesitum a loco moveret, et inpositum feretro pro metu Danorum ad deferendum aliosum pararet.* See also earlier recounting, PL 149:53–54. At the same time, the chronicler sought to reinforce the bishop's rights by alluding to the Benedictine Rule's injunction in support of the bishop's jurisdiction over the affairs of the monastery, "If the community elects someone who encourages their wickedness, and this is made known to the bishop of the diocese or other abbots and good Christians in the locale, these in turn should annul the choice, and they should choose a worthy overseer of God's house." *The Rule of St. Benedict,*

chronicler records the most important quality of Richard as an abbot, in the eyes of the episcopal hierarchy.

> The count entrusted the banished abbey to that most religious man Richard, to be ruled with the bishop overseeing and regulating (it). He [Richard] built up the rules of religious discipline among the many brothers . . . The evil Fulrad having been expelled, he [Richard] always appeared subject with all reverence to the lord bishop, and he complied with him in all things with the pure sign of love, as is proper.[23]

In addition, the *Gesta* glowingly reports the many instances of cooperation between Abbot Richard and Bishop Gerard in reforming the monastic houses of the region, such as Hautmont and Lobbes.[24] Interestingly, the same is not entirely true of episcopal relations between Gerard and Richard's successor, Leduinus, even though the bishop participated in the selection of the new abbot.[25] David C. Van Meter has recently revealed a notable blip in the traditionally smooth cooperation between the abbot and the bishop in the decades after Fulrad was deposed. Apparently, soon after he was installed, Leduinus either revised an old, forged episcopal exemption purportedly granted by the seventh-century bishop Vindician, or fabricated it anew, in an attempt to reassert the abbey's autonomy.[26] By

---

trans. Anthony C. Meisel and M. L. del Mastro (Garden City, N.Y., 1975), Chap. 64, p. 99. PL 149:109. *Porro iste, qui contendebat disciplinam et increpationem episcopi declinare, et contra evangelicae et apostoliae institutionis auctoritatem a jugo episcopi cervicem deditionis excutere, male intelligebat sententiam sancti benedicti, ubi, tractans ordinando abbate, inter cetera dicit: "Episcopus, ad cuius diocesim ipsum monasterium pertinet."* See Cowdrey, 23–24, on the Rule and episcopal influence.

[23] PL 149:119. *Quare et huic amotam abbatiam Richardo religiossimo viro comes, providente episcopo atque ordinante, moderandam commisit. Qui in tantum fratres norma disciplinatae religionis extruxerit . . . Hic etiam, extincta Fulradi malicia, semper domno episcopo cum tota reverentia subjectus extitit, eique in omnibus, sicuti decet, intermerato amoris signaculo obsecundavit.*

[24] PL 149:147 on Hautmont, 150 on Lobbes, and 151 on Florennes.

[25] PL 149:151.

[26] David C. Van Meter, "Eschatological Order and the Moral Arguments for Clerical Celibacy in Francia Around the Year 1000," in *Medieval Purity and Piety: essays on medieval clerical celibacy and religious reform*, ed. Michael Frassetto (New York, 1998), 149–175. Copies of the Vindician charter survive both in the twelfth-century Guimann Cartulary, in Louis De Bréquigny, François La Porte du Theil and Jean-Marie Pardessus, *Diplomata, chartae, epistolae, leges, aliaque instrumenta res Gallo-Francicas spectantia* II (Paris, 1849), 180 and E. Van Drival, *Cartulaire de l'abbaye de Saint-Vaast rédigé au XIIIe siècle par le moine Guiman* (Arras, 1875), 18–22, and in Douai BM MS 795 (753) fols. 67–69, a manuscript from the first half of the eleventh century containing the earlier *Chronicon Vedastinum*. This version was published along with the *Chronicon* in MGH SS XIII, ed. Georg Waitz (Hanover, 1881), 697–698. Van Meter does not address the doubts raised by Jean Lemarignier about whether this early

1031, in the wake of the Peace of God crisis that will be described below, Gerard had been forced to confirm the fraudulent charter, which was later included in the abbey's twelfth-century Guimann Cartulary.[27] Nonetheless, a close reading of the charter granted by Gerard reveals that he was able to avoid compromising the principle of episcopal control outright. The privilege from Gerard to Leduinus refers to one of these forgeries as *libellum quod a beato Vindiciano eiusdem sedis episcopo*. It sets out clearly the bishop's responsibility to protect the monastery from disturbances (*omni seculari inquietudine et mundana potestate*) by secular lords and powers (*neque comes nec aliqua regia postestas vel judiciaria*), quoting from the earlier forgery. The earlier customary's explicit exclusion of the bishop, *Si autem talis extiterit causa, ut merito episcopus accersiri debeat, nisi vocatus ab abbate vel a monachis, aliter, ut diximus, nec alicui liberum ingressum consentimus*, however, is elided in the later document, to *Si autem extiterit causa ut merito episcopus accersiri debeat, vocatus ab abbate veniat*.

Despite this disagreement, Gerard and Leduinus managed to maintain cordial relations and set about reforming and founding monasteries together.[28] Still, if the *Gesta episcoporum Cameracensium* was written at his request, as seems likely, clearly the issue of episcopal jurisdiction weighed very heavily on the mind of Bishop Gerard. Perhaps in reaction to the recent history of discord, he sought through the

charter should be associated with Leduinus. While two early exemptions attributed to Bishop Vindician and the eighth-century Pope Stephen II have long been recognized as forgeries, Lemarignier noted that the invention of such documents during an era of cooperation between Abbot Leduinus and Bishop Gerard must be highly suspect (Lemarignier, "L'exemption monastique," 335–340). He redated the Vindician charter to the abbacy of Fulrad, c. 988–1004, and interpreted it as ammunition in the lasting dispute between the decadent abbot and two of Gerard's predecessors, Rothard and Erliunus, especially because the *Gesta episcoporum Cameracensium* (PL 149:109), written under Gerard, alleged that Fulrad claimed that he had a Vindician charter during his contest with the abbot: *Hoc profecto versutus incentor ad ampliandas discordias cum subdola et verisimili assertione addebat, se habere videlicet sancti Vinditiani ejusdem sedis episcopi privilegia, apostolica auctoritate confirmata, in quibus decretum esset, monachos sancti Vedasti non debere habere, respectum ad pontificem aecclesiae Cameracensium.* Even if the forgery predated Leduinus, however, most significant for us is that Gerard felt compelled to reaffirm a version of it during Leduinus's abbacy. For the early privileges from Saint-Vaast, Van Drival, 17–64. Once again, because the cartulary was compiled in the late twelfth century, when Saint-Vaast had long been under Cluniac control, the reliability of all of these documents remains to be established. On the origins and editing of the cartulary, see above, chapter one, note 10.

[27] Van Drival, *Cartulaire*, 61–63 and Van Meter, "Eschatological," 161.

[28] PL 149:133 on Marchiennes, 131 on Billi-Berclau, 133 on Denain, and 134–135 on Haspres.

Gesta to foster cooperation between himself and the abbots of Saint-Vaast.

While the evidence provided by the *Gesta* for successful relations between the Bishop of Cambrai and the abbots of Saint-Vaast comes mainly from the episcopal viewpoint, the Arras Bible was copied and decorated within the monastic scriptorium at Saint-Vaast. Its Jeremiah illustration provides proof that in the monastic context as well, despite the controversy surrounding the false Vindician charter, the bishop must have been regarded in a positive light (pl. IV). The Jeremiah figure, dressed in episcopal regalia, is surrounded with the insignia of divine authority, including angels, haloes, and the apocalyptic lamb. Because the dating of these illustrations falls broadly within the first third of the eleventh century, it is impossible to assign this image to either the period before the false charter affair or to its aftermath, when the abbey may have wanted to curry favor with an offended bishop. The details of the image imply that the illustrator, or programmer, of the Bible viewed the episcopal office as that of a legitimate governor. Once again, this belief can be aligned specifically with Richard and his reform movement, for it certainly was not common to all monastic reformers of this period, Cluny being the best known example.

Gerard's attempt to control the actions of the local abbot didn't end with the flattering depictions of Richard and even Leduinus in the *Gesta*, or with his reworking of the Vindician charter to allow episcopal intervention. He also sought to exert control over them from the moment of their elevation to office. Traditionally, the ceremony for the consecration of bishops included a pledge of obedience to higher authority made during the examination of the candidate for the episcopal seat. Such pledges were usually absent, on the other hand, from ordines for the consecration of abbots.[29] Two different

---

[29] Edmond Martène, *De antiquis ecclesiae ritibus libri*, 4 vols. (Antwerp, 1736), II, 409. The Roman Pontifical, the Romano-Germanic Pontifical, and the Leonine, Gelasian and Gregorian Sacramentaries included no such pledge. See Michel Andrieu, *Le Pontifical Romain au Moyen-âge*, Studi e Testi LXXXVI–LXXXVIII and IC (Vatican City, 1964–1965), Jean Deshusses, *Le sacramentaire grégorien* (Fribourg, 1971), Sieghild Rehle, *Sacramentarium Gelasianum mixtum von Saint-Amand* (Regensburg, 1973) and Cyrille Vogel and Reinhard Elze, *Le pontifical Romano-Germanique du dixième siècle*, Studi e Testi CCXXVI, CCXXVII and CCLXIX (Vatican City, 1963–1972). In the near contemporary *Liber tramitis* from the Cluniac reformed monastery of Farfa, the local bishop is permitted to oversee the election and to consecrate the new abbot, but

ordines for the consecration of an abbot originating in the diocese of Arras-Cambrai, however, reveal that there the abbot was required to bow to the authority of the bishop and his successors.[30] The first is found in the Cologne Pontifical, Erzbischöfliche Diözesan Dombibliothek, Dom MS 141.[31] Textually, this manuscript can easily be localized to the archdiocese of Reims. In the litany, only the names of Vedastus, or Vaast, and Benedictus are written in capital letters. The litany also ends with the name of Gaugericus, first bishop of Cambrai, implying that this manuscript was produced for the bishop of Arras-Cambrai. The references to St. Vaast, Benedict, and Gaugericus combine to suggest that the manuscript was copied and decorated at Saint-Vaast for the local bishop.[32] This is reinforced by the style of the manuscript's decoration, which lies purely within the later Saint-Vaast school, recalling strongly the hurried line-drawing style seen in English manuscripts c. 1000, but now carried out in a painted form with white highlights and red-line drawn features.[33] In

---

not to obtain a pledge of loyalty. *Liber tramitis aevi Odilonis abbatis*, ed. Peter Dinter, CCM X (Siegburg, 1980), 208–210.

[30] Cologne, Erzbischöfliche Diözesan Dombibliothek, Dom MS 141, and Arras BM MS 745. Laurent Jégou, "L'évêque entre autorité sacrée et exercice du pouvoir. L'exemple de Gérard de Cambrai (1012–1051)," *Cahiers de civilisation médiévale, X^e–XIIe siècles* XLVII (2004), 37–55, has recently speculated that the Romano-Germanic Pontifical was introduced into the diocese of Arras-Cambrai in the early-eleventh century specifically in order to shore up the prestige of the episcopacy. Surprisingly, he does not mention either the redaction of Cologne Dom MS 141, whose author borrowed heavily from the Romano-Germanic Pontifical, or the sacrament found in Arras BM MS 745, discussed below.

[31] *Ornamenta Ecclesiae* I, 423–425 and *Handschriftcensus Rheinland*, ed. Günter Guttermann (Wiesbaden, 1993), 654–655, n. 1105. The complete series of ordines found in the manuscript was published in a most abbreviated way by Michel Andrieu in *Les ordines romani du haut moyen age*, Spicilegium sacrum lovaniense; études et documents, fasc. 11, 23–24, 28–29, 5 vols. (Louvain, 1931–1961) I, 108–114.

[32] Schulten, *Münchner Jahrbuch*, 64–66. Andrieu argued that the manuscript was probably written in a Benedictine monastery in the joint diocese of Arras-Cambrai, most likely in the Arras region of the diocese (*Les ordines romani* I, 108, and IV, 475).

[33] Schulten identified the roots of the Cologne manuscript's decoration in that of the 'präzisen Zeichners,' one of the artists who provided initials in the Bible. The style of initials and vegetal ornament in Cologne Dom MS 141 is much closer to that found in other Saint-Vaast manuscripts than the figure illustrations. Although Schulten compared the historiated initial of Christ on fol. 33 of Cologne Dom MS 141 with the seated Christ found in the Bible's Acts illustration, volume III, fol. 141, particularly in the proportions of the figures and the design of the drapery (Schulten, *Münchner Jahrbuch*, 66), this was not carried out by the same artist. Further reinforcement for the origin of the manuscript comes from Dijon BM MS 130. This manuscript was copied for Stephen Harding at the time of his visit to Saint-Vaast in 1125. On fol. 104 the artist, Oisbertus, has depicted Henry of Saint-Vaast

fact, Sigrid Schulten concluded in her 1956 study of the scriptorium
that the Pontifical was created at Saint-Vaast for the Bishop of Arras-
Cambrai, very possibly in connection with the production of the
early manuscripts such as the Bible. She rightly suggested a date of
the second half of the eleventh century, possibly soon after Gerard's
death.[34] This is within a few years of the production of the Saint-
Vaast Bible, when the same concerns were likely to have been current in people's minds, and in the wake of Leduinus's attempt to
reexert the abbey's exemption from episcopal control.

On fol. 134v, the ceremony for the consecration of an abbot begins
with an admonition that the bishop must celebrate mass in the presence of two or three other abbots, and then give the candidate a
staff, shoes and a copy of the Benedictine Rule. A lengthy examination of the candidate by the bishop follows. On folio 135, as part
of this examination, the bishop asks the abbot to indicate his willingness to acknowledge episcopal authority. "Do you desire to show
obedience and subordination to the holy Church of . . . . and to
me and to my successors according to canonical authority and the
decrees of the holy bishops?"[35] Like the other ceremonies for consecration found in this manuscript, the *Ordo ad benedicendum abbatem*
was apparently compiled from a variety of sources.[36] Although the
greater part of this ceremony was adapted from that found in the
tenth-century Romano-Germanic Pontifical, the examination of the
candidate and pledge of loyalty made to the episcopal seat are both
interpolations, demonstrating that the ordo has been adapted to suit
circumstances in eleventh-century Arras.

---

and Stephen Harding of Cîteaux offering their abbeys to the Virgin Mary. His
work is so close to that of the Cologne Pontifical that he either was the artist of
that manuscript many decades before or was trained by him. Yolanta Zaluska,
Manuscrits enluminés de Dijon (Paris, 1991), 127–129.

[34] Schulten, *Münchner Jahrbuch*, 66.

[35] *Vis sanctae . . . . aecclesiae et mihi meisque successoribus subiectionem et oboedientiam
exhibere secundum canonicam auctoritatem et decreta sanctorum pontificum.* At some point in
the manuscript's history, the name of the church was scratched out. Michel Andrieu,
in his study of medieval ordinals, speculated that this lacuna originally read *camera-
censis*, and that after the division of the diocese between Arras and Cambrai in
1093, when Arras was removed from the jurisdiction of the Cathedral of Cambrai,
the word was effaced (*Les ordines romani* I, 108 and *Ornamenta Ecclesiae* I, 423). This
demand mirrors that found in the ceremony to consecrate a bishop from the same
manuscript. On fol. 124 the archbishop asks of the candidate, "Vis fidem et subiectionem sanctae ecclesiae matri remensi omnes dies vitae tuae servare."

[36] Vogel and Elze, Ordo XXVI, 62–69.

An early-twelfth-century edition of the Benedictine rule produced at the Cathedral of Arras, today Arras BM MS 745, shows that this practice persisted for at least fifty years.[37] The Rule of Saint Benedict is followed by a series of ordines including an *ordo ad monachum abbatem faciendum*, which is almost entirely different from the ordo in the Cologne Pontifical, and contains only one prayer borrowed from the Romano-Germanic Pontifical.[38] The directions for the selection of the abbot prefacing the examination of the candidate emphasize the right of the bishop to observe and confirm this choice.[39] Then follows an examination that is similar but not identical to the one in the Cologne Pontifical ordo. On fol. 22, the bishop once again demands of the candidate a pledge of obedience to the episcopacy: "Do you wish to be subject to the holy church of Arras, and to me and all my successors, according to the rule of the blessed Benedict?"[40] Then, the candidate is instructed to write out this pledge:

> I, the following, now being ordained abbot, to the following church, promise to show subjection and reverence by the decree of the holy fathers, and obedience according to the precept and rule of Saint Benedict, to this holy church of Arras, and to you father, the following bishop, and to your successors forever, and I confirm this with my own hand.[41]

The manuscript was probably composed before c. 1115, for by that date Saint-Vaast and the other monasteries in the diocese had been forcibly converted to Cluniac observance, although manuscripts copied by the cathedral may have preserved such a form after it had fallen

---

[37] *Catalogue général* IV, Arras, 408. The manuscript can be attributed to the cathedral based on a contemporary inscription, *Liber beate Marie Atrebatensis*, on the first guard page.

[38] For a group of similar ordines, see Martène, 428, 432 and 436 and Aimé Martimort, *La documentation liturgique de Dom Edmond Martène: Étude codicologique*, Studi e Testi CCLXXIX (Vatican City, 1978), nos. 56, 103, 248, 259 and 260.

[39] Arras BM MS 745, fol. 21. *Deinde episcopo in cuius diocesi abbas est ordinandus, ipsa electio perscriptum et testes presentetur, quatinus per episcopum si digne facta fuerit confirmetur, et statuto tempore electus ab illo consecretur. Si autem electio in presentia episcopi facta et confirmata fuerit, dicatur.*

[40] *Vis sanctae atrebatensi aecclesiae et mihi et successoribus meis esse subiectus secundum regulam beati benedicti.*

[41] Fols. 22–22v. *Ego, illum, nunc ordinandus abbas, ad titulum illum, subiectionem et reverentiam a sanctis patribus constitutam et oboedientiam, secundum preceptum et regulam sancti benedicti, huic sanctae atrebatensi, tibi que pater illum episcope, et tuis successoribus perpetuo me exhibiturum promitto, et propria manu confirmo.* This same pledge can be found in manuscripts from Besançon, Tours, and Reims. Martène, 428, 432 and 436.

from practical use.[42] Despite the differences between them, both the
ordines in the Cologne Pontifical and in the Arras Benedictine Rule
demonstrate how important monastic obedience to the authority of
the bishop remained in the diocese where Saint-Vaast is located.
This tradition of obedience set these monasteries apart from the contemporary Cluniac movement. In this environment, a manuscript
containing an illumination like the Jeremiah image that glorified the
authority of the bishop would have been timely and appropriate.

Episcopal exemption was not one of the original founding principles of Cluny, which had stressed immunity from interference in its
temporal affairs, but had not demanded exemption from the spiritual
guidance of its local ecclesiastical hierarchy.[43] Rather, exemption only
developed over time into a defining characteristic of the Cluniac
movement. The push to remove Cluny from episcopal influence was
first made in the 990's, and culminated in 1024 with the full exemption of Cluny from the control of local bishops granted by Pope
John XIX.[44] The Pope soon found the opportunity to ask King
Robert the Pious of France to offer his support for this exemption,
drawing the secular ruler into the debate.[45] Robert's involvement did
not go unnoticed by the bishops of the Capetian realm. They protested
against the undue influence they saw exercised over the king by the
abbot of Cluny, whom they believed was usurping the role traditionally played by the bishops. In the poem *Carmen ad Rotbertum regem*,
Adalbero of Laon, Gerard of Cambrai's fellow bishop and cousin,
names Odilo of Cluny as his nemesis. Through parody, he warns
the king of the dangers of a world where monks have overstepped
their traditional role and assumed that reserved for consecrated religious leaders, the bishops.[46]

This controversy, along with its local manifestation in the form of
Leduinus's apparent demand for a renewel of Vindician's charter,

---

[42] Hallinger, *Gorze-Kluny*, 473–492. The pledges, both spoken and written, testify
to the fact that the manuscript was written after 1093, since the church to which
obedience is given is Arras. No mention is made of Cambrai, which was split off
from the diocese of Arras in 1093.

[43] Cowdrey, 6–8, and on Cluniac exemption, above chapter 2.

[44] Cowdrey, 23, 28–34, Lemarignier, "L'exemption monastique," 298–322, and
Georges Duby, *The Three Orders: Feudal Society Imagined*, trans. Arthur Goldhammer
(Chicago, 1980), 140–141.

[45] Cowdrey, 35. See PL 141:1145–6.

[46] Adalbéron de Laon, *Poème au roi Robert*, Les classiques de l'histoire de France
au moyen âge XXXII, ed. Claude Carozzi (Paris, 1979), 2–13. See Duby, 53–55.

was brewing at precisely the time when the pictorial statement of monarchical and episcopal precedence and cooperation was laid out in the Saint-Vaast Bible. The monks of Saint-Vaast were certainly aware of the furor surrounding exemption, and knew the opinions of their leaders, Bishop Gerard of Cambrai and Richard of Saint-Vanne. Richard and Gerard obviously shared an ideology of rule in which monks answered to the ultimate authority of the bishop, otherwise Richard would not have found the path smoothed for his reform in the diocese of Arras-Cambrai. In supporting Richard and his reform, Gerard was undoubtedly, at least in part, attempting to work against the threat to his authority posed by Cluny, and the danger he thought it represented to the power of kings.[47]

The fact that an image such as the Jeremiah illumination (pl. IV), which obviously seeks to glorify the episcopal office, is found in the Arras Bible, is amply justified by the Richardian reform movement's philosophies. The *way* in which the bishop is glorified, however, is more reasonably defined through an understanding of the political beliefs of Gerard of Cambrai, recorded in the writings associated with him, including the *Gesta episcoporum Cameracensium* and the *Acta synodi Atrebatensis*.

The Christological Bishop in the Jeremiah Miniature

A trio of contemporary manuscripts from the region, including the Arras Bible, share a variety of motifs proclaiming the divine origin of the bishop's power as well as his likeness to Christ. A *Vita Sanctorum* produced at the nearby monastery of Saint-Bertin in Saint-Omer includes on two facing folios a pair of dedication images (figs. 33–34).[48]

---

[47] Duby, 139–140, on Gerard's probable distinction between Richard of Saint-Vanne and Cluny.

[48] Boulogne BM MS 107, fols. 6v–7. Claire Kelleher, "Illumination at Saint-Bertin at Saint-Omer under the Abbacy of Odbert," Ph.D. Dissertation, University of London, 1968, 63–66. Kelleher, p. 32, believes this manuscript was illuminated by Abbot Odbert himself, and can therefore be dated ca. 990–1012. She identifies the unlabeled central figure on both folios as St. Bertin (p. 64), presumably because the images preface a mass for St. Bertin. Yet, as St. Bertin was apparently never ordained, and certainly never consecrated a bishop, it would have been inappropriate to depict him wearing the chasuble, dalmatic and stola and holding a maniple as in fol. 7. The wearing of the chasuble and dalmatic in combination was restricted to bishops (Braun, 249). It is more likely, therefore, that the images depict

In one, a haloed bishop stands with book and crozier flanked by two deacons, while above him, framed in a circle, is a nimbed Apocalyptic lamb. On the facing page, the bishop receives a book from a kneeling monk, while the hand of God descends from above. The Saint-Vaast artists rearranged the building blocks used in this image to create their new and suggestive composition that highlights the prophet's ability to signify both the importance of the bishop, and the supernatural source of his authority by visually aligning him with the heavenly lamb.

Although in the Carolingian era Jeremiah had been depicted in conjunction with the Lamb of the Apocalypse in *maiestas* images that included other prophets, he was never singled out as the sole prophet to be associated with the Lamb.[49] The Ezra Master in the Arras scriptorium has isolated him, while the Acts Master combined the two motifs of the divine hand and the Apocalyptic lamb drawn from the Saint-Bertin images to create a redundancy: the Lamb, as a manifestation of Christ, needs no blessing.[50] The blessing is surely intended for the bishop below, who receives his power through the grace of the Lamb. The bishop's glory is signalled not only by the choir of angels surrounding him, but also by the full-body mandorla that encloses him. The mandorla was an attribute typically reserved in the eleventh century for Christ or Christological symbols, as in the lobed mandorla that surrounds the Lamb hovering above Jeremiah. The two artists intended to make a visual parallel, which attributes Christ-like qualities to the figure dressed as a bishop below.

The Saint-Vaast Bible was not the only Saint-Vaast manuscript in which a vertical link was made between Christ and a bishop. The Ezra Master was also responsible for drawing the dedication page of the contemporary manuscript that combines Augustine's *Confessiones* and *De vera religione*, Arras BM MS 616 (548) fol. 1v (fig. 35), where

---

a historical or contemporary bishop, although one cannot rule out the possibility that the artists mistakenly invested St. Bertin with an office that he had never attained.

[49] Herbert L. Kessler, *The Illustrated Bibles from Tours* (Princeton, 1977), 42–58. He was sometimes chosen as one of the four prophets to surround the Lamb, accompanied by the four evangelist symbols, in *maiestas agni* frontispieces to the Gospels, such as that in the Touronian Bamberg Bible, Bamberg, Staatsbibliothek Misc. class. Bibl. 1, fol. 339v, or in the St. Gauzelin Gospels now in the Cathedral Treasury at Nancy, fol. 3v.

[50] *Lexikon der christlichen Ikonographie* III, 7–14.

Augustine kneels before the enthroned Christ. Directly below, a kneeling scribe pays homage to an enthroned bishop, presumably the patron saint, St. Vaast, of the monastery for which the manuscript was copied.[51] The intended parallel between Christ and Bishop Vedastus could not be more obvious.

A wealth of historical documents surround the Arras Bible and explain the sudden appearance of this innovative iconography in early-eleventh-century Arras. The writings associated with Gerard of Cambrai have never before been connected with the Saint-Vaast Bible, although they originated in the same period and region. Gerard is now best remembered for his handling of a heresy that arose in Arras in the season of Epiphany in 1025. Either he or an assistant documented the synod called to deal with this outbreak in the *Acta synodi Atrebatensis*, and in the process also recorded Gerard's theories on kingship and episcopal power. In the course of defending the institutional church against the threat supposedly posed by this heresy, Gerard defined the episcopal office in a way that explains, in large part, the iconography of the Jeremiah miniature.

The heresy at Arras was not an isolated occurrence, but one of the earliest examples of what Jeffrey B. Russel calls 'reform dissidence.'[52] The rise of heresy in early-eleventh-century France was yet another symptom of the shifting social structures that had led to the series of monastic reforms that washed across Northern Europe at the same time. The heresies reflected, in the doctrines of their adherents, dissatisfaction with the corrupt state of the contemporary Church, and presaged many of the reforms that would later become Church policy under Gregory VII. Like so many of the contemporary heretical movements, this one was espoused by the disenfranchised. The *Acta* reports that the Arras heretics were tortured during their incarceration, suggesting that they weren't entitled to the rights traditionally

---

[51] Schulten, "Die Buchmalerei," 57–58, believes this drawing was carried out by the 'zweite Werkstattgruppe,' the same group responsible for much of the illustration in the Bible, including parts of the Jeremiah image.

[52] Jeffrey B. Russel, *Dissent and Order in the Middle Ages: The Search for Legitimate Authority* (New York, 1992), 21, and idem, *Dissent and Reform in the Early Middle Ages* (Los Angeles, 1965), 20. This heresy has been discussed generally many times. See, for example, Robert I. Moore, *The Birth of Popular Heresy* (London, 1975), 15–20, idem, *The Formation of a Persecuting Society: Power and Deviance in Western Europe, 950–1250* (New York, 1987) 17–19, and idem, *The Origins of European Dissent* (Toronto, 1994, orig. 1977), 9–20.

accorded freedmen.[53] Furthermore, after the sentence had been read
in Latin, it had to be translated into the vernacular for the benefit
of the heretics, who signed it only with crosses.[54] This and other
details of the account hint that Gerard's intended readership for the
Acta were literate clerics and nobles who shared his concerns about
hierarchy.

The *Acta synodi* themselves suggest that Gerard carefully stage-man-
aged the event to allow himself an opportunity to express his own
views. Bishop Gerard had just celebrated Christmas of 1024 in
Cambrai when, as was his custom, he departed to spend a few days
in Arras. When he reached Arras, he was informed that a group of
heretics had arrived from Italy, and were preaching their beliefs. He
had the adherents seized and brought before him, where he questioned them. Agreeing that they were indeed heretics, Gerard ordered
them imprisoned for three days. He then convened a synod and
processed into the Cathedral with his retinue singing the antiphon
Exsurgat Deus. Surrounded by all the clergy of Arras, including abbots
and priests, archdeacons, and all the rest seated according to their
rank, Gerard called the synod to order and the unfortunates were
brought before him so that he could question them yet again.[55]

The *Acta synodi Atrebatensis* are allegedly the records of this examination.[56] Erik van Mingroot has argued on the basis of orthography and literary style that the *Acts* were composed by the same cleric
who composed the *Gesta episcoporum Cameracensium*, and probably around

---

[53] Robert I. Moore, "Literacy and the Making of Heresy, c. 1000–1150," in
Heresy and Literacy, 1000–1530 (Cambridge, 1994), 26, note 23, accepts the translation in *Heresies of the High Middle Ages*, eds. Walter L. Wakefield and Austin P. Evans
(New York, 1969), 84, of *supplicia* as 'tortures' in Gerard's letter to Bishop R.: PL
142:1270. *Verum illi quoque qui, missi ab eis ad seductionem huiusmodi, ad nos devenerant,
comprehensi multa dissimulatione renitebant, adeo ut nullis suppliciis possent cogi ad confes-
sionem....* This assumption can be questioned, however, for not only were laws
regarding torture in a state of flux in the eleventh century, but also, although in
the Greek and Republican legal canons only slaves could be tortured, already in
the third century anyone in the lower ranks of society, whether slave or free, could
be tortured, and all ranks could be tortured in the case of accusations of treason
or heresy (see Malise Ruthven, *Torture: the Grand Conspiracy* [London, 1978], 36–52).
[54] PL 142:1312, Moore, *The Formation of a Persecuting Society*, 17.
[55] PL 142:1271.
[56] The *Acta synodi Atrebatensis* are most accessible in PL 142:1269–1312. They
were first published in Luc D'Achéry, *Veterum aliquot scriptorum quo in Galliae bibliothecis, maxime Benedictinorum latuerant, Spicilegium* XIII (Paris, 1677) republished as Luc
D'Achéry and Louis De La Barre, "*Synodus attrebatensis a Gerardo...*", *Spicilegium, sive
collectio veterum aliquot scriptorum qui in Galliae bibliothecis delituerant* I (Paris, 1723),
606–624, reprinted by the Gregg Press (1967).

the same time.[57] The earliest copy of the text known is a twelfth-century Cîteaux manuscript now in Dijon, BM MS 582. Here, the *Acts* are immediately prefaced by an epistle to a certain Bishop R., upbraiding him for his laxity in allowing heresy to flourish in his diocese, and letting it spread unchecked to neighboring dioceses. Most scholarship on the texts themselves has been restricted to uncovering the identity of R., the recipient of the letter.[58] But the intended recipient of the letter is of less interest here than the ideas espoused in the records of the synod itself.

Scholars have long noted that there seems to be a sizeable discrepancy between the beliefs admitted by the heretics in their own statements, and those with which they were charged by Gerard in the *Acta*.[59] During the single opportunity given them to speak, the heretics stated that they were followers of the Italian Gundulf, who had taught them to accept from the Bible only the precepts of the Gospels and the Apostles, to abandon the world, to restrain the desires of the flesh, to live by the labor of their own hands, to injure no one, and to share with those of the same faith. Furthermore, they saw no merit in baptism, because children could not knowingly commit to its responsibilities, but also because the baptized often took up again what they had renounced at the font, and the ministers who performed this sacrament were not free from sin themselves.[60]

---

[57] On the *Gesta episcoporum Cameracensium* see above, chapter two. Erik Van Mingroot, "Acta Synodi Attrebatensis (1025): problèmes de critique de provenance," in *Melanges G. Fransen*, ed. Stephan Kuttner, 2 vols. (Rome, 1976), II, 224–225. Brian Stock, *The Implications of Literacy: Written Language and Models of Interpretation in the Eleventh and Twelfth Centuries* (Princeton, 1983), 121, using the evidence of Van Mingroot, but advancing with more caution, argues on the other hand that the *Acta* may only have been revised by the author of the *Gesta*, presumably some time before the death of the recipient in 1042.

[58] The literature involved in this debate is immense. The two most popular candidates have been Réginard, Bishop of Liège, and Roger, Bishop of Châlons-sur-Marne. See the recent summary of the controversy in Van Mingroot, *"Acta Synodi Attrebatensis,"* 203–229. The most recent proposals have been by Jeffrey B. Russel, "A propos du synode d'Arras en 1025," *Revue d'histoire ecclésiastique* LVII (1962), 66–87, who prefers Réginard de Liège and believes the synod actually took place in 1026, and J. M. Noiroux, "Les deux premiers documents concernants l'heresie aux Pays Bas," *Revue d'histoire ecclésiastique* IL (1954), 842–855, a partisan of Roger of Châlons-sur-Marne. Van Mingroot argues convincingly in favor of a date of 1025, and Roger as the intended recipient.

[59] Moore, "Literacy and the Making of Heresy," 26–27, and idem, *The Origins of European Dissent*, 14–16 and 288–289. Also Russel, *Dissent and Reform*, 22–23, and Stock, 126.

[60] PL 142:1271–1272.

Bishop Gerard, however, did not restrict himself to attacking these confessed beliefs, but rather accused the heretics of a host of other false doctrines, which he rebutted one by one in great detail in the over 20,000 words of the *Acta*. Even before the accused had finished their confession, it seems, he interrupted to add that they also rejected the sacrament of the body and blood of Christ, the legitimacy of marriage, and the efficacy of penance, while denying the existence of the Church and the value of confessors, believing that only apostles and martyrs should be venerated.[61] In the body of the *Acta* he further accused them of not praying for the dead and denying the need for Christian burial, rejecting holy orders and the Church hierarchy, and condemning the singing of psalms, the offices, and the decoration of churches with images and the cross. Gerard appears to have been most disturbed by the possible threat to the hierarchy of the Church represented by these heretics, a threat probably already familiar to him from the other heresies then known to be making their way north from Italy.[62]

Without waiting for the heretics to either confirm or deny these accusations, Gerard proceeded to counter each of the admitted or imputed doctrines of the heretics. He bolstered his argument with a wealth of examples taken from both the Old and New Testaments, underlining the importance of tradition and the societal hierarchy instituted by God as the most meaningful precedents for determining what is heretical.

One may ask with some justification if Gerard could really have delivered this lengthy discourse in one day, in the presence of the wilting, illiterate heretics and crowds of clergy described. It is much more likely that the composition and dissemination of an account of the synod was used by Gerard after the fact as an opportunity to air views that had less to do with the Arras heretics themselves than with the changing power relationships in that time period that threatened the established hierarchy of the Church.[63]

---

[61] PL 142:1271.

[62] See Russel, *Dissent and Reform*, 27–38, and Moore, *The Origins of European Dissent*, 25–35 on the early-eleventh-century heresies at Orléans and Monteforte.

[63] Stock, 122, and Moore, *The Origins of European Dissent*, 15. See also the recent revisiting of this event in Michael Frassetto, "Reaction and Reform: Reception of Heresy in Arras and Aquitaine in the Early Eleventh Century," *Catholic Historical Review* LXXXIII (1997), 385–400. Frassetto argues that a similar dynamic operated between the heretics of Aquitaine and Ademar of Chabannes from 1018 into the 1030s.

Both of the scholars who have shaped recent interpretation of the *Acta* agree that Gerard must have been attempting to protect the status of the bishop and the traditional prerogatives of the Church, which was then in the midst of a fury of protest and reform, when he directed the *Acta synodi* to be written. Brian Stock proposes, for instance, that the sermon could have been intended at least in part for participants in the contemporary debate over the reform of the Church.[64] Gerard defended current Church practices not because they were customary, but because these practices or similar ones were instituted in the text of the Bible.[65] Like the heretics, Gerard used arguments based on biblical precedents. While the heretics had stated that they wished to discard the accumulated customs of the institutional church and return to the simpler practices exemplified by the mandates of the evangelists and the apostles, Gerard wished to preserve them.[66]

Georges Duby sees the text as, above all, a defense of order, both of the trifunctional division of society regulating the roles of all humans, and of the hierarchy established within the structure of the Church.[67] In addition, the order here on earth that Gerard was justifying reflected the order present in heaven, with one major exception. Whereas on earth the leadership of the ecclesiastical and secular realms was divided between two officers, the king and the bishop, in the heavenly sphere, one entity combined these two functions: Christ.[68] Gerard was attempting to preserve the rights he saw as essential to the consecrated leaders who took Christ's roles on earth against those who would level society. According to Duby, Gerard's belief in the parity between king and bishop, and the gulf that separated holders of these two offices from everyone else, were both

---

[64] Stock, 129.

[65] Stock, 129–135.

[66] Stock, 127–129. PL 142:1271. *At illi referunt se esse auditores Gundulfi, cuiusdam ab Italiae partibus viri, et ab eo evangelicis mandatis et apostolicis informatos, nullamque praeter hanc scripturam se recipere, sed hanc verbo et opere tenere.* Stock considers the contrast between these differing interpretations of the roots of Church custom in the Scriptures as the crux of the disagreement between Gerard and the heretics. Through his explanations, Gerard argues against the free access of uneducated laymen to the text, as without the preparation to understand its teachings, they may misinterpret its directives and fall into just such a heresy. The authority of the Church's practices and its right to act as intermediary between the text and the public is therefore reinforced (Stock, 137).

[67] Duby, *The Three Orders*, 31–32.

[68] Duby, *The Three Orders*, 33.

antiquated ideas reminiscent of the Carolingian era, but no longer relevant in the early-eleventh century. He thus sees Gerard as a conservative who sought to preserve a dying tradition.[69] I believe both of these interpretations are relevant to an understanding of the miniature program in the Saint-Vaast Bible. Both Stock and Duby see the primacy of the bishop as an essential component of Gerard's outlook.[70] Gerard's defense of the authority of bishops in the *Acta synodi* sets the stage for the image cycle in the Saint-Vaast Bible. Gerard called on biblical and heavenly precedents as a justification for the eleventh-century status quo, as did the artists of the Saint-Vaast Jeremiah illustration.

In the *Acta synodi Atrebatensis*, Gerard defended the authority of the bishop to govern the Church based on two grounds, both of them rooted in the Bible. First, the institution of a governing hierarchy in the Church was established in the Old Testament. The eleventh-century incarnation of a head priest, the bishop, was simply the most recent version of a biblically mandated leader. It is therefore not surprising that an Old Testament figure was chosen to carry episcopal regalia in the Saint-Vaast Bible, and that a Bible was chosen as the appropriate locale to demonstrate the bishop's rights. Second, in taking up his office, if not in his personal characteristics, a bishop was made a type of Christ. This was achieved through the act of consecration anointment, when the bishop was imbued with the grace of Christ, an event typologically related to the Baptism of Christ. Here Gerard joined a well-established tradition reflected in consecration liturgies, in the writing of authors such as the twelfth-century Norman Anonymous as well as in the *Acta*. All make abundantly clear that this belief was a constant from at least the ninth to the twelfth centuries.

It will be very revealing to take a closer look at some of Gerard's repeated references to the importance and origins of the office of bishop in the *Acta*. In chapter fifteen, entitled "About the ruling orders of the Church," Gerard defended the ecclesiastical hierarchy,

---

[69] Duby, *The Three Orders*, 163.

[70] Jégou, 46–55, also argues that Gerard used the *Gesta episcoporum Cameracensium* and the *Acta synodi* to shore up the prestige of his office, but asserts that this was necessary because it had been undermined in the eyes of the local cathedral chapter and townspeople by his exercise of secular power. Jégou thus applies a rather anachronistic standard for the separation of Church and State to eleventh-century politics.

with the bishop at its head, using the example of the Old Testament as the precedent for the New:

> Therefore, we read that in the Church of the old people, which is usually called by the name synagogue, the orders were arranged by God through Moses, who and what kind, and how and when they must govern the rest or be governed by the rest, or rule the rest or be ruled by the rest, and how they must serve in separate offices. But also now in the Church, which is called the Kingdom of Heaven in likeness to the heavenly order, we read and know the ministers to have been lucidly arranged through the institution of the Lord and apostolic tradition . . .[71]

In order to defend his own office, Gerard explained that the special status of the bishop came from the belief that he was a type of Christ. He began, as usual, with the roots of this office in the Church of the Old Testament and its replication in the apostolic period, in chapter six, "About the sacred orders."

> Moses, placing his hand upon Joshua's head, gave to him the spirit of virtue and the leadership of the people of Israel. So also fulfilling the Law and the prophets, our Lord Jesus Christ blessed the Apostles. Also in the Acts of the Apostles, at the order of the Holy Spirit, a hand was placed on the Apostles Paul and Barnabas in bishophood, and so they were sent forth to evangelize. The head indicates the chief of the mind, and just as the body is ruled by the mind, so the Church, which is the body of Christ, is ruled through the bishops.[72]

Both of these passages refer to Moses as the origin of this hierarchy, and as we will see below, Moses plays a very important part in the visual program of the Saint-Vaast Bible. Here it is most important to note that Gerard described the typological connection between Christ and the contemporary bishop as the fruit of his consecration anointment, which immediately elevated the bishop to a rank above

---

[71] PL 142:1308. *Igitur ordines in Ecclesia veteris populi, quae usitato nomine Synagoga vocatur, fuisse legimus per Moysen a Deo dispositos, qui et quales et qualiter ac quando ordinare caeteros vel ordinari a caeteris, vel regere caeteros, vel regi a caeteris deberent. Sed et nunc in Ecclesia, quae regnum coelorum appellatur, ad instar coelestium ordinum, ministros Domini institutione et apostolica traditione legimus et cognoscimus distincte esse compositos . . ."*

[72] PL 142:1294. *Moyses, super caput Josue manum imponens, dedit ei spiritum virtutis et ducatus in populo Israel. Sic et suppletor legis et prophetarum, Dominus noster Jesus Christus, apostolos benedixit. Et in Actibus apostolorum ex praecepto sancti Spiritus Paulo et Barnabae apostolis manus imposita est in episcopatum, et sic missi sunt ad evangelizandum. Caput enim principale mentis designat; et sicut mente corpus regitur, ita per episcopos Ecclesia, quae est corpus Christi, regitur.*

the unanointed by imbuing him with the grace of God.[73] Once again, this was instituted by Moses in the Old Testament with the priesthood of Aaron, whom he compared to bishops. In chapter four, dealing with incense and unction, he quoted Psalm 44:8, "Therefore God, thy God, hath anointed thee with the oil of gladness above thy fellows," and commented:

> When he calls them colleagues (fellows), what else does he consider them unless bishops, who, about to receive the grace of unction from him, who is the true priest according to the order of Melchisedech, he foresaw in prophetic spirit as vicars of Christ to rule the holy Church? Moreover, Christ is our head, therefore the high priest, who is made the vicar of Christ, is anointed on the head. By imitating him, who is the head of the whole Church, he himself is also made the head of the whole Church through this mystery of unction.[74]

Gerard then made a further parallel between the bishop and Christ, identifying the New Testament precedent for unction in the Baptism of Christ.

> Just as Christ speaks on behalf of the universal Church, so the bishop [speaks] on its behalf given to him. Into him, therefore, whom it is said was anointed Christ by the prophet before his colleagues, penetrated the gift of spiritual grace, in which Christ was anointed before the rest of his colleagues, meaning the saints, the unction of whom was performed in that time when he was baptized in the Jordan and the Holy Spirit in the form of a dove descended over him and remained with him.[75]

---

[73] The consecration anointment of the bishop on the head is well documented already in the Carolingian period, in Archbishop Hincmar of Reims' epistle describing the process of consecration to Adventius of Metz in 869–870. See Michel Andrieu, "Le sacre épiscopal d'après Hincmar de Reims," *Revue d'histoire ecclésiastique* XLVIII (1953), 39, part 9: *Ut autem ventum fuerit ad loca, in quibus sunt cruces signatae, accipiat consecrator vas chrismatis in sinistra manu et cum dextro pollice, cantans quae ibidem continentur, per singula loca faciat crucem de crismate in verticem consecrandi.* Philippe Buc has discussed how early medieval commentators frequently used the same technique of making typological parallels to Biblical rituals in order to elevate the kingly office. These similarities proved that the royal ritual contained an element of all-powerful "mysterium," granting the recipient sacred status. "Ritual and Interpretation: the Early Medieval Case," *Early Medieval Europe* IX (2000), 189–191.

[74] PL 142:1290. "*Unxit te Dominus Deus tuus oleo laetitiae prae consortibus tuis.*" *Quando consortes nominavit, quos alios intuebatur nisi episcopos, quos, Christi, vicarios spiritu prophetico ad regendam sanctam Ecclesiam praevidebat, qui hanc unctionis gratiam ab eo accepturi erant, qui est verus sacerdos secundum ordinem Melchisedech? Porro caput nostrum Christus est, ideo pontifex in capite ungitur, qui Christi vicarius efficitur. Imitando enim illum, qui est totius caput Ecclesiae, per hoc unctionis mysterium fit et ipse caput Ecclesiae sibi commissae.*

[75] PL 142:1290. *Et sicut Christus pro universa interpellat Ecclesia, ita episcopus pro sibi*

Furthermore, he distinguished the Christological consecration anointing of a bishop from that of a priest, for while bishops are anointed on the head, signifying their Christ-like nature, priests are anointed only on the hands.[76]

According to Gerard, the power of the bishop did not spring from any merit inherent in the pre-existing man, but was a gift of grace. This was a powerful argument against heretics who believed that the sinfulness of individual priests rendered the sacraments they delivered invalid. A bishop, no matter what the failings of his human nature, had received the right to govern through his consecration. Gerard compared the election of contemporary bishops to the election of the original Apostles. "And bishops, who were appointed through the world in the seats of the Apostles, succeeded the same Apostles in ordination. (They) are not now elected from the race of flesh and blood as at first, but each and every one through the merit which divine grace confers in him."[77]

 . The Jeremiah miniature in the Saint-Vaast Bible, produced in the same diocese as the *Acta*, in the same era, and at a monastery strongly under Gerard's sway, expresses the same beliefs in a visual form. In the *Acta*, Gerard repeatedly defended the office of bishop by recalling its origins in the Old Testament and in the apostolic era. He stressed the similarity between the sacramental anointing of the bishop at his elevation and the Baptism of Christ. He made a symbolic parallel between Christ and the bishop as the 'head' of the earthly Church, the body of Christ. In the miniature, the artists or programmer have chosen an Old Testament prophet as the vehicle to demonstrate the importance of this clerical office. The bishop's Christ-like role is emphasized both by the vertical alignment of the bishop and the Lamb of the Apocalypse, and by the mandorlas which surround both the bishop and the Christological lamb above, signifying that both received the gift of spiritual grace, Christ at his baptism,

---

commissa. *In eo autem quod ait propheta unctum Christum prae consortibus suis, spiritualis gratiae donum, quo Christus prae consortibus, id est caeteris sanctis, unctus est, insinuat, cuius unctio illo expleta est tempore, quando baptizatus est in Jordane, et Spiritus sanctus in specie columbae descendit super eum, et mansit in illo.*

[76] PL 142:1290. *Igitur hunc unctionis morem in ordinandis episcopis sancta adhuc servat Ecclesia; ipsi etiam episcopi in consecrandis presbyteris, manus eorum ungunt in oleo, ut mundi sint ad offerendum Deo hostias, et largi ad caetera officia pietatis.*

[77] PL 142:1294 . . . *et ipsis apostolis ordinantibus successerunt episcopi, qui sunt constituti per mundum im sedibus apostolorum, qui non iam ex gente carnis et sanguinis eliguntur sicut primum, sed pro uniuscuiusque merito, quod in eum divina gratia contulit.*

the bishop at his ceremonial anointment, the moment when he was imbued with the ability to lead.

Another miniature crafted in the same scriptorium reinforces this interpretation. Between 1060 and 1070, Abbot Seiwold of Bath gave the Arras scriptorium a manuscript, today Arras BM MS 732 (684), that included the Pseudo-Jerome letter *Cogitis me*, a tract which discusses with skepticism the possibility of bodily Assumption.[78] Soon after its arrival, Master A, who painted the Esther miniature in the Saint-Vaast Bible, so an artist familiar with the Bible's program, added an image of the Virgin Mary's Assumption into Heaven before the letter, on fol. 2v (fig. 36).[79] Master A used several motifs to indicate Mary's transition from her earthly home to her heavenly throne alongside her son.[80] He surrounded her with a full body mandorla overlapped at the top by a hand of God. On either side, angels with draped hands hover, in a visual echo both of the *Koimesis*, where angels sometimes carry the soul of Mary aloft, and of the Baptism of Christ, where angelic bystanders frequently hold clothes for the drying of the newly baptised Christ.[81] The combination of the angelic

---

[78] Philip Grierson, "Les Livres de l'abbé Seiwold de Bath," *Revue bénédictine* LII (1940), 109, described as "lib. de assumptione sanctae Mariae," in the record of the donation in Arras BM MS 849 (539), fol. 159. For the text of *Cogitis me*, PL 30:122–142. On the authorship of the text, C. Lambot, "L'homilie du Pseudo-Jérome sur l'Assomption et l'évangile de la Nativité de Marie d'après une lettre inédite d'Hincmar," *Revue bénédictine* XLIV (1934), 265–282.

[79] Schulten, "Die Buchmalerei," 86–88. This artist also carried out parts of Boulogne BM MS 9, the Gospel book from Saint-Vaast.

[80] Images of the bodily Assumption of the Virgin Mary did not become common until the twelfth century. Contemporary artists almost always chose to represent Mary's death and acceptance into heaven with the *Koimesis* (see for instance the Pericope book of Henry II, Munich, Bayerische Staatsbibliothek MS Clm 4452, fols. 79v–80, which show both the Assumption of the soul of Mary and its glorification). The only reasonably similar contemporary images are the Assumption of Mary in the Augsburg Sacramentary, London BL MS Harley 2908, from the first half of the eleventh century, where Mary is shown surrounded by a mandorla held by bare-handed angels, and the sacramentary from Mont St. Michel, New York Pierpont Morgan M. 641, fol. 142v (on the history of the western iconography, see Gertrud Schiller, *Iconographie der christlichen Kunst*, 5 vols. [Gütersloh, 1966–1991], IV/2, 95–107, and J. J. G. Alexander, *Norman Illumination at Mont-Saint-Michel 966–1100* (Oxford, 1970), 155–157 and plate 42a. Henry Mayr-Harting argues that such images, though they may be mistaken for the bodily Assumption, merely represent the glorification of Mary's soul as described in the Pseudo-Jerome letter (Mayr-Harting, *Ottonian Book Illumination; an Historical Study*, 2 vols. [New York, 1991], I, 151).

[81] The heavenly baptismal assistants appeared in the sixth century, in works such as the *Sancta Sanctorum* reliquary casket and the throne of Archbishop Maximianus in Ravenna. They continued to be popular in Carolingian and Anglo-Saxon art,

towelbearers and the mandorla, in fact, mirrors closely the Anglo-Saxon Benedictional of Aethelwold's Baptism of Christ miniature. Here, Christ's Baptism is shown in the mode of a coronation anointing, with its two vials of Chrism, and an epiphany, through the mandorla. Like Christ, whose grace was made manifest at the moment of his Baptism, Mary received Christological grace at the Annunciation. Because she remained in a state of grace throughout her life, she was assumed to heaven, as indicated by the mandorla that surrounds her and the hand of her welcoming son.[82] The artists of Saint-Vaast consciously used the mandorla as a symbol of grace. Similarly, they intended the Jeremiah miniature of the Saint-Vaast Bible to show that the bishop partook in the glory of Christ.

Gerard was certainly not alone in believing that bishops were types of Christ. In fact, this notion was then becoming a commonplace in Anglo-Saxon and Ottonian art and literature. The Norman Anonymous, possibly the pro-imperial Bishop Guillaume de Bona Anima, wrote an early scholastic discourse perhaps seventy-five years later that argued in dialectical fashion for Christocentric rulership.[83] He described kings and bishops as *personae geminae*,[84] blending spiritual and secular power through the institution of consecration and unction.[85] In his *De consecratione pontificum et regnum*, the author explained

---

for instance in the Baptism on the ninth-century Brunswick casket in the Herzog Anton Ulrich Museum and in the Anglo-Saxon Benedictional of Aethelwold, London BL MS Add. 49598, fol. 25. See Schiller, I, 143–150 and Robert Deshman, *The Benedictional of Aethelwold* (Princeton, 1995), 45–54.

[82] PL 30:126–127 and Deshman, 47.

[83] Ernst H. Kantorowicz, *The King's Two Bodies: a Study in Medieval Political Theology* (Princeton, 1957), 42–61 and idem, "Deus per Naturam, Deus per Gratiam: a Note on Mediaeval Political Theology," in *Selected Studies* (Locust Valley, 1965), 124–125, where he points out the similarity between the Norman Anonymous' view of Christological kingship and that expressed by Pope John VIII in 877, referring to the consecration of Charles the Bald. In addition, see George H. Williams, *The Norman Anonymous of ca. 1100 A.D.; Towards the identification and evaluation of the so-called Anonymous of York* (Cambridge, Mass., 1951), 125–7, Roger E. Reynolds, "The Unidentified Sources of the Norman Anonymous: CCC MS 415," *Cambridge Bibliographical Society* V (1970), 122–131 and Wilfried Hartmann, "Beziehungen der Normannischen Anonymus zu frühscholastischen Bildungszentren," *Deutsches Archiv für Erforschung des Mittelalters* XXX (1975), 108–142, for a discussion of the authorship of the treatise.

[84] *De Consecratione pontificum et regnum*, ed. H. Boehmer, MGH Libelli de lite III, imperatorum et pontificum saeculis XI et XII (Hanover, 1897), 664. *Itaque in unoquoque gemina intelligitur fuisse persona, una ex natura, altera ex gratia, una in hominis proprietate, altera in spiritu et virtute.*

[85] MGH Libelli de lite III:663. *Ad hanc itaque regendam reges in consecratione sua*

that both kings and bishops, through their ordination anointings, imitate the anointings of the Old Testament kings of Israel, or *christi* as he calls them, because they foreshadow the *Christus* of the New Testament.[86] The king's and the bishop's power became the same as that of Christ, and because they acquired grace through anointment, they both paralleled in their double human and divine natures the two-natured Christ.[87]

Remarkably, Gerard of Cambrai used the same term, *personae geminae*, to describe the bishop and the king nearly three-quarters of a century earlier, in the *Gesta episcoporum Cameracensium*, although he used it in a different way.[88] The Norman Anonymous defined *personae geminae* as the twin natures in one person given by grace, one human and one divine, in the image of Christ. Gerard, in contrast, described the king and bishop as twins of each other through their God-given roles.

The Saint-Vaast artists who built the Jeremiah image, as we have already seen, borrowed motifs that were current in episcopal imagery in Northern France, as witnessed in the depictions of bishops in the St. Bertin *Vita sanctorum* and the Arras Augustine manuscript, to build the Jeremiah image in the Arras Bible. Their familiarity with the iconography of Christ-centered rulership was not restricted to the resources of the County of Flanders, however. The artists of the Saint-Vaast workshop were clearly fluent in the visual vocabulary of the Carolingians and Ottonians, and drew on it liberally. At the same time, taking into account the current threat to the status of

---

accipiunt potestatem, ut regant illam et confirment in iudicio et iusticia et disponant eam secundum christianae legis disciplinam ... Ad hoc ipsum etiam et episcopalis ordo instituitur et sacra unctione et benedictione consecratur, ut et ipse regat sanctam aecclesiam secundum formam doctrinae a Deo sibi traditam.

[86] MGH Libelli de lite III:664. *Sed ut verum esse liqueat, quod vir unctus oleo sancto et divina benedictione sanctificatus mutetur in virum alium, id est in Christum Domini, et habeat in se spiritum Dei et virtutem, sine quibus christus non potest, et cum quibus non potest non esse christus ... "Ecce unxit te Dominus super hereditatem suam in principem, et insiliet in te spiritus Domini et prophetabis et mutaberis in virum alium."*

[87] MGH Libelli de lite III:664. *Quoniam et istae duae personae in veteri testamento olei sancti unctione consecrate et divina benedictione sanctificate leguntur ad hoc, ut in regendo populo Christi Domini figuram vicemque tenerent et in sacramento preferrent imaginem. Ad ipsam quippe unctionem et divinam benedictionem insiliebat in eos spiritus Domini et virtus deificans, per quam Christi figura fierent et imago ...* See Kantorowicz, *The King's Two Bodies*, 46–61 on the origin of the *personae geminae* concept and how it is used by the Norman Anonymous.

[88] PL 149:158. *Hoc etiam modo sanctae aecclesiae statum confundi, quae geminis personis, regali videlicet ac sacerdotali, administrari precipitur. Huic enim orare, illi vero pugnare tribuitur.*

bishops, they updated it to reinforce that bishops, like kings, shared in the glory of consecrated leadership. The striking parallels between the Saint-Vaast Jeremiah image and a famous Ottonian ruler image shows that the artists were taking part in a Europe-wide dialogue about rulership even though the scriptorium lay far from the French and Ottonian capitals. They must have borrowed from current royal iconography that reflected the Christ-centered rulership later described in texts such as *De consecratione pontificum et regnum*, for surviving miniatures from the Ottonian realm show that this concept was alive in the visual domain well before the Norman Anonymous put pen to parchment around 1100.

As we will see below, by the turn of the millennium artists working in monasteries and court scriptoria throughout Northern Europe had perfected a visual language of motifs intended to signal the inner, divine qualities of those in leadership positions, particularly secular leaders. The same bishops who monopolized ever more power as the ruling dynasties became weaker and more dependent on their bureaucracy were also the main patrons of medieval scriptoria. Thus surviving Carolingian and Ottonian manuscript illuminations tend to emphasize the very qualities that had brought these rulers under the sway of the church in the first place, namely the divine grace imbued during their consecration anointing, which was performed by the church. Between the early-ninth century and the late-tenth, the visual language of what Walter Ullmann has called "the theology of royal grace charisma"[89] became progressively more elaborate and at the same time more broadly applied, even while the policy was at times threatened by rulers who objected to interference in what they considered affairs of state by powerful bishops and later the pope.

The Arras artists may have been inspired in part by the iconographic *topoi* popular among the Carolingians. In the Psalter frontispiece of the Carolingian First Bible of Charles the Bald, fol. 215v (fig. 37), King David was represented as a type of Christ by placing him in a composition comparable to the Bible's *Maiestas Domini* image (fig. 38).[90] Standing in the middle of a blue Christological mandorla, David is surrounded by six figures, four of them seated

---

[89] Walter Ullmann, *The Carolingian Renaissance and the Idea of Kingship* (London, 1969), 43–55.
[90] Kessler, *The Illustrated Bibles from Tours*, 106–108.

musicians echoing the seated writing evangelists in the *Maiestas Domini*. Furthermore, as Herbert Kessler has pointed out, this typology was part of a larger series meant to encompass not only the Old Testament King David, but also the ruler portrait of Charles the Bald in the same Bible, fol. 423 (fig. 39), by giving both kings the same crown and similar facial features.[91] The composition of the First Bible of Charles the Bald's Psalter illustration, in surrounding a Christ-like figure with a series of sitting and standing figures, also parallels that of the Arras Bible Jeremiah illustration.

The Saint-Vaast artists, however, may have encountered this motif through the intermediary of an Ottonian artwork. Ernst Kantorowicz has pointed out that the Norman Anonymous' ideas about Christological kingship were paralleled iconographically in a ruler image possibly from Reichenau, produced around the year 996. In the Aachen Gospel book, Aachen Cathedral Treasury, fol. 16 (fig. 40), the Emperor Otto III is depicted partaking of the nature of Christ.[92] The artists of the Gospels drew on their Carolingian patrimony, using a *Maiestas Domini*, or Christ in Majesty, composition to invoke the presence of Christ. In the *Maiestas Domini* in the Carolingian First Bible of Charles the Bald, fol. 329v (fig. 38), Christ is shown enthroned in a figure-eight mandorla, surrounded by evangelist symbols, busts of four prophets, and seated, writing evangelists.[93] In the Aachen Gospels image the artists have made a startling transformation. Christ has been supplanted by the Emperor, while the other attributes of Christ, including his gesture, the evangelist symbols, and the mandorla, have been retained. The Emperor is shown enthroned on a cushioned bench, carried by a personification of the earth, and surrounded by a mandorla. A hand of God places a diadem on Otto's head. Around Otto's mandorla are the four apocalyptic beasts, and

---

[91] Kessler, *The Illustrated Bibles from Tours*, 109. See Herbert L. Kessler "A Lay Abbot as Patron: Count Vivian and the First Bible of Charles the Bald," in *Committenti e produzione artistico-letteraria nell'alto medioevo occidentale*, SSCISAM XXXIX (1992), 662–668, on the broader political implications of the comparison between David and Charles the Bald.

[92] Kantorowicz, *The King's Two Bodies*, 61. Kantorowicz, following early twentieth-century opinion, dated the manuscript to c. 973, and identified the ruler pictured as Otto II. More recently, Mayr-Harting, I, 60, assigned the manuscript to the Liuthar group of Reichenau manuscripts and accepted a date of ca. 996, during the reign of Otto III. See Mayr-Harting, I, 217 note 4, for further bibliography.

[93] See Kessler, *The Illustrated Bibles from Tours*, 36–58, on the construction of the Gospel frontispieces at Tours.

below are a group of his subjects. The artists have represented the Emperor's two natures, the human part with which he was born below, with his feet on the earth, and the divine part bestowed by the royal consecration above, with his head in heaven, the two parts separated from each other by a scroll-shaped form.[94] Otto himself was crowned emperor on Ascension day of 996, making this depiction of Otto receiving grace as he floats up towards heaven particularly apt.[95]

The artists of the Arras Bible have used the same tools to visualize the bishop's divine nature, granted during his consecration as a gift from Christ. As in the Aachen Gospels ruler image, the Ezra Master has surrounded the prophet in his episcopal regalia with a mandorla and a heavenly hand appears above (pl. IV), where it blesses the Apocalyptic Lamb of Christ in its own mandorla. The Old Testament prophet Jeremiah therefore simultaneously takes on both the attributes of a bishop, the chasuble and crozier, and of Christ himself, the mandorla, and receives heavenly sanction through the blessing hand.

Bishop Gerard and Richard of Saint-Vanne and their companions were probably predisposed to use a typological comparison between an Old Testament prophet and a bishop because contemporary writers routinely flattered their subjects by assimilating them to Old Testament models. Both Richard and Gerard had probably been exposed to the hagiography written about Archbishop Adalbero of Reims, their teacher, in the early-eleventh-century Chronicle of Mouzon. The anonymous author described how after the voyage of the relics of Saint Arnulf against the current in a ship guided only by an eagle on its prow, Adalbero interpreted, like the holy prophet Ezekiel, the appearance of the eagle for the assembled throng.[96]

---

[94] Kantorowicz, *The King's Two Bodies*, 63–67.

[95] Mayr-Harting, I, 65 and Hagen Keller, "Herrscherbild und Herrschaftslegitimation. Zur Deutung der ottonischen Denkmäler," *Frühmittelalterliche Studien* XIX (1985), 290–311. See also Steffan Patzold, "*Omnis anima potestatibus sublimioribus subdita sit.* Zum Herrscherbild im Aachener Otto-Evangeliar," *Frühmittelalterliche Studien* XXXV (2001), 243–272. He prefers to see the miniature as containing a more admonitary message, signaling the necessary virtues of the ideal ruler.

[96] *Chronique, ou, livre de fondation du monastère de Mouzon*, ed. Michel Bur (Paris, 1989), 156–157, Ez. 17:3,7, and Michel Bur, "Adalbéron, archevêque de Reims, reconsidéré," *Le roi de France et son royaume autour de l'an mil*, Actes du colloque Hugues Capet 987–1987. La France de l'an mil, Paris-Senlis, 22–25 juin 1987 (Paris, 1992), 61.

When Adalbero and his followers lay siege to the fortress of Warcq, a cow wandered up to the river that blocked their way to the walls, and exposed a hidden ford. Adalbero prophetically interpreted the cow as a messenger from God, guiding them through the water as the Red Sea had been divided by God so that the people of Israel passed through and the Pharaoh's army was engulfed.[97] Clearly the vision of the bishop as a leader in the style of an Old Testament prophet was alive and well in the archdiocese of Reims in the early-eleventh century.

Lest one think that the typological details and anachronistic vestments in the Jeremiah image were simply the ad hoc additions of unschooled artists without a greater agenda, the same artist who created the figure of Jeremiah, the Ezra Master, used the same tools in a second miniature to craft a related message. The illustration for the Book of Ezra, like the Jeremiah miniature, reveals Gerard and Richard's political viewpoint. Both leaders relied on cooperation with secular leaders to carry out their reforms and maintain order in their spheres of influence. Both were educated in a milieu, the late-tenth and early-eleventh-century school of Reims, which throve with the support of the French and Ottonian rulers. The iconography of the Ezra miniature makes clear that Gerard and Richard believed that the Church and State, though separate entities, could achieve their goals only through cooperation if each component abided by its biblically defined roles.

Ezra, Artaxerxes and the Ideal of Royal-Priestly Cooperation

The Saint-Vaast Bible's image prefacing the Book of Ezra, volume III, fol. 29 (pl. VII), encodes the ideal of religious and secular leaders governing together under the guidance of divine law. On the incipit page for Ezra, the artist inserted two tiny roundels into the oval interlace frame surrounding the incipit for the text. Inside them a king and a Christian priest, who is, like Jeremiah, identified through the anachronistic use of vestments, cooperate in the distribution of the scriptures. To the right, the king sits enthroned on a faldstool,

---

[97] *Chronique de Mouzon*, 153–154, Ps. 135:13–15.

a footstool under his feet and a knobbed lily scepter in his left hand. He is crowned with a lily crown and gestures with his right hand towards the roundel on the left. Here, a bearded man wearing a long robe stands on a small hillock and gazes heavenward. He holds an open book in hands protected by a maniple and seems to address another bearded man in a short tunic standing to his left.

The Ezra Master or his director appears to have invented this composition anew. The Book of Ezra was not a popular source for narrative illustrations in the pre-Romanesque period when even author portraits of the scribe are few and far between.[98] The precise moment depicted in the Saint-Vaast Bible is also not immediately obvious. Several kings appear in the Book of Ezra, but the king shown to the right in the Arras Bible has no distinguishing characteristics, making it difficult to identify him. Yet in combination with the pendant roundel to the left, a probable subject for the two medallions emerges. At first glance, it might seem that the two images could illustrate the very first verses of the first Book of Ezra,

---

[98] The only vaguely similar Ezra image that may date before the Arras Bible is that found in the nearly contemporary Ripoll Bible, Rome BAV cod. Vat. lat. 5729, fol. 312. Here a man stands above the initial 'I', for the first words of the text, "In anno primo," and holds in his left hand a scroll inscribed with the *incipit* that unfurls over the opening of the Book of Ezra. Below him a bearded man wearing a pointed cap and seated on a bench, presumably Ezra, addresses a group of five men seated on the ground. In this example, only the content, Ezra preaching, is similar to the Saint-Vaast Bible illustration. One author portrait survives in the seventh-century Syrian bible, Paris BnF MS syr. 341, fol. 212, where Ezra is shown standing as an orant in a veiled, colonnaded enclosure (Kurt Weitzmann, *Late Antique and Early Christian Book Illumination* [New York, 1977], 17 and 29). Another example is found in the Codex Amiatinus, Florence, Biblioteca Laurenziana, MS Amiatinus 1, fol. 5, which depicts Ezra in the style of a seated, writing evangelist, in front of a cupboard holding the volumes of the Bible (Weitzmann, *Late Antique and Early Christian*, 24 and 29, and R. L. S. Bruce-Mitford, "The Cassiodorus-Ezra Miniature in the Codex Amiatinus," in Thomas D. Kendrick et al., *Codex Lindisfarnensis* (Lausanne, 1960), and idem, "The Art of the Codex Amiatinus," *Journal of the British Archaeological Association* XXXII [1969], 1–25). See also more recently, Richard Marsden, "Job in his place: the Ezra miniature in the Codex Amiatinus," *Scriptorium* IL (1995), 3–15, and Paul Meyvaert, "Bede, Cassiodorus and the Codex Amiatinus, *Speculum* LXXI (1996), 827–883. Meyvaert, 872–876, shows that the Ezra figure in the Wearmouth-Jarrow manuscript was most likely inspired by a portrait of Cassiodorus, rather than an earlier image of Ezra. Neither type of image could have provided any visual inspiration for the unprecedented Saint-Vaast illustration, although if Meyvaert is correct in speculating that Ezra was intended to be a type of Christ (pp. 881–882), the Amiatinus and the Arras Ezra images may share an underlying symbolism.

> In the first year of Cyrus king of the Persians, that the word of the Lord by the mouth of Jeremiah might be fulfilled, the Lord stirred up the spirit of Cyrus king of the Persians: and he made a proclamation throughout all his kingdom, and in writing also, saying: Thus saith Cyrus king of the Persians: The Lord God of heaven hath given to me all the kingdoms of the earth, and he hath charged me to build him a house in Jerusalem, which is in Judah.[99]

This would accord with the Saint-Vaast artists' customary practice in the Arras Bible of illustrating the opening of a book with the first events described in the text.[100] This would also tie the illustration in the Saint-Vaast Bible to that found in the twelfth-century English Winchester Bible. The three vertically aligned quatrefoils on fol. 342 of the Winchester Bible show three vignettes from the book of Ezra. In the top quatrefoil, a seated king holds an unfurled, now tarnished, silver scroll. In the middle quatrefoil, two priests hold a second gold scroll, while in the third quatrefoil, one of the priests from above holds a rotulus and preaches to an attentive throng. Claire Donovan believed that the first quatrefoil illustrates King Cyrus holding this proclamation.[101] According to Donovan, the proclamation is distributed in the quatrefoil below, while in the lowest quatrefoil Ezra brings the Law to the children of Israel after the building of the Temple was thwarted as described in II Ezra.

> And the seventh month came: and the children of Israel were in their cities. And all the people were gathered together as one man to the street which is before the water gate, and they spoke to Ezra the scribe, to bring the book of the law of Moses, which the Lord had commanded to Israel. Then Ezra the priest brought the law before the multitude of men and women, and all those that could understand, in the first day of the seventh month.[102]

While this is a tempting identification for the Saint-Vaast Ezra illustration as well, it is more likely that the two roundels illustrate instead a moment from elsewhere in the Book of Ezra which not only fits the visuals provided more exactly, but is also more in keeping with the message found in the works associated with Gerard of Cambrai.

---

[99] I Ezra 1:1–2.

[100] Instances where part or all of the subject matter illustrated comes from later chapters include the miniatures for III Kings, IV Kings, Esther and the *Passio Machabeorum*.

[101] Claire Donovan, *The Winchester Bible* (London, 1993), 57.

[102] II Ezra 8:1–2.

I Ezra 7 describes the cooperation between Artaxerxes, King of the Persians, and Ezra, the leader of the Israelites, in ending the Babylonian exile.

> This Ezra went up from Babylonia and he was a ready scribe in the law of Moses, which the Lord God had given to Israel: and the king granted him all his request, according to the hand of the Lord his God upon him . . . For Ezra had prepared his heart to seek the law of the Lord, and to do and to teach in Israel the commandments and judgement. And this is the copy of the letter of the edict, which King Artaxerxes gave to Ezra the priest, the scribe instructed in the words and commandments of the Lord, and his ceremonies in Israel. Artaxerxes king of kings to Ezra the priest, the most learned scribe of the law of the God of heaven, greeting. It is decreed by me, that all they of the people of Israel, and of the priests and of the Levites in my realm, that are minded to go into Jerusalem, should go with thee. For thou art sent from before the king, and his seven counsellors, to visit Judah and Jerusalem according to the law of thy God, which is in thy hand.[103]

This text seems to account for several distinctive details of the illustration. First, the horizontal parallel between the two roundels, and the gesture made by the king towards Ezra and his companion, imply communication, or at least contemporaneity, between the king and Ezra. This would be difficult to explain with the first texts, for Ezra is not described as living under the reign of King Cyrus. The text also specifies that the Law of Moses is "in thy [Ezra's] hand," a detail that is depicted explicitly, in that the Law rests on Ezra's manipled hand. This piece of medieval liturgical gear invests Ezra with a new meaning. Wearing this maniple, he becomes not just the Old Testament head priest of the Levitical order, but also a Christian priest. Because Ezra was described in the text as a high priest above the other Levites, one can assume that he is intended to signify here a high priest of the Christians, a bishop. Again, this was a technique used already in Carolingian art. In the Grandval Bible, as Martina Pippal has observed, Aaron the high priest also holds a maniple draped across his left hand, thereby becoming a priest of the Christian, Frankish church.[104] The cooperation between king and bishop implied by this pair of roundels illustrating the Book of Ezra harmonizes

---

[103] I Ezra 7:6, 10–14.
[104] London BL MS Add. 10546, fol. 25v. Martina Pippal, "Distanzierung und Aktualisierung in der Vivianbibel: Zur Struktur der touronischen Miniaturen in den 40er Jahren des 9. Jahrhunderts," *Aachner Kunstblätter* LX (1994), 70.

with the cooperation prescribed and celebrated by Gerard of Cambrai in his writings, particularly in those militating against the Peace of God in the *Gesta episcoporum Cameracensium*, as we will see below.

Furthermore, several details used to depict King Artaxerxes signal that he, like Ezra, was intended to stand in for contemporary leaders. Enthroned on a faldstool that seems to float incongruously in the air, the king wears a lily crown and carries a prominent knobbed lily scepter. These insignia are not generic but instead were taken from contemporary royal portraits from specific regimes. The short-staffed, knobbed, lily scepter first began to appear in portraits of Carolingian rulers, but was used consistently only in the early Ottonian period, when seals showed Otto II and Otto III bearing the lily scepter.[105] Contemporary with the Saint-Vaast Bible's redaction, early-eleventh-century Ottonian seals and the famous ivory situla now in the cathedral at Aachen also all depict Emperor Henry II carrying the knobbed lily scepter.[106] At the same time, the only surviving contemporary image of the Capetian king Robert the Pious, a seal that copied the details of Carolingian seals, showed Robert with a short knobbed lily scepter.[107] Artaxerxes's scepter, then, was a replica of eleventh-century royal insignia.

His crown, on the other hand, resembles more closely late-tenth- and early-eleventh-century Anglo-Saxon crowns. Like the lily scepter, the lily crown was first adopted by Carolingian rulers. Bejeweled versions can be seen in several well-known depictions of Charles the Bald, Saint-Vaast's former patron.[108] By the early-eleventh century, however, Ottonian artists were much more likely to depict crowns with arched tops or the angular mural crown than the lily crown.

---

[105] Percy Ernst Schramm, *Die deutschen Kaiser und Könige in Bilder ihrer Zeit; 751–1190*, ed. Florentine Mütherich (Munich, 1983), pl. 88, a seal of Otto II and pl. 97, a seal of Otto III, and pl. 104, the depiction of Otto III on the cover of the Codex Aureus Epternacensis, produced at Trier between 985–991, now in the German National Museum at Nürnberg.

[106] Schramm, *Die deutschen Kaiser und Könige*, pls. 113–116.

[107] J. Roman, *Manuel de sigillographie française* (Paris, 1912), 73 and pl. II, no. 2.

[108] Schramm, *Die deutschen Kaiser und Könige*, 167–174. See in particular the Prayerbook of Charles the Bald, c. 860, Munich, Schatzkammer der Residenz, fol. 38v, the Psalter of Charles the Bald from before 869, Paris BnF MS lat. 1152, fol. 3v, and the equestrian statue tentatively identified as Charles the Bald, c. 870, now in the Louvre. Percy Ernst Schramm, "Die Kronen des frühen Mittelalters," *Herrschaftszeichen und Staatssymbolik*, MHG Schriften XIII/2 (Stuttgart, 1955), II, 414–415. See also the surviving lily-crown now decorating the Essen Madonna, Schramm, "Die Kronen des frühen Mittelalters," fig. 55.

The use of the simple, unjeweled lily crown like that in the Saint-Vaast Bible is more common in Anglo-Saxon manuscripts, for instance in the New Minster Charter, where King Edgar sports a lily crown.[109] In fact, the simple lily crown appears especially in Anglo-Saxon depictions of holy figures, such as the crowned Christ in Majesty in the early-eleventh-century Trinity Gospels and the Sherborne Pontifical (fig. 28), or the choirs of confessors and virgins in the Benedictional of Aethelwold.[110] Once again, however, it is also seen in the single surviving early Capetian seal portrait of Robert the Pious.[111] Artaxerxes's lily crown was therefore taken either from now lost early Capetian royal portraits or from the Anglo-Saxon models that would have been so easily available to the artists of Saint-Vaast.[112] Artaxerxes, the Syrian king who ended the Babylonian exile, was used as a visual stand in for contemporary rulers, because in cooperating with his religious counterpart, the high priest Ezra, he embodied the virtue that Bishop Gerard sought in a ruler.

Gerard of Cambrai and Eleventh-Century Augustinianism

As a defender of the ecclesiastical status quo, Gerard of Cambrai sought not just to preserve the ancient rights of bishops, but also with them the divinely sanctioned rights of kings, which he saw as being similar because both offices were granted through the same type of anointing. Gerard seems to have developed his philosophy of ecclesiastical leadership in response both to his education and to his role as bishop of a conflicted diocese. As the product of the imperial patronage system for bishops, he was intimately familiar with the workings of court politics and his potential to act as a religious powerbroker. His noble background and his early education also prepared him for a life in the service of the State. Yet because

---

[109] The most similar version crowns Edgar in the New Minster Charter, London BL MS Cotton Vespasian A VIII, fol. 2v. Like Artaxerxes's crown, these crowns are simple gold bands with projecting trefoils, without the jeweled decoration found on the Carolingian and Ottonian crowns of the same shape.

[110] The Trinity Gospels, Cambridge, Trinity College MS B.10.4, fol. 16b, the Sherborne Pontifical, Paris BnF MS lat. 943, fol. 5b and the Benedictional of Aethelwold, London, BL MS Add. 49598, fols. 1–2 (*The Golden Age of Anglo-Saxon Art*, 55 and 68).

[111] Roman, 73 and pl. II, no. 2.

[112] See above, chapter 1.

the territory of his diocese straddled the border between Capetian
France and the Holy Roman Empire, he was forced into a delicate
balancing act both in the realm of ecclesiastical reform and that of
secular politics.

Scholars of the twentieth century were often preoccupied with
Gerard's political allegiances. In addition, modern historians have
found Gerard a convenient pawn in their own attempts to reinter-
pret the genesis of the modern states of France and Germany. Three
scholars have examined in detail Gerard of Cambrai's actions in the
realms of secular and ecclesiastical politics in the early-eleventh century. Yet in many ways they remain as opaque as ever, for each
scholar's work was clouded by the politically charged context of its
creation.

The first scholar to write extensively about Gerard was Theodor
Schieffer, who published an article entitled "Ein deutscher Bischof
des elften Jahrhunderts" in the newly founded *Deutsches Archiv für
Geschichte des Mittelalters* in 1937.[113] This set the tenor for almost all
subsequent discussions of Gerard by concentrating on his role in the
sphere of eleventh-century politics. Schieffer's conclusions about
Gerard's loyalties are signaled already in the words of his title: *Ein
deutscher Bischof.*

Born in the Rhineland, Schieffer demonstrated a life-long interest
in the religious and political leaders of the Carolingian and Ottonian
eras in the borderland between what later became France and
Germany.[114] His article on Gerard was published when Schieffer was
27 years old and working at the *Monumenta Germaniae Historica* as an
apprentice, and is best understood in the context of the time and
place in which it was written. Schieffer advanced quickly in the academic climate of the Third Reich, working from 1939 to 1945 as
an assessor at the Prussian State archives in Berlin, and spending
from the summer of 1940 until 1942 in Paris as a member of the
German archives commission after the fall of France.[115] In later life,

---

[113] "Ein deutscher Bishof des elften Jahrhunderts: Gerhard I. von Cambrai
(1012–1051)," *Deutsches Archiv für Geschichte des Mittelalters* I (1937). Interestingly, this
journal's editorial board was completely replaced in the immediate postwar era and
its name changed to *Deutches Archiv für Erforschung des Mittelalters*. Schieffer's article
on Gerard was ignored by the author of his eulogy, Heribert Müller.

[114] Heribert Müller, "Theodor Schieffer. Leben und Werk," in *Theodore Schieffer,
1910–1992* (Munich, 1992), 3.

[115] Müller, 5–6. The regime's use of German intellectuals in important academic

colleagues lauded his wartime actions, pointing out that he maintained his connection with his Jewish teacher, Wilhelm Levison, at
a time when many German academics cut ties with racially suspect
faculty members.[116] In spite of this, his 1937 assessment of the eleventh-
century political role of Gerard on the frontier of two realms resonates with the territorial concerns of two nations that, in the twentieth
century, would soon be at war.[117]

Schieffer's article stood as the major study of Gerard of Cambrai
until 1970, when Heinrich Sproemberg's portrait of the bishop was
posthumously published in his collected papers.[118] Originally written
about 1960, possibly in preparation for his related encyclopedia entry
in the Belgian *Biographie nationale*, this study at first blush appears to
mimic Schieffer's article, repeating many of the same incidents from
the life of Gerard in the same order.[119] A closer examination, however, shows that Sproemberg's assessment of Gerard's role in the
political life of eleventh-century northern Europe is markedly different.
His interpretation probably comes closest to the Augustinian approach
displayed in the Saint-Vaast Bible, as will be discussed below, because
he refused to see Gerard as loyal to any ruler in particular. Rather,
he recognized that Gerard's actions ultimately grew from his allegiance to his flock.

Born in Berlin in 1889 and educated at the University of Berlin,
Sproemberg was roughly twenty years older than Schieffer, and his
career followed a very different path. Discriminated against in Weimar
Germany, according to later commentators, because of his opposition to official historical studies, Sproemberg by 1933 was a frequent
guest-lecturer in the Netherlands and Belgium and spent much of
the war in the Low Countries. In the introduction to his collected
papers, Sproemberg was characterized as an anti-fascist and a
Democrat, in the East German sense, who worked to overcome a

---

and administrative posts both in Germany and abroad is explored in Jerry Z. Muller,
The Other God that Failed. Hans Freyre and the Deradicalization of German Conservatism
(Princeton, 1987). See the useful introduction, 3–24.
[116] Müller, 5. See Schieffer's eulogy for Levison, "In Memoriam Wilhelm Levison,"
Rheinische Vierteljahrsblätter XL (1976), 225–242.
[117] Norman Cantor, *Inventing the Middle Ages* (New York, 1991), 86–89 on the
rightward swing of German academia in the pre-war years.
[118] *Mittelalter und demokratische Geschichtsschreibung*, 103–106.
[119] Heinrich Sproemberg, "Gérard Ier, évêque de Cambrai," *Biographie nationale*
XXXV, Supplément VII (Fascicule Ier) (Brussels, 1969), 286–299.

Germano-centric view of European history.[120] Sproemberg attempted
to trace the growth of the communal movement as the middle classes
rose up against the feudal nobility.[121] By 1950 he was granted a
position at the University of Leipzig, newly renamed Karl Marx
University, as part of the eastern Bloc's post-war policy to Sovietize
the University.[122] In 1959 he moved to the University of Berlin. This
was the setting for his work on Gerard of Cambrai.

The most recent lengthy interpretation of Gerard of Cambrai and
his contemporaries was provided by Georges Duby.[123] Duby's assessment of Gerard, in many ways, provides a striking contrast to his
self-stated goals as an historian. Beginning in World War II, when
Duby was a pacifist, he rejected the study of the great individual
and the Nation in favor of an examination of social systems and
their outcomes using the methods of the *Annales* school.[124] Later in
his career he experimented with the label of Marxist historian.[125]
Nonetheless, Duby's search for social stratification in medieval culture
in his 1978 book *The Three Orders, Feudal Society Imagined* takes as its
starting point the motivations of one of the best known thinkers of
the early-eleventh century, Gerard of Cambrai, and works to remake
him as a champion of France.[126] In the words of Alain Peyrefitte,
who delivered a panegyric on the occasion of Duby's reception into
the *Académie Français*, "You have become one of the high priests of
our national conscience. A medievalist, you impose on us, more than
an historian of less distant eras, the obligation to situate ourselves—

---

[120] Gerhard Heitz et al., "Vorwort," *Mittelalter und demokratische Geschichtsschreibung*,
vii–x.
[121] Heitz et al., x, on this overarching theme in his work.
[122] *Wer is Wer? Das Deutsche Who's Who* XII (1955), 1138. Muller, 317–321, on
the University of Leipzig in the post-war period.
[123] Duby, *The Three Orders* and Duby, "Gérard de Cambrai."
[124] Alain Peyrefitte, "Réponse," in *Discours de réception de Georges Duby à l'Académie
française et réponse d'Alain Peyrefitte* (Paris, 1988), 59 and Georges Duby, *History Continues*,
trans. Arthur Goldhammer (Chicago, 1994), 1–3.
[125] Duby, *History Continues*, 62–65.
[126] Theodore Évergates, "The Feudal Imaginary of Georges Duby," *Journal of
Medieval and Early Modern Studies* XXVII (Fall, 1997), 644, 650–653, examines Duby's
problematic methodology, which, for instance, takes medieval ecclesiastical writers'
use of a trifunctional division as proof of that hierarchy in society, even though
secular documents reveal little evidence that it was applied. See Giles Constable,
"The Orders of Society," in *Three Studies in Medieval Religious and Social Thought*
(Cambridge, 1995), 251–341, esp. 283–288 for a critique of this idea as applied in
the eleventh century.

France of the present—through comparison with France of so long ago."[127] In addition, Duby's reason for studying this great man was to chart his interpretation of the development of the feudal ideal, including the contest between those who supported a strong king and those who put their faith in the ever more powerful nobles. His study does not have the disdain for the French feudal nobility that taints the articles of Schieffer, because of his pro-German nationalism, and Sproemberg, because of his internationalist respect for the proletariat, and yet his view of Gerard is distorted by his attempts to remake the bishop into a defender of the French.

It is necessary to strip away the rhetoric that has accumulated around the actions of Gerard in order to interpret the relationship between his politics and the Saint-Vaast Bible's program of illustrations. I believe that the best understanding of the Saint-Vaast Bible's pictorial program, as it expresses the political philosophies of Bishop Gerard and his allies, comes from exploring the theological underpinnings of his approach to secular leadership, and the intricacies of his immediate context. Gerard was able to satisfy the many, seemingly conflicting, demands in the first years of his episcopacy using a political philosophy founded on the Augustinianism taught in the cathedral school at Reims. Gerard and the clerics who surrounded him during his schooling and career, including Richard of Saint-Vanne, Frederick of Verdun, Adalbero of Reims, and Gerbert of Aurillac, all subscribed to an Augustinian belief system. A reading of the imagery of the Saint-Vaast Bible is better served by looking into the philosophical framework of Gerard's actions than dwelling on Gerard's attachment to individual leaders. In the constantly shifting sands of eleventh-century politics, Gerard's interactions with these rulers were driven by pragmatism and expediency rather than long-term loyalty or familial tradition, as often believed by the twentieth-century scholars who studied him.

The variety of Augustinianism fostered at Reims was an outgrowth of the Carolingian age. Augustine, in attempting to combat the Donatist heresy, propounded that it was the duty of the good Christian to bow before a legitimate Christian ruler as he would bow before

---

[127] "Vous êtes devenu l'un des grands prêtres de la conscience nationale. Médiéviste, vous nous imposez, plus qu'un historien d'époques moins reculées, l'obligation de nous situer—nous, Français du temps présent—par rapport à cette si longue durée." *Discours de réception de Georges Duby*, 42–43.

God. To question one's loyalty to a ruler recognized by the Church would be to assert free will "against the hidden ways of God," as expressed by Peter Brown.[128] Drawing on the book of Jeremiah, Augustine advised that even as a captive in an unfriendly state, the Christian should take advantage of the peace this state provides.[129] Relying on statements such as Paul in Romans 13, "Let every soul be subject to the governing powers, for there is no power but from God; these, coming from God, are subject to his ordering," he made no distinction between good and evil leaders.[130] It was God, Augustine pointed out, who caused the triumphs of the Persians, even though his reasons for giving power to such an empire were hidden.[131] Moreover, although peace was the desirable condition of society, Christian subjects were obliged to fight in a war if declared by the lawful authority.[132]

More useful in Gerard's situation was Augustine's cooperative model of governance. Already in *The City of God*, Augustine had established that he expected the emperor to act as an arm of the Christian Church, preserving its values and protecting its members.[133] Although a society guided only by moral precepts was the ideal, political government was required because of the sinfulness of human kind, which inevitably leads to conflict.[134] Given human propensity towards violence and sin, it is only because the State had charge of certain aspects of society, including judgement and punishment, that order could be maintained.[135] Christian rulers were not simply to create order, however. It was the duty of the Christian ruler to spread the worship of God and to defend the doctrines of the Church

---

[128] Peter Brown, "Saint Augustine," in *Trends in Medieval Political Thought*, ed. Beryl Smalley (Oxford, 1965), 9.

[129] Brown, 14, after Jeremiah 29:7 in *The City of God against the Pagans*, trans R. W. Dyson, Cambridge (1998), 19:26.

[130] Brown, "Saint Augustine," 5.

[131] Paul Weithman, "Augustine's Political Philosophy," in *The Cambridge Companion to Augustine*, eds. Eleonore Stump and Norman Kretzmann (Cambridge, 2001), 245 after *The City of God*, 4:33 and 5:21.

[132] Weithman, 247 and *Contra Faustum Manichaeum*, ed. Josephus Zycha, CSEL XXV (Vienna, 1891–1892), 22:74.

[133] Brown, 17, and *The City of God* 5:26, 47.

[134] Weithman, 239.

[135] Brown, 14, after Sermon 302:xiv, 13–17, *Sermones*, PL 38. Also *Epistula* 153:6:16, *Epistulae*, ed. A. Goldbacher, CSEL XXXIV/1–2, XLIV, LVII–LVIII (Vienna, 1895–1923), XLIV.

against heresy.[136] The Church and the State were therefore partners in the achievement of Christian goals.

The Ezra illustration in the Saint-Vaast Bible (pl. VII) makes manifest the doctrines of Augustinian political philosophy as it was probably understood by Gerard and his contemporary, Richard of Saint-Vanne, and their teacher, Archbishop Adalbero of Reims. Ezra the priest is shown cooperating with a secular ruler, the Persian king Artaxerxes, who was not one of the Chosen People, and indeed ruled the Jews as a subjugated population. Nonetheless, Ezra and his followers were right to remain pliant, as the king provided them with a peaceful environment in which to pursue their true goal, the love of God. In this image he is also shown encouraging the return of the Jews to Jerusalem, and therefore fostering the worship of God.

Gerard's outlook on the relationship between ecclesiastical and secular rulers did not necessitate exclusive loyalty to one ruler. Because of the volume of his political writing, and the copious records of his life, scholars have felt compelled to designate the leader he would have supported, despite the fact that Gerard, of necessity, served more than one. Gerard's true loyalty lay with his Church. His actions with the secular leaders were driven by its interests. As I will show below, the kingship program in the Bible is not directed towards one particular ruler. There is no ruler portrait in this Bible, unlike in the Carolingian Bibles. Instead, the Bible expresses a theology of rulership applicable to whomever was in power, so long as he had been legitimately consecrated by the Church. Capetian or Ottonian, these rulers were required to work with the bishop to protect the rights of Christians, particularly against the assaults of local, unconsecrated secular lords such as the Counts of Flanders.[137] Without this framework for understanding both the writings of Gerard of Cambrai and the miniature program in the Saint-Vaast Bible, produced at a scriptorium within his sphere of influence, it is easy to interpret both

---

[136] Weithman, 246 and *The City of God*, 5:24 and R. W. Dyson, *The Pilgrim City. Social and Political Ideas in the Writings of St. Augustine of Hippo* (Rochester, N.Y., 2001), 188–191 and *Epistula* 87:7–9, *Epistulae*, CSEL XXXIV/2.

[137] Gerard does not seem to have taken Augustinianism to the extremes of the next generation, during the Investiture Controversy, when Augustine's writings were used as an excuse for the Church to direct the State, rather than simply cooperating with it (Dyson, 181–182).

through a veil of anachronistic political concerns. Because throughout Gerard's life he faced challenges to his authority and opportunities to work with powerful leaders to advance the interests of the
Church, his interactions with these leaders have been analyzed repeatedly for signs of political bias. Rulers such as the kings of France,
the Ottonian and Salian emperors, and local counts and castellans
figure prominently in the records of Gerard's life. These references,
the details of Gerard's genealogy, his educational background, and
the evidence of his participation in affairs of state as described in the
Gesta episcoporum Cameracensium, gave Theodor Schieffer and the scholars
who followed valuable tools for constructing a political identity for
the bishop even if the overarching conclusions they ultimately drew
from the material foundered.[138] Tracing the history of the study of
Gerard of Cambrai and his environment will nonetheless help us to
understand the true nature of his political philosophy.

Schieffer began his study of Gerard of Cambrai with a defense of
the bishop's loyalty to the German realm. Gerard, he explained,
although born in a family firmly established in Lorraine and related
to Adalbero, Archbishop of Reims, was still ultimately more sympathetic to the concerns of the Empire than to Capetian France, in
whose sphere of influence Reims was located. Schieffer's evaluation
of Gerard's episcopacy is littered with terminology that reinvents the
politics of the eleventh century as the first phase of the modern
conflict between France and Germany. The Treaty of Verdun, which
had divided the Carolingian Empire into the parts that would later
become Capetian France and Ottonian Germany, with the problematic territory of Lotharingia in between, was less than 200 years
old. The people of the former western part, as Schieffer acknowledges, still termed themselves *Karlenses*, in reference to their Carolingian
heritage.[139] Nonetheless, Schieffer consistently refers to the two realms
as France and Germany, and their inhabitants as French and German,
nationalistic distinctions that would have been unimaginable to people still so closely connected by the ties of family, and until just a
few decades before, related ruling dynasties.[140]

---

[138] On the *Gesta*, see above, chapter two.

[139] Schieffer, "Ein deutscher Bishof," 324.

[140] Ethnically, the inhabitants of these states identified themselves much more
closely with regions led by minor lords than with the overarching ruling dynasty.
Timothy Reuter, "The Making of England and Germany, 850–1050: Points of

Sproemberg, on the other hand, after probing Gerard's family ties for evidence of his political commitments, asserted that Gerard's ties to France through his mother's family outweighed the status of his father's family as minor Lotharingian nobles. Sproemberg believed that Gerard was most likely brought up speaking a Romance, as opposed to Germanic, language.[141] He points out that intermarriage between different regions at this time was so common that no national antagonism could develop. Gerard was thus sent to Reims for his education because of its reputation as the center of learning for the French church. There is little evidence, according to Sproemberg, that Gerard had more than fleeting contact with the pro-imperial teacher Gerbert. Instead, he was most likely educated by his great-uncle on his mother's side, Archbishop Adalbero of Reims.[142] The time spent by the future Bishop of Arras-Cambrai under the tutelage of an archbishop unencumbered by imperial loyalties must have been crucial. Nonetheless, Sproemberg underlined that Reims under Adalbero was sympathetic to the imperial promotion of cooperation between Church and State, and that this eased Gerard's entry into service at the chapel of Henry II.[143]

Duby emphasized the location of Reims, where the young Gerard had studied, as the site of the consecration of the kings of France and the heart of what he called 'Francia.' Like Sproemberg, Duby asserted that Gerard spoke a Romance, not Germanic, language, and was tied equally to the king of France and to the emperor. Duby recalled that Robert the Pious had also been educated at Reims, where he was equally indoctrinated in the belief of cooperation between Church and State.[144] Thus these three scholars, using the same fragments of information, were able to interpret them in contradictory ways. The same is true about approaches to the bishop's later life.

Comparison and Difference," in *Medieval Europeans. Studies in Ethnic Identity and National Perspectives in Medieval Europe*, ed. Alfred P. Smyth (New York, 1998), 57–58. Although the kingdom was occasionally called 'Germania,' this was apparently not considered an ethnic identification but a regional name recalling that used by the Romans. The inhabitants did not speak a common language or recognize themselves as having a common heritage. Reuter, 64–65.

[141] Sproemberg, *Mittelalter und demokratische Geschichtsschreibung*, 106.

[142] Sproemberg, *Mittelalter und demokratische Geschichtsschreibung*, 103–105 and *Biographie nationale*, 289.

[143] Sproemberg, *Mittelalter und demokratische Geschichtsschreibung*, 107.

[144] Duby, *The Three Orders*, 15–17.

   Gerard's chronicle is unabashed in admitting that he received the
bishopric of Cambrai through imperial favor.[145] Henry II appointed
him to the seat in 1012 while the previous bishop was still alive,
possibly in an effort to forestall a similar move by the count of
Flanders.[146] Although early scholars sometimes maintained that Gerard
and his successor, Lietbert, were both invested at court, Gerard,
according to his chronicle, successfully avoided the Emperor's desire
to oversee his consecration as bishop.[147] In book three, chapter two
of the *Gesta*, Gerard's chronicler describes the circumstances of his
consecration. Henry II apparently commanded Gerard to the imperial court to be consecrated following correct Lotharingian tradition,
in an apostolic mass and surrounded by his cobishops and abbots.[148]
Gerard, however, claiming a sentimental attachment to the city where
he was schooled, Reims, asked if he could be consecrated there
instead. Henry II seemingly gave way gracefully, asking only that
the ceremony take place according to an ordo that he gave to Gerard,
so that no irregularities would occur as a result of the consecration
taking place in the realm of the Capetian sovereign, Robert the
Pious.[149]

---

[145] PL 149:141–142. *Domnus imperator Henricus, ut superius diximus suorum principium
unanimi consilio usus, Gerardo suo capellano, adhuc diacono, non infimis parentibus Lothariensium
atque Karlensium edito, apud Arvitam villam Saxoniae Kalendis Februarii* (1012) *donum largitus est episcopii, Hunc in puericia Albero Remensium archiepiscopus, pro consanguinitate, sed et
pro praediis quae ex patre matris in ipsa terra habebat hereditario jure tenendis, secum permissione parentum abduxit, et sub regula canonica degetem familiariter educavit.*

[146] PL 149:122. *Qui* [Azelinus] *etiam paulo antequam domnus Erluwinus ex hoc seculo
decederet, suae ambitioni consulere estimans, suos imperatori legatos dirigere festinavit, per quos
eius benivolentiam fortasse empturus ad episcopii prerogativam pertingeret . . . . His autem repul-
sis, communi suorum usus consilio, potius Gerardum suum capellanum estimavit donandum.* The
bias of the chronicler, however, makes this assessment slightly suspect.

[147] Alfred Cauchie, *La querelle des investitures dans les diocèses de Liège et de Cambrai*
(Louvain, 1890), xxxii. See Sproemberg, "Gérard Ier," 286–299, as well. Gerard
was, however, ordained a priest at court in 1012, before he could accept the position of bishop. PL 149:143. *Hoc autem in loco ipsum* [Nimwegen] *domnum Gerardum in
sua presentia fecit ordinari presbyterum.*

[148] According to Schieffer, "Ein deutscher Bishof," 333, Henry's demand that he
consecrate Gerard as bishop was part of a larger policy to remove the diocese of
Arras-Cambrai from the jurisdiction of the archdiocese of Reims.

[149] PL 149:144. *Post haec vero monuit illum imperator, ut secum ad novum episcopum
dedicandum, in civitatem videlicet Bavenberg, una proficisceretur, ibique in sua presentia a missis
apostolicis multisque coepiscopis sive abbatibus, qui illuc ad encenia templi convenire deberent,
ordinaretur episcopus. Qui et si honorabilius et disciplinatius coram regia pompa et Lothariensi
sollertia sciret se ordinandum: tamen loci amore, quo nutritus fuerat, captus, a nullo quidem nisi
a metropolitano Remensium archiepiscopo ordinatum iri velle respondit; quippe satis provide ac
competenter causam considerans, ne forte videlicet eo etiam ipse consuetudini sedis metropolitanae*

Schieffer believed that Gerard's education at the Cathedral school at Reims under Gerbert, an imperial sympathizer, led directly to Gerard's call to service in the Imperial chapel at Aachen. Soon thereafter he was chosen by the Emperor to fill the episcopal seat in Cambrai, all signs that he had been firmly inserted into the *Reichskirche* system.[150] Although Schieffer admitted that it would be anachronistic to characterize Germany as a Nation-state with its own *Volk* in the tenth century, he termed the situation on the Lotharingian borderland a war with French and German fronts.[151] According to Schieffer, here, as was also the case in the Rhineland, the German emperor systematically installed a series of bishops who could stand as bulwarks against the threat of encroachments by the French king and his unruly nobles. Schieffer saw Gerard as one of these bishops.[152]

Sproemberg's article on Gerard of Cambrai shadowed Schieffer's article closely, but he removed all references to the nation of Germany and denied that the Ottonians had as yet developed a German national character. Sproemberg's study shied away from the nationalism that flavored Schieffer's examination of Gerard, while at the same time succumbing to a different agenda: the internationalization of medieval politics. Sproemberg's article asserted that the composer of the *Gesta episcoporum Cameracensium*, from which both he and Schieffer drew most of their information about Gerard's life, was a fierce critic of the French.[153] The author of the *Gesta*, according to Sproemberg, viewed the events in the life of Gerard, like his election as bishop, through a lens of anti-French bias, thus coloring his reporting of Gerard's loyalties. While Sproemberg acknowledged the Emperor's desire to defend his sphere of influence in Lotharingia, as already suggested by Schieffer, his explanation for Gerard's participation in this plan was very different. In recounting Gerard's refusal to be consecrated to his office at Bamberg, Sproemberg credited Gerard with greater loyalty to the western ecclesiastical city of

---

contraire videretur, quod domnus Erluinus episcopus ob supradictum contentionem, Romae ordinationem. Quo audito, imperator altioris consilii illum advertens, libenter acquievit, dataque reditus licentia, largitus est ei librum consecrationes clericorum et ordinationem episcopi continentem, ut per hunc videlicet consecratus, haud fortasse quidem indisciplinatis moribus Karlensium irregulariter ordinaretur. Unde mox ad sua cum honore et prosperitate concessit.

[150] Schieffer, "Ein deutscher Bishof," 332–333.
[151] Schieffer, "Ein deutscher Bishof," 323–324.
[152] Schieffer, "Ein deutscher Bishof," 325.
[153] Sproemberg, *Mittelalter und demokratische Geschichtsschreibung*, 116–117.

Reims than had been allowed by Schieffer. More importantly, Gerard's decision to be consecrated by the archbishop of Reims, according to Sproemberg, signified his strong desire to protect the rights of the Church, a desire imbedded in him during his education at Reims.[154] Gerard had developed a healthy respect for the power of a ruler who could protect the interests of the Church against the infringements of warring feudal nobles. In the early-eleventh century, the kings of Capetian France were still hopelessly disorganized and unable to control the nobles even within the acknowledged boundaries of France. Gerard's only choice as a protector of the Church was the Ottonian Emperor. In Sproemberg's words, to Gerard and his circle of Northern bishops *Imperium* wasn't a national but rather an international institution. Gerard's ideal was a close cooperation and harmony between the Church and the State, not the Church and the Nation of Germany. Thus Sproemberg acknowledged Gerard's loyalty to the Emperor, but claimed that the reason for it was not nationalism, as suggested by Schieffer, but a pragmatic choice in the interests of the Church and its people against its oppressors, the nobles.[155]

If Sproemberg was right, as I believe, in his interpretation of Gerard's impetus, then the bishop was simply following a path already shown him during his schooling at Reims. In fact, Gerard's teacher, Archbishop Adalbero of Reims, had already apparently modeled a solution to this very conflict for both Gerard and Richard in the time when they had been students at Reims.[156] Although Adalbero's actions, like Gerard's, are seen through the veil of his biographers' personalities and loyalties, one can still discern in them an attempt to use his ecclesiastical power to serve the often-overlapping interests of both his archdiocese and the secular leaders of the Holy Roman Empire and France.[157] Reims fell under the sway of the Ottonians, and Adalbero had served as a counselor to Theophanu

---

[154] Sproemberg, *Mittelalter und demokratische Geschichtsschreibung*, 109.
[155] Sproemberg, *Mittelalter und demokratische Geschichtsschreibung*, 118.
[156] Bur, "Adalbéron," 55–63.
[157] There are three principle sources on Adalbero. The late-tenth-century Richer of Saint-Remi's *History* highlights Adalbero's work in the city of Reims. The letters of the monk and teacher Gerbert of Reims, written both for and about Adalbero, feature Adalbero's political interaction with surrounding leaders. The chronicle of a monastery founded by Adalbero, the early-eleventh-century *Chronique de Mouzon*, emphasizes his monastic reforms and his spiritual life. On Adalbero's continuing role in tenth-century politics, see Geoffrey Koziol, *Begging Pardon and Favor. Ritual and Political Order in Early Medieval France* (Ithaca, 1992), 113–116.

as well as urging Imperial bishops to remain loyal to Otto III. In addition, Adalbero's scribe and associate, the pro-imperial Gerbert of Reims, had testified to his loyalty to Otto III.[158]

Adalbero also felt no compunction about interfering in the succession politics of France, which geographically, if not practically, governed Reims. When Louis V, heir to the throne of France, died in 987, Adalbero participated in the election of a new king, lobbying against the Carolingian descendent and in favor of Hugh Capet.[159] The chronicler Richer of Saint-Remi recorded Adalbero's arguments for rejecting Charles of Lower Lotharingia as the new king. Charles, he said, lacked wisdom, honor and virtue and had debased himself by marrying the daughter of a vassal. Because of this it was Adalbero's duty as a vicar of Christ to support another more suitable candidate, one who would better serve Christianity.[160] Adalbero, as the archbishop of Reims, in addition to advising and consecrating kings, was entitled to rule on who would be eligible for the throne.[161] At the cathedral school of Reims, Gerard would have been educated that the duties of a bishop were the same. When he was appointed to lead a diocese that straddled the boundaries of both the Holy Roman Empire and France, the complications of his office mirrored Adalbero's to a surprising degree. A vassal of the Ottonian emperor, he was at the same time an advisor and supporter of the French king, and needed, in his role as God's consecrated Church leader, to cooperate with both.[162] Although Gerard had been chosen for his office by Emperor Henry, the Arras Bible's image program could easily have been addressed to the French king in whose realm Arras fell.

An interesting comparison could perhaps be found in the actions of Gerard's near contemporary, Abbo of Fleury. Abbo, who was both abbot and chronicler of the ancient and famous abbey at Fleury, espoused the ideology of political Augustinianism as well, but local

---

[158] Gerbert of Reims, *Die Briefsammlung Gerberts von Reims*, ed. Fritz Weigle, MGH Die Briefe der deutschen Kaiserzeit II (Weimar, 1966), pp. 48–50 letters 26–27, pp. 64–66, letters 37 and 39, p. 113, letter 85, pp. 116–117, letter 89, pp. 133–134, letter 103.

[159] Gerbert, 77–78, letter 48, 87–90, letters 57–58, 92–93, letter 61.

[160] Richer, *Histoire de son Temps*, ed. Georg Heinrich Pertz (Paris, 1845), IV:10–IV:11.

[161] Richer, IV:8.

[162] *Chronique de Mouzon*, 152, describes how Adalbero was elevated by Lothar, King of the Franks, after he was elected by the clergy and people and approved by the nobles.

circumstances led him to apply his beliefs differently.[163] Abbo subscribed to the understanding that both religious and secular leaders
were invested with a special power by God, and that humanity was
bound to follow them because of this. Abbo had spent much of his
career defending the material wealth and autonomy of his abbey
against the ambitions of the local bishop, Arnulf of Orleans. Not
surprisingly, then, Abbo implied that power was supposed to be
shared by secular rulers and the pope, rather than his bishops. Using
anthropomorphic imagery borrowed from Paul's epistle to the Romans,
Abbo explained that just as the earthly church is the body of Christ
and its limbs are her officers, the head is the governing pope.[164]
When Gerard had called on similar anthropomorphic imagery in
the *Acta synodi Atrebatensis*, he had made the bishops into the 'head'
of the 'whole Church,' which was the body of Christ.[165] While Abbo
believed, like Gerard, that the foremost offices of the ecclesiastical
and secular world had been created by God, he asserted that it was
the pope, not the bishops, who had inherited the apostolic tradition,
and thus shared the responsibility for guiding society with the king
or emperor.[166]

Gerard may have felt bound to cooperate with both the French
and Ottonian rulers based on his ideology, but his public activities
were more visibly undertaken on behalf of the Emperor. Immediately
after the consecration Gerard began a long career as a diplomat in
imperial service, starting with his journey to assist the Emperor at
the seige of Metz just after arriving at Cambrai to take up his new
episcopal seat. Between Gerard's consecration in 1012 and the death
of Henry II in 1024, the chronicle describes many missions undertaken by Gerard for his imperial patron.[167] Gerard also acted as a

---

[163] Marco Mostert, *The Political Theology of Abbo of Fleury: A Study of the Ideas about
Society and Law of the Tenth Century Monastic Reform Movement*, Middeleeuwse Studies
en Bronnen 2 (Hilversum, 1987), 85.

[164] Romans 12:4–7. "For as in one body we have many members, but all the
members have not the same office: so we being many, are one body in Christ, and
every one members one of another. And having different gifts, according to the
grace that is given us, either prophecy, to be used according to the rule of the
faith; or ministry, in ministering; or he that teacheth, in doctrine." Mostert, 128–129.

[165] PL 142:1294, 1290.

[166] Mostert, 125–128.

[167] PL 149:145. This chapter also describes how in October of 1013, Gerard
went with Balderic, Bishop of Liège, as Henry's legate to a synod at Coblenz.

mediator in both secular and ecclesiastical affairs.[168] Schieffer identified
the public activities of Bishop Gerard in light of his perceived role
as defender of the Empire. Schieffer attributed his presence at a
1018 synod at Reims to his function as a diplomatic ambassador of
the Emperor, and believed that at the Compiègne summit in 1023
and at another at Ivois, despite the lack of any statement to that
effect in the sources, he must have been negotiating on behalf of
the Emperor.[169] Schieffer also called the now-lost, and never described,
early-eleventh-century cathedral of Cambrai a part of the flowering
of the 'Saxon' Romanesque style, a monument to German rule built
under the influence of the German princes of the Church then
installed in the west.[170]

Schieffer believed that Gerard saw Germany as an island of political stability, in contrast to the seething feudal discord prevalent in
the weakened and dissolute Capetian realm. Emblematic of Schieffer's
analysis is his interpretation of Gerard's ongoing battle with the local
castellan of Cambrai. According to the *Gesta episcoporum Cameracensium*,
Walter of Lens, a minor noble loyal to Count Baldwin V of Flanders,
repeatedly assaulted the bishop and his property, while remaining
safely within his own fortress in Cambrai.[171] Walter, however, was
not a free agent. He was acting at least in part at the behest of
Count Baldwin, and King Robert the Pious, both of whom hoped
to gain a foothold in Cambrai, thereby encroaching on imperial territory.[172] In fact, the chronicle records that soon after Gerard's consecration, Walter actually called on Robert the Pious to assist him
in appeasing Gerard after burning part of the town. Robert sent a
delegation led by a Capetian bishop, Harduin of Noyon, to support
Walter's negotiations in Cambrai.[173] The castellan, according to

---

[168] Chapter seven of book three describes how Gerard worked to secure the
recognition of the emperor's protégé, Duke Godfrey of Verdun, the newly-appointed
duke of Lower Lotharingia, from the counts of Louvain and Hainaut (PL 149:159–160).
Later, in the 1023 synod attended by the Emperor at Aachen, Gerard settled a
dispute between the imperial bishops of Liège and Cologne over their rival claims
to authority over a local monastery (PL 149:160).

[169] Schieffer, "Ein deutscher Bishof," 335.

[170] Schieffer, "Ein deutscher Bishof," 351.

[171] PL 149:120–122 and 144–145.

[172] See Duby, *The Three Orders*, 23, for a general overview and David C. Van
Meter, "Count Baldwin IV, Richard of Saint-Vanne and the Inception of Monastic
Reform in Eleventh-Century Flanders," *Revue bénédictine* CVII (1997), 130–148.

[173] PL 149:145. *Nam Robertum regem et Odonem comitem precatores sibi et adjutores para-
vit, et ut domnum episcopum placaturi, suae temeritati veniam rogarent, obtinuit. Verum hii circa*

Schieffer, was the type of feudal noble then prevalent across the border in France: unruly, uncontrollable, and a constant thorn in the side of the rightful representative of the Emperor, Bishop Gerard, who was attempting to establish the order, *Ordnung*, of the state. Supported, apparently, by the French king, Robert the Pious, Walter was, in the words of Schieffer, a party to a power struggle, a *Machtkampf*, typical of contemporary French-German relations, whose theater in this case was the town of Cambrai.[174] He was an agent in the bitter war with the French-oriented local aristocracy.[175]

Our introduction to Robert the Pious in the chronicle is thus in the role of an adversary. Despite Gerard's self-identified strong connection to Henry, and his pride in his importance as the Emperor's advisor made obvious in the chronicle, Duby nonetheless chose to interpret Gerard's motivations through the lens of his allegiance to the French king. According to Duby, however, in spite of his sometimes adversarial relationship with Robert, Gerard owed allegiance to the king of France and took seriously his duty to advise him and to foster his interests. Duby's interpretation of Gerard can be summed up in a single statement. "Gerard of Cambrai-Arras was a member . . . of a circle of bishops who gravitated towards the Capetian king. As 'Orators' they spelled one another in insuring that the monarch was exposed to an uninterrupted disquisition on morality, or rather, that he was engaged in a continuous moralizing dialogue."[176]

Duby's view of Gerard may have been swayed by a desire to make his political beliefs accord with those of Adalbero of Laon, Gerard's cousin, the author of the *Carmen ad Rotbertum regem*. This tract, composed between 1027 and 1031, explicitly addressed the French king about threats to his capacity to rule, especially from the ever more powerful reform movement of Cluny. As Adalbero's cousin and fellow French bishop, in Duby's eyes Gerard should have been an equally strong proponent of the French king's rights.[177] Duby's interpretation, however, takes several liberties with the evidence. Aside from Gerard's statements associated with the Peace of God, there is

---

negocium aliud occupati, Harduinum Noviomensum episcopum cum aliis etiam oratoribus usu vicario ad Gerardum pontificem delegarunt. Schieffer, "Ein deutscher Bishof," 335.

[174] Schieffer, "Ein deutscher Bishof," 335–336.
[175] Schieffer, "Ein deutscher Bishof," 359.
[176] Duby, *The Three Orders*, 17.
[177] Duby, *The Three Orders*, 17.

very little proof that Gerard spent much time meeting or communicating with Robert the Pious, or considering his interests. Arras, in the county of Flanders and dominated by Counts Baldwin IV (988–1035) and Baldwin V (1035–1067), was a long way from the very limited power base of the French king, and Robert the Pious never visited Arras during Gerard's episcopate. Gerard's own *Gesta episcoporum Cameracensium* credits the king and his troops with looting the town and its churches during their visit in 1006.[178] Even Duby, in an earlier version of his study, had suggested that Gerard's fight against the Peace of God had been undertaken in the first instance as a way to defend Lotharingia against incursions from the west, meaning from Capetian nobles.[179] Furthermore, Olivier Guyotjeannin, in an article that identified bishops in the French royal entourage, did not include the bishop of Cambrai.[180] On the only occasion he noted where the bishop of Cambrai played a role in a royal ceremony, Guyotjeannin ascribed his appearance to his loyalty to his archbishop rather than to the king.

Gerard of Cambrai, the Peace of God and the Saint-Vaast Bible

Perhaps Gerard's biggest political challenge was provided by the Peace of God movement that swept through France in the early-eleventh century. The Peace of God was first proposed to Gerard by the bishops of Soissons and Beauvais at the royal conference at Compiègne in 1023, where Gerard and his friend Richard of Saint-Vanne may have been sent as envoys to Robert the Pious from Henry II, charged to arrange a formal meeting between the two sovereigns.[181] Then, in August of 1023, Henry II and Robert II met at Ivois on the Meuse to negotiate a State-sponsored peace. Although

---

[178] PL 149:117 and Van Meter, "Count Baldwin IV," 136.

[179] Duby, "Gérard de Cambrai," 144–145.

[180] Olivier Guyotjeannin, "Les évêques dans l'entourage royal sous les premiers Capétiens," in *Le roi de France et son royaume autour de l'an mil.* Actes du colloque Hugues Capet 987–1987. La France de l'an mil, Paris-Senlis, 22–25 juin 1987 (Paris, 1992), 93.

[181] Roger Bonnaud-Delamare, "Les institutions de paix dans la province ecclésiastique de Reims au XIe siècle," *Bulletin philologique et historique du Comité des travaux historiques et scientifiques* (Paris, 1957), 175–176. The *Gesta* does not explain where this took place, but circumstantial evidence suggests it must have been at Compiègne, where all are recorded as having gathered.

the preparatory meeting at Compiègne is not well described in the chronicle, Gerard's argument with several fellow bishops over their proposal for the church-led Peace of God dominates the account. Chapter thirty-seven of the chronicle records in detail the summit at Ivois, attended not only by the King and the Emperor, but also by other nobles, bishops and abbots.[182] Here, the two rulers themselves pondered how to restore peace within all of Christianity.[183] It was also decided at that time that both Robert and Henry would in the future travel to Pavia to meet in the presence of Pope Benedict VIII. This meeting was prevented by the death of Henry II in 1024. Nonetheless, the records of these meetings provide us with some of our best information about Gerard's view of royal government and its relationship with the Church and the keys to understanding the Jeremiah and Ezra miniatures in the Arras Bible. Drawn from the beginning of his episcopacy into the diplomatic sphere, Gerard developed a healthy respect for the secular hierarchy. Gerard would have accepted, based on the Augustinian model he had learned at Reims, that although he was not an instrument of the state, as bishop he could best serve the interests of his diocese by cooperating with the legitimate secular authority sanctioned by the Church. All the same, he sought to protect a division between Church and State.

The Peace of God movement challenged Gerard's model of Church and State cooperation at its very foundations. In an effort to repress the ever-increasing threat from marauding minor nobles such as Walter of Lens, the Castellan of Cambrai, leading clerics proposed that a general peace be sworn, not just by the commonly identified culprits, but by society at large, led by the clergy. It was thought that this oath made over relics, along with the requisite penance and fasting and the threat of excommunication, would put responsibility for enforcing the peace and preventing violence into the hands of lay-people.[184] In the *Gesta episcoporum Cameracensium*'s description of

---

[182] PL 149:157–158. Better evidence of the presence of Gerard and Richard is provided by a charter written by Guérin of Beauvais, presumably at the time of the meeting. Lemarignier, "Paix et réforme," 444–445.

[183] PL 149:161–162: . . . *certe pacis et justituae summa diffinitio mutuaeque amicitiae facta reconciliatio; ibi quoque diligentissime de pace sanctae Dei aecclesiae maxime tractatum est, et quomodo Christianitati, quae tot lapsibus patet, melius subvenire deberent.* Lemarignier, "Paix et réforme," 452–453.

[184] See generally Henri Platelle, "La violence et ses remèdes en Flandre au XIe siècle," *Sacris Erudiri* XX (1971), 101–173, Egied I. Strubbe, "La paix de Dieu dans

this meeting, the author made clear that Gerard recognized the danger of this idea from the beginning. The author, in chapter twenty-seven of book three, explained that Bishops Beroldus of Soissons and Walerannus of Beauvais, who suggested this solution to Gerard at Compiègne, were inspired by the practices in Burgundy, which they felt, if adopted in the archdiocese of Reims, would halt the decline of law in the region.[185] He then described the Burgundian model as a sacramental bond constraining clergy and laity alike to be the servants of peace.[186] The Bishop of Arras-Cambrai immediately argued against the proposal, because it confused the duties of Church and State, thereby undermining the powers traditionally held by both the secular office of the king and the ecclesiastical office of the bishop. He thought that the two proponents of the plan were taking advantage of the, in his words, *inbecillitate regis*, to weaken royal authority by proposing the Peace of God, for the oath would have covered almost exclusively the territory of the archdiocese of Reims, most of which fell within the realm of *Francia*, governed by the politically impotent King Robert the Pious.[187]

Schieffer argued that Gerard rejected the Peace of God proposed by the Burgundian bishops out of loyalty to the German emperor.[188] Duby, on the other hand, believed it was rejected instead because of the damage it could cause to the rights of kings in general, and the French king in particular. Duby saw the original 1024/1025 part of the *Gesta episcoporum* as having been produced with one goal in mind: to portray Gerard of Cambrai as the proponent of a 'true

---

le Nord de la France," *Recueil de la Société Jean Bodin* XIV, no. 1 (1961) 489–501, and more recently, Geoffrey Koziol, "Monks, Feuds, and the Making of Peace in Eleventh-Century Flanders," in *The Peace of God: Social Violence and Religious Response in France around the Year 1000*, ed. Thomas Head and Richard Landes (Ithaca, 1992), 239–258. On the peace proposed at Compiègne and carried out at Douai, Lemarignier, "Paix et réforme," 457–461, and Bonnaud-Delamare, 165–200 and David C. Van Meter, "The Peace of Amiens-Corbie and Gerard of Cambrai's Oration on the Three Functional Orders: the Date, the Context, the Rhetoric," *Revue belge de philologie et d'histoire* LXXIV (1996), 633–657.

[185] PL 149:157. *Ipso in tempore videntes episcopi Beroldus Suessionensium et Walerannus Belvacensium, prae inbecillitate regis peccatis quidem exigentibus statum regni funditus inclinari, jura confundi, usumque patrium et omne genus justitiae profanari; multum rei publicae succurrere arbitrati sunt, si Burgundiae episcoporum sententiam sequerentur.*

[186] PL 149:158. *Hii nimirum totius auctoritatis expertes, commune decretum fecerunt, ut tam sese quam omnes homines sub sacramento constringerent, pacem videlicet et justitiam servaturos.*

[187] PL 149:157–158.

[188] Schieffer, "Ein deutscher Bishof," 345, and Bur, "Adalbéron," 61.

peace,' the peace of kings, as opposed to what he saw as the 'false peace' being promoted at that time, the Peace of God.[189] Gerard's opposition to the Peace of God was motivated, however, not simply by personal loyalties to particular rulers, but by his long-held belief in the cooperative model of government between bishops and kings fostered at Reims, the belief that led him to support Henry II as a ruler. In his original argument against the Peace of God, as recorded in the chronicle in connection with the meeting at Compiègne, Gerard explained his view of the special roles set aside for bishops and kings. Kings, according to his *schema*, were assigned the job of suppressing mutinies, allaying wars and expanding peace. Bishops, on the other hand, were supposed to advise kings and to pray for their victories.[190] The Peace of God, by making the enforcement of peace the function of an episcopal oath, therefore removed this duty from the regal sphere and reassigned it to the clerical. The Ezra illustration in the Saint-Vaast Bible pictured the two offices governing these spheres, king and high priest, as separate, equal and interdependent, the same model described by Gerard in his argument against the Peace of God as recorded in the *Gesta episcoporum*.

Despite his misgivings, Gerard finally did lead the Peace of Douai in 1024, after having been pressured by Abbot Leduinus of Saint-Vaast, Abbot Roderic of Saint-Bertin in Saint-Omer, both disciples of Richard of Saint-Vanne, and by Baldwin IV, the Count of Flanders.[191] Gathering in a field at Douai, in the center of the diocese of Arras-

---

[189] Duby, "Gérard de Cambrai," 139–142 and Duby, *The Three Orders*, 21–22.

[190] PL 149:158. *Hoc enim non tam inpossibile quam incongruum videri respondit, si quod regalis juris est, sibi vendicari presumerent. Hoc etiam modo sanctae aecclesiae statum confundi, quae geminis personis, regali videlicet ac sacerdotali, administrari precipitur. Huic enim orare, illi vero pugnare tribuitur. Igitur, regum esse seditiones virtute compescere, bella sedare, pacis commercia dilatare; episcoporum vero, reges ut viriliter pro salute patriae pugnent monere, ut vincant orare.*

[191] The involvement of Leduinus and Roderic is reported in the *Gesta*, PL 149:158. The date of this peace has been disputed, because its retelling in the *Gesta* is found in book three, chapters 53–54, a section originally thought to describe events from the year 1036. Duby, however, believed that this description, and the other documentary evidence of the peace, date from 1024, and were inserted into a later section of the chronicle when it was reworked after Gerard's death (See above, chapter two). This suggestion is convincing, as it puts the eventual execution of the Peace much closer to the time it was suggested, instead of allowing an unexplained lapse of twelve years between the two events. Duby, *The Three Orders*, 25–26. For the later dating of these documents, see Bonnaud-Delamare, 188–189 and 191 and Van Meter, "The Peace of Amiens-Corbie," 644–645.

Cambrai but on the border between France and the Holy Roman Empire, Gerard led the crowd in saying a pledge over relics brought from every part of the diocese. In this peace, Gerard, true to his stated beliefs, reserved for the king the right to make war, a situation that would not obtain in later north-French peace agreements.[192]

Just before the description of the Peace of Douai in the chronicle the author inscribed a speech in which Gerard reiterated his argument against the Peace of God, this time using illustrative examples taken from the Old and New Testaments. Gerard states that he based his system on the example of the Old Testament kings and patriarchs Abraham, Joshua, and David, who, like the contemporary *pugnatores* of Gerard's era, were to be supported by the *sacerdotes* of the Church through which they gained their right to lead.[193] He again described his vision of the three different segments of society, made up of those who pray, those who labor or farm, and those who fight. All worked to support each other: the *pugnatores* protected the *oratores* from worldly cares, while the *oratores* provided them spiritual sustenance in return; the *agricultores* furnished their worldly and spiritual protectors with food and material sustenance while the *oratores* sought to lift them up to heaven through prayer and the *pugnatores* guarded them against danger while still on earth.[194] Once again, Gerard reinforced the notion that although the ecclesiastical and secular hierarchies, led by the king and the bishop, must cooperate in

---

[192] The text of the promise of peace made at Douai that day is preserved in an eleventh-century codex originally from the abbey of Marchiennes and now in Douai, BM MS 856, fol. 91. Bonnaud-Delamare, 196–198. The document is transcribed in p. 184bis. *Ceterum in hac pace nullus nisi rex caballicationem aut hostilitatem faciat et quicumque in caballicatione aut hostilitate regis fuerit in hoc episcopatu nihil plusquam sibi ac suis equis necessaria sunt ad victum accipiant.*

[193] PL 149:171. *Quibus—dum Abraham et Josue et David ex voce Domini arma tulisse in prelium vetus ostendit pagina, et sacerdotes gladio accingunt reges, regnante gratia in nostra matre aecclesia Dei sponsa—officium non est in culpa, si deest peccatum in conscientia.* According to Van Meter, "The Peace of Amiens-Corbie," 646, this speech may instead of have been delivered in response to the Peace of Amiens-Corbie in 1033–1034. This proposed redating however, doesn't change the significance of its content to our interpretation of the Saint-Vaast Bible's imagery.

[194] PL 149:170–171. *Genus humanum ab initio trifarium devisum esse monstravit, in oratoribus, agricultoribus, pugnatoribus; horumque singulos alterutrum dextra laevaque foveri, evidens documentum dedit: "Oratorum a saeculi vacans negotii dum ad Deum vadit intentio, pugnatoribus debet, quod sancto secura vacat otio; agricultoribus, quod eorum laboribus corporali pascitur cibo. Nihilominus agricultores ad Deum levantur oratorum precibus, et pugnatorum defensatur armis. Pari modo pugnatores, dum reditibus agrorum annonantur et mercimoniis vectigalium solatiantur armorumque delicta piorum quos tuentur expiat precatio sancta, foventur ut dictum est mutuo."*

order to create a civil society, at the same time they must not trespass on each others' clearly defined duties. Furthermore, he argued
against a suggested component of the Peace that would prohibit the
return of booty, again reinforcing the traditional rights of kings, who,
he explained, were taught by the holy fathers to protect the goods
of the Church and return what had been unjustly taken.[195]

That the Ezra Master depicted Jeremiah and Ezra in the roles of
bishop and king (pls. IV and VII) would not be enough to set out
a coherent program of consecrated rulership for the miniature cycle.
The Saint-Vaast Bible is, however, replete with other images of kingship, many by the same artist, and many of which borrow aspects
of the philosophy of divinely inspired rule promulgated by Gerard
of Cambrai in the two most important writings associated with his
episcopate, the *Gesta episcoporum Cameracensium* and the *Acta synodi
Atrebatensis*. As I will demonstrate in chapter four, taken in combination, the images of episcopal authority discussed above and the
representation of the rights of the king together make visual the political philosophy found in the chronicle and in the *Acta*.

---

[195] PL 149:171. *Inde reges per sanctos patres edocti, statuerunt firmas leges, ut res suas injuste
sublatas aecclesia vel quilibet juste repeteret; quas legaliter cogeretur qui rapuerat, restituere.*

CHAPTER FOUR

KINGS, PRINCES, AND POLITICS

Since the Carolingian period, when Hincmar of Reims had taken up the standard of monarchical rights, the elite had understood that the offices of king and bishop were inherently similar. The Carolingian ordines for the consecration of kings and bishops were continually reworked to strengthen the connection between these two office-holders, both through the prayers that were said and the symbolic insignia they received.[1] From that point on, the king and the bishop recognized each other as spiritual kin who labored within the same 'ministerium,' and relied on each other to maintain their shared status.[2] If the king's divine right to govern were undermined, the bishop's authority would suffer as well.

We have already seen how Gerard of Cambrai pragmatically adapted this belief, and applied it using an Augustinian political philosophy, to his own unique circumstances. In fact, the political realism we have observed among these late-tenth and early-eleventh-century religious leaders is simply a continuation of the tradition established early in the Carolingian era. Although early scholars painted a picture of great uniformity in the cooperative model of government established

[1] Carra Ferguson O'Meara, *Monarchy and Consent. The Coronation Book of Charles V of France* (London, 2001), 63, notes that while Archbishop Hincmar of Reims added an oath to the royal consecration that echoed a bishop's oath of office, Archbishop Ebbo of Reims added a staff to the insignia with which a bishop was invested, similar to the insignia of the king. Michel Andrieu, "Le sacre épiscopal d'après Hincmar de Rheims," *Revue d'histoire ecclésiastique* XLVIII (1953), 22–73, Pierre Batiffol, "La liturgie du sacre des évêques," *Revue d'histoire ecclésiastique* XXIII (1923), 732–63 and Janet Nelson, "Kingship, law and liturgy in the political thought of Hincmar of Reims," *English Historical Review* XCII (1977), 241–279. These concepts have been thoroughly explored by Arnold Angenendt, "*Rex et Sacerdos.* Zur Genese der Königssalbung," in *Tradition als historische Kraft: interdisziplinäre Forschungen zur Geschichte des frühen Mittelalters*, ed. N. Kamp and J. Wollasch (Berlin, 1982), 100–118.
[2] Hincmar of Reims introduced the idea of the joint ministry of bishops and kings in the Protocol of 869 for the crowning of Charles the Bald as King of Lotharingia at Metz. O'Meara, 73 and Richard A. Jackson, *Ordines coronationis Franciae. Texts and Ordines for the Coronation of Frankish and French Kings and Queens in the Middle Ages*, 2 vols. (Philadelphia, 1995–2000), I, 87–109.

by the Carolingians, and its continuation under the Ottonian *Reichskirche* system,[3] in reality the relationship between rulers and leading churchmen was constantly renegotiated in the course of the eighth through eleventh centuries.[4] A close examination of any region or locality tends to reveal a much more nuanced series of machinations, or adjustments, in the interactions of rulers and bishops. Matthew Innes, for instance, has recently charted the flip-flopping of political allegiances that took place in the Middle Rhine Valley between 843, in the wake of the Treaty of Verdun, and the Ottonians' rise to ascendancy.[5] Bishops, counts and kings constantly reworked their alliances in the face of the rising and falling power of each office-holder, and the constantly shifting geographical boundaries of their realms.

The same dynamic was at work in the intricate politics of the diocese of Arras-Cambrai in the early eleventh century. Led by his Augustinian political philosophy, and hoping to gain the upper hand in his relationship with the ambitious counts of Flanders, Gerard clung to the idea of royal hegemony based on each ruler's connection with God. In early eleventh-century Flanders especially, no consecrated ruler held the reins of power securely, contributing to Gerard of Cambrai's constant problems with the local nobility. David C. Van Meter has recently explored Baldwin IV's political machinations, and charted a series of events in Arras and Cambrai that would have profoundly affected Gerard's experience as bishop, incidents typical of the relationship between a powerful bishop, local nobility, and distant rulers in ninth through eleventh-century Europe.[6]

Gerard of Cambrai fought for over a decade with the local castellan of Cambrai, Walter of Lens. Count Baldwin IV of Flanders twice

---

[3] See, for instance, the overview provided by Walter Ullmann, *The Carolingian Renaissance and the Idea of Kingship* (London, 1969), 111–128.

[4] Janet L. Nelson, "Kingship and Empire in the Carolingian World," in *Carolingian Culture: Emulation and Innovation*, ed. Rosamund McKitterick (Cambridge, 1994), 52, and Rudolf Schieffer, "Bischofserhebungen im westfränkisch-französischen Bereich im späten 9. und im 10. Jahrhundert," in *Die früh- und hochmittelalterliche Bischofserhebung im europäischen Vergleich*, ed. Franz-Reiner Erkens (Cologne, 1998), 59–82.

[5] Matthew Innes, *State and Society in the Early Middle Ages: The Middle Rhine Valley, 400–1000* (Cambridge, 2001), 210–250.

[6] David C. Van Meter, "Count Baldwin IV, Richard of Saint-Vanne and the Inception of Monastic Reform in Eleventh-Century Flanders," *Revue bénédictine* CVII (1997), 130–148. See also the work of Laurent Jégou, "L'évêque entre autorité sacrée et exercice du pouvoir. L'exemple de Gérard de Cambrai (1012–1051)," *Cahiers de civilisation médiévale, X^e–XIIe siècles* XLVII (2004), 37–55.

attempted, unsuccessfully, to install his own uncle as bishop of Arras-Cambrai. When this ploy failed, he installed Walter as castellan in anticipation of Gerard's arrival in Cambrai, even though Cambrai fell outside Baldwin's domain. Walter prevented the burial of Gerard's predecessor and occupied the episcopal palace until a deal could be struck between Gerard, Walter, and Baldwin.[7] Gerard must have longed for the past, when Carolingian rulers such as Charles the Bald and his wife Ermintrude had lavished attention on Saint-Vaast and Arras, and royal authority had remained relatively unquestioned. His *Acta synodi Atrebatensis* and *Gesta episcoporum* certainly reflect this desire, by resurrecting the Carolingian idea of the divinely appointed sovereignty of the king and the authority of the bishop.

Furthermore, although Richard of Saint-Vanne, the abbot of Saint-Vaast, and Leduinus, his successor, have routinely been depicted as allies of Count Baldwin, in fact their own allegiances were as complicated and prone to frequent adjustments as Gerard's. In 1012, as part of his campaign to further his own reforms, Richard circulated a letter describing two visions experienced by one of the monks of Saint-Vaast.[8] In the second vision, the monk was led by the Archangel Michael through Purgatory, where he saw a locale replete with leaping hellfire and writhing worms. The angel explained that this region was especially reserved for Count Baldwin. Interestingly, the monk was perplexed that the count, who had endowed an ersatz 'royal' cult at the monastery of Saint-Bertin in Saint-Omer, would be left to suffer such punishment. The monk suggested that because the count had a wealth of gold and silver, and thus the limitless potential for good works, he could yet be saved. The angel replied that Baldwin was already beyond the pale as he turned a deaf ear to any admonishment. According to Van Meter, by circulating this letter, Richard was most likely attempting to manipulate Count Baldwin into supporting his attempts to reform Saint-Bertin.[9] This document is a telling indication that Richard and Baldwin's relationship was

---

[7] Van Meter, "Count Baldwin IV," 132–141.

[8] Van Meter, "Count Baldwin IV," 142, idem, "Apocalyptic Moments and Eschatological Rhetoric of Reform in the Early Eleventh-Century: The Case of the Visionary of St. Vaast," *The Apocalyptic Year 1000: religious expectation and social change 950–1050*, ed. Richard Landes (Oxford, 2003), 311–325, and Hugh of Flavigny, *Chronicon*, PL 154:234–235.

[9] Van Meter, "Count Baldwin IV," 143–144.

not seamless, and that Richard was not above using epistolary propaganda to influence the powerful lord. Visual propaganda such as
that found in the Saint-Vaast Bible, which was intended to elevate
the occupants of real royal cults and their partners, the bishops,
would only have furthered his goals.

By the eleventh century bishops had essentially cornered the market on king-making in Western Europe. Once the king was no longer
chosen in a secular election from among his peers but received his
office by birthright, the bishops stepped in to assert their right to
bestow God's approval, and the anointing through which God's grace
was imbued in the new ruler. The ceremony for king-making, as
Carra Ferguson O'Meara has so cogently pointed out, was consistently included in the pontifical, the book of sacraments performed
specifically by a bishop. At the same time, imagery of the elevation
of the ruler disappeared from the public sphere to reappear almost
exclusively in liturgical manuscripts.[10]

The diocese of Arras-Cambrai fell within the archdiocese of Reims,
where the coronation and consecration of the French king took place
and where so recently Archbishop Adalbero had orchestrated the
downfall of the Carolingian dynasty and the elevation of the Capetians.
When the scriptorium at Saint-Vaast copied and illustrated the
Cologne Pontifical sometime after the middle of the eleventh century, it contained ordines for the consecration of both the king and
the bishop.[11] Indeed, Saint-Vaast stands out in the history of coronation rituals, because the oldest surviving ordo for the consecration
of a king, the First English Ordo, was copied into the Leofric Missal,
which may have been made at Saint-Vaast for English use in the
tenth century.[12] This manuscript would have left Arras by the time

---

[10] O'Meara, 64–65.
[11] Cologne, Erzbishöfliche Diözesan Dombibliothek, Dom MS 141. See above, chapter 2.
[12] On the Leofric Missal (Oxford, Bodleian Library MS Bod. 579) at Saint-Vaast, see above, chapter 1. Janet Nelson, "The Earliest Surviving Royal Ordo: Some Liturgical and Historical Aspects," in *Authority and Power: Studies on Medieval Law and Government Presented to Walter Ullman on his Seventieth Birthday* (Cambridge, 1980), 29–48. Nicholas Orchard, editor of the most recent edition of the Leofric Missal, has argued that the earliest section (A) of the manuscript was instead redacted in England by a foreign scribe using a manuscript from Saint-Vaast as one of his sources. The manuscript faithfully copies the frames and initials then being created at Saint-Amand and Saint-Vaast, has Flemish style-script, and relies heavily on a sacra-mentary that combined material from Arras and Tours (*The Leofric Missal*, Henry

the Bible project was begun, but the insistence in its royal ordo on the Old Testament models for the consecration of the king set the stage for later western ordines, and is clearly echoed in the Bible's pictorial program. Although neither manuscript contains images of consecrations, the Saint-Vaast Bible, the most lavish and important manuscript produced by the eleventh-century scriptorium, pictorial-izes the elite's expectations of their office-holders.

These themes have already emerged from a careful examination of the illuminations prefacing the Books of Jeremiah and Ezra. The choice of scenes used to illustrate these books of the Bible, and the details with which they were illustrated, served to interpret the bib-lical narrative in the light of the religious and political concerns cur-rent in Flanders in the first half of the eleventh century. I believe that the writings of Gerard of Cambrai, the ordines in the Cologne Pontifical from Saint-Vaast, and the images of the Saint-Vaast Bible worked in harmony to reinforce the divine right of not only bishops, but also kings, to govern. As we have already seen, of the eighteen narrative illustrations in the Bible, two show figures wearing clerical vestments. In addition, nine images show biblical kings or governors, most of whom bear royal insignia reminiscent of those seen in Carolingian, Capetian, Anglo-Saxon and Ottonian ruler portraits. Solomon alone appears four times, and each time is singled out as an anointed ruler who embodies the kingly and priestly virtues granted by the grace delivered at his unction. These images make clear that the theme of the divine sanction of the offices of bishop and king, and the heavenly origin of the Law that was their basis, underlies the cycle of miniatures.

King Solomon and 'royal grace charisma' in the Saint-Vaast Bible

King Solomon, along with King David, had been set up as a pro-totype for western kings so frequently since the eighth century that the comparison had become commonplace. Almost all royal conse-

---

Bradshaw Society CXIII–CXIV [London, 2002], 16–131). Furthermore, Orchard himself notes many Franco-Saxon liturgical books that were produced for export (17–18, 24). The reverse could therefore be true. The Leofric Missal may have been crafted in Northern France specifically for export to Canterbury, hence its many English elements.

cration ordines from the First English Ordo onwards, for instance, compared the anointing of the king to the unction of Solomon by the priests Nathan and Zadok when he was elevated to rule. Not surprisingly, then, the programmer of the Saint-Vaast Bible chose the author portrait of Solomon found before the Book of Wisdom, fol. 144, vol. 2 (pl. VI), for the most explicit defense of a king's God-granted right to rule. By applying the same type of Christological imagery found in the miniature of Jeremiah to King Solomon, the artist, once again the Ezra Master, also expressed the king's Christ-like persona, the quality that made his rule divine.

Although at first glance the Solomon image appears to be nothing more than a fairly straightforward author portrait, a closer examination reveals that the artists used both obvious and subtle details to signal that Solomon was different from other leaders. Solomon sits on a bench-throne within the initial D. An interlace frame encases the initial and text, and corner medallions hold courtiers who blow horns and, on the left side, confront leaping dogs. Most immediately striking is that, like the bishop illustrating the opening of the Book of Jeremiah (pl. IV), King Solomon, who was consecrated to his reign through unction, is also represented surrounded by a full-body mandorla.[13] None of the other kings in the Bible, even those who share Solomon's other insignia, are shown with a mandorla. In this case it is divided into an almond shape behind his body, and a circle behind his head, an interesting inversion of the typical Christological mandorla depicted around the enthroned Christ in other Saint-Vaast manuscripts.[14] Perhaps this was intended to highlight his head, the part that received the anointing that elevated him to kingship, and made him a good representative for contemporary eleventh-century kings.

The Ezra Master has also borrowed from older and contemporary images of kings and bedecked Solomon in a combination of royal and priestly insignia. Like King Artaxerxes in the Ezra illustration, Solomon's insignia are not generic, but instead are carefully chosen adaptations of royal symbols of rank that reveal the breadth of the artists' contacts with Carolingian, Capetian, Anglo-Saxon, and Ottonian models. Solomon's hand stretches out over the side of the

mandorla to grasp a delicate, knobbed Capetian or Ottonian lily scepter that is silhouetted against the green background.[15] His lily crown resembles closely late-tenth and early-eleventh-century Anglo-Saxon crowns or that seen on the single surviving portrait of Robert the Pious, on a late tenth-century seal.[16] Although the lilies on the crowns that inspired those worn by Solomon were perhaps ultimately suggested by biblical descriptions of decorations of the tabernacle of the Law and Temple, another detail that has been added shows that the vision of kingship expressed by Solomon's author portrait is Christological.[17]

The artist distinguished Solomon's crown from the Saint-Vaast Bible's many other crowns by adding dangling pendants that swing out from either side, terminating in foliate ends that were empha-sized with particularly heavy pen strokes. These decorations, which did not appear on King Artaxerxes's crown (pl. VII), for instance, must have been meant to signal some special attribute of Solomon's rule. Unfortunately, identifying the purpose of these pendants is chal-lenging because no crowns survive from the period, and depictions of crowns can be very generalized, especially in their most common carrier, coins. On the one hand, these additions vaguely resemble *pendilia*, the beaded pendants that dangled from the sides of Byzantine crowns. According to the Annals of Saint-Bertin, Charles the Bald surprised the assembled crowd at the 876 Synod of Ponthion when on the last day he appeared wearing Byzantine regalia, which prob-ably included *pendilia*.[18] He and his son Louis the Stammerer were

---

[15] Percy Ernst Schramm, *Die deutschen Kaiser und Könige in Bilder ihrer Zeit; 751–1190*, ed. Florentine Mütherich (Munich, 1983), pl. 88, and pl. 97. See above, chapter 3.

[16] See above, chapter 3. The most similar crowns Edgar in the New Minster Charter, London BL MS Cotton Vespasian A VIII, fol. 2v. Like Solomon's crown, these crowns are simple gold bands with projecting trefoils, without the jeweled dec-oration found on the Carolingian and Ottonian crowns of the same shape. However, the Anglo-Saxon crowns have no *infulae* or pendants, such as those seen on Solomon's crown.

[17] Schramm believed that the Carolingian lily-scepter and lily-crown were both inspired by the texts of Exodus and Kings, where God requested that Moses and Solomon decorate the implements of the tabernacle and later the Temple, both of which were meant to contain the tablets of the Law, with lilies. See Exodus 25:31–34 and 37:17–20, and III Kings 7:19–22 and 49. Schramm, "Die Kronen des frühen Mittelalters," *Herrschaftszeichen und Staatssymbolik*, MHG Schriften XIII/2 (Stuttgart, 1955), II, 412–413.

[18] Hincmar of Reims, the reputed author of this section of the Annals, described him as "clad in the Greek fashion and wearing his crown." *The Annals of St-Bertin*,

also depicted wearing *pendilia* on a silver casket made for Charles'
second wife, Richildis.[19] *Pendilia* became much more popular on
Ottonian crowns in the wake of Otto II's marriage to Theophanu,
when many motifs from Byzantine imperial regalia were adopted by
Ottonian rulers. Nonetheless, the pendants on Solomon's crown can
be distinguished from Byzantine, Carolingian and Ottonian *pendilia*
because they do not have the characteristic beaded shape, they are
too long and they don't hang straight down, like Byzantine-inspired
pendilia.

On the other hand, these may be *infulae*. *Infulae*, or fillets, are most
well known today from bishop's miters and papal tiaras. The modern ceremonial version of an *infula* is a stiff strip of cloth with a tas-
seled end that is sewn onto the back of a miter or tiara and hangs
against the wearer's neck. These are derived, however, from ancient
flexible woolen strips that were wrapped around the heads of priests
or sacrificial animals and tied, or used to secure imperial diadems.[20]
In the depiction of Solomon before II Chronicles (vol. I, fol. 170,
pl. III) that will be discussed below the Ezra Master depicted Solomon
seated in profile with his foliate-ended strips swirling behind his head.
Here we see the fillets designed to tie a royal diadem, as depicted
in the profile portraits of kings and emperors on Carolingian, Ottonian
and Anglo-Saxon bulls, seals and coins that drew on ancient Roman
coin conventions.[21] By the early-eleventh century, such *infulae* were
commonly shown attached to the back of crowns, as in Solomon's
II Chronicles portrait, rather than to simple diadems. If artists
attempted to depict *infulae* on a full-face portrait, they might be

---

trans. Janet L. Nelson (Manchester, 1991), 194. The Annals of Fulda criticized his
new fashions, explaining that "he used to go to church on Sundays and feast-days
dressed in a dalmatic down to his ankles and with a sword-belt girded over it, his
head wrapped in a silk veil with a diadem on top. For, despising all the customs
of the Frankish kings, he held the glories of the Greeks to be best, and so that he
might show his overweeningness more fully he put aside the name of king and
ordered that he should be called Emperor and Augustus of all kings on this side
of the sea." *The Annals of Fulda*, trans. Timothy Reuter (Manchester, 1992), 79.

[19] Schramm, *Die deutschen Kaiser und Könige*, 61 and pl. 48. The Ellwangen casket
was made around 876 or 877.

[20] Ann M. Stout, "Jewelry as a Symbol of Status in the Roman Empire," in *The
World of Roman Costume*, eds. Judith Lynn Sebesta and Larissa Bonfante (Madison,
2001), 82.

[21] Schramm, *Die deutschen Kaiser und Könige*, 199, fig. 101a, Bull of Otto III, where
the *infulae* have been attached to a foliate crown rather than a diadem, as in the
Saint-Vaast Bible.

expected to swing outwards from behind the head as do the pendants in the Solomon portrait from the book of Wisdom. Anglo-Saxon, Norman, and Ottonian kings were sometimes depicted full-face on seals and coins with what have been described as Byzantine-derived *pendilia* that were longer, swung outwards and terminated in three lobes, similar to those in the Saint-Vaast Wisdom and II Chronicles images.[22] All of these artists may have intended to show not swinging *pendilia* but *infulae*. Such a full-face coin or seal portrait of a ruler with crown and *infulae* could easily have been available to artists at Saint-Vaast.

Because the contemporary Anglo-Saxon and Ottonian societies especially subscribed to a belief in Christological kingship, however, these *infulae* attached to royal crowns may have taken on a more Christological meaning. Originally considered the insignia of pagan priests and sacrifices, from early Christian times, *infulae* were considered part of the garb of the high priest, the bishop, although where on the body these bands were to be worn was not specified.[23] By the tenth and eleventh centuries the connection between *infulae* and ecclesiastical honor was well established. Flodoard, in his tenth-century history of the church of Reims, described how a local priest discovered the tomb of a certain Scotigena at the burial church of St. Hilarius, and "looking in he saw the body uncorrupt and crowned (or perhaps 'bound') with *sacerdotalibus infulis*."[24] Carolingian and later glosses also made the connection between the priestly *infulae* and royalty by explaining that in Prudentius's *Cathemerinon* King David was called 'rex sacerdos infulatus' because as a priestly king he could be dressed in the garb of the high priest.[25] Although some writers may

---

[22] See, for instance, the 'third seal' of Henry I (1100–1135) or the first seal of Stephen (1135–54). *English Romanesque Art 1066–1200* (London, 1984), 302–303, figs. 330 and 331. Full-face coin portraits of Conrad II, the Salian emperor who ruled 1024–1039, may be of this type, but are too generalized to be very informative. Schramm, *Die deutschen Kaiser und Könige*, figs. 139.23–26. The closest surviving example chronologically is the 'Penny of Facing Bust-Pyramids Type' struck in 1065 at Cricklade by the moneyer Leofred, depicting Edward the Confessor on its obverse. *The Golden Age of Anglo-Saxon Art 966–1066*, ed. Janet Backhouse, D. H. Turner, and Leslie Webster (London, 1984), 185, fig. 234.

[23] Popes Gelasius I (*Epistola* IX, c. 9, PL 59:51), Gregory of Tours (*Liber miraculorum* ch. 58, *De sancto Eugenio*, PL 71:758) and Innocent I (*Epistola* 17, c. 1, PL 20:528) all spoke of the *infulae* as being connected with high ecclesiastical office. Joseph Braun, *Die liturgische Gewandung im Occident und Orient* (Darmstadt, 1964), 427.

[24] Braun, 427, *Historia ecclesiae Remensis*, PL 135:322. *Introspiciensque videt corpus integrum sacerdotalibus infulis redimitum.*

[25] Braun, 427, *Cathemerinon* 9:5 (PL 59:862),

have used the term *infula* to refer to the bishop's garments and insignia generally,[26] the artists of the Saint-Vaast Bible may have been attempting to depict Solomon as a priestly king and assimilate him to a bishop by placing an unusual emphasis on his crown's *infulae*.

The early-eleventh-century Anglo-Saxon Eadui Psalter from Christ Church, Canterbury, which is almost exactly contemporary with the Saint-Vaast Bible, contains an image of the monks of Christ Church presenting Saint Benedict with a copy of his rule.[27] Benedict is crowned with a diadem inscribed 'Timor dei,' while fillets with gold terminals spring from behind his head. This miniature copies an earlier version of the same composition that is preserved in a damaged mid-eleventh-century Christ Church manuscript of the reforming *Regularis Concordia* and the Benedictine Rule.[28] In this version, Benedict's diadem has lost much of its inscription, but the *infulae* are so oversized that they dwarf Benedict's head. This image may have been designed by Bishop Aethelwold of Winchester in order to emphasize that Benedict, like the bishops who then led the monastic reform in England, was assimilated by his diadem to the earthly king and the heavenly ruler, Christ, and was ultimately responsible for his flock.[29] By the early-eleventh century, Anglo-Saxon art was replete with images of a diademed Christ, meaning that Benedict's diadem with *infulae* would have been a recognizable reference to Christ as King of kings and Priest of priests.[30] As we've already seen, Anglo-Saxon England was one of the chief sources of style and iconography for the Saint-Vaast artists, who also maintained connections to

---

Christus est, quem rex sacerdos adfuturum protinus
Infulatus concinebat voce, chorda, et tympano
glossed in 860 by the monk, Iso, and in the tenth century in Rome BAV cod. Vat. lat. 5821.

[26] Braun, 428.

[27] London BL MS Arundel 155, fol. 133, probably illustrated between 1012 and 1023.

[28] London BL MS Cotton Tiberius A. III, fol. 117v.

[29] Robert Deshman, "*Benedictus monarcha et monachus:* Early Medieval Ruler Theology and the Anglo-Saxon Reform," *Frühmittelalterliche Studien* XXII (1988), 204–240.

[30] Robert Deshman, "*Christus rex et magi reges*: Kingship and Christology in Ottonian and Anglo-Saxon Art," *Frühmittelalterliche Studien* X (1976), 367–405. Just one of many Anglo-Saxon examples of Christ wearing a diadem is found in the Boulogne Gospels, Boulogne BM MS 11, fol. 10, illustrated by an English artist visiting the monastery of Saint-Bertin in Saint-Omer in the late-tenth century. See *The Golden Age of Anglo-Saxon Art*, 60–65.

English reformed houses. It is possible they could have encountered this iconography through an imported insular manuscript.

At the same time that the artists of Saint-Vaast ornamented Solomon's crown with *infulae*, and the artists at Canterbury crowned Benedict with a diadem and *infulae*, the miter with pendant *infulae* was becoming a recognized liturgical vestment. In the early-eleventh century, Italian artists depicted bishops wearing miters in Exultet rolls,[31] while literary documentation shows that by the middle of the eleventh century the pope had awarded miters to a series of northern bishops.[32] Dressing both bishops and kings in prominent *infulae* was particularly appropriate since both were considered types of Christ and both took on a priestly function through their anointing. Even though the 'bishop' Jeremiah in the Saint-Vaast Bible does not wear a miter (pl. IV), educated onlookers would have understood the Christological implication of attaching *infulae* to either a miter or a royal crown, especially in the case of King Solomon, who had been anointed to rule in a ceremony that sealed him as God's chosen ruler.[33] Like Jeremiah's chasuble and crozier and Ezra's maniple, Solomon's priestly *infulae* would have signaled that the Old Testament ruler was being used to embody a modern idea, in this case that of the Christian priest-king then being defended by the clerical elite. The Ezra Master, or whoever directed his work, has made Solomon, framed by a mandorla like Jeremiah's and invested with royal and priestly regalia, Jeremiah's companion in his visual explanation of the rights of contemporary bishops and kings.

---

[31] Guglielmo Cavallo, *Exultet. Rotoli liturgici del medioevo meridionale* (Rome, 1994). These include Bari, Archivio del Capitolo Metropolitano MS Exultet 1, p. 137, from the second quarter of the eleventh century, and Troia, Archivio Capitolare MS Exultet 2, p. 198, in which the bishop's miter is embellished with prominent *infulae* that swing out from behind his head.

[32] Braun, 448–449.

[33] Although bishops were not generally depicted wearing miters in the first half of the eleventh century, they must have been worn at least occasionally, because in 1049 Pope Leo IX was documented as bestowing a miter on the archbishop of Trier (Braun, 447). The miter was developed from the turban worn by Old Testament high priests as described in Exodus 28:36–38. The bishop saint Erhard is depicted wearing this turban miter in the early-eleventh-century Uta Codex, Munich, Bayerische Staatsbibliothek Clm. 13601, fol. 4. Adam S. Cohen, *The Uta Codex. Art, Philosophy and Reform in Eleventh-Century Germany* (University Park, PA, 2000), 85.

Solomon's Priestly Kingship in Context

Already, the addition of *infulae* to Solomon's crown has suggested
that this king was intended to be seen in a sacred, Christian, light.
The scholarly literature surrounding the sacral nature of medieval
kingship is immense, and recently the discussion about rituals, texts
and images that served to depict and construct the king and his
office has become contentious. From the time of its publication in
1957, Ernst Kantorowicz's *The King's Two Bodies: A Study in Mediaeval
Political Theology* (Princeton), inspired generations of scholars in their
interpretation of royal and sacred imagery of the Carolingian, Ottonian,
Anglo-Saxon, and Capetian realms. In the last decade, however,
reassessments of both Kantorowicz's scholarly context and the materials on which he based his assumptions have led to a renewed debate
about the meaning of the very images that, as we will see below,
are most similar to the Saint-Vaast Bible's Solomon portrait.[34]

Kantorowicz's assessment of Ottonian Christ-centered kingship has
been criticized because it relied on an armature of extracts from
texts that were examined outside their original context.[35] In particular, recent students of Ottonian kingship have questioned whether
the overarching theme of Christ-like kingship that has been threaded
through modern interpretations of the Ottonian literary and artistic
legacy really was the driving principle behind the choices made by
writers and artists alike.[36] Because most often the patrons and recipients of the works remain unknown, attempts to pin the political
agenda of legitimizing a given ruler to a portrait or writing are spec-
ulative at best. My explanation of the Saint-Vaast Bible's political
message, on the other hand, is buttressed by a minute examination
of the immediate political dynamic in Arras and the County of
Flanders. The political philosophy of the prevailing religious leader
at the time and in the town where it was produced, Gerard of

---

[34] Johannes Fried, "Ernst Kantorowicz and Postwar Historiography. German and
European Perspectives," in *Ernst Kantorowicz: Erträge der Doppeltagung, Institute for Advanced
Study, Princeton, Johann Wolfgang Goethe-Universität, Frankfurt*, ed. Robert L. Benson and
Johannes Fried, Frankfurter Historische Abhandlungen XXXIX (Stuttgart, 1997),
180–201.
[35] Jean-Philippe Genet, "Kantorowicz and the *King's Two Bodies*: A non Contextual
History," in *Ernst Kantorowicz: Erträge der Doppeltagung*, 265–273.
[36] Ludger Körntgen, *Königsherrschaft und Gottes Gnade. Zu Kontext und Funktion sakraler
Vorstellungen in Historiographie und Bildzeugnissen der ottonisch-frühsalischen Zeit* (Berlin, 2001).

Cambrai, is a matter of public record. The literary tropes used by Gerard and his clerks were shared by the artists working in the local scriptorium. We are on much firmer ground when interpreting the pictorial program produced under his sway in the light of the challenges he himself faced as a subject of two kings whose authority was consistently undermined in his relatively remote diocese.

Furthermore, the political agenda that I will trace in the kingship program of the Saint-Vaast Bible served Gerard's most immediate interest of elevating his rule as it did the same for the distant kings. A firm explanation of the political undercurrents that can be detected in the Wisdom miniature serves to reinforce Kantorowicz's hypothesis, that manuscripts made in the monastic setting could nonetheless have addressed the origins and authenticity of royal power, although it does not, of course, prove that the same understanding of similar texts and images can be assumed for all times and all places.[37]

Not surprisingly, an examination of some of the same textual and artistic resources that shed light on the iconography of the Jeremiah illumination can also enhance our understanding of this image of Solomon (pl. VI). From the early Carolingian era through the eleventh century, commentators on royal status borrowed repeatedly from the Old and New Testaments to create a biblical setting for kingship and inspire respect for the anointed ruler.[38] Artwork from the Carolingian, Ottonian and Anglo-Saxon dynasties all used similar visual *topoi* to express their claims that kings attained a special and unquestionable status. Around fifty years after Gerard of Cambrai's death,

---

[37] Timothy Reuter, "Pre-Gregorian Mentalities," *Journal of Ecclesiastical History* XLV (1994), 473. Reuter has pointed out the difficulties inherent in attempting to connect the kind of "closed and self-mirroring system of aesthetics and theology" frequently associated with tenth- and early-eleventh-century art and politics to a wider dialogue in which other levels of society might have participated. I do not in the least intend to imply that my interpretation of the writings and images associated with Gerard and his circle represented part of a Europe-wide understanding of the symbolism inherent in the motifs, words or rituals involved. Gerard's anachronistic use of Carolingian and Ottonian visual language may have effectively removed him from a mainstream artistic current, if such a thing even existed. Even if Gerard hoped for a broader audience, the messages encoded in his writings, in the ordines composed in his circle, and in the Saint-Vaast Bible's imagery may have been understood only by those within the "closed and self-mirroring system" of the noble and ecclesiastical community in and around the scriptorium of Saint-Vaast.

[38] For the use of this technique within descriptions and depictions of political rituals, see especially Philippe Buc, "Ritual and interpretation: the early medieval case," *Early Medieval Europe* IX (2000), 189–191.

the 'Norman Anonymous,' most likely Bishop Guillaume de Bona Anima, wrote *De consecratione pontificum et regnum* as a dialectically argued defense of the concept of divinely sanctioned kingship.[39] Although he identified the source of power in the offices of both king and bishop as the same, resting in their initiation through sacramental anointment, he ultimately saw the king as preeminent over the bishop. While strengthening the authority of the episcopate in an effort to reinforce at the same time that of the king, he still placed the king first as *christus Domini*, the true image of Christ. In the words of George Williams, "As the king was the recipient of the same unction in a more representative way than any of his bishops, he was both more royal and more priestly than they were."[40] He also argued that the dual nature, both human and divine, of contemporary kings had already been established in the Old Testament with the anointment of the kings of Israel, who were types of Christ reigning in eternity.[41] Both this text and the illustrative cycle of the Saint-Vaast Bible may have attempted to demonstrate that the authority of contemporary kings to rule was rooted in their typological connection to Old Testament and Christological prototypes and that they shared important characteristics imbued in them through their consecration.

The Norman Anonymous was simply updating two concepts that had already been amply explored by Carolingian commentators on kingship: that the office of king and its attributes had been established by Old Testament and New Testament prototypical leaders, and that from the beginning this office combined both royal and priestly functions.[42] The connection between Old Testament kings, particularly David and Solomon, and contemporary kings was well established in the Carolingian period. King Louis the Pious, like earlier Carolingian kings, was addressed in panegyrics as 'the New

---

[39] On the Norman Anonymous, see above, chapter three.

[40] George H. Williams, *The Norman Anonymous of ca. 1100 A.D.; Towards the identification and evaluation of the so-called Anonymous of York* (Cambridge, MA, 1951), 199. See especially *De consecratione pontificum et regnum*, ed. H. Boehmer, MGH Libelli de Lite III imperatorum et pontificum saeculis XI et XII (Hanover, 1897), 669.

[41] MGH Libelli de Lite III:666. *Nam et ideo Saul et David electi dicuntur a Deo et uncti super hereditatem dei Israel et sederunt in solio et sede regni in Hierusalem, super quod et a propheta et ab angelo sessurus esse Christus in aeternum describitur.*

[42] Walter Ullmann, *The Carolingian Renaissance and the Idea of Kingship* (London, 1969), esp. 43–55 on the change from rulership based on blood kinship to rulership based on divine grace.

David' and 'the New Solomon.'[43] As described in chapter three above, in the Carolingian First Bible of Charles the Bald, produced at Tours in the mid-ninth century, a series of images visually parallel King Charles (fig. 39) with King David (fig. 37), and also, through the similarity of facial features and compositions, with Christ himself (fig. 38). In fact, Christological kingship had been even more overtly portrayed in several other Carolingian manuscripts. In a copy of Rabanus Maurus's *Carmen figuratum de laudibus sanctae crucis*, a nimbed, diademed Louis the Pious is shown as the Christian soldier of the Pauline Epistle to the Ephesians, followed a few folios later by an image of Christ crucified.[44] In the Prayerbook of Charles the Bald, Munich, Residenz, fols. 38v–39, the kneeling ruler assimilates himself to Christ on the cross by humbling himself, as Christ was humbled on the Cross. In the late eighth century this concept appeared in England as well, for by 785 the Anglo-Saxon kings were also anointed as *christus Domini*.[45]

If the king was assimilated to the 'King of kings' in his capacity as the royal leader, then it was logical that at the same time he would resemble Christ's other role as the 'Priest of priests,' the bishop. At the Synod of Frankfurt in 794, the attending bishops declared Charlemagne 'Rex et Sacerdos' after he pronounced on the issues of iconoclasm and Spanish Adoptionism.[46] We have already seen that the Carolingians had picked up on Prudentius's identification of King David as a 'rex sacerdos infulatus,' a king who was also a high priest,

---

[43] Ernst Kantorowicz, *The King's Two Bodies: a Study in Medieval Political Theology* (Princeton, 1957), 81, quoting Amalarius of Metz, *De ecclesiasticus officiis libri IV*, PL 105:988. See also Ullmann, *The Carolingian Renaissance*, 44.

[44] Rome BAV cod. Reg. lat. 124, fol. 4v, Deshman, "*Benedictus Monarcha et Monachus*," 210–211 and Elizabeth Sears, "Louis the Pious as *Miles Christi*; the Dedicatory Image in Hrabanus Maurus's *De laudibus sanctae crucis*," in *Charlemagne's Heir; New Perspectives on the Reign of Louis the Pious (814–840)*, eds. Peter Godman and Roger Collins (Oxford, 1990), 605–628 and *Rabani Mauri in honorem sanctae crucis*, ed. Michel Perrin, Corpus Christianorum, Continuatio Mediaevalis C (Turnhout, 1997), plates A5 and B1. Belief in Christological kingship was also demonstrated in the Carolingian period by Smaragdus's *Via regia*, written as a *Speculum principis* for Louis the Pious.

[45] Ernst H. Kantorowicz, *Laudes regiae: A Study in Liturgical Acclamations and Mediaeval Ruler Worship*, University of California Publications in History XXXIII (Berkeley, 1946), 57, note 148.

[46] Kantorowicz, *Laudes regiae*, 47 and 57, and *Concilium Francofurtense* (794), MGH Leges Sectio III, Concilia II, Concilia Aevi Karolini I (Hanover, 1906), ed. Albert Werminghoff, 141.

in his *Cathemerinon*.[47] It was but a small step, after all, to elevate the ruler from 'priestly' to 'episcopal', in the eyes of Carolingian panegyricists and the redactors of Carolingian coronation ordines, who used these initiation ceremonies to parallel the bishop and the king.[48]

The Carolingians, however, had slipped from power in the region at least a century before the Saint-Vaast Bible was illustrated, and the Norman Anonymous may have written as much as seventy-five years later. Although the artists of the Capetian dynasty would later pick up the themes first expounded by the Saint-Vaast artists and perfect them into finely honed propaganda, they had not yet produced any identifiable art of moment when the Arras Bible was being copied and decorated.[49] The only eleventh-century manuscript that has been connected with French royal patronage is the Gaignières Evangeliary (Paris BnF MS lat. 1126), which was written and decorated at the abbey of Fleury by a visiting Lombard artist and has no figural illustrations.[50] The eleventh-century Saint-Vaast artists may have been familiar with the iconography that had been popular in Carolingian scriptoria, especially because their own Franco-Saxon manuscripts had been embellished with narrative imagery. Nonetheless, chronologically the closest sources were the manuscripts then being produced by Ottonian and Anglo-Saxon workshops.

As we have already seen, the artists of the Saint-Vaast scriptorium drew liberally on the many visual resources that must have been available to them from the Ottonian and Anglo-Saxon worlds when they constructed their own didactic language. The Solomon image is a pastiche of motifs taken from the art of the Carolingian, Anglo-Saxon, and Ottonian societies, each of which had a well-developed propaganda of kingship. The iconography of biblically-inspired

---

[47] *Cathemerinon* 9:5 (PL 59:862), glossed in 860 by the monk, Iso.

[48] See Angenendt, 100–121.

[49] Henry Mayr-Harting, *Ottonian Book Illumination: An Historical Study*, 2 vols. (1991) I, 47–55, posits that the explanation for the dearth of surviving early Capetian art lies in the fact that French artists in that period preferred metalwork, especially reliquaries, to manuscript art. Because of the inherent value of its materials, metalwork is much less likely to survive to the present day than manuscripts, which cannot so easily be converted to currency.

[50] Carl Nordenfalk, "Miniature ottonienne et ateliers capétiens," *Art de France* IV (1964), 49–54. Nordenfalk described Fleury as a 'royal' school where Robert the Pious imported a workman in order to propagate a new style. I think given that only two manuscripts survive from the school, and only one of these can be firmly labeled as royal, this may be an overstatement.

kingship became ever more explicit under the Ottonians.[51] Otto III and his successors moved away from the Carolingian's emphasis on Old Testament prototypes to concentrate on the likeness between the ruler and Christ, using some of the same motifs favored by the Saint-Vaast artists. The image of the enthroned Emperor Otto III elevated to the position of Christ in the Ottonian Aachen Gospels, Aachen Cathedral Treasury, fol. 16 (fig. 40), discussed above, made the Carolingian visual *topos* of Christ-like rule more specific by removing the intermediary of the Old Testament king. In this case, Otto III, surrounded by his mandorla and hovering evangelist symbols, stepped in for Christ in a *Maiestas Domini* composition that would have been immediately recognizable to the artistically literate elite.

Ottonian artists went one step further when they depicted his successor, Emperor Henry II, sharing a mandorla with Christ himself. In the Regensburg Sacramentary, Munich, Bayerische Staatsbibliothek, Clm 4456, fol. 11, Henry's 1002 coronation is shown overlapping the heavenly realm. Henry stands and receives the Holy Lance and sword from hovering angels, while his arms are supported by the bishop saints Udalric of Augsburg and Emmeram of Regensburg.[52] At the top of the composition, Christ in his mandorla reaches down to crown the king, gripping the arched Ottonian crown, while his mandorla hangs downward behind Henry, encompassing his head and shoulders. As O'Meara has pointed out, like in the Carolingian First Bible of Charles the Bald, Christ and Emperor Henry have been given the same facial features.[53]

Perhaps the most similar statement of beliefs about Christological kingship in an Ottonian artwork can be found in the Warmund Sacramentary, Ivrea Bibl. Capitolare MS LXXXVI. Created around 1000 for Bishop Warmund, a Lombard favored by Emperor Otto III, the miniature cycle in the sacramentary may have played a part of Warmund's attempt to shore up his own authority. Like Bishop Gerard of Cambrai, Warmund was an imperial appointee who lived

---

[51] On sacral kingship under the Ottonians, see Karl J. Leyser, *Rule and Conflict in an Early Medieval Society. Ottonian Saxony* (Bloomington, 1979), 75–107.

[52] Mayr-Harting, *Ottonian Book Illumination* I, 66, points out that the saints here perform the same actions as Aaron and Hur, who supported the arms of Moses while he prayed for the triumph of the Israelites over the Amalekites in battle. Thus the king is more subtly assimilated to Moses.

[53] O'Meara, 82, and Mayr-Harting, *Ottonian Book Illumination* I, 64.

on the borderland of the Empire and faced constant harassment from the local lord, in this case the margrave of Ivrea, Arduin, who later became the king of Italy.[54] Arduin, taking advantage of the emperor's preoccupation with battles elsewhere, attempted to gain hegemony in episcopal cities like Vercelli and Ivrea by attacking not only the churches, but also the serfs who served the bishops on the cathedrals' estates.[55] In 997 he assassinated Bishop Peter of Vercelli and burned his body in his church.[56] Although Bishop Warmund appealed to the pope and the emperor for help, Arduin was only excommunicated by Sylvester II at the Synod of Pavia in 999, and Ivrea's cathedral community was finally granted immunity by the emperor in July of 1000.[57] Pierre-Alain Mariaux points out, however, that Warmund was not simply an imperial lackey. Warmund did not follow the train of the emperor assiduously through the empire, but instead stayed for the most part in his own diocese, wrestling with its concerns. Like Gerard, in Warmund's case, in the words of Michel Parisse, "The close connection between episcopacy and royalty is a general, and not specifically imperial, phenomenon."[58] Left to fall back on his own resources, he may have directed the Warmund Sacramentary's image cycle in order to demonstrate that bishops, like kings, should be respected because of the grace that had been instilled at their consecration to office.

In a series of images depicting the sacraments included in the manuscript's text, the artists have constructed a careful parallel between Christ, the ruler, and the bishop.[59] The image of the coronation and consecration unction of the king, fol. 2 (fig. 41), departs from a strict visualization of the text, because an acolyte behind the king holds two *ampullae* of chrism, even though the king was anointed only once. Robert Deshman hypothesized that the artists visually

---

[54] Pierre-Alain Mariaux, *Warmund d'Ivrée et ses images: Politique et création iconographique autour de l'an mil*, Publications universitaires Européennes, Série XXVIII, Histoire de l'art CCCLXXXVIII (Bern, 2002).

[55] Mariaux, 31.

[56] Mariaux, 22.

[57] Mariaux, 35–36.

[58] Mariaux, 53, and Michel Parisse, "Princes laiques et/ou moines, les évêques du Xe siècle," in *Il secolo di ferro: mito e realtà del secolo X*, SSCISAM XXXVIII (Spoleto, 1991), I:501.

[59] Robert Deshman, "Otto III and the Warmund Sacramentary: A Study in Political Theology," *Zeitschrift für Kunstgeschichte* XXXIV (1971), 1–20.

assimilated the king's unction to that of Christ at his Baptism, fol. 27, and Constantine at his baptism, fol. 23v, through the appearance in all three images of the motif of the double *ampullae*. This implication of a double anointing, which did not, in fact, take place, expressed a political theology current among the Ottonian ecclesiastical and secular hierarchy that kings held both royal and priestly powers.[60] Furthermore, the miniature of the king's coronation may have been invented specifically to match compositionally that of the consecration of the bishop, the next image in the book (fol. 8), implying a similarity between both offices.[61] Both miniatures, alone of the sixty-two illuminations in the manuscript, lack frames and *tituli*, and both have been highlighted with gold.[62]

Unlike the ruler portraits in the Sacramentary of Henry II or the Aachen Gospels of Otto III, which share iconographic motifs with the Saint-Vaast Bible's Jeremiah and Wisdom images, the illustrative scheme in the Warmund Sacramentary uses an entirely different pictorial language. Nonetheless, the artists have attempted to transmit the same theme, for the same reason: Christ, the king, and the bishop shared innate characteristics that in themselves served as a justification of their authority. The Saint-Vaast Bible's artists created a similar parallel between the king and the bishop for the same end, but using different tools and motifs.

A comparison with the near contemporary Life of Saint Amand (Valenciennes BM MS 502) from Saint-Amand-les-Eaux, also from Flanders, demonstrates that when confronted with a different historical dynamic, artists could choose to depict bishops and kings very differently. Barbara Abou-el-Haj has argued that the miniature cycle of this Saint's *vita*, executed in the late-eleventh or early-twelfth century, was designed to broadcast the local episcopacy's allegiance with the papacy in the long-running Investiture Controversy.[63] In this case, the artists managed to imply through a subtle arrangement of architectural elements and figures that, first, the saintly bishop had been

---

[60] Deshman, "Otto III and the Warmund Sacramentary," 11.

[61] Roger E. Reynolds, "Image and Text: The Liturgy of Clerical Ordination in Early Medieval Art," *Gesta* XXII (1983), 30–31, expands this interpretation, suggesting that the scene may depict the consecration of the "summum pontificem," the pope.

[62] Mariaux, 74.

[63] Barbara Abou-el-Haj, "Consecration and Investiture in the Life of Saint Amand, Valenciennes BM MS 502," *Art Bulletin* LXI (1979), 342–358.

wrongly compelled towards consecration by the king (fol. 11r) and
then that St. Amand had argued against the king's attempt to invest
him with the insignia of office (fol. 22r).[64] In the first miniature, the
artists relegated the saint, in the process of being consecrated at the
order of the king, to a position underneath a column, as if to deface
the objectionable action. In the second miniature, the saint stands
under a dome-like arch, as if in a church rather than the palace,
and seems to reject the insignia proffered by the king. Pope Gregory
VII had banned lay investiture in 1078, and the abbey of Saint-
Amand had become enmeshed in an investiture debate from the
death in 1092 of the bishop of the neighboring diocese, Gerard II
of Cambrai, until the dispute was finally settled around 1105 with
the installation of Bishop Odo.[65] The monks of Saint-Amand-les-
Eaux, whose possessions were rendered particularly vulnerable by
this prolonged dispute between the local Counts of Flanders, the
Ottonian Emperors, and the Pope, were as interested in the relationship between the bishops in their neighborhood and secular rulers
as the monks of nearby Saint-Vaast had been fifty to seventy-five
years earlier when the Saint-Vaast Bible was painted. In this case
as well, their viewpoint was shaped by the local contemporary concerns, but because of this they argued against the mutually dependent and ritually enacted relationship between bishops and kings that
the Saint-Vaast artists appeared to favor.

The Saint-Vaast Bible artists were manifestly familiar with Ottonian
iconography. In Arras BM MS 732 (684) (fig. 36), copied in the
early-eleventh-century and illustrated by Master A, who contributed
the Esther illumination to the Bible, Mary's Assumption is depicted
using a motif borrowed directly from Ottonian art. As she floats
heavenwards within an atmosphere of billowing clouds, angels hover
beside and above her, and the hand of God descends from above.
A mandorla overlaps both the frame at the top and the head and
shoulders of the Virgin, echoing almost exactly the arrangement of
the nearly contemporary Sacramentary of Henry II's coronation
image. However, the Saint-Vaast artists generally did not subscribe
to the purely Christological iconography of Ottonian monuments.
The case of the Saint-Vaast Bible's Wisdom miniature is emblem-

---

[64] Abou-el-Haj, 342–350.
[65] Abou-el-Haj, 352–355.

atic of their approach (pl. VI). The Ezra Master borrowed a motif popular in contemporary Ottonian workshops, in this case the full-body mandorla that frames the king, and applied it to the Old Testament prototype inspired by the Carolingian tradition, making him an intermediary for the king's Christ-like attributes. The Saint-Vaast artist thus created a synthesis of Carolingian and Ottonian artistic ideas, but didn't favor the dynastic art of either group.

The idea of Christ-centered ecclesiastical and secular rulership was also current in Anglo-Saxon England, and was expressed in manuscript illuminations.[66] The composition of a ruler portrait found in the New Minster charter illustrated at Winchester, London BL MS Cotton Vespasian A.VIII, fol. 2b, shows King Edgar in the act of offering the New Minster charter itself to Christ, who is enthroned above in a mandorla carried by angels. The ruler below is flanked by Mary and Peter in imitation of a *Deesis* composition, perhaps intended to assimilate Edgar to Christ in a manner quite reminiscent of the ruler image in the Aachen Gospels.[67] In addition, King Edgar and the bishops pictured with him in the Christ Church Canterbury *Regularis Concordia*, Bishop Aethelwold of Winchester and Archbishop Dunstan of Canterbury, jointly rule the worldly and spiritual kingdoms because both the offices of king and bishop derive from Christ, their model.[68]

The artists gave the Christ-like king in the Saint-Vaast Bible priestly insignia that had first been combined with royal elements in Anglo-Saxon manuscripts. The *infulae* that spring from behind Solomon's Anglo-Saxon style crown echo those seen in the English images of Saint Benedict in the Eadui Psalter and the *Regularis Condordia*, where Benedict had gained the royal diadem that so frequently crowned Christ in Anglo-Saxon monuments. The English diademed or crowned Christ expressed that country's belief in Christological kingship much like the Ottonian ruler portraits with mandorlas. The Saint-Vaast artist has used this potent iconographic combination to make references to both traditions.

---

[66] Deshman, "*Benedictus Monarcha et Monachus*," 228–231 and idem, *The Benedictional of Aethelwold*, 210.

[67] Deshman, "*Benedictus Monarcha et Monachus*," 224.

[68] London BL MS Cotton Tiberius A.III, fol. 2v, from around the mid-eleventh century, may copy an earlier model. Deshman, "*Benedictus Monarcha et Monachus*," 210.

Unlike the images in the Anglo-Saxon *Regularis Concordia* manuscript, or in the Ottonian Aachen Gospels (fig. 40) or Sacramentary
of Henry II, in the Arras Bible particular rulers and bishops are not
represented. Instead, the illuminator applied Christological attributes
and office-specific regalia to Old Testament figures who could stand
as ciphers for unnamed leaders, in keeping with the Augustinian
political philosophy espoused by Gerard of Cambrai.

The Cologne Pontifical and Christ-like Kingship

The Saint-Vaast Bible was not the only document created in eleventh-
century Arras that expressed these values. A coronation ordo written in the Cologne Pontifical, Erzbischöfliche Diözesan Dombibliothek,
Dom MS 141 fols. 153–165v, a manuscript copied and illustrated
in Arras in the second half of the eleventh century, synthesizes all
of these ideas in liturgical form.[69] The manuscript actually contains
not one, but three separate ordines for royal and imperial consecrations: an *ordo ad consecrandum regem*, fols. 153–165v, an *ordo ad benedicendam reginam*, fols. 168v–171v, both of which have been recently
edited and published by Richard A. Jackson as Ordo XVI,[70] and
separating these two ordines an *ordo Romanus ad benedicendum impera-
tore*, edited by Reinhard Elze in 1960 as Ordo IX.[71] The king's coronation ordo, especially, draws together the themes of the Old Testament
prototypes for kingship, the similarity between the king and the
bishop, and the Christological nature of the king, to parallel the
many details expressed visually in the Solomon illustration. Drawing
on the Carolingian tradition of coronation ordines and paralleling
the Anglo-Saxon and imperial ordines then in use, the Royal Ordo
was devised to address the needs of an elite which saw the rights of
its king threatened.

Percy Schramm and Jackson agree that the Cologne manuscript's
Royal Ordo was never used in Capetian France, where the text was
redacted. Jackson points out, however, that because it was compiled

---

[69] See above, chapter two.
[70] Jackson, I, 201–216.
[71] *Ordines coronationis imperialis: Die Ordines für die Weihe und Krönung des Kaisers und
der Kaiserin*, MGH Fontes iuris Germanici antiqui in usum scholarum separatim editi
IX (Hanover, 1960), 20–22.

in the joint diocese of Arras-Cambrai, which straddled the border of the Empire and France, this seemingly uninfluential ordo is quite important.[72] At the same time, he seems not to have been aware that Sigrid Schulten localized the manuscript to the scriptorium of Saint-Vaast itself in her study of Saint-Vaast manuscripts.[73] Because the Cologne Pontifical was copied at Saint-Vaast the Royal Ordo is an invaluable piece of evidence for the way in which kingship was regarded during the episcopate of Gerard of Cambrai, since the manuscript was probably produced immediately after his reign under the direction of his student, nephew and successor, Lietbertus of Lessines.[74] Gerard had been educated under the tutelage of Adalbero of Reims, who seems to have appreciated the powerful messages that could be transmitted through royal rituals to both participants and witnesses, and who mastered the art of royal propaganda. Adalbero had already brought political ritual to the forefront of church practice in his archdiocese by the end of the tenth century.[75] Adalbero's emphasis on rituals, including coronations, may have rubbed off on Gerard and his associates. The Cologne ordo is replete with typological imagery that justifies the king's right to rule through his similarity to Old and New Testament prototypes, the same language used by Gerard to explain the authority of the bishop in his *Acta synodi*. In addition, as the ordo was compiled from two preexisting ordines of the late Carolingian era, once again the Saint-Vaast scriptorium underlined its allegiance to the same older ideals of kingship that were being reworked by the Anglo-Saxons and Ottonians in both texts and images.[76]

The Royal Ordo, as laid out in Cologne MS 141, fols. 153–165v, not surprisingly prescribes the same chain of events seen in most ordines since the Carolingian period. From the first sentence, the ordo makes clear that while the king is nominally elevated by the 'clergy and people' of the realm, the bishops are the sole instruments

---

[72] Percy Ernst Schramm "Ordines-Studien II. Die Krönung bei den Westfranken und des Franzosen," *Archiv für Urkundenforschung* XV (1938), 23–24 and Jackson, 29.

[73] See above, chapter two.

[74] *Gesta episcoporum Cameracensium: Continuato—Gesta Lietberti episcopi*, PL 149:177–192.

[75] Geoffrey Koziol, *Begging Pardon and Favor. Ritual and Political Order in Early Medieval France* (Ithaca, 1992), 113–121.

[76] Jackson, 202–203. The Royal Ordo is a compilation from the Romano-Germanic Pontifical of Mainz and the Ratold Ordo, which may have originated in the Archdiocese of Reims.

of the change. At the same time, any witnesses familiar with the ceremony for the consecration of a bishop would have recognized that the redactors of the ordo were determined to call the office of bishop to mind when creating the king. The ceremony began in the palace throne room, where two bishops prayed over the king before leading him in a solemn procession from the palace to the door of the church. The king and his bearers were preceded by the Gospels, incense and a crucifer, while responsories and antiphons were sung, all mirroring the entrance of a celebrant during the mass. After a second prayer, the two bishops led him to the choir where the metropolitan awaited him, as a candidate for bishop would have been led from the sacristy by two bishops to confront the waiting metropolitan according to the *ordo qualiter ordinetur episcopus* in the same manuscript.[77]

While his regalia lay before the altar, the candidate for royal consecration was examined, and pledged his willingness to defend the Church and its bishops. The parallels between this examination and the one used during the ceremony to consecrate a bishop would not have been lost on anyone who had witnessed both, especially when the king prostrated himself before the altar while the litany was sung, like a bishop-elect.[78] Then, two bishops led a series of prayers that asked for wisdom for the king, one of the virtues that he was supposedly granted through his anointing, and the peace and prosperity that should logically follow. The metropolitan led a prayer of consecration, affirming towards the beginning with the phrase "whom we have chosen for the kingship," the clergy's ultimate power to select, install and depose a king. This prayer listed the Old Testament prototypes of the contemporary king, and asked for the cooperation of the Lord in making his reign equally well guided.

> . . . you who made your faithful servant Abraham triumph over enemies, who bestowed great victory to Moses and Joshua displayed before your people, who lifted up your humble boy David to the summit of the kingdom, and freed him from the mouth of the lion and the hand

---

[77] Cologne, Erzbischöfliche Diözesan Dombibliothek, Dom MS 141, fol. 123v. O'Meara, 79–80, on these parallels.

[78] Jackson, 205, nos. 13 and 14. *Promitto vobis, sanctissimi patres, et perdono, quia unicuique de vobis et ecclesiis vobis commissis canonicum privilegium et debitam legem atque iustitiam servabo et defensionem quantum potuero, adiuvante Domino, exhibebo, sicut rex in suo regno unicuique episcopo et ecclesiae sibi commissae per rectum exhibere debet,* and Kantorowicz, *Laudes regiae,* 91, on royal prostration.

of the beast and Goliath but also from the spiteful sword of Saul and from all his enemies, and who deigned to reward Solomon with the ineffable gift of peace and wisdom, consider favorably the prayers of our humility and upon this your servant, whom we have chosen for the kingship in suppliant devotion, give greatly of your blessings, and surround him always with the right hand of your power, just like the aforesaid Abraham strengthened in faith, Moses supported in gentleness, Joshua defended with strength, David exalted in humility, distinguished with the wisdom of Solomon, . . .[79]

Moses, Joshua, David, and Solomon, the very kings and prophets who are pictured in the Saint-Vaast Bible's pictorial program, were listed repeatedly as leaders chosen by God and filled with virtues who were to serve as models for the king then being consecrated.

Already primed to envision the ceremony in terms of its Old Testament heritage, the witnesses were pulled into this biblical context even further with the king's anointing, when the clerics were instructed to sing the antiphon that had first been introduced into the Leofric Missal's coronation ordo, "Zadok the priest and Nathan the prophet anointed Solomon king in Gihon, and those approaching rejoiced and said: may the king live in eternity."[80] The consecration prayer then continued:

> Whence you anointed priests, kings and prophets and martyrs, who conquered kingdoms through faith and were occupied with justice and attained promises. Let this most holy unction flow over his head and descend into his interior and penetrate the inmost of this heart, and with the promises that the most victorious kings attained, let him be made worthy of your grace, and just as also in the present time he may reign happily, let him succeed to the society of them in the reign of heaven, through our Lord your son Jesus Christ, who was anointed with the oil of joy before his colleagues . . .[81]

---

[79] Jackson, 206–207. . . . *qui Abraham fidelem famulum tuum de hostibus triumphare fecisti, Moysi et Iosue tuo populo praelatis multiplicem victoriam tribuisti, humilem quoque puerum tuum David regni fastigio sublimasti, eumque de ore leonis et de manu bestiae atque Goliae sed et de gladio maligno Saul et omnium inimicorum eius liberasti, et Salemonem sapientiae pacisque ineffabili munere ditasti, respice propitius ad preces nostrae humilitatis, et super hunc famulum tuum, quem supplici devotione in regnum pariter eligimus, benedictionum tuarum dona multiplica, eumque dextera tuae potentiae semper ubique circumda, quatinus praedicti Abrahae fidelitate firmatus, Moysi mansuetudine fretus, Iosue fortitudine munitus, David humilitate exaltatus, sapientia Salomonis decoratus . . .*

[80] Jackson, 207. *Unxerunt Salomonem Sadoch sacerdos et Nathan propheta regem in Gion, et accedentes laeti dixerunt, "Vivat rex in aeternum."*

[81] Jackson, 207. *Unde unxisti sacerdotes, reges et prophetas ac martyres, qui per fidem vicerunt*

Thus as the oil allowed the infusion of the Holy Spirit into the anointed, the archbishop's prayer connected the anointing of Old Testament kings, priests and prophets to the baptismal anointing of Christ, the King of heaven and the celestial prototype for the new ruler.[82] The prayer after the unction continued in the same vein, picking out in particular the Old Testament leaders of the Israelites as prototypes for the contemporary ruler. "You ordained your servant Aaron as priest through the unction of oil, and afterwards, through infusion of this unguent you made priests, kings and prophets to rule your people Israel, and the appearance of the Church you predicted in oil rejoicing through the prophetic voice of your servant David . . ."[83] A second prayer added yet another comparison to Christ. "God, son of God Jesus Christ our Lord, who was anointed with the oil of exaltation by his father before his colleagues, let him pour the same blessing, by means of the immediate infusion of the

---

regna et operati sunt iustitiam atque adepti sunt promissiones. Cuius sacratissima unctio super caput eius defluat atque ad interiora descendat et cordis illius intima penitret, et promissionibus quas adepti sunt victoriosissimi reges, gratia tua dignus efficiatur, quatinus et in praesenti seculo feliciter regnet et ad eorum consortium in caelesti regno perveniat, per dominum nostrum Iesum Christum filium tuum, qui unctus est oleo laetitiae prae consortibus suis . . .

[82] Interestingly, the ordo for imperial blessing in the same manuscript does not make some of the same parallels. According to the text of the ordo published by Elze, 22, section 8, anointment does not take place on the head, but rather on the wrists and between the shoulders: *Hic ungat ei de oleo sancto compagem brachii dextri et inter scapulas.* The prayer before consecration does include references to the Old Testament predecessors of the emperor, Elze, 21, section 4: *Deus inenarrabilis auctor mundi, conditor generis humani, gubernator imperii, confirmator regni, qui ex utero fidelis amici tui patriarchae nostri Abrahae praeelegisti reges saeculi profuturos . . . Visita eum sicut Moysen in rubo, Iesu Nave in proelio, Gedeon in agro, Samuelem in templo, at illa eum benedictione siderea ac sapientiae tuae rore perfunde, quam beatus David in psalterio, Salomon filius eius te remunerante percepit e caelo . . .* Also, the prayer after unction makes reference to priests, kings and prophets, as in the Royal Ordo. Yet no mention is made of the baptismal anointing of Christ, therefore, no Christological typology is constructed. Michel Andrieu does note, however, *Les ordines romani*, IV, 477, that the words for consecration directly preceding anointment are borrowed from the traditional rite for the consecration of a bishop. Kantorowicz, *Laudes regiae*, 142, notes that as the eleventh century progressed, the pope assumed many of the prerogatives that had once been shared with the emperor, leading to the lessening of the stature of the emperor's anointing, so that it was carried out with unblessed oil and on the arms and shoulders rather than the head, to symbolize that the emperor was the protector of the highest leader, the pope.

[83] Jackson, 208. . . . *Aaron famulum tuum per unctionem olei sacerdotem sanxisti, et postea per huius unguenti infusionem ad regendum populum tuum Israheliticum sacerdotes, reges ac prophetas perfecisti, vultumque ecclesiae in oleo exhilarandum per propheticam famuli tui vocem David esse praedixisti . . .*

holy unguent of the paraclytic spirit, upon your head and cause it
to penetrate into the interior of your heart."[84]

By now, the witnesses to the ceremony would have been thoroughly aware of the expectation that the king's ritual anointing
allowed a fundamental change to occur. The Holy Spirit appeared
and was infused into his head and heart though the agency of the
oil applied by the spiritual authority, the archbishop, and thus the
king was filled with a series of virtues that entitled him to rule. That
accomplished, the ceremony could then continue with the invest-
ment of the king with the royal regalia, his visible symbols of rank,
the ring, sword, crown, scepter and staff, each of which was accompanied by a prayer for the Christian qualities of rulership, and the
continued protection of the Church. Repeated references are made
to priestly consecration and the parallel duties of the king. For
instance, at the bestowal of the ring, the metropolitan intoned,
"because today you are ordained head and prince of the realm and
the people, you will persevere as supporter and establisher of
Christianity and the Christian faith . . ." When the bishops and archbishop crowned him, they explained, "do not misunderstand, through
this you are a partner in our ministry, so that just as we are understood to be shepherds and rulers in innermost things, so you [are
seen as] God's true nurturer in outer things and vigorous defender
of the Church of Christ against all misfortunes and of the realm
given to you by God and [committed] to you through the office of
our benediction . . ."[85] The prayer over the conferring of the sword
included a justification for the participation of bishops. "Accept this
sword through the hands of the bishops, although unworthy, [they
are] however also consecrated by the authority of the holy Apostles,
[it is] imposed upon you magnificently in the office of our benediction,
divinely ordained in defense of the holy Church of God . . ."[86]

---

[84] Jackson, 208. *Deus, Dei filius, Iesus Christus dominus noster, qui a Patre oleo exultationis unctus est prae participibus suis, ipse per praesentem sacri unguinis infusionem Spiritus par-
acliti super caput tuum infundat benedictionem eandemque usque ad interiora cordis tui penitrare
faciat . . .*

[85] Jackson, 209. *. . . et per hanc te participem ministerii nostri non ignores, ita ut, sicut nos
in interioribus pastores rectorsque animarum intelligimur, tu [appareas] quoque in exterioribus verus
Dei cultor strenuusque contra omnes adversitates ecclesiae Christi defensor regnique a Deo tibi dati
et [commissi] per officium nostrae benedictionis. . . . . .*

[86] Jackson, 209. *Accipe gladium per manus episcoporum, licet indignas, vice tamen et auctoritate sanctorum apostolorum consecratas, tibi regaliter impositum nostraeque benedictionis officio,
in defensionem sanctae Dei ecclesiae divinitatus ordinatum . . .*

After the royal regalia were conferred, the king was blessed, and a series of ten petitions were made. The king was then led to the throne just as a newly consecrated bishop would be led to his cathedra.[87] Finally, after a kiss of peace, the mass was said, with the king participating as the bearer of the bread and wine in the offertory.[88]

Because those who drafted the Cologne Pontifical's Royal Ordo and the artist of the Saint-Vaast Bible's Solomon portrait (pl. VI) all labored in the same workshop, it is hardly surprising that they used the same vocabulary to express the ideals of contemporary kingship in words and images. All of the themes hinted at using pictorial details in the Wisdom miniature are echoed in the text of the ordo's prayers. Wisdom itself is mentioned no less than four times, and Solomon's wisdom twice, in the course of the consecration ceremony, meaning that the biblical book of Wisdom was an ideal location for the Saint-Vaast Bible's visual explanation of the king's virtues. The choice of Solomon as the representative of an ideal king is most appropriate given that in the prayer before the consecration the contemporary king's right to rule was justified by his similarity to his Old Testament predecessors, Abraham, Moses, Joshua, David and Solomon, the king's unction is paralleled to Solomon's unction, and at the end of the ceremony God is asked to grant the new king a reign as peaceful as Solomon's.[89] According to the Cologne Pontifical, God granted the new king the same virtues and blessings that are ascribed to these prototypical rulers, making him the same kind of divinely recognized king.

In the Saint-Vaast Bible, Solomon does not merely represent the virtues of Old Testament kingship as favored by the Carolingians and modeled in their manuscripts, however (pl. VI). The artist framed him in Christ's mandorla, making him the prototype for contemporary eleventh-century kings using the same tools popular in Anglo-Saxon and Ottonian art. The ordo amplifies the same biblical typology by suggesting the similarity of royal unction to that received by Christ at his Baptism. These parallels between both Old and New Testament recipients of unction were repeated and elaborated in the prayers

---

[87] Cologne, Erzbishöfliche Diözesan Dombibliothek, Dom MS 141, fol. 132.

[88] Jackson, 214. A note at the end of the ordo explains *In hac missa offerat rex ad manus archiepiscopi panem et vinum et, completa missa, communicetur, et sic agat Deo gratias.*

[89] Jackson, 212. *Da ei, Domine Iesu, in tuo spiramine cum mansuetudine ita regere populum, sicut Salomonem fecisti regnum optinere pacificum.*

after consecration, when Aaron and the religious and secular leaders of Israel were mentioned again, and God was asked to infuse the king with the Holy Spirit through unction just as he did to Christ during Christ's baptismal unction.

Any of the eleventh-century residents of or visitors to Saint-Vaast who had paged through the Saint-Vaast Bible would have encountered another mandorla around the prophet Jeremiah (pl. IV), who was dressed as a bishop, and pondered the connection between the priestly prophet and the Christ-like king. Solomon's priestly and royal *infulae* served to underline the overlap in the roles played by these two Old Testament figures in the Saint-Vaast Bible's program, just as observers of the king's consecration by the archbishop, many of whom were most likely intimately familiar with liturgical language, may have recognized borrowings from the ceremony for consecrating a bishop. The examination of the candidate set out the relationship between the royal office and the Church by making one of the king's principal duties the defense of the Church and its clergy, while at the same time this series of demands directly paralleled those asked of a candidate for episcopacy, thus comparing the king's office to that of the bishop. The archbishop and bishops reminded the king that he became a partner in Christian ministry with specific duties. Finally, the bishops explained that God gave the kingdom to the king using the agency of the bishops, who participated in the ceremony because their office was instituted by the Apostles.

This ordo and others like it were clearly written by bishops and their assistants, for in many cases their language seems to glorify the presiding archbishops and bishops as much as it does the king. The bishops, vested in elaborate robes like the king's and repeatedly intoning comparisons between themselves and the king, used the ceremony to remind the witnesses that they retained the right to choose, consecrate and direct the ruler. The same clerics probably played some role in the design of the Saint-Vaast Bible's program, where the responsibilities of the king and the bishop find their justification in visual terms.

This biblical typology of royal consecration was obviously not invented by the composer of the Royal Ordo in Cologne MS 141, who compiled the *ordo ad consecrandum regem* from at least two other older ordines that were available in Flanders: the English-influenced late-tenth-century Ratold Ordo, and the Romano-Germanic Mainz

Ordo of ca. 950.[90] Already in the Carolingian period, anointing may
have implied parallels between Old Testament and Carolingian kings
and contemporary and Levite priests.[91] Similarities between royal and
episcopal consecration, with their references to the Christological
nature of both offices, were also not innovations of eleventh-century
Flanders. The anointing of Charles the Bald on the head in 848,
Janet Nelson speculates, may have been inspired by the increasing
popularity of anointing bishops on the head in that period. This was
when the coronation oath demanding that the king support the people and their Church, an oath based on that made by candidates
for the office of bishop before their anointing, was also introduced.[92]
At the same time, Frankish bishops took over from the pope in consecrating kings to rule, and therefore gained spiritual jurisdiction over
this office.[93] The tradition of royal unction and the biblical typology
it implied, along with the prominent role of bishops, was therefore
well established as part of the inaugural ceremony of a monarch in
France by they end of the tenth century. At this point, the Capetian
dynasty succeeded the Carolingian, beginning with the consecration
of Hugh Capet by Archbishop Adalbero of Reims in 987 and Hugh's

---

[90] Jackson, 29 and 201. Although its earliest origins are contested, it is clear that
by the era of the Carolingians, anointing was an accepted part of royal ceremonial in Frankish lands. Competing theories for the Carolingian practice of anointing kings ascribe the origins to Ireland, Visigothic Spain, or simply the contemporary
anointment during baptism. For a summary of this debate, see Angenendt, 100–118.
Also, more recently, Michael J. Enright, *Iona, Tara and Soissons: The Origin of the Royal
Anointing Ritual* (Berlin, 1985), and Robert-Henri Bautier, "Sacres et couronnements
sous les Carolingiens et les premiers Capétiens: Recherches sur la genèse du sacre
royal français," *Annuaire-bulletin de la Société de l'histoire de France*, 1987 (1989), 10–11.
Pippin the Short was anointed at least twice, first in 751 and again in 754, and
Charles the Bald was anointed in 848. See Bautier, "Sacres et couronnements,"
8–9, 11–13 and 34, for documentary evidence for the anointings of Pippin and
Charles the Bald. Janet L. Nelson believes that regular anointing of Anglo-Saxon
kings probably began as early as 787, and was a part of the ceremonial inauguration in all the main kingdoms by the mid-tenth century. See "Inauguration rituals," in *Early Medieval Kingship*, ed. P. H. Sawyer and Ian N. Wood (Leeds, 1977),
52–54.
[91] Nelson "Inauguration rituals," 58.
[92] On ninth-century episcopal anointings, see also *Les ordines romani* IV, 40–43.
Nelson, "Inauguration rituals," 61–62, and idem, "Kingship, law and liturgy,"
258–260, and above, note 1. On the implications of the oath and of the media-
tion of bishops, see idem, "National Synods, Kingship as Office, and Royal Anointing,"
in *Studies in Church History* VII (1971), 41–59, reprinted in *Politics and Ritual in Early
Medieval Europe* (London, 1986), 239–258, and above, note 2.
[93] Nelson "Kingship, law and liturgy," 245–250.

association of his son, Robert II, to the throne through unction in Orléans later that year.[94] These coronation rituals must have been reviewed and revised in the face of the demands of a new dynasty, and yet these themes remained unchanged.

Christological Kingship in Eleventh-Century Flanders

Why would the concept of Christocentric kingship, so firmly established under the Carolingians, Ottonians, and Anglo-Saxons, have appealed to Gerard of Cambrai, who didn't live directly under the sway of any of these dynasties? The ideals expressed in the Royal Ordo of the Cologne Pontifical and the Saint-Vaast Bible's pictorial program are all the more striking given that Arras lay at the periphery of Capetian France, where the dynasty had not yet created its own Christological propaganda, and in the County of Flanders, which was dominated by a feudal noble rather than a king. The nearby Count of Flanders was most likely responsible for the assaults perpetrated on Gerard and his Cambrai cathedral properties by Walter of Lens, the Castellan of Cambrai.[95] Gerard, pulled between the distant Ottonian and Salian emperors and the weak Capetian king, witnessed first hand the dangers of existing in a royal no man's land where no powerful divinely appointed ruler protected him from being buffeted by the assaults of lesser nobles. Faced with this threat to the traditional hegemony of both the bishop and the king, Gerard clung fiercely to the ideology he had learned at Reims, under his uncle, Archbishop Adalbero. Bishops and kings were, according to his beliefs, natural allies in the battle to protect the Christians who were their charges. Both had been consecrated through a ceremony that elevated them to a Christ-like status that made their authority unquestionable, even in the face of material powerlessness.

Gerard's perception that royal power had been weakened and needed to be reinforced emerges from the recounting of the royal conference at Ivois in the *Gesta episcoporum Cameracensium*.[96] The bishops of Soissons and Beauvais suggested the Peace of God as a possible

---

[94] Bautier, "Sacres et couronnements," 52.
[95] See above, chapter 3.
[96] See above, chapter 3.

remedy for the disorder plaguing a region where the king was too powerless to prevent war and plunder among his own subjects. When Gerard protested against the Peace of God and its infringement on royal authority and the prerogatives of the royal office, he attributed the bishops' initiative to the *inbecillitate regis peccantis quidem exigentibus statum regni funditus inclinari, jura confundi, usumque patrium et omne genus justitiae profanari*.[97] These two French bishops were, in Gerard's mind, taking advantage of a momentary powerlessness on the part of the ruler in order to abrogate his traditional rights, a short-sighted tactic that would ultimately disempower the bishops with whom the kings shared their *ministerium*.

Gerard shared these fears with his cousin and fellow bishop, Adalbero of Laon. George Duby likened Gerard's textual defense of the offices of bishop and king to that of his cousin, Bishop Adalbero of Laon.[98] Adalbero, an advisor to King Robert the Pious, composed an elaborate and esoteric poem, the *Carmen ad Rotbertum regem*, between 1027 and 1031.[99] Adalbero of Laon did not blame French bishops for undermining the king, however. Rather than criticizing the Peace of God movement, like his cousin Gerard, Adalbero attacked the leaders of Cluniac monasticism as lay people greedy for power, who desired to displace the bishops as advisors of the king and would ultimately lead to his downfall.[100]

The Cluniac policy of advocating the exemption of their monasteries from the jurisdiction of the local bishop should not have immediately lessened the authority of the king.[101] Also, it does not appear that the Cluniac reform made any significant inroads into monasteries in either the diocese of Gerard of Cambrai or of Adalbero of Laon under their respective episcopates. Both bishops, however, no

---

[97] PL 149:157.

[98] Georges Duby, *The Three Orders: Feudal Society Imagined*, trans. Arthur Goldhammer (Chicago, 1980), 44–55 and 139–144. On Adalbero of Laon, see Robert T. Coolidge, "Adalbero, Bishop of Laon," in *Studies in Medieval and Renaissance History* II (1965), 1–114, especially chapter 5, "Adalbero and Robert the Pious, 1000–1031," 66–93, where Coolidge assesses Adalbero's interaction with the Cluniacs.

[99] Adalbéron de Laon, *Poème au roi Robert*, ed. Claude Carozzi, Les classiques de l'histoire de France au moyen âge XXXII (Paris, 1979). Carozzi proposes that the poem was begun after the consecration of Henry, son of Robert, in 1027, and was left unfinished at Adalbero's death before the middle of 1031 (Carozzi, cxvi–cxvii).

[100] Coolidge, 73.

[101] See above, chapter two.

doubt felt threatened by the philosophy behind this movement, and it certainly could have been one of the reasons that Gerard backed Richard of Saint-Vanne's reform so strongly. More relevant to the present discussion is the increasingly important role in advising King Robert played by Odilo of Cluny, who was present along with Adalbero of Laon at the consecration of Robert's son Henry to the throne in 1027.[102] Odilo, an abbot rather than a bishop, who had not been consecrated to office, did not share with the king those qualities that could only be delivered through unction.

Adalbero described the king's attributes, or better, qualifications for rule, in his *Carmen*. He used two terms to describe the two natures of a good ruler: *imago iuventutis*, which is the powerful, proactive, and warlike aspect of the ruler to which the first part of the poem was addressed, and *sapientia*, the gift of God which makes him govern wisely, the aspect which Adalbero addressed in the second part of the poem.[103] Adalbero outlined the heavenly origin of this wisdom, saying:

> *Munera concessit Pius omnibus his meliora*
> *Dans intellectum quae sit sapientia vera,*
> *Per quem scire potes quae sunt caelestia semper.*[104]

Adalbero therefore reinforced in his poem the characteristic of king-ship which we have already encountered in the Royal Ordo of the Cologne Pontifical, where *sapientia* is mentioned four times, and twice as one of the kingly attributes of Solomon, given by God.[105]

Gerard of Cambrai's connection to King Robert the Pious is more tenuous than Adalbero of Laon's. Nonetheless, the Saint-Vaast Bible's pictorial program reveals that Gerard and his colleagues in Arras were equally preoccupied with this royal virtue. Although it must have been very challenging to find the means to represent the trans-mission of such an immaterial quality, no less than three times in the Saint-Vaast Bible Old Testament kings are shown receiving wis-dom. The first of these images also hints that Gerard and his col-leagues had more than a passing familiarity with royal inheritance practices used by the Ottonians and Capetians.

---

[102] Coolidge, 78 and Carozzi, cxvi.
[103] Carozzi, cxxvi–cxxx and Duby, 1978, 45–47.
[104] *Carmen*, v. 190–192 in Carozzi, 14–15.
[105] Jackson, 206–207. . . . *et Salemonem sapientiae pacisque ineffabili munere ditasti . . . sapientia Salomonis decoratus.*

III Kings

The Ezra Master was also responsible for the two-tiered miniature prefacing the third Book of Kings, vol. III, fol. 128v (pl. II), where two Old Testament kings are depicted receiving the quality of divine wisdom. The artist has borrowed a visual formula used since classical times to indicate dreams or visions, the figure reclining in bed, for in the III Kings miniature, both registers are dominated by enormous, lion-footed beds holding, above, King David, and below, King Solomon. The Carolingians had already revived this artistic trope and applied it to Biblical kings. Two ninth-century manuscripts, the Stuttgart Psalter, Württembergische Landesbibliothek, Cod. bibl. 23, and the Utrecht Psalter, Bibliotheek der Rijksuniversiteit, Utrecht, cod. 32, are filled with images of King David, the reputed author of the Psalms, lying in bed while sleeping, addressing Christ or being protected by him.[106] The artist used this motif in the Saint-Vaast Bible's image to prime the viewer to seek something revelatory in the events depicted, because biblical dreams were so often the vehicles for communication with the divine. As it happens, however, only one of these two vignettes depicts a dream.

Helpful *tituli* above both images identify the characters in each scene. In the top register, the *titulus* explains "Here David is warmed by the young girl and Solomon [stands] before him whom he admonishes to be strengthened in the commandments and ways of the Lord."[107] This scene represents two moments. One is taken from the first chapter of III Kings, where David's advisors, realizing that their elderly king was no longer able to warm himself, brought him a Shunammite maiden, Abishag, who could warm him.[108] The presence of Solomon, his son and successor, who holds a foliate scepter of office and is accompanied by a sword bearer, was inspired by a later moment in the next chapter, where David called to his son after Solomon had been anointed as his heir, and admonished that he be strengthened in the commandments of God.[109]

---

[106] Paul E. Dutton, *The Politics of Dreaming in the Carolingian Empire* (Lincoln, NE, 1994), 17–19.

[107] *Hic David calefit ab adolescentula et salomon ante eum que monet ut confortetur in mandatis et in. . . . viis domini.*

[108] III Kings 1:1–4.

[109] III Kings 2:1–9.

Although the depiction of David introduced to, or warmed by, Abishag was to become very popular in Giant Bibles of the later Romanesque period, the Arras Bible image is the earliest known example.[110] Surviving images of David's last charge to Solomon from the Byzantine East and early medieval Spain hint, however, at a much earlier visual tradition for this scene that may have provided some inspiration to the Saint-Vaast artist. If this is the case, the choices that this artist made in creating this compilation speak volumes about his intentions. The Spanish versions of David's charge to Solomon differ dramatically from that in the Arras Bible, for instead of being bedridden and crownless, David is shown enthroned and crowned.[111] The Byzantine examples, by contrast, are compositionally very close. A Byzantine manuscript of the Book of Kings, Vatican gr. 333, fol. 72v, includes a column illustration of David, crowned and sitting up in bed, instructing an already crowned Solomon who sits at the end of the bed while a fan bearer stands behind the bed.[112] Furthermore, the miniature prefacing the third Book of Kings in the thirteenth-century Arsenal Old Testament, Paris, Bibliothèque de l'Arsenal MS 5211, fol. 183v (fig. 42), parallels the Saint-Vaast image in both its content and the probable intentions of its artists. Daniel Weiss has proposed that the miniature cycle in this manuscript, carried out in the Holy Land scriptorium of Saint Jean d'Acre, may have encompassed a program intended to make David and Solomon into biblical *exempla* for Louis IX during his conquest of the Holy Land. The full-page miniature for III

---

[110] The only similar earlier image might be the depiction of a bedridden, elderly David visited by Bathsheba in the *Sacra Parallela* of John of Damascus, Paris BnF MS gr. 923, fol. 323, where Bathsheba is shown standing behind David's bed. In this image, however, both figures are markedly argumentative in gesture. The content of the scene is clearly different. For the *Sacra Parallela* see Kurt Weitzmann, *The Miniatures of the Sacra Parallela, Parisinus graecus 923*, Studies in Manuscript Illumination VIII (Princeton, 1979).

[111] In the Spanish examples, a crownless Solomon approaches the seated David from the right with both hands outstretched. See the León Bible of 960, San Isidoro MS 2, fol. 142v, and León, San Isidoro MS 3, vol. I, fol. 142, a twelfth-century Bible which is thought to copy the same model as the earlier Bible. On the León Bible of 960, John Williams, *Early Spanish Manuscript Illumination* (New York, 1977), 55–61. On the relationship between the various Bibles, also idem, "A Castilian Tradition of Bible Illustration: the Romanesque Bible from San Millán," *Journal of the Warburg and Courtauld Institutes* XXVIII (1965), 66–85.

[112] Jean Lassus, *L'illustration byzantine du livre des Rois, Vaticanus Graecus 333*, Bibliothèque des cahiers archéologiques IX (Paris, 1973), 79, fig. 98.

Kings is comprised of six scenes from the beginning of the book that may reflect column illustrations found in Byzantine books available to the artists in Acre.[113] In the upper left hand quatrefoil David lies in bed, while two advisors introduce a young girl who approaches from the right. Following this, a series of scenes show the royal succession being decided. First, Bathsheba petitions David on behalf of Solomon, then Solomon is paraded on a mule by David's servants, is anointed by Nathan and Zadoc, and in the lower left hand corner, a crowned Solomon flanked by an advisor addresses a crowned David on his deathbed before, in the last quatrefoil, King David is buried.

The Saint-Vaast artist may have been inspired by a Byzantine Book of Kings manuscript like the one available to the Acre artists, or some similar source, to combine the scenes of Abishag and Solomon before David to create the top register of the Arras Bible III Kings illustration (pl. II). In addition to fusing these two moments in the story, the artist rearranged minor details, for Solomon stands at the end of the bed instead of behind it, and carries a scepter instead of wearing a crown, and David is shown without a crown.

Peter Brieger, in his article "Bible Illustration and Gregorian Reform," cited this miniature as one of the most meaningful in the manuscript.[114] He believed that the two-register image, along with the miniature prefacing the Book of Esther, was intended to demonstrate "God's ordinance of Kingship and the Church," by picturing royal succession and its divine origin. Despite the inscription identifying the woman in the top scene as Abishag, however, Brieger felt that she represented Bathsheba pleading for the succession of her son, Solomon.[115] Because the *titulus* dates from the same time that the miniature was painted, it is unlikely that the scribe made such an error. In fact, the inclusion of Abishag in this scene actually reinforces Brieger's hypothesis.

According the text of III Kings, Solomon had already been anointed as king by Nathan and Zadoc when his last interview with David took place.[116] Even though Solomon is not crowned in this image,

[113] Hugo Buchthal, *Miniature Painting in the Latin Kingdom of Jerusalem* (Oxford, 1957), 54–61, and Daniel Weiss, "Biblical History and Medieval Historiography: Rationalizing Strategies in Crusader Art," *MLN* CVIII (1993), 710–737.
[114] *Studies in Church History* II (1965), 154–164.
[115] Brieger, 156.
[116] III Kings 1:39.

the Ezra Master has signaled his kingship by placing a foliate scepter in his hand. The top image, therefore, shows the two living kings together in the brief interlude between the elevation of the younger and the death of the elder. Such a scenario would have been very familiar to the clerics of Northern Europe, for among both the Capetians and the Ottonians it was standard practice to insure the succession of the chosen heir by 'associating' him to rule even before the death of his predecessor.[117] Pope John XIII crowned both Otto I and his son, Otto II, as emperors at St. Peter's in 972, although Otto II had been considered a co-emperor since 967.[118] Adalbero of Reims anointed Hugh Capet, the first Capetian king, in 987. That same year, Hugh associated his son, Robert the Pious, to the throne by having him consecrated and crowned.[119] Robert himself associated his elder son Hugh in 1017, and after Hugh's premature death, associated his younger son Henry in 1027.[120] All of these ceremonies were attended by an audience of clergy, in addition to the celebrants. In the Arras Bible image, Solomon is advised by his still-living father to rule with the guidance of God, in whose power he would be strengthened, just as eleventh-century divinely appointed monarchs were charged by their consecrators to follow Christian precepts as one of the duties of their office. But further, David's introduction to Abishag is used to demonstrate one of the most important characteristics of the divinely sanctioned ruler in early-eleventh-century belief: wisdom.

Angelom of Luxeuil, a Carolingian commentator, built on an idea first expressed by Jerome by interpreting Abishag in this way: "Who

---

[117] Andrew W. Lewis, "Anticipatory Association of the Heir in Early Capetian France," *American Historical Review* LXXXIII (1978), 906–927, challenges the popularly held view that anticipatory association was exclusively a mechanism of weak kings bent on shoring up questionable dynasties. He argues instead that the practice reflects a trend common to the higher levels of noble society at that time. While he grants that Hugh Capet's association of his son Robert in 987 was clearly an effort to continue a dynasty still seen by some as usurpers, by the time Robert associated his two sons, Capetian kingship was already considered hereditary (Lewis, 908–909).

[118] Mariaux, 18.

[119] Bautier, "Sacres et couronnements," 52, and idem, "L'avènement de Hugues Capet et le sacre de Robert le Pieux," *Colloque Hugues Capet, 987–1987, La France de l'an mil (1987) Le roi de France et son royaume autour de l'an mil*, ed. Michel Parisse and Xavier Barral i Altet (Paris, 1992), 27–37.

[120] See above.

is this Shunammite wife and virgin, so hot that she could warm the
cold man, and yet so holy that she would not provoke excitement
and passion, except *sapientia*?"[121] The votive crown hanging over
Abishag signals the divine quality ascribed to *sapientia* in this context, as pendant votive crowns in this period were used almost exclusively to indicate the presence of the holy.[122]

The scene in the lower register reinforces this message. An inscription sketched over two dark bands between the two scenes describes
the moment: "After the death of David, the Lord appeared to
Solomon in a dream, saying 'Ask what you desire so that I may
give it to you.'"[123] Once again, a ruler, identified by the inscription
as Solomon, reclines on the bed. At his feet, under an arched door-
way, stands a host of six guards, while above his head dangles another
votive crown. From a multicolored glory above appear Christ-logos
carrying a cross-staff and two angels. Once again, the artist has found
one of the Bible text's very rare opportunities to show a king receiving heavenly wisdom.[124] According to III Kings, after David's death,
Solomon sought to follow his father's advice and continued the practice of offering holocausts in the high places. After one such sacrifice
of 'a thousand victims' on the altar at Mount Gibeon, in Jerusalem,

---

[121] *Enarrationes in libros Regum*, PL 115:393. *Quae est igitur ista Sunamitis uxor et virgo,
tam fervens, ut frigidum calefaceret, et tam sancta ut calentem ad libidinem non provocaret, nisi
sapientia* . . .
[122] The dangling votive crown was a very popular motif, especially in Ottonian
manuscript art. See, for example, the Gospel book of Saint Bernward of Hildesheim,
Cathedral Treasury MS 18, fol. 17, where votive crowns dangle from the arches
of an arcade over the enthroned Virgin and two flanking angels, and fol. 111,
where one is found hanging over the altar in the temple at the Annunciation to
Zacharias (Marlis Stähli, *Die Handschriften im Domschatz zu Hildesheim*, Mittelalterliche
Handschriften in Niedersachsen VII [Wiesbaden, 1984], 17–50). In the Aachen
Gospels of Otto III, Aachen, Cathedral Treasury, fol. 129v, three votive crowns
hang over a scene of the Presentation in the Temple, and they also appear in several other miniatures (Ernst Grimme, *Das Evangeliar Kaiser Ottos III im Domschatz zu
Aachen* [Freiburg, 1984], 62). The Carolingian Drogo Sacramentary includes a votive
crown suspended over the altar in an historiated initial for *Te Igitur*, Paris BnF MS
lat. 9428, fol.15v, and in numerous other liturgical scenes (Florentine Mütherich
and Joachim Gaehde, *Carolingian Painting* [New York, 1976], fig. 28). Votive crowns
were also used in Anglo-Saxon art, for instance in the c. 1025–1050 Benedictional
of Archbishop Robert, Rouen BM MS Y 7 (369), fol. 54v, scene of the Death of
the Virgin (*The Golden Age of Anglo-Saxon Art*, 60, and Deshman, *The Benedictional of
Aethelwold*, 267–268).
[123] *Post mortem David apparuit dominus salomoni per somnium dicens, postula quod vis ut
dem tibi.*
[124] III Kings 3:5–12.

the Lord appeared to him in a dream. Solomon acknowledged that the Lord had made him king over the Chosen People, and asked in addition for an understanding heart so that he could rule well.[125]

This scene is unknown in earlier art, although it does appear in two early-eleventh-century Spanish Bibles.[126] In the Roda Bible Solomon is visited by a single winged angel carrying a scepter. In the Ripoll Bible, by contrast, a full-length Christ-logos seated in a mandorla held by angels hovers over Solomon's bed, while two spear-holding attendants stand at the end.[127] Both scenes are vaguely similar in composition, but not enough to warrant undue speculation about a common model. Biblical commentators discussing this moment emphasized that the most important desire of Solomon, and his greatest gift from God, was divine wisdom. According to the III Kings 3:11–12, God answered Solomon's request for an understanding heart, "Because thou hast asked this thing, and hast not asked for thyself long life or riches, nor the lives of thy enemies, but hast asked for thyself wisdom to discern judgement, behold, I have done for thee according to thy words, and have given thee a wise and understanding heart." The commentator Claudius of Turin, writing in the mid-ninth century, refined this, saying, "And so Solomon went up to Gibeon, and there he made a burnt offering to the Lord, where the Lord appeared to him during the night, and listened to his plea, which he demanded, and gave to him wisdom and knowledge . . . After having received this wisdom from heaven, soon it is tried because of the judgement of base women."[128] The Arras III Kings

---

[125] III Kings 3:1–9.

[126] The Roda Bible, Paris BnF MS lat. 6, vol. 11, fol. 75 and the Ripoll Bible Rome BAV cod. Vat. lat. 5729, fol. 95, see Wilhelm Neuß, *Die katalanische Bibelillustration um die Wende des ersten Jahrtausends und die altspanische Buchmalerei* (Bonn, 1922), 77–79. The Roda Bible's version of this scene is actually found not before III Kings, but rather before II Chronicles. A later similar scene might be the depiction of the Solomonic bed found in the *Hortus Deliciarum* of Herrad of Landsberg. Here, Solomon, as a type of Christ, was shown asleep in a bed that was identified in an inscription as the Church, the typological womb of Christ's mother, Mary. Behind him is a crowd of guards. Although superficially similar to the Saint-Vaast illustration, this image is missing the visionary apparition that would identify it as the same scene. See Herrad of Landsberg, *Hortus Deliciarum* (New Rochelle, 1977), pl. LIII.

[127] This actually illustrates a different moment than that described in the Arras Bible inscription, for it shows God's second appearance to Solomon in III Kings 9, after the construction of the Temple, which is pictured before the dream in the Ripoll Bible miniature. Nonetheless, a similar composition could have inspired the Arras artists.

[128] *Commentarii in libros Regum*, PL 50:1103. *Abiit itaque Salomon in Gabaon, et immolavit*

miniature (pl. II), therefore, in both the upper and lower registers
depicts Old Testament kings, the prototypes of the contemporary
eleventh-century kings, receiving the essential trait which set them
apart from lesser nobles and justified their authority: God-given
wisdom.

Could the Ezra Master or his director have decided to pair these
scenes simply because both gave him the opportunity to use the
composition inspired by Solomon's dream vision of God? By the end
of the Carolingian age, after all, the literature of royal dreams and
visions was extensive and had bred a popular artistic form, the reclining biblical king.[129] This seems unlikely. The combination of moments
found in the upper scene, where two different incidents from the life
of David are depicted, joined to the event chosen for the lower scene,
transmits a very specific message about the duties of kings and the
quality delivered at their unction that made them eligible to rule.
Furthermore, later Capetian propagandists mined the same material
in order to explain the same theme.

The underlying meaning of the Saint-Vaast illumination recalls
that found in the Arsenal Old Testament's visual program (fig. 42).
As a product of the thirteenth-century crusader kingdom, the Arsenal
program itself had a mission. Daniel Weiss argues that by including
three portraits of Solomon in the Arsenal manuscript's Book of
Proverbs, all seated beneath a temple-like baldachin strongly reminiscent of Louis IX's baldachin over the Grande Châsse in the Sainte-
Chapelle, the artist compared Solomon to King Louis. Visual parallels
between depictions of Louis and Solomon in the stained glass program of the Sainte-Chapelle continue this typology.[130] Like the Arras
Bible, other Old Testament miniature pages in the Arsenal manuscript also show the divine institution of rulership by prefacing a
series of scenes with an image of God appearing to the protagonist.[131] Furthermore, according to Weiss, the III Kings frontispiece

---

*ibi holocaustum Domini, ubi apparuit ei Dominus per noctem, et exaudivit deprecationem quam
postulavit, deditque ei sapientiam et scientiam,..Post acceptam autem divinitus sapientiam, mox
turpium mulierum de causa judicio tentatur.*

[129] Dutton, *The Politics of Dreaming*, 50–80, shows, however, that for the most part
Carolingian dreams by and about royal figures were negative and admonitory.

[130] Daniel Weiss, "The Three Solomon Portraits in the Arsenal Old Testament
and the Construction of Meaning in Crusader Painting," *Arte medievale*, Ser. II, VI/2
(1992), 15–38.

[131] Weiss, "The Three Solomon Portraits," 21.

in the Arsenal Old Testament is meant to depict the orderly transition of rule between David and his heir, Solomon, by including
scenes of David's instruction to anoint Solomon, the anointing itself,
and David's final charge to Solomon. This, he feels, was an appropriate program because David and Solomon were understood as
royal *exempla*. In addition, like the Saint-Vaast Bible, the Arsenal
miniature depicts the practice of anticipatory association, where the
chosen heir is crowned before the death of the reigning king.[132]

Differences in detail in the Saint-Vaast image, however, give it a
subtly different meaning from that implied in the Arsenal manuscript's program. Specifically, by combining the introduction of Abishag
as a personification of Holy Wisdom with David's final charge to
Solomon, the artist has emphasized that Solomon's, and by extension the contemporary ruler's, real qualification for just rulership is
the possession and exercise of God-given wisdom. In adding to the
top register's scenes the dream imagery of the bottom register, where
Solomon asks the apparition of God for wisdom, this intention of
the program is further underlined. In the context of the rest of the
Ezra Master's miniatures depicting kings and clergy, where the Christ-
like nature of rulership is alluded to repeatedly, this miniature's
admonitory message is clear.

What is striking, however, is the remarkable continuity in the use
of imagery of David and Solomon as prototypes of contemporary
kings. Well established in the Carolingian period with the First Bible
of Charles the Bald's illuminations of David and King Charles, and
rejuvenated in the illustrative program of the Arras Bible, the use
of David and Solomon as *exempla* persisted into the later Capetian
era, where artists, still consulting the same pictorial and exegetical
sources available to the earlier generations of artists, inventively combined and altered these programs to create messages directed at
specific rulers and contexts.

Furthermore, this series of images of Solomon does not end with
the miniature prefacing III Kings. Instead, Solomon appears yet
again, and in what may be a second depiction of the same moment
shown in the bottom register of the III Kings image.

---

[132] Weiss, "Biblical History and Medieval Historiography," 731.

II Chronicles and Solomon's Dream at Gibeon

The first Book of Chronicles, fol. 158 of volume I, is prefaced only with a full-page decorated initial. Possibly the artists were discouraged from attempting to illustrate the book by the nine chapters of tedious genealogies that initiate it. Before the second Book of Chronicles, volume I, fol. 170 (pl. III), however, the Ezra Master drew his fourth image of Solomon in the Saint-Vaast Bible, a portrait we already encountered when investigating the *infulae* attached to Solomon's crown in the miniature for Wisdom. The second Book of Chronicles begins with a reprise of the transference of power already depicted in the illustration of III Kings. "And Solomon the son of David was strengthened in his kingdom, and the Lord his God was with him, and magnified him to a high degree."[133] The Ezra Master recycled some of the same motifs used in the III Kings (pl. II), Wisdom (pl. VI) and Jeremiah (pl. IV) images, including the vertical parallel and royal regalia, in creating his II Chronicles image. Inside a quatrefoil frame surrounding this text is a two-level composition: in the top lobe, an enthroned Christ-logos is flanked by two angels, while in the initial C nestled inside the left hand lobe below, Solomon sits on an animal throne, crowned with a trefoil crown with fluttering *infulae* and holding a lily-scepter, regalia much like that adorning Solomon in the miniature for the Book of Wisdom. In this case, however, he sits in profile and makes a speaking gesture towards the impassive figure of Christ-logos, above. Outside the frame one finds a set of fantastic animals in the upper spandrels, and two facing shield- and spear-bearing soldiers in the lower spandrels. At the very top of the illumination, a pair of tiny, closed, green doors sits atop the frame.

The biblical Books of Chronicles never provided popular subjects for figural illustration, and no earlier examples of Chronicles illustration survive. In the contemporary Spanish Catalan Bibles, where the Books of Chronicles were prefaced with cycles of illustrations, either entirely different subjects were chosen for illustration, or the scene in question, the sacrifice at Mount Gibeon, is illustrated with material inspired by the description from III Kings.[134] Because the

---

[133] II Chronicles 1:1.
[134] See the Ripoll Bible, Rome BAV cod. Vat. lat. 5729, fols. 159v-161, for extensive cycles of unrelated scenes from IV Kings and Chronicles, and the Roda Bible,

Chronicles for the most part simply recount the same events that are also described in the other canonical books of the Octateuch and Kings, artists seeking source material need only have referred to illustrations of the more popular incidents from those books in other contexts. The illustration for II Chronicles in the Saint-Vaast Bible itself has the appearance of an ad hoc creation.

This miniature is, undeniably, one of the most artistically inept in the entire manuscript. Christ in majesty between his angelic companions has been awkwardly squeezed into the top lobe in such a way that the frame truncates the angels' wings. Meanwhile, the figure of Solomon below twists sideways on his seat, his legs knotted under him, while the front half of a standing animal whose back end and hind legs are missing is used for his throne, rather than the fald-stool or masonry seat found in the Bible's other royal images. The artist has articulated the arms and legs of both Solomon and Christ with multiple rubbery joints. Even the text dwindles below the initial to leave an unsatisfactory and uneven well of empty parchment. Despite its inharmonious composition, however, the artist cogently assembled the image's contents to remind the viewer that Solomon, like a contemporary king, ruled through the grace of God and in the image of the heavenly King of kings.

The Carolingian commentator Rabanus Maurus glossed the first words of II Chronicles, the very words framing the image, thus: "What does it mean, that it says Solomon, the son of David, strengthened in his kingdom, except that he shows our Savior most stead-fastly to have sovereignty, in the name of whom and in the building of the house of the Lord Solomon offered a type."[135] The first words of the text of II Chronicles, and the popular commentary of Rabanus Maurus, certainly may provide a straightforward explanation for most of the components of this miniature. Solomon, enthroned below Christ, can be considered his type, at the same time that his reign,

---

Paris BnF MS lat. 6, fols. 63 and 75. The three-register illumination on fol. 75, prefacing II Chronicles, shows Solomon acclaimed, the sacrifice at Gibeon, and Solomon's vision, where an angel visits him while he sleeps. As will be demonstrated below, this depiction is closer to the text of III Kings than II Chronicles. See Neuß, 77–81.

[135] PL 109:414. *Quid est, quod confortatum dicit Salomonem filium David in regno suo, nisi quod ostendit Salvatorem nostrum, cujus Salomon in nomine et in aedificatione domus Dei typum praeferebat, firmissimum habere imperium.*

symbolized by his regalia and the flanking guards below him, was
'strengthened in the Lord.' This portrait of Solomon, like the miniature prefacing the Book of Wisdom, thus serves as an even more
explicit visualization of Solomon's Christological kingship.

Two details of the image, however, remain perplexing. First,
Solomon appears, through his gesture, and his profile posture, not
just to imitate Christ but also to address him. Second, the tiny doors
surmounting the top lobe of the frame may be intended to symbolize Rabanus's notation that Solomon 'in the building of the house
of the Lord,' prefigured Christ's Church-building. They could, on
the other hand, refer to the very next event of the text.

> And Solomon went up thither to the brazen altar, before the taber-
> nacle of the covenant of the Lord, and offered upon it a thousand
> victims. And behold that night God appeared to him, saying: Ask what
> thou wilt that I should give thee. And Solomon said to God: Thou
> hast shewn great kindness to my father David: and has made me king
> in his stead . . . Give me wisdom and knowledge that I may come in
> and go out before thy people; for who can worthily judge this thy
> people, which is so great?[136]

Perhaps the doors are intended to represent the tabernacle, before
which Solomon made his sacrifice. Unlike the II Chronicles recounting, the text of III Kings did not specify that Solomon's sacrifice
was made before the tabernacle.[137] Like the description of the sacrifice
at Mount Gibeon in III Kings, the Chronicles version once again

---

[136] II Chronicles 1:6–8, 10.

[137] Similar doors appear in two Carolingian manuscripts of the Apocalypse, the
Trier Apocalypse, Trier, Stadtbibliothek MS 31, fol. 11v, the letter to Philadelphia
(Apoc. 3:7–13), and 14v, the First Vision (Apoc. 4), and a slightly later copy of the
Trier manuscript, Cambrai BM MS 386, fol. 7v, the letter to Philadelphia and fol.
10v, the First Vision. In these texts, 'door' refers to the door of Heaven. For the
Trier Apocalypse, see *Trierer Apokalypse: vollständige Faksimile-Ausgabe im Originalformat
des Codex 31 der Staatsbibliothek Trier*, Codices selecti phototypice impressi XLVIII
(Graz, 1974–1975) and Paul Huber, *Apokalypse. Bilderzyklen zur Johannes-Offenbarung in
Trier, auf dem Athos und von Caillaud d'Angers* (Düsseldorf, 1989), 23–35, with recent
bibliography. Lawrence Nees has pointed out in *The Gundohinus Gospels* (Cambridge,
Mass., 1987), 185–188, that the positioning of angels labeled CYRUBIN with wings
raised to protect Christ in that manuscript may have been intended to recall the
cherubim of the Ark of the Covenant. The angels with raised wings flanking Christ
in the II Chronicles miniature of the Saint-Vaast Bible may therefore be meant to
allude to the doors above as the Ark or the tabernacle, and to Christ below as a
New Ark.

emphasizes that Solomon was visited by God, who gave him the opportunity to ask for some favor, and that Solomon pleased him by asking for the gift of wisdom. Unlike the III Kings version, however, in the II Chronicles rendition, there is no mention of either dreaming or sleep, meaning that the II Chronicles illumination, which shows Solomon in wakeful communication, accurately reflects the text that inspired it.

If the Ezra Master intended his combination of tabernacle doors and Solomon addressing Christ-logos to refer to Solomon's sacrifice on Mount Gibeon, it is possible to further inflect Solomon's role as represented in the Saint-Vaast Bible. Interestingly, in Rabanus Maurus' commentary for the Book of Chronicles version of Solomon's vision after his sacrifice at Gibeon, unlike his commentary connected with III Kings, wisdom is just as necessary to the governance of priests, the 'rectoribus sanctae Dei Ecclesiae,' as it is to that of kings.

> If Solomon, made king in the earthly Jerusalem, did not seek from God gold nor wealth nor substance, neither worldly glory, so much more greatly is it necessary to the rectors of the Church of God, to whom has been commended the care and the governance of souls, that they do not seek earthly substance or worldly wealth, but desire wisdom and knowledge of the laws of God and the wealth of virtue, so that they may be able worthily to judge the people of God, and to demonstrate to him teaching reasonably and rightly his going in to faith and coming out to the appearance of eternal blessedness.[138]

These images of David and Solomon form the core of the Saint-Vaast Bible's statement on Biblical kingship. The artist has made several, in some ways, surprising choices. Incidents from the lives of David and Solomon such as David killing the lion, David and Goliath, the unction of David, David composing the Psalms, the unction of Solomon, or the judgment of Solomon were better known and had a much richer tradition of illustration, particularly in the art of the Carolingians. With the illuminations prefacing the books of Kings, Chronicles and Wisdom, the Ezra Master, however, seems to have

---

[138] Rabanus Maurus, *Commentaria in Paralipomena*, PL 109:415–416. *Ubi moraliter considerandum est: si Salomon, rex factus in terresti Jerusalem, non aurum, nec divitias, non substantiam, neque gloriam mundanam a Deo petivit, quanto magis necesse sit rectoribus sanctae Dei Ecclesiae, quibus commendata est cura et regimen animarum, ut non substantiam terrenam vel divitias mundi quaerant, sed sapientiam et scientiam legis Dei atque divitias virtutum appetant, ut possint populum Dei digne judicare, et ingressum eius ad fidem atque egressum ad speciem aeternae beatitudinis rite ac rationabiliter docendo ei demonstrare.*

moved beyond a simple attempt to show that the office of king had been instituted in the Bible and that David and Solomon were good kings. Instead, he emphasized the qualities of a king that entitled him to rule, including his Christological persona and the wisdom that was imbued into him at the time of his unction. The viewer who paged through the manuscript would have repeatedly encountered King Solomon, especially, in an aura of ever-increasing glory. First, in the miniature for III Kings, the realm was passed to him by his father, and he received wisdom during his vision of God. The next miniature in the manuscript depicted him enthroned below Christ, possibly again experiencing this heavenly vision in which wisdom was granted and, at the least, in a composition that emphasizes his Christ-like rule. Finally, in the miniature prefacing the Book of Wisdom, Solomon received the mandorla of Christ himself while priestly *infulae* swirl from behind his head. The artist or programmer has truly hammered home the Christological nature of kingship, while all three miniatures also make reference to the theme of divine wisdom.

This does not mean that the origins of secular and ecclesiastical offices in the Bible were not signaled in the Saint-Vaast Bible's pictorial program. In fact, the very first pair of narrative illustrations in the Bible, framing the beginning of Deuteronomy, explained the hierarchy of offices and the need for leaders who could act as intermediaries between God and his Chosen People.

The writings of Gerard of Cambrai and other contemporary documents, such as the consecration ordo, again and again defended the conception of divinely sanctioned kingship and episcopal rule using the explanation that both offices had been instituted in the Bible. Therefore, the king and bishop were merely the most recent holders of offices already held by their biblical prototypes, including David, Solomon, and the Apostles, and most importantly, their heavenly exemplar, Christ, who combined both offices in one ruler. According to Gerard, one of the primary reasons for opposing the Peace of God was that it undermined the division of leadership roles already instituted in biblical times when Abraham, Joshua and David wielded the sword, while the priests supported them with prayer.[139]

---

[139] See also above, chapter three. *Gesta pontificum Cameracensium*, PL 149:171. *Quibus—dum Abraham et Joshua et David ex voce Domini arma tulisse in prelium vetus ostendit pagina, et sacerdotes gladio accingunt reges . . .*

Gerard further believed that this division of roles was specifically mandated by God through Moses when the Law was handed down to the Israelites, as for instance, when he defended the episcopal office by pointing out that Moses had created the hierarchy within the Church of the Old Testament.[140] Thus it is not surprising that the very first narrative illustration in the Saint-Vaast Bible depicts the moment when secular and clerical leadership was instituted, setting the stage for the defense of these leaders in many of the Bible's other miniatures.

The Deuteronomy Illustrations

To scholars familiar with the illustrated Carolingian Bibles of the ninth century, and the Romanesque Bibles that would follow in the later-eleventh and twelfth centuries, it must seem incongruous that the Saint-Vaast Bible was never provided with the otherwise standard illustrations for the Old Testament Books of Genesis and Exodus. The pictorial programs of even the most sparely illustrated Carolingian and Romanesque Bibles began with the creation of the world, either in a full-page miniature or a series of vignettes inserted into the historiated initial 'I' that prefaced the beginning of the text: *In principio creavit Deus caelum et terram.*[141] In the Arras Bible, instead, the first illustration of the Pentateuch is found before Deuteronomy, the last book of Moses.

The two folios of this opening, fols. 53v and 54 of volume I (figs. 2–3), mirror each other, with almost identical double-lobed frames surrounding, on the left hand side, the display capitals opening the text and, on the facing page, the densely written text itself. While the space inside the frame of the left hand folio is dominated by

---

[140] See also above, chapter three. *Acta synodi Atrebatensis*, PL 142:1308. *Igitur ordines in Ecclesia veteris populi, quae usitato nomine Synagoga vocatur, fuisse legimus per Moysen a Deo dispositos, qui et quales et qualiter ac quando ordinare caeteros vel ordinari a caeteris, vel regere caeteros, vel regi a caeteris deberent.*

[141] For the Genesis illustrations in the Touronian Bibles, see Herbert L. Kessler, *The Illustrated Bibles from Tours* (Princeton, 1977), 13–35. See also, on the San Paolo Bible, Joachim Gaehde, "The Touronian Sources of the San Paolo Bible," *Frühmittelalterliche Studien* V (1971), 359–400. On Romanesque illustrations of Genesis, Walter Cahn, *Romanesque Bible Illustration* (Ithaca, 1982), 175–182.

extra-textual elements such as birds battling serpents and a tunic-
and chlamys-wearing bugler, the artist, once again the Ezra Master,
has squeezed the narrative images into the spandrels above the frame.
Relegated to the outside of the frame in this way, the components
of the narrative at first appear to be afterthoughts. In fact, the artist
has cleverly situated the figures so that the text of their conversa-
tions falls within the frames below them, almost like comic speech
bubbles. In addition, he has constructed a chain of pendant figures
across the top of the opening that implies equivalencies while mov-
ing the visual action forward. The first miniature, fol. 53v, is topped
by a *titulus* sketched into a box, 'The Lord speaks to Moses.'[142] Rather
than the more typical image familiar from Byzantine, Carolingian,
and Anglo-Saxon art of Moses gazing heavenwards at the Creator,
the artist has created a unique and startling parallel between Christ
and Moses. Christ-logos and Moses are enthroned on the same level,
and gesture to each other in a conversation of equals. Christ-logos,
on an architectural throne with his feet on a globe, is identified by
his cross-nimbus inscribed '*PAX*.' Moses, enthroned on a faldstool,
the medieval sign of episcopal or secular jurisdiction, gestures towards
Christ-logos.[143]

The artist planned the first Deuteronomy miniature to introduce
the typological kingship program of the Saint-Vaast Bible. Moses, of
course, was not a king and did not receive unction. Nonetheless, just
as Christ was the first *rex et sacerdos* of the Christians, Moses combined the roles of ruler and priest of the Israelites before these functions were separated under his jurisdiction. Perhaps this is what
allowed him to become, like David and Solomon, a typological predecessor for medieval kings. In Carolingian writings, Pepin was repeatedly addressed as '*novus Moyses*,' although the authors acknowledged
that Moses's rule was not such a perfect prototype for a Carolingian
king as that of the anointed king David.[144] By the early-eleventh century, Moses was included in the Royal Ordo of the Cologne Pontifical

---

[142] *Dominus ad moysen loquitur.*

[143] On medieval faldstools, see Ole Wanscher, *Sella Curulis: the Folding Stool, an Ancient Symbol of Dignity* (Copenhagen, 1980), 191–238.

[144] Kantorowicz, *Laudes regiae*, 57, note 148. MGH Epist. III, Epistolae Merovingici et Karolini aevi I, Wilhelm Gundlach, Ernst Dümmler (Hanover, 1892), 480 no. 3, 540 no. 33, 552 no. 39, 554 no. 42, and 649 no. 98. On the superiority of David over Moses as a prototype, MGH Epist. III:540 no. 33.

as one of the many Biblical role models set up for the king-elect.[145] Helgaud of Fleury, in the *Epitoma vitae regis Rotberti pii*, explained that the Capetian king Robert the Pious resembled Moses because he triumphed through being a humble servant of God and in likening himself to the cross when faced with his enemies, as Moses had during the Israelites' triumph over the Amalekites.[146] In Ottonian manuscripts the emperor was made a type of Moses when Henry II was depicted in the posture of Moses at the Battle of the Amalekites, his arms supported by two bishops, as Moses' had been by Aaron and Hur.[147] In the Saint-Vaast Bible, while Moses is not crowned, he is enthroned on a commonly acknowledged symbol of sovereignty, the faldstool, and paralleled compositionally with the King of kings, Christ. Moreover, the representation of Moses as a type of Christ was prevalent from an early period, and used to imply that the Old Law as transferred through him was but a foreshadowing of the New Law to be introduced by Christ.[148]

Our interpretation of the first Deuteronomy miniature is nuanced, however, both by the miniature that faces it and the contemporary writings of Gerard of Cambrai. On the facing folio, fol. 54 (fig. 3), a similar exchange is taking place: Moses, holding a cross staff, stands and blesses three bowing figures, two men and a woman. Again, the event is described by an inscription placed in a darkened band between Moses and the facing group, *Moyses ad filios israel loquitur*, 'Moses speaks to the children of Israel.' Thus, according to the inscriptions, this pair of scenes illustrates the end of the Book of

---

[145] Jackson, 206–207, *Omnipotens sempiterne Deus, creator ac gubernator caeli et terrae, conditor et dispositor angelorum et hominum, rex regum et dominus dominorum, qui Abraham fidelem famulum tuum de hostibus triumphare fecisti, Moysi et Josue tuo populo praelatis multiplicem victoriam tribuisti . . . benedictionum tuarum dona multiplica, eumque dextera tuae potentiae semper ubique circumda, quatinus praedicti Abrahae fidelitate firmatus, Moysi mansuetudine fretus . . .*

[146] Exodus 17:9–13. *Vie de Robert le pieux/ Epitoma vitae regis Rotberti pii*, Sources d'histoire médiévale I, eds. Robert-Henri Bautier and Gillette Labory (Paris, 1965), 100 and Meyer Schapiro, *Words and Pictures. On the literal and the symbolic in the illustration of a text* (The Hague, 1973), 21.

[147] Schapiro, 24, describing the Sacramentary of Henry II, Munich, Bayerische Staatsbibliothek Clm. 4456, fol. 11 and the Pontifical of Henry II, Bamberg, Staatsbibliothek, Lit. MS 53, fol. 2v.

[148] See Archer St. Clair, "The Basilewsky pyxis: typology and topography in the exodus tradition," *Cahiers archéologiques* XXXII (1984), 16–17.

Numbers, where God dictates the Law to Moses, and the beginning of Deuteronomy, when Moses transmits the Law to the Israelites.[149]

The same type of illustrations had been employed by the Carolingian artists of Tours almost 200 years earlier to transmit a similar message. Two Exodus miniatures from Touronian Bibles are so similar to the Saint-Vaast Bible's Deuteronomy illuminations in both theme and intent that they could easily have demonstrated to later artists the potential for these scenes to carry political messages. Important differences, however, underline that the Arras Bible images were created with a different message in mind, for while the Carolingian miniatures emphasized the foundation of the Levitical priesthood and its foreshadowing of the Christian Church, the Arras Bible's images have as their primary theme the institution of kingship.

In both the Grandval Bible and the First Bible of Charles the Bald, the artists have used subtle details in the Exodus illustrations to Christianize the transmission of the Law to Moses and its transferal to the Israelites.[150] In both illuminations, Moses receives the tablets of the Law from the hand of God and then, accompanied by Joshua, transfers the teachings of the Lord to his followers, either the Israelites as a whole or the Levite priesthood.[151] In the Grandval Bible (fig. 43), rather than simply choosing two moments from Exodus, the artists paired the episode of Moses receiving the Law from the hand of God in the upper register with a moment from Deuteronomy, when Moses preaches to the priests and elders, here labeled 'filii Israhel.'[152] The Grandval Bible's Exodus frontispiece was part of a broader program to invest the Bible with a Christian typological meaning. Moses has been given facial features that had been assigned to Paul in other Carolingian manuscripts, and the scene takes place inside the tabernacle, imitating Paul preaching in the Synagogue, instead of out of doors as would be appropriate in the Pentateuch

---

[149] Roughly, Numbers 25:10–Deuteronomy 30.

[150] London BL MS Add. 10546, fol. 25v and Paris BnF MS lat. 1, fol. 27v.

[151] Kessler, *The Illustrated Bibles from Tours*, 59–68. Also idem, "Traces of an Early Illustrated Pentateuch," *Journal of Jewish Art* VIII (1981), 20–27.

[152] Deuteronomy 31:10. Kessler, "Traces of an Early Illustrated Pentateuch," 24, based this identification on comparisons with the fifteenth-century Rovigo Bible, Rovigo, Accademia dei Concordi, MS 212 and London BL MS Add. 15277, which he believes preserves the iconography of an Early Christian Pentateuch cycle. Here, Kessler has reassessed his original supposition that the lower scene represented Exodus 34:29–33, Kessler, *The Illustrated Bibles from Tours*, 62.

to all but the priesthood, the only people holy enough to enter the tabernacle.[153] Martina Pippal proposed that in the Grandval Bible image Moses is shown both as the prototypical leader of the people and as the founder of the Church in the act of dividing these offices between Joshua and Aaron, both of whom hold foliate scepters.[154]

Likewise in the First Bible of Charles the Bald (fig. 44), an image of Moses receiving the tablets of the Law has been paired with the moment of his transfer of the commandments to the Levite priesthood just before his own death, another moment from Deuteronomy.[155] Again, the scene has been Christianized, this time by the addition of a cross in the pediment of the basilica that has replaced the wilderness tent described in the text, and on the tablets Moses transfers to the Levites where there is a quotation from Deuteronomy which was later, according to the Gospels, repeated by Christ.[156] In the First Bible of Charles the Bald, Moses is again made a type of Paul, taking on Pauline facial features. Furthermore, an obvious counterpart to the image is the frontispiece to the Pauline epistle in the same Bible, fol. 386v, where at the bottom of the page Paul preaches to a similar audience in a similar architectural setting.[157] The typology connecting the two images emphasizes the continuity of the Old and the New Law as revealed by God.[158] The Carolingian artist thus subtly adjusted these Old Testament scenes with Christian motifs to represent the importance of the Christian mission to the Franks, the Chosen People of the ninth century, who were led by King Charles the Bald and his court, the audience for this picture cycle.[159]

An important subtext in the Exodus illustration in the First Bible of Charles the Bald foreshadows the theme in the Saint-Vaast Bible's

---

[153] Archer St. Clair, "A New Moses: Typological Iconography in the Moutier-Grandval Bible Illustrations of Exodus," *Gesta* XXVI (1987), 21–25.

[154] Martina Pippal, "Distanzierung und Aktualisierung in der Vivianbibel: Zur Struktur der touronischen Miniaturen in den 40er Jahren des 9. Jahrhunderts," *Aachener Kunstblätter* LX (1994), 62–63, 71–72.

[155] Deuteronomy 31:9. Kessler, *The Illustrated Bibles from Tours*, 64.

[156] Deuteronomy 6:5. *Diliges Dominum Deum tuum ex toto corde tuo* . . . Matthew 22:37 and Mark 12:30. Herbert L. Kessler, "An Apostle in Armor and the Mission of Carolingian Art," *Arte medievale* II/4 (1990), 32.

[157] Kessler, "An Apostle in Armor," 32.

[158] See Herbert L. Kessler, "A Lay Abbot as Patron: Count Vivian and the First Bible of Charles the Bald," in *Committenti e produzione artistico-letteraria nell'alto medioevo occidentale*, SSCISAM XXXIX (1992), 658–659, for a summary of recent research on this theme.

[159] Kessler, "An Apostle in Armor," 35.

illustration. Søren Kaspersen demonstrated that the Exodus illustration in the First Bible of Charles the Bald (fig. 44), where Moses
hands the book of the Law to the Levite priesthood observed by his
appointed successor, a scepter-bearing figure of Joshua, may also
show the division by Moses of the offices of *regnum* and *sacerdotium*
between Joshua and Aaron, just as the Grandval Bible's Exodus illustration had (fig. 43). Moses, who here takes an intermediate position between the two leaders, has power over both offices. The
institution of kingship is therefore made an important part of biblical history, and its relationship with the Church standardized.[160] Yet
Pippal suggested that in the First Bible of Charles the Bald the institution of the powers of the Church was the most important theme,
with the priest defined as the guardian of the *ius divinum*. The artists
have represented the high priest Aaron as a Christian bishop through
the use of liturgical garments such as an alb, *tunicella* and *clavi*.[161]

The Ezra Master once again borrowed from Carolingian visual
tradition in building his Deuteronomy images (figs. 2–3). Like the
Exodus illustrations in the two Touronian Bibles, the Deuteronomy
images in the Saint-Vaast Bible depict the Lord giving the Law to
Moses, and Moses subsequently transferring it to his followers. This
meaning is enhanced by the fact that within the pair of tablet-shaped
frames between and below both groups of figures, the text of the
Law itself, as it was preserved in the Book of Deuteronomy, is transcribed.[162] In addition, a Christological attribute, in this case, Moses's
cross staff, establishes that, as in the Carolingian Bibles, some sort
of typological connection with the New Testament is intended. In
almost every other way, however, the Saint-Vaast Bible Deuteronomy
miniature differs from its Carolingian predecessors. First, in the Saint-

---

[160] Søren Kaspersen, "Cotton-Genesis, die Toursbibeln und die Bronzetüren—
Vorlage und Aktualität," in *Bernwardinische Kunst: Bericht über ein wissenschaftliches
Symposium in Hildesheim vom 10.10 bis 13.10.1984* (Göttingen, 1988), 87–91.

[161] Pippal, 62–63, 71–72. This is in addition to being distinguished from the
other Levite priests by his elaborate crown and *rationale*.

[162] My thanks to Jeffrey Hamburger for pointing out the similarity between the
tablets of the Law, and the shape of the frame in this opening, which could be
intended to create a tablet-diptych opening out of these pages. This would help to
convey that, although Moses is not shown transferring the tablets of the Law,
nonetheless, his pronouncements, and the government he instituted, have their basis
in the framework, so to speak, of the Mosaic Law.

Vaast image the moments depicted are different from those found in the Carolingian images. Moses does not receive the tablets of the Law from God, but instead converses with him, and his transmittal of the Law to the Israelites takes place orally.[163] This can be accounted for by the fact that the scenes preface a different text, Deuteronomy, where Moses is described in the first words of the text as retelling to the people all that the Lord had commanded.[164] Second, rather than supplicating a heavenly God from Mount Sinai, Moses is enthroned as a ruler in the presence of God, a depiction that is, as far as I know, unprecedented. This unusual motif signals the true purpose of this pair of miniatures within the Saint-Vaast Bible's pictorial program. If the viewer glances from the left-hand miniature to the right-hand folio, he or she sees Moses speaking to the Israelites the very words written into the right-hand diptych below, recalling the establishment of the ruling hierarchy of Israel as it took place years before during the Exodus:

> And I said to you at that time: I alone am not able to bear you: for the Lord your God hath multiplied you, and you are this day as the stars of heaven, for multitude . . . I alone am not able to bear your business, and the charge of you and your differences. Let me have from among you wise and understanding men, and such whose conversation is approved among your tribes, that I may appoint them your rulers. Then you answered me: The thing is good which thou meanest to do. And I took out of your tribes men wise and honorable, and appointed them rulers, tribunes, and centurions, and officers over fifties, and over tens, who might teach you all things.[165]

---

[163] The combination of moments pictured in the Arras Bible is also found in the Anglo-Saxon Aelfric Hexateuch, London BL MS Cotton Claudius B.IV, fol. 99v, an illustration for Exodus 20–24.3, where Moses kneels before the Lord on Mount Sinai, and then returns with empty hands to the waiting Israelites, below. This image is too different in detail to have provided anything more than a very general model for the Saint-Vaast illustration. On the Hexateuch, see *The Golden Age of Anglo-Saxon Art*, 153 (unillustrated), and C. R. Dodwell and P. Clemoes, *The Old English Illustrated Hexateuch*, Early English Manuscripts in Facsimile XVIII (London, 1974), fol. 99v.

[164] Deut. 1:1–3. "These are the words, which Moses spoke to all Israel . . . Moses spoke to the children of Israel all that the Lord had commanded him to say to them . . ."

[165] Deut. 1:9, 12–15. This folio contains Deut. 1:1–18, in which Moses recounts the battle with the Amorrhites, the gift of the Promised Land, and the institution of rulership.

Moses's kinsman Jethro had visited and remarked on his habit of sitting in judgment over the Israelites in every question and dispute, no matter how trifling. Jethro suggested that because Moses was no longer able to manage alone the leadership of all the Israelites, he should establish a hierarchy of rulers below him, with only the highest matters reserved for his personal attention.[166] Thus while Moses sits enthroned as a ruler on the left hand side of the opening, on the right he stands and reminds the bowing Israelite multitude that he was the leader of an elaborate hierarchy of government.

Finally, the second figure of Moses in the Arras Bible speaks to the Israelite throng, which includes a woman with a veiled head, rather than the Levitical priesthood and thus he cannot be establishing the ecclesiastical hierarchy alone. Although the label states clearly that Moses is speaking to the children of Israel, his blessing gesture and the bowed heads of his audience suggest instead that this image may have been inspired by a model that depicted Moses blessing the Israelites just before his death, as described in the Book of Deuteronomy, chapter 33. Such an image can be found in the contemporary Anglo-Saxon Aelfric Paraphrase, London BL MS Cotton Claudius B.IV, fol. 139v, where Moses holds a rod and blesses a group of standing Israelites to the right.[167] As Martina Pippal has recently pointed out, before his final blessing in Deuteronomy, Moses instructed the Israelites to install a king over themselves as directed by God once they reached the Promised Land.[168] This king was to be guided by the Law, kept in the possession of the Levites.

> When thou art come into the land, which the Lord thy God will give thee, and possessest it, and shalt say: I will set a king over me, as all nations have that are round about; thou shalt set him whom the Lord thy God shall choose out of the number of thy brethren . . . But after he is raised to the throne of his kingdom, he shall copy out to himself the Deuteronomy of this law in a volume, taking the copy of the priests of the Levitical tribe, and he shall have it with him, and shall read it all the days of his life, that he may learn to fear the Lord his God, and keep his words and ceremonies, that are commanded in the law.[169]

---

[166] Exodus 18:13–26.
[167] See *The Golden Age of Anglo-Saxon Art*, 153 (unillustrated), and Dodwell and Clemoes, fol. 139v.
[168] Pippal, 73.
[169] Deuteronomy 17:14–19.

In both this text and that found in chapter one, the text surrounded by the framed narrative opening, the Book of Deuteronomy established the secular hierarchy of rulership and the relationship between the priestly and kingly orders. The Ezra Master combined references to these two incidents, the first by placing the Saint-Vaast Bible's second Deuteronomy image over the relevant text, and then the second through the depiction of Moses blessing, in order to signal that the intended theme was the institution of all hierarchical governments in the Bible, and their interdependence.

The early-eleventh-century monks in the Saint-Vaast workshop certainly had the opportunity to consider Moses and his good works while writers in the diocese copied Gerard of Cambrai's *Acta synodi Atrebatensis* for distribution to surrounding dioceses.[170] Because the stated intention of the *Acta synodi* was to record how Gerard had defended the institutional Church against the allegations of heretics who sought to dismantle it, it is not surprising that its content should lean towards an explanation of the biblical roots of ecclesiastical rather than secular institutions. The *Acta* exhibit Gerard's, or his ghost-writer's, encyclopedic knowledge of scripture by calling on the examples set by Old and New Testament figures throughout, and yet Moses was clearly his favorite subject. He referred to Moses at least twenty times, more than any other Old Testament figure, and while glossing over Moses' encounter with the Burning Bush, his leadership of the Exodus from Egypt and his wandering in the wilderness, he glorified Moses' role as the builder of the secular and ecclesiastical hierarchy, in particular his inauguration of the practice of anointing. Although Gerard focused on the creation of the Levitical priesthood because they were the predecessors of contemporary priests, Moses, he pointed out, anointed both Aaron, the first priest, and Joshua, the secular leader, to their offices, following the directions of God.[171]

The differences between the Carolingian images and that in the Saint-Vaast Bible underline that almost two hundred years elapsed between their respective production. Whereas the illustrators of the Touronian Bibles were attempting to depict the origins of the Christian

---

[170] See above, chapter 3, for the possibility that the *Acta* were composed as a political tract meant for a wide audience.
[171] PL 142:1287, 1289, 1290, 1294.

mission of the Franks in the Old and New Testaments (figs. 43 and 44), the miniatures in the Saint-Vaast Bible instead emphasize royal leadership on the model favored by the medieval clergy (figs. 2–3). Moses in both miniatures is made a Christological leader, in the first when he is enthroned like the pendant Christ-logos, and in the second by carrying a cross staff, though in neither case is he made either priest or king. Moses nonetheless embodies one of the roles set out for the king in the ordines we have already encountered, including the Royal Ordo of the Cologne Pontifical. While the king-elect was led to his throne by the bishops, the metropolitan advised him that he had become the 'mediator between God and men' as well as the mediator between the clergy and the people.[172] This is literally what is shown in these images, where Moses, the Christ-like leader, stands between the enthroned Christ-logos and the *filii Israel* and repeats to them what God said.

Although the Ezra Master may have drawn on such images as the Exodus illustrations in the Touronian Bibles, he has shifted the meaning of the scene in the Saint-Vaast Bible both by placing the illustration of the transmission of the Law before Deuteronomy, and by changing details of the image. In illustrating Deuteronomy, rather than Exodus or Leviticus, he was able to avoid showing the transmission of the tablets of the Law, although that tablets existed was implied by the tablet-shaped frame around the opening text of Deuteronomy. Instead of transmitting the Law simply to the guardians of the tablets, the Levitical priesthood, Moses transmitted the Law orally to all the children of Israel. The artist underlined this by including women within the image, for women were obviously not eligible for priesthood. Moses's enthronement in the presence of the Lord indicated that the Lord entrusted to him the institution of rulership.

Furthermore, the very next image in the Saint-Vaast Bible emphasizes that, not only were leaders ultimately appointed and inspired by God, but they ruled only within and through the Law that had been handed down to Moses.

---

[172] Kantorowicz, *Laudes regiae*, 81, and Jackson, 212. *Et quanto clerum sacris altaribus propinquiorem prospicis, tanto ei potiorem in locis congruis honorem impendere memineris, quatinus mediator Dei et hominum te mediatorem cleri et plebis in hoc regni solio confirmet . . .*

Joshua Inspired by the Lord

The narrative imagery that the Ezra Master contributed to the first folio of the Book of Joshua on fol. 72, vol. I (fig. 4) is so minimal compared to other openings in the Bible that it might escape notice. A frame surrounds a large initial, in the foliage of which is entwined a nude man with a tendril piercing his throat. The narrative image is confined to the two roundels in the top corners of the frame. A bust-length Christ-logos is shown on the left, holding a cross-staff and gesturing towards the opposite roundel. There, a bust-length Joshua returns the gesture, and holds a book in his left hand. Between the two and above the frame is an inscription, '*Dominus iosue monet ut confortetur ad docendum filios israel.*' It is clear from the inscription that the scene is intended to show God's support for the rule of Joshua, who had been invested with the leadership of the Israelites by Moses before his death.[173] The image may refer obliquely to Joshua 1:8, "Let not the book of this law depart from thy mouth: but thou shalt meditate on it day and night, that thou mayst observe and do all things that are written in it: then shalt thou direct thy way, and understand it."

The Saint-Vaast Bible's Joshua image represents a striking departure from tradition, for almost all images of Joshua show him in the persona of a warrior.[174] Joshua, as described in the Bible, was much less likely to be preoccupied with books than with the battle to conquer the Promised Land, and most cycles of Joshua illustration concentrate on these campaigns. No earlier images resemble that in the Arras Bible, although the early-eleventh-century Roda Bible displays some similarities in its column illustration prefacing the Book of

---

[173] Deut. 34:9. "And Joshua the son of Nun was filled with the spirit of wisdom, because Moses had laid his hands upon him. And the children of Israel obeyed him, and did as the Lord commanded Moses."

[174] See *Lexikon der christlichen Ikonographie*, ed. Engelbert Kirschbaum, 8 vols. (Basel, 1968–1976), II, 436–442. The most famous images of Joshua depict him at war, such as the mosaics in Santa Maria Maggiore and the Joshua Roll (Rome BAV cod. Vat. Palat. gr. 431). However, even images where Joshua is not depicted making war often nonetheless show him garbed in battle-dress, witness the images in the Grandval Bible and the First Bible of Charles the Bald, London BL MS Add. 10546, fol. 25v, and Paris BnF MS lat. 1, fol. 10v. In the Bible from San Paolo fuori le mura in Rome, which unlike the two Tours Bibles does include a frontispiece for the Book of Joshua on fol. 58, Joshua is not shown in the tunic of a soldier, but is shown in the midst of battle.

Joshua.[175] In choosing to illustrate the Book of Joshua in this way,
the Ezra Master or his advisor may simply have been attempting to
visualize some of the first words of the text, which admonished Joshua
to rule within the Law. These words are not found on the same
folio as the illustration, however, where instead the Lord promises
Joshua that he will conquer the land beyond the Jordan. Instead,
the artist was probably elaborating on the theme already introduced
within the Deuteronomy image: that the model for the secular and
ecclesiastical hierarchy had been instituted by Moses at the direction of the Lord, and that rulers thus chosen were to rule within
the Law as it had been handed down to Moses.

Altogether, the Ezra Master contributed five miniatures in volume
I, two in volume II, and one in volume III to the program intended
to elevate kings and bishops in the Saint-Vaast Bible. Because we
do not know his identity, when he lived, or what his connection was
to the key historical players in Arras, Richard of Saint-Vanne and
Gerard of Cambrai, it is impossible to know if he was educated well
enough, and given enough artistic freedom, to invent the program
on his own. Although at nearby Saint-Bertin at almost exactly the
same time the abbot himself, Odbert, had served as the abbey's foremost artist, at Saint-Vaast the design of such an important and
expensive program of miniatures may have been the responsibility
of a leader such as the librarian, while the artist simply followed his
directions. Furthermore, the Ezra Master shared the burden of carrying out this cycle, at least in part, with another artist: the Acts
Master. The fact that more than one artist participated in this project increases the likelihood that a director of some sort planned the
program in its entirety before it was carried out or while it was in
progress.

Although in combination, the Ezra Master's miniatures prefacing
the Books of Deuteronomy and Joshua emphasize the origin of secular kingship in the Bible, the institution of the Church and its leadership was not ignored in the Saint-Vaast Bible's miniature cycle.
Instead, the Acts Master used an illustration from the New Testament
and its typological connection to Moses in Deuteronomy to estab-

---

[175] Paris BnF MS lat. 6, vol. I, fol. 89r. Here, the Lord, standing in a round
glory, hands the book of the Law to Joshua, who lifts it in his draped hands to
shield his face from the radiance of the Lord.

lish that the Church of the New Testament, and thus the contemporary Church, was simply the Christian continuation of an institution and hierarchy established by Moses and sanctioned by God.

The Acts Illustration

As we have already seen, in the Carolingian First Bible of Charles the Bald a typology was created between Moses, the Old Testament patriarch, and a New Testament figure, Paul the Apostle. The artists of the Arras Bible created a similar typology between the protagonists of the Deuteronomy and Acts illustrations. In the Saint-Vaast Bible, the counterpart of Moses is not Paul, but Christ. In the Deuteronomy illustrations themselves Moses had been assimilated to Christ both compositionally by showing him enthroned like Christ, and by giving him the Christological attribute of the cross-staff. The Acts illustration's oblique reference to Moses would only have been understandable to viewers familiar with the writings of Gerard of Cambrai.

The framed initial page introducing the book of Acts in volume III, fol. 141 (pl. X), shows two narrative moments just as the pair of images prefacing Deuteronomy. In this case, however, the Acts Master has shown two different types of action. In the initial P at the top of the page, we again see the transmission of the text, where the author Luke speaks to its recipient the first lines, "The former treatise I made, O Theophilus, of all things which Jesus began to do and to teach."[176] Below, the narrative content of the text is depicted, as an enthroned Christ preaches to the twelve Apostles.

There was no earlier tradition for the illustration of the Book of Acts in the medieval West. Depictions of Luke addressing his speech to Theophilus are unknown in earlier western art, although examples do exist in the margins of Byzantine Gospel and lectionary manuscripts.[177] The lower half of the image with Christ enthroned

---

[176] Acts 1:1.

[177] See the examples in an early-eleventh-century Gospel book, Paris BnF MS gr. 64, fol. 102v, and a lectionary, Venice, St. Giorgio dei Greci, fol. 384v, where the evangelist Luke can be found preaching to a standing Theophilus across a column of text, usually Luke 1:3, which includes Luke's reference to his scribe, Theophilus. For Paris BnF MS gr. 64, Henri Omont, *Les plus anciens manuscrits grecs*

among the seated Apostles, on the other hand, draws on a visual *topos* that had been popular since the early Christian period. In the Roman catacombs, for instance, in the cubiculum of Damasus in the Catacomb of Marcus and Marcellianus, Christ is shown enthroned on a high backed throne with seated rows of Apostles sloping away from him on either side.[178] Such images were used to decorate apses after the legalization of Christianity, as in the apse of the Chapel of Sant'Aquilino in the Church of San Lorenzo in Milan.[179] This composition was still current in the Carolingian period, when artists adapted it to the top level of the miniature silver Einhard reliquary arch.[180] According to drawings that record the imagery from the now lost reliquary Christ was depicted enthroned on a bench throne with a footstool and holding a book while the apostles were seated on long, arcade-fronted benches in groups of three, ranged around the front and sides of the arch.

Even though manuscript illustrations of Christ preaching to the Apostles exist, it is unlikely that they could have inspired the Saint-Vaast Acts image, because they almost never show both Christ and the Apostles seated. In cases where Christ is shown seated on a

---

de la Bibliothèque nationale (Paris, 1926). Sirarpie Der Nersessian also identified a similar iconography prefacing the Book of Acts in Washington, D.C., Dumbarton Oaks MS 3, fol. 215, a Psalter and New Testament dating from 1084. Here, a barely visible Theophilus faces Luke, who has become the upright of the initial T. No image of Christ and the Apostles is found in this manuscript. "A Psalter and New Testament Manuscript at Dumbarton Oaks," *Dumbarton Oaks Papers* XIX (1965), 161. For a discussion of the 'witness' motif of Luke with Theophilus and its later history, see George Galavaris, *The Illustrations of the Prefaces in Byzantine Gospels* (Vienna, 1979), 53–56.

[178] Josef Wilpert, *Die Malerei der Katakomben Roms* (Freiburg, 1903), pl. 177 (1). Other examples include a niche fresco in the catacomb at the Giordani cemetery which shows Christ seated surrounded by Apostles who overlap in a way more reminiscent of the Saint-Vaast image. Pasquale Testini, *Le catacombe e gli antichi cimiteri cristiani in Roma* (Bologna, 1966), fig. 130. Early Christian sarcophagi also portray scenes of an enthroned Christ teaching, flanked on either side by a row of seated Apostles, such as the example from the Cathedral of Nîmes. Josef Wilpert, *I sarcofagi cristiani antichi* (Rome, 1929), I, pl. XLIII (5).

[179] Christa Ihm, *Die Programme der christlichen Apsismalerei vom vierten Jahrhundert bis zur Mitte des achten Jahrhunderts* (Wiesbaden, 1960), 5. The hypothesis of Ihm's first chapter, "Der lehrende Christus und die himmlische Kirche," 5–10, is that apse decorations such as that at San Lorenzo would have provided the model for catacomb and sarcophagus images of a similar subject.

[180] Hans Belting, "Die Einhardsbogen," *Zeitschrift für Kunstgeschichte* XXXVI (1973), 100–104, and *Das Einhardkreuz: Vorträge und Studien zum Münsteraner Diskussion zum arcus Einhardi*, ed. Karl Hauck (Göttingen, 1974).

bench throne, such as the Byzantine representations of Christ and the Apostles used to illustrate the Gospel, Paris BnF MS gr. 74, fols. 19v and 74v, the Apostles grouped on either side are shown standing.[181] Nonetheless, whether the artist copied a monumental model or created a new composition *ad hoc*, as is suggested by the awkward position of the apostles' legs, any artist monk at Saint-Vaast would have had the opportunity to observe a contemporary equivalent of this apostolic gathering. Apse decorations such as that at San Lorenzo in Milan directly mirrored, and were inspired by, the arrangement of the bishop flanked by priests and other clerics that would have been found regularly in the apse below, making visual the commonly understood typology that the bishop was a type of Christ, and the clergy types of the Apostles. The introduction of the *Acta synodi Atrebatensis* even describes such a gathering. As he convened the synod in 1024, Bishop Gerard took his place in his *consistorium* in the cathedral, while the rest of the lesser clergy were arranged on either side of him in declining order according to rank, . . . *utrinque abbatibus, religiosis atque archidiaconis, caeterisque secundum ordinationis suae gradum discumbentibus* . . .[182]

Furthermore, the two events pictured in the Acts illustration were connected by Gerard of Cambrai in his *Acta synodi Atrebatensis* where he himself explained the typology that was made visual in the Saint-Vaast Bible. Gerard compared the founding of the Christian church by Christ described in Acts to the foundation of the Church of the Old Testament through Moses. Defending the institutional church, Gerard writes, "Finally, Luke, writing to Theophilus, said that the Lord Jesus 'showed himself alive to his apostles by many proofs after his passion, appearing to them for forty days, and speaking of the Kingdom of God (Acts 1:3).' What did he say about the Kingdom of God, unless to set in order the state of the Church, which is called the Kingdom of God?"[183] Gerard also drew a connection

---

[181] Henri Omont, *Evangiles avec peintures byzantines*, 2 vols. (Paris, 1908). Sirarpie Der Nersessian, "Recherches sur les miniatures du Parisinus Graecus 74," *Jährbuch der Österreichischen Byzantinistik* XXI (1972), 109, laments the overuse of this particular composition. An exception is found in the problematic Montecassino version of Rabanus Maurus' *De Universo*, Cod. Casinensis 132, p. 73, where Christ and a semicircular ring of Apostles are shown seated in front of an arcade, with an eagle-shaped lectern in front of Christ and a disembodied hand rising behind.

[182] PL 142:1271.

[183] PL 142:1286. *Postremo Lucas ad Theophilum scribens, ait quia Dominus Jesus "post*

between the institution of the priesthood in the Book of Acts and the institution by Moses of the Levitical priesthood. He saw both events as justifying the early-eleventh-century hierarchical church. He described how, in the Book of Numbers, Moses was instructed by the Lord to invest the tribe of Levi with the maintenance of the Temple, serving under the priest Aaron. Gerard then connected this with the Book of Acts, where the Apostles gathered together to choose seven followers to serve as deacons, freeing themselves to preach.[184]

The miniatures for Deuteronomy which introduce the narrative program of the Bible (figs. 2–3), and the miniature for Acts which closes it (pl. X), therefore would have served as bookends, imbuing the Biblical narrative with a particular meaning for those in early-eleventh-century Arras. These images, the first the Deuteronomy illustrations showing Moses instituting the secular government and the Church as instructed by God, and the other the Acts illustration depicting Christ instituting the Church of the New Testament, are connected through their content: in both cases these leaders instituted heavenly sanctioned orders. In addition, Moses was made to prefigure Christ not simply through his actions, which foreshadowed those of Christ, but visually, by carrying the cross staff.

The two sets of images, seen in the context of the concerns of early-eleventh-century Flanders, interpret the Bible as the story of the secular and ecclesiastical governance of the Christian world. From the Book of Deuteronomy, where Moses divided the kings from the priests, inventing the Levitical priesthood and instructing the Israelites to choose a king, to the Book of Acts, where Christ, through the Apostles, instituted the hierarchy of the Christian Church, the Bible thus becomes the model-book for contemporary rule.

---

passionem suam, discipulis seipsum vivum praebuit in multis argumentis, per dies quadraginta apparens eis et loquens de regno Dei." Quid est loqui de regno Dei, nisi de statu Ecclesiae, quae regnum dicitur Dei, ordinare?

[184] PL 142:1292. *Cui vero otium fuerit Vetus Testamentum revolvere, inveniet ab eo hos sumpsisse exordium, nec minus etiam eos qui supersunt, id est, Levitas et sacerdotes, quorum gradus quia altior est, paulo plus in eis nobis est immorandum. Nam, sicut liber Numerorum refert: Locutus est Dominus ad Moysen, dicens "Applica tribum Levi, et fac stare in conspectu Aaron sacerdotis, ut ministrent ei, et excubent, et observent quidquid ad cultum pertinet multitudinis coram tabernaculo testimonii, et custodiant vasa tabernaculi, servientes in ministerio eius* (described in Numbers 1:50)." *De his scriptum est, in Actibus apostolorum, quia "convocantes duodecim multitudinem discipulorum, dixerunt: Non est aequum nos derelinquere verbum Dei et ministrare mensis. Considerate ergo, fratres, viros ex vobis boni testimonii septem, plenos Spiritu sacto et sapientia, quos constituamus super hoc opus; nos vero orationi et ministerio verbi erimus instantes* (Acts 6:2–4)."

The miniatures in between make more specific the rights and attributes of the rulers thus instituted. The offices of the king and the bishop, through the miniatures for Jeremiah (pl. IV) and Wisdom (pl. VI), are justified by the belief that the office-holders become types of Christ upon their elevation to office. The miniatures of III Kings (pl. II) and II Chronicles (pl. III) demonstrate God's gift to kings, the divine wisdom that allows them to rule justly. The miniatures of Joshua (fig. 4) and Ezra (pl. VII), furthermore, delimit these offices. The first serves to show that kings must rule within and through the Law, which was guarded by the priests. The second demonstrates that kings and Church leaders, or bishops, must also cooperate in the creation of a civil society.

In choosing which books to illustrate, the programmer or artists repeatedly passed over the more popular or commonplace choices or the first books in a series, such as Genesis, I Kings or I Chronicles, and selected instead books whose content provided material for this program. At the same time that this ideology of rule was pictorialized in the Saint-Vaast Bible, it was also set out in words in such documents as the *Gesta episcoporum Cameracensium*, the *Acta synodi Atrebatensis*, and the *Ordo ad consecrandum regem* in the Cologne Pontifical. By examining all of these together, a very clear picture of the troubled state of the government of northern France, both secular and ecclesiastical, arises, as does the solution proposed by those in power, such as Gerard of Cambrai.

CHAPTER FIVE

LESSONS FOR A QUEEN

The series of miniatures in the Saint-Vaast Bible that addressed the offices of king and bishop was simply one component of a campaign whose traces can also be found in the *Acta synodi Atrebatensis* by Gerard of Cambrai, the contemporary *Gesta episcoporum Cameracensium* and the liturgical ordines of the Cologne Pontifical. Gerard of Cambrai and his chroniclers had nothing to say, on the other hand, about the office of queen. Nonetheless, two pieces of evidence reveal that the duties, responsibilities and dangers of queens were most likely a topic of conversation in eleventh-century Arras. Both the artists of the Saint-Vaast Bible and the redactors of the *ordo ad benedicendam reginam* in the Cologne Pontifical drew on well-established traditions to construct a vision of queenship using biblical models. While images of actual Carolingian and Capetian queens are rare before the thirteenth and fourteenth centuries, in the Anglo-Saxon and Ottonian worlds royal women were much more frequently depicted. In all of these dynasties, however, clerical writers developed a series of literary *topoi* that frequently utilized *exempla* from the Bible to outline how they desired the queen to use her status as a role model and her influence as a presence in the royal court. The same *topoi* find a visual parallel in Biblical manuscripts meant for the eyes of powerful clerics and their noble patrons, and perhaps even for the eyes of the queen herself.

From the Carolingian period onwards, artists and programmers used the illuminated Bible as a vehicle for imagery directed at royal women and their contemporaries. As I will discuss below, the artists of the dedication image in the ninth-century Bible of San Paolo fuori le mura depicted the reigning queen next to King Charles the Bald, perhaps as a mark of her recent coronation and in recognition of the court's hopes for her fertility (fig. 45).[1] They also mined the Bible's text for virtuous prototypes for the queen. In a frontispiece

---

[1] Rome, San Paolo fuori le mura, fol. 1.

to Rabanus Maurus's *Expositio in librum Judith*, probably produced at Reims around 830, the second wife of King Louis the Pious, also named Judith, is shown receiving a crown from the hand of God in a *carmen figuratum*.[2] This was probably intended as part of a flattering dedicatory comparison between Queen Judith and her namesake, a biblical prototype of queenship. This practice lasted well beyond the ninth century. In the thirteenth century two royal monuments included cycles of images of Old Testament female role models joined to their extensive programs dedicated to the idea of heavenly-sanctioned Capetian kingship. The miniatures prefacing the books of Judith, Esther, and Ruth in the Arsenal Old Testament,[3] produced at Saint-Jean d'Acre between 1250 and 1254 may have been intended indirectly for the glorification of Blanche of Castile, queen-mother of Louis IX. The stained glass lancets depicting Judith and Esther at the Sainte-Chapelle in Paris, dedicated in 1248, may have had a similar purpose to the Arsenal Old Testament.

The designers of the Saint-Vaast Bible followed in the footsteps of their Carolingian predecessors in using Old Testament prototypes to construct a vision of queenship appropriate to the political circumstances then facing the monarchy and their partners in government, the Church. They also chose the same didactic tool popular with Carolingian royal clerical advisors, the Bible. Rather than using a dedication image, however, the Saint-Vaast artists, as they had in their kingship program, once again referred to their theme tangentially, through the language of Biblical models. They drew from diverse books of the Bible, including a poetical book (the Song of Songs), a pseudepigraphical tale of martyrdom (the Passion of the Maccabees), and a heroic novella (the Book of Esther). The artists of the Arras Bible wove together a series of diverse filaments by uniting the themes of marriage, motherhood, and the partnership of the king and queen in these three frontispieces dedicated to Old Testament prototypes of the ideal wife and mother. All of these components were necessary to confront the issues facing the Church: the politics of royal marriage, the role of women in relation to the Church, and the duties of the queen to her own family and to the realm, within the royal household and outside it.

---

[2] Geneva Bibliothèque publique et universitaire MS lat. 22, fol. 3v, PL 109:542.
[3] Paris, Bibliothèque de l'Arsenal MS 5211.

Sponsus-Sponsa: the Song of Songs

The Saint-Vaast Bible's illustration prefacing the Song of Songs, fol. 141v of volume II (pl. V), drawn by the Ezra Master, is one of the most flamboyantly decorated and carefully organized miniatures of the entire Bible. Within a zodiac circle formed from an unfurling white tendril, Christ-logos sits enthroned before a heavenly city constructed of an architectural encyclopedia of turrets, doors, roofs, and posts. Christ has been captured in the midst of a conversation with a veiled woman standing to his left. Compared with the ad hoc appearance of many of the other miniatures, this illustration seems both more carefully planned and designed to take advantage of the relationship between text and image. This is not an historiated initial (as the text starts complete with the word *Osculetur* below), but the circular shape of the zodiac mirrors the first letter of the text.

The Song of Songs illustration in the Saint-Vaast Bible is the very first, and also the largest, in what would become a long series of Song of Songs illustrations picturing the mystical union between Christ and his Church, often called the *Sponsus-Sponsa*, or husband and wife, image. Later artists showed the union between the heavenly couple in a much more explicit manner, depicting not just the kiss of the first word of the text, but occasionally even an intimate embrace. In one case, the *Sponsus* even grasps the naked breast of the *Sponsa*.[4]

The Ezra Master, in exploring this theme seemingly for the first time, chose to restrict the relationship between the bride and bridegroom to a chaste dialogue. Nonetheless, he has created one of the most complex surviving illustrations of this love poem between Christ and *Ecclesia*. Combining a series of familiar symbols, such as the zodiac and the heavenly city of Jerusalem, the composition implies a subtext about contemporary issues facing the Church. This illumination, along with several others in the Bible, addresses the changing status of marriage in the eleventh and twelfth centuries and the Christian vocation of the married woman, especially the one who served as the primary role model for upper-class society: the queen.

The Ezra Master was truly breaking new ground, for this miniature is the first surviving illustration of the Song of Songs in a Bible.

---

[4] Reims BM MS 18, fol. 149.

The erotic nature of the first-person poetry of the book must have stymied previous generations of artists, for it made a straightforward literal visualization next to impossible in a Christian context. The Saint-Vaast artist, unable to turn to an existing Song of Songs tradition for inspiration, borrowed the bulk of this illustration almost wholesale, it seems, from the Carolingian commentator Rabanus Maurus' *De rerum naturis*. This is an encyclopedia of the earth and heavens compiled in the mid-ninth century primarily from Isidore of Seville's *Etymologiae* that survives in several illustrated copies, although none predates the eleventh century. An early eleventh-century copy of *De rerum naturis* from Montecassino, probably based on a Carolingian model, illustrates Book Nine with personifications of the sun and moon as busts of a man and woman shown side by side within a zodiac circle.[5] The resemblance between the Montecassino *De rerum naturis* illustration and the Saint-Vaast Bible Song of Songs miniature is striking enough to suggest that the Ezra Master had a very similar source available to him when he set out to compose his own illustration. The Christian allegorical interpretation of the heavens attached to the *De rerum naturis* miniature in its original context provides a ready explanation for this borrowing. Not surprisingly, Rabanus interprets the sun as Christ, while its counterpart the moon is interpreted as *Ecclesia*. Book Nine's description of the heavens doesn't specifically mention the zodiac.[6] Rabanus Maurus's *De laudibus sancti crucis*, however, provides an even more direct explanation for the arrangement of the image by exploring the Christian numerology of twelve. After comparing the number of zodiac signs to the number of winds, months, and hours of the day with sun, as well as patriarchs and tribes of Israel, Rabanus describes the home of Christ and *Ecclesia* in the celestial Jerusalem as a bejeweled city with twelve sacraments, twelve gates and twelve foundations.[7] The writings

---

[5] Montecassino, cod. Casinensis Ms 132, fol. 118. Diane O. Le Berrurier, *The Pictorial Sources of Mythological and Scientific Illustrations in Hrabanus Maurus' De rerum naturis* (New York, 1978), 60–62. Le Berrurier suggests that the artist of the model for the Montecassino manuscript probably borrowed his illustration, in turn, from Aratus of Soloi's *Phaenomena*, for which a similar illustration survives in Rome BAV cod. Vat. gr. 1087.

[6] *De rerum naturis*, PL 111:263–264. Rabanus does interpret the twelve months of the year as the twelve apostles or perhaps obliquely as the different orders of the earthly church. *De rerum naturis*, PL 111:267, 269, 301.

[7] *Rabani Mauri in honorem sancti crucis*, ed. Michel Perrin, Corpus christianorum, Continuatio mediaevalis C (Turnhout, 1997), 77–79.

of Rabanus and associated surviving illustrations provide sources for
almost all the visual details in the Saint-Vaast Bible's Song of Songs
image.

The Ezra Master mined these sources in order to visualize the
allegorical interpretation assigned to the text by Christian commentators on the Song of Songs. Although his illustration stands at the
beginning of a long line of conceptually similar miniatures, the Arras
Bible's version of this scene predates the next surviving example by
perhaps as much as fifty years. What inspired him to create such
an original illustration, one of the most carefully composed and compositionally successful in the entire Bible? Several possibilities present themselves.

The first and most obvious is suggested by the text immediately
following the image. The scribe inserted a series of rubrics into the
text that interpret the words of the Song of Songs as a conversation between a cast of characters that includes Christ, *Ecclesia*, and
Synagoga.[8] Inspired by such works as Bede's and Alcuin's commentaries on the Song of Songs, these rubrics were incorporated into
even the pre-Jerome *Vetus Latina* version of the Bible.[9] By the eighth
and ninth century, they had become a standard part of the text of
the Song of Songs, although they are unfortunately seldom edited
in critical editions of the Vulgate, and aren't even mentioned in discussions of Song of Songs illustration.[10] Examples are found in such
well-known illustrated Bibles as the Codex Amiatinus, a Hiberno-
Saxon Bible copied at the Roman-influenced scriptorium of
Wearmouth-Jarrow in the early-eighth century,[11] and in two of the
surviving ninth-century illustrated Tours Bibles, the Moutier-Grandval
Bible and the First Bible of Charles the Bald.[12] At least six, and
probably more, versions of these rubrics had developed by the end

---

[8] Diane J. Reilly, "Picturing the monastic drama: Romanesque Bible illustrations
of the Song of Songs," *Word & Image* XVII (2001), 389–400.

[9] Donatien De Bruyne, "Les anciennes versions latines du Cantique des Cantiques,"
Revue bénédictine XXXVIII (1926), 97–122, and idem, *Sommaires, divisions et rubriques
de la Bible latine* (Namur, 1914), 558–561.

[10] For instance, the most recent critical edition of the Vulgate, the *Biblia sacra
iuxta Latinam vulgatam versionem ad codicum fidem*, ed. Henri Quentin et al., 18 vols.
(Rome, 1926–1995), XI, makes no mention of these rubrics.

[11] Florence, Biblioteca Laurenziana MS Amiatinus 1.

[12] London BL MS Add. 10546, fol. 260v and Paris BnF MS lat. 1, fol. 243v.

of the Romanesque era, but the version chosen by the scribe to elaborate the text of the Arras Bible was the oldest; that found in the Codex Amiatinus, and the illustrated Touronian Bibles: Variant A.[13]

Because the Saint-Vaast Bible was used for refectory and choir reading, one must assume that the intent behind including this series of rubrics was that they should be read aloud to a listening body of monks. In fact, a later manuscript from the Cistercian abbey of Vauclair specifically directs the refectory lector, "In the Canticle of Canticles, 'The Voice of Christ' and 'The Voice of the Church' shall be said."[14] The listener would have heard the Song of Songs as a theatrical dialogue, with the voices divided up using identifying labels pronounced by the reader. These sets of rubrics were not rigidly codified sequences, however. Although Donatien De Bruyne, the editor of the biblical rubrics, divided them into a set typology, a survey of over forty surviving manuscripts with Song of Songs rubrics inserted into their texts reveals that no two sets of rubrics are exactly alike.[15] The scribes seem to have had considerable leeway in picking and choosing which rubrics to include and where to insert them, meaning that each manuscript version of the Song of Songs would be interpreted slightly differently when read out loud.

In the Arras Bible, the conversation between Christ and the Church begins in chapter one, verse five. The monks listening to the reading in the refectory would have heard: "[Voice of the Church]— Shew me, O thou who my soul loveth, where thou feedest, where thou liest in the midday, lest I begin to wander after the flocks of my companions. [Voice of Christ]—If thou know not thyself, O fairest among women, go forth, and follow after the steps of the flocks, and feed thy kids beside the tents of the shepherds." The scribe here has chosen to emphasize the dialogue of the mystical couple, Christ and *Ecclesia*, at the expense of the rest of the usual participants. In other Bibles that include Variant A rubrics the voices of Mary Magdalene and the Synagogue are soon heard. In the Arras

---

[13] De Bruyne's Variant A, DeBruyne, *Sommaires*, 559.

[14] Chrysogonus Waddell, "The Song of Songs in the Stephen Harding Bible," *Liturgy* XVIII/2 (1984), 29.

[15] This survey was undertaken in 1999 using the microfilm collection of the Hill Monastic Manuscript Library at St. John's University, Collegeville, Minnesota, and included manuscripts from across Western Europe, from the early Medieval period to the beginning of the Gothic era.

Bible, these characters have been left out. In the first four chapters
only Christ and the Church speak. These changes to the rubrics
have important implications for how we interpret the Song of Songs
illustration.

Peter Brieger, in the first investigation of the iconography of the
Saint-Vaast Bible, interpreted this miniature as an address to unchaste
clergy. Brieger set the miniature within the theological debate over
the marriage of priests and the predominance of simony in the early-
eleventh century.[16] He felt that the presence of *Ecclesia* in what is
clearly the heavenly Jerusalem is meant to reflect Bede's interpretation of the Song of Songs. "Grace, mother and progenitor of the
Church which nourishes and protects her now in the unity of Catholic
peace, will raise her in times to come to the joys of a heavenly
fatherland, leaving behind her the crowds of schismatics."[17] According
to Brieger, the architectural vista behind her may refer to an anonymous Carolingian commentator's interpretation of Songs 1:16, "the
cedarbeams of our house." These were "the heart of the elect incor-
ruptible like cedar wood in whom Christ rests as under a roof." The
same commentator speaks of the future union of the Church with
the Heavenly Jerusalem after the expulsion of the sinful, specifically
the concubines and *adulescentularum*.[18] Thus the Saint-Vaast miniature
could picture the Church's rightful arrival in Jerusalem after her
relief from the threat of corrupt clergy.

While this interpretation does address the general context of the
creation of the Saint-Vaast Bible and some features of the miniature, it ignores the figure at the very heart of the illustration, Christ,
and the dialogue he holds with *Ecclesia*. Surely the core meaning of
the miniature should be found in these two figures rather than their
backdrop! Nonetheless, Brieger's interpretation and his sources provide a clue to a more compelling interpretation for the miniature.

---

[16] Peter Brieger, "Bible Illustration and Gregorian Reform," *Studies in Church History*
II (1965), 156–157.

[17] PL 91:1183.

[18] Paris BnF MS lat. 2822, fol. 141, *Tigna donorum nostrarum cedrina: Tecta domorum
corda sunt electorum, quae per incorruptionem cedris comparantur, in his enim Christus velut sub
tecto quiescit*, and fol. 147, *Una est matri suae, electa genetricis suae; matri suae scilicet
Jerusalem, una est ergo illi sancta electorum ecclesia, quia expulsis cunctis reprobis, quos sub
nomine concubinarum et adulescetularum appellat, ipsi tantummodo sociabuntur illi*, as quoted
in Helmut Riedlinger, *Die Makellosigkeit der Kirche in den lateinischen Hohelied-Kommentaren
des Mittelalters* (Münster Westfalen, 1958), 92, n. 13.

This *Sponsus-Sponsa* composition, as the name suggests, may indeed refer to the problems surrounding marriage in the eleventh century. Instead of addressing the issue of those who should not marry in the eyes of the Church, namely the clergy, the miniature's message refers to those whose marriages are ideally modeled on the mystical union between Christ and the Church: the laity.

A series of events and documents surrounding the Bible point in this very direction. The issue of lay marriage, from the highest levels of society down to the peasant masses, was at that time vexing the leaders of the Church, including Gerard of Cambrai. A series of events involving the bishops of Arras-Cambrai and revealed by the documents they left behind illuminates the meaning of this and several other images in the Saint-Vaast Bible.

Henry and Anne and royal marriage in the eleventh century

In the spring of 1051, the Capetian King Henry I concluded marriage negotiations with Prince Jaroslav of Kiev for the hand of his daughter, Anne.[19] The choice of Anne of Kiev may reflect Henry's experience as the son of a domineering and powerful mother, Constance of Arles. Third wife of Robert the Pious, Constance had arrived at court armed with a party of noble supporters who were willing to stop at nothing, including murder, in her aid.[20] After bitterly fighting repudiation by her husband, Constance then favored her younger son, also named Robert, in the succession battle that followed the king's death.[21] Anne of Kiev, by contrast, traveled so far for her nuptials that she was unable to bring a substantial coterie of supporters, and remained politically impotent and dependent on her husband for the remainder of his life.

Henry had been made a widower in 1044 by the death of his first wife, Matilda, a daughter of the Imperial household. When this first betrothal was negotiated, it was intended to shore up power in

---

[19] Robert-Henri Bautier, "Anne de Kiev, reine de France, et la politique royale au XIe siècle. Étude critique de la documentation," *Revue des études slaves* LVII (1985), 539–564.

[20] Marion F. Facinger, "A Study of Medieval Queenship: Capetian France 987–1237," *Studies in Medieval and Renaissance History* V (1968), 5–6.

[21] Bautier, 543, 547.

the succession dispute following King Robert's death. After Matilda's death, Henry may have married yet another Imperial daughter for her value as a pawn in the process of forming political alliances.[22] When this princess also died still in childhood, Henry seems to have found the next best thing. In Anne he received a wife who was not too closely related to him by blood, but who provided a political alliance on the other side of the Ottonian Empire.[23] Yet she came to the court unknown, unrevered, and possibly even unable to speak the local language.[24]

Thus prevented from beginning any immediate political intrigue, Anne nonetheless could fulfill the functions visualized for her by contemporary clerics. But what was a queen, in their eyes? To establish the sanctioned role of the medieval queen, both the abstract definition invented by their contemporaries and the real role played by living queens, involves an examination of a variety of different kinds of documents. Letters written to queens by their spiritual advisors, admonitory literature about the royal office, hagiography, panegyric and criticism written about historical queens, and visual documents depicting queens and their prototypes all reveal a strikingly consistent picture. From the early Middle Ages onwards, the office of the Christian queen had been very narrowly defined by her most important critics, the clergy. Merovingian, Carolingian, and Capetian queens all worked within a definition of queenship intended to make them as harmless yet as useful as possible by limiting their contributions to the realms of modest and supportive wife, progenitor and educator of royal children, and proponent of the Church. The degree to which the actions of the queen conformed to this model, however, varied greatly depending upon the stability and power of the monarchy, and is most often revealed in the castigation delivered by this very same institution, the Church.

---

[22] Bautier, 543–544 and note 1, p. 544. The sources seem confused on this issue because both princesses, the first the daughter of Emperor Conrad and Empress Gisela, and the second the daughter of Liudolf of Frisia and Gisela's granddaughter, bore the name Matilda.

[23] Bautier, 545, 549.

[24] Marion F. Freidson (Facinger), "A Study of Medieval Queenship. Capetian France 987–1237," Ph.D. Dissertation, University of Chicago, 1964, 33. No contemporary commented on her possible multilingualism, but apparently in 1063, thirteen years after her arrival, she signed an act in Cyrillic characters, hinting that Russian may still have been her customary language (Freidson, 32 n. 1).

Many early queens were praised for their holiness and held up as role models for their successors. Rathier of Verona, writing in the middle of the tenth century, suggested that queens who desired eternal life should imitate, in addition to the Virgin Mary, Empress Helena, mother of Constantine, Queen Radegond, wife of Chlothar, Queen Clothilde, wife of Clovis, and Empress Galla Placidia, daughter of Theodosius.[25] Other queens, such as Constance of Arles, were routinely pilloried for their perceived interference in the affairs of state.[26] Marion Facinger has pointed out that the loose definition of the early Capetian realm and the monarchy's royal powers may, in fact, have increased the ability of the queen to influence affairs of state and to participate in the government of the royal household, and by extension, the kingdom.[27] The early Capetian monarchy had no permanent capital and the government moved along with the rulers. Because the court was centered in the familial residence of the king and queen, the queen was present for discussions of the administration of the kingdom, and was often a member of the *curia regis*, witnessing documents and arguing on behalf of petitioners to the court.[28] Achille Luchaire in his 1891 study of the Capetian monarchy invented a term for the power structure that developed: the Capetian trinity. The queen joined the crowned king and his heir, who, as we have seen,[29] was often formally associated to rule at a relatively young age, in governing the then still very limited realm.[30] This was made possible by the weakness of the Capetian monarchy in the early eleventh century, and the lack of a developed bureaucracy. In this period of monarchical decline, the king's family members

---

[25] Suzanne Fonay Wemple, "Le pouvoirs des femmes en Europe occidentale au Xᵉ siècle," in *La femme au moyen âge*, eds. Michel Rouche and Jean Heuclin (Maugeuge, 1988), 347, commenting on *Praeloquiorum libri sex*, II, tit. IV 20, PL 136:206B.

[26] Her biggest critics include Aimon and André de Fleury, *Miracula sancti Benedicti*, ed. E. de Certain, Société de l'histoire de France (Paris, 1858), repr. 1968, Radulfus Glaber, *Historiarum libri quinque*, ed. Neithard Bulst, trans. John France and Paul Reynolds (Oxford, 1989), and Helgaud de Fleury, *Vie de Robert le pieux. Epitoma vitae regis Rotberti pii*, ed. Robert H. Bautier and Gillette Labory, Sources d'histoire médiévale I (Paris, 1965).

[27] Facinger, 24.

[28] Facinger, 26–27.

[29] Above, chapter 4.

[30] *Histoire des institutions monarchiques de la France sous les premiers capétiens (987–1180)* (Paris, 1891), I, 133–134.

and the minor nobles who surrounded the court served by necessity
as the court's officials.[31]

Recent research on the scope of action for women in medieval
France describes an emerging dichotomy between queens and aristocratic women.[32] The powers of the queen seem to have eroded in
the course of the eleventh century as her role was circumscribed
through the intervention of the Church, the newly developed royal
bureaucracy and changes in the structure of the family.[33] Aristocratic
women, on the other hand, subject to much less interference from
these institutions, continued to exercise considerable power, especially
as sole inheritors of a fief, or in the absence of their husbands. In
the eleventh and twelfth centuries, northern French wives are well
documented as ruling as subsidiaries to their husbands in their presence, and as serving in the capacity of lords after their husbands'
deaths, or while they were away on military campaigns.[34] In those
cases they could supervise pious gifts, command groups of knights,
render judgement in secular courts and conduct diplomatic negotiations. What both royal and noble women seemed to share, however, was a series of functions seemingly relegated to the domestic
realm but which necessarily bled over into affairs of state.[35] The
queen and the noblewoman could provide heirs for a dynasty, defend
the interests of the church before her husband, and finally, she could
raise her children in a manner suitable to future leaders and yet
respectful of the teachings of the Church.[36] These were the roles

[31] Jean F. Lemarignier, *Le gouvernment royale aux premiers temps capétiens (987–1108)*
(Paris, 1965), 75–76.
[32] Kimberly LoPrete and Theodore Evergates, "Introduction," in *Aristocratic Women
in Medieval France*, ed. Theodore Evergates (Philadelphia, 1999), 1–5.
[33] Jo Ann McNamara and Suzanne Wemple, "The Power of Women Through
the Family in Medieval Europe, 500–1100," *Feminist Studies* I (1973), 126–42, reprinted
in *Women and Power in the Middle Ages*, ed. Mary Erler and Maryanne Kowaleski
(Athens, 1988), 83–101, and Facinger, 3–48.
[34] Kimberly LoPrete, "Adela of Blois: Familial Alliances and Female Lordship,"
in *Aristocratic Women in Medieval France*, 7–43 and Karen Nicholas, "Countesses as
Rulers in Flanders," in *Aristocratic Women in Medieval France*, 111–128.
[35] Susan Mosher Stuard, "Fashion's Captives: Medieval Women in French
Historiography," in *Women in Medieval History & Historiography*, ed. Susan Mosher
Stuard (Philadelphia, 1987), 68–69, 74, points out that the permeable membrane
between public and private life caused the exclusion of many powerful medieval
women from twentieth-century histories until very recently.
[36] Sharon Farmer, "Persuasive Voices: Clerical Images of Medieval Wives," *Speculum*
LXI (1986), 517–526.

assigned to both royal and aristocratic women within the family from at least the Merovingian period onwards, when queens such as Balthild are described as directing almsgiving from the court treasury, supervising the education of the youths of the palace, and influencing their husbands in the interests of the Church.[37]

In the Carolingian era, the office of queen as something akin to a co-ruler with the king was much more readily acknowledged.[38] While several documents of this period express the ideal role of the queen, Hincmar of Reims was probably the most effective codifier of the Carolingian idea of queenship. Not only did he craft two coronation ordines for queens that would serve as models for future generations, but his *De ordine palatii* picked up where the ordines left off, describing the duties of the queen after her coronation. The queen was to oversee the smooth administration of the palace, which was extended to cover the diplomatic functions of the state. The concerns of the Church were to be brought before both the king and the queen.[39] Sedulius Scottus's *speculum principis* "On Christian Rulers" pointed out that the choice of a royal wife should be made with care, because the king should be able to rely on her advice, especially in spiritual matters.

> A ruler, therefore, should perspicaciously endeavor to have a wife who is not only noble, beautiful and wealthy, but also chaste, prudent, and compliant in holy virtues . . . Not only unbelieving but also pious and orthodox princes often ponder and give heed to the marvelous prudence in their wives, not reflecting on their fragile sex, but, rather, plucking the fruit of their good counsels.[40]

Writings by the clergy frequently sanctioned the spiritual leadership provided by the royal wife. By the eleventh century, the literature depicting women as patrons of churches either using their own wealth or that of their husbands was extensive, for not only could aristocratic

---

[37] Janet Nelson, "Queens as Jezebels: the Careers of Brunhild and Balthild in Merovingian History," in *Medieval Women*, ed. Derek Baker (Oxford, 1978), 31–77.

[38] Franz-Reiner Erkens, "'Sicut Esther regina.' Die westfränkische Königen als *consors regni*," *Francia* XX (1993), 15–20.

[39] Hincmar of Reims, *De ordine palatii* editio altera, ed. Thomas Gross and Rudolf Schieffer, MGH Fontes iuris Germanici antiqui III (Hanover, 1980), chap. 22, 72–73.

[40] *On Christian Rulers and the Poems*, trans. Edward G. Doyle, Medieval and Renaissance Texts and Studies XVII (Binghamton, 1983), 59–60.

wives influence their husbands' actions, they could even make up for their husbands' misdeeds behind their backs.[41] In England, like in France, the queen was glorified as a pious intercessor and a powerful patron. In the early-twelfth century, Queen Matilda, wife of Henry I of England, was known as a consistent and generous benefactor of the Church. She also attested her husband's charters, was present at meetings of the royal curia, and even served as regent when the king was away, overseeing the administration of government.[42] Matilda's contribution to the health of the realm was recognized by her contemporaries. A letter from Hildebert of Lavardin after the birth of one of her children praised her as one who "preserves reverance for the laws and the undamaged state of the church."[43] In addition, a third of the life of St. Margaret, written in the early-twelfth century by the cleric Turgod for her daughter, Queen Matilda, is dedicated to explaining Margaret's efforts to reconcile the practices of the Scottish church with those of Rome.[44] Even during the life of Queen Anne, wife of the Capetian King Henry, clerics referred in their writings to these already codified norms.

After Henry's death, Anne's precipitous remarriage to a prominent and already-married noble seems to have effectively removed her from the scandalized court.[45] During her brief nine-year reign as queen, from her marriage in 1051 until Henry's death in 1060, however, Anne functioned in the way Henry had most likely anticipated. In addition to giving birth to three sons and patronizing a series of religious foundations together with her husband,[46] she developed a working relationship with the leadership of the Church.[47]

---

[41] Farmer, 535–538, and Jean Leclercq, "Rôle et pouvoir des épouses au moyen âge," in *La femme au moyen âge*, eds. Michel Rouche and Jean Heuclin (Maugeuge, 1988), 91–92 and 95–96.

[42] Lois L. Huneycutt, "'Proclaiming her Dignity Abroad': The Literary and Artistic Network of Matilda of Scotland, Queen of England 1100–1118," in *The Cultural Patronage of Medieval Women*, ed. June Hall McCash (Athens, GA, 1996), 157.

[43] Huneycutt, 161–162.

[44] Huneycutt, 162.

[45] Bautier, 553–559 and Andre Poulet, "Capetian Women and the Regency: the Genesis of a Vocation," in *Medieval Queenship*, ed. John Carmi Parsons (New York, 1993), 101, 106–107.

[46] Diplomata Henrici I Francorum Regis, *Recueil des historiens des Gaules et de la France* XI, Congrégation de Saint-Maur (Paris, 1767), 559–600, charters XXXI–XXXIII list her name as one of the witnesses.

[47] Bautier, 551.

A letter from Pope Nicholas II to Anne written near the end of Henry's life exhorted her to carry out the duties incumbent upon her as queen.[48] Nicholas reminded her that her fecundity was a gift from God, which must be repaid by her efforts to rear her sons as future leaders who revere the Church above money and power. This somewhat formulaic injunction about her role as mother is, however, prefaced by a much more telling description of her duty as a wife. Anne's influence as a model and companion made her the ideal instructor of her husband, as well. She was to use her wiles to influence the king to protect the interests of the Church. Doing this allowed her to follow in the footsteps of a rather surprising pair of Old Testament wives of wise kings: Abigail and the Queen of Sheba.

Nicholas compared Anne to Abigail, who assuaged the anger of David, and thus preserved her husband Nabal from the sword.[49] Likewise, he stated, Anne should lead her husband to preserve "those who are of God." Further, Anne's marriage should rise above the concerns of the flesh to focus on its spiritual benefits. "In what manner," he asked, "are those wives believed to love their husbands, who love in them the shells, as such I will say, of the body, but they do not turn towards the gold of the spirit which is buried in them?"[50] Nicholas reinforced his recasting of royal marriage as a spiritual partnership with yet another comparison to a royal couple. "For Queen Sheba came not to see the wealth but to hear the wisdom of Solomon. That which she did not desire, all the same most plentifully she brought back."[51] Just as the Queen of Sheba, according to Nicholas, had sought out Solomon because of his reputation for wisdom, David chose Abigail to be his wife after the death of Nabal because of her demonstrated wisdom and good council, which had prevented him from tainting his hands with blood. This was the model of marriage then preferred by the Church, a spiritual union entered into not on the basis of land holdings or family contract but

---

[48] *Recueil des Historiens des Gaules et de la France* XI, 653.

[49] I Kings 25.

[50] *Recueil des Historiens des Gaules et de la France* XI, 653. *Alioquinquo pacto viros suos illae conjuges amare credantur, quae in eis capsas, ut ita loquar, corporum diligunt; sed animarum aurum, quod in eis reconditur, non attendunt?*

[51] *Recueil des Historiens des Gaules et de la France* XI, 653, referring to III Kings 10:1–13.

rather for spiritual gain.[52] The Church's interest in regulating royal marriage must have been directly related to their desire that the king choose a helpmeet who would work on their behalf, guided by them to appeal to the king's spiritual strengths.

The picture of holy matrimony painted by Nicholas is strikingly at odds with the form practiced by European royal and noble dynasties well beyond the eleventh century. From the time of Louis the Pious the Church had taken a more active interest in the regulation of marriage as one of the best means for the laity to avoid sin. Although the Church had long participated, at least to some extent, in marriage ritual, they now sought to intervene in the decision of who would marry whom and how long these marriages would last. The 829 Council of Paris set out several guidelines for proper marriage. Divorce was allowable only in cases of fornication, incest must be avoided, and consanguinity was prohibited to the seventh degree.[53] Later commentators on marriage pointed out that the union between husband and wife should mirror "the mystical union between God and his creation," and thus that marriage should be primarily a spiritual, rather than a sexual, joining of two Christians.[54] For the royalty and nobility, however, the Church's definition of marriage interfered with their more pragmatic approach, in which marriage was a fundamental tool in establishing political and familial alliances, as well as creating heirs. Prohibitions against endogamy, and the inability to repudiate barren or politically useless wives, were roadblocks thrown up by the Church in the negotiation of what had been, until then, a primarily civil matter.[55]

The marriage ceremony of Anne of Kiev to King Henry in the spring of 1051 after her arrival from Russia reveals much about the way marriage was seen in the middle of the eleventh century, the relationship between the Church and the kingdom, and the status

---

[52] Georges Duby, *Medieval Marriage. Two Models from Twelfth-Century France* (Baltimore, 1978), 16–17.

[53] Georges Duby, *The Knight, the Lady and the Priest: The Making of Modern Marriage in Medieval France* (New York, 1983), 30–31, 36 and Council of Meaux-Paris, *Die Konzilien der karolingischen Teilreiche, 843–859*, ed. Wilfried Hartmann, MGH Concilia III, Concilia aevi Karolini DCCCXLIII–DCCCLIX (Hanover, 1984), 81–131.

[54] Duby, *The Knight, the Lady and the Priest*, 31, Jonas of Orleans from *De istitutione laicali*, PL 106:121–278.

[55] Duby, *The Knight, the Lady and the Priest*, 48.

of the royal wife. According to the *Vita Lietberti*, written well after the event by Rudolfus, Abbot of St. Trond, King Henry heard that the new Bishop of Arras-Cambrai had been designated and was about to be consecrated by the Archbishop of Reims. He petitioned that the blessing and coronation of his new bride take place at the same time.[56] Thus both ceremonies were celebrated on the nineteenth of May, 1051. The blessing of a royal bride and her consecration were ceremonies that had been combined already in the Carolingian era when Hincmar of Reims wrote a Coronation ordo for the marriage between Judith, daughter of Charles the Bald, and an Anglo-Saxon king.[57] Although the idea that a bishop's consecration was a type of marriage between the bishop and his church was commonly understood from at least the ninth century, joining this event to an actual wedding was an innovation.[58]

In the *Vita Lietberti*, Rudolfus critiqued this unusual combination of ceremonies. While the king of the Franks wed a carnal spouse, he described, the bishop instead wed the Holy Church. How much better and holier was this union, said Rudolfus, for while one generated carnal offspring through corruption, the other bred holy progeny through adoption and virginity. The daughter of the earthly king was led to the king of the Franks, while the wife (*Ecclesia*) of the King of kings (Christ), was committed to the bishop, Lord Lietbert.[59] Even as the Church struggled to change the common understanding of the nature of marriage from carnal to spiritual and to restructure marriage and subsume it within its own series of sacraments, as witnessed by this unique joint consecration, Rodulfus, who died in 1138, still clung to the popular belief that lay marriage was an institution born of carnal needs. As we will see, a group of documents contemporary with the wedding, rather than the *Vita Lietberti* which dates from fifty years later, shows that the religious and political issues surrounding marriage in the early-twelfth century had dominated ecclesiastical thought even at the time when Henry and Anne's union took place.

---

[56] Facinger, 17, *Vita sancti Lietberti*, PL 146:1459.

[57] *Ordines coronationis Franciae: Texts and Ordines for the Coronation of Frankish and French Kings and Queens in the Middle Ages*, ed. Richard A. Jackson, 2 vols. (Philadelphia, 1995–2000), I, 24.

[58] Jean Gaudemet, "Note sur le symbolisme médiéval: le mariage de l'évêque," in *La société ecclésiastique dans l'occident médiéval* (London, 1980), 71–80.

[59] *Vita sancti Lietberti*, PL 146:1460.

The Saint-Vaast Bible's Song of Songs illustration (pl. V), with its depiction of the ideal spiritual marriage between Christ and *Ecclesia*, is only our first hint that mystical marriage was a subject of discussion among the clergy of Flanders in the middle of the eleventh century. Although no records survive of the exact content of Henry and Anne's marriage ceremony, two other texts complement the Arras Bible's message about marriage. The first is the *Acta synodi Atrebatensis*. A veritable *summa* on the questions facing Church authority in the first half of the eleventh century, it was written on the occasion of Bishop Gerard of Cambrai's trial of the heretics of Arras in 1025 as already discussed in chapters three and four. It records his opinion that marriage was a necessary and acceptable form of union at a time when marriage was, it seems, slowly migrating from the domain of civil into ecclesiastical law.

The second text, the Cologne Pontifical, Cologne, Erzbishöfliche Diözesan Dombibliothek, Dom MS 141, has been described as a "very free adaptation of the Romano-Germanic Pontifical" that was then becoming the standard sacramental text for northern Europe.[60] Copied at Saint-Vaast in Arras in the decades around the marriage of Henry and Anne, it preserves two important and topical ceremonies: the nuptial blessing of a couple and the coronation ordo for a queen.

The Cologne Pontifical and Medieval Marriage

Robert the Pious, Henry's father and the second Capetian king, must have seemed to the Church to epitomize the problem with the royal practice of marriage. Married three times in succession, Robert repeatedly repudiated wives who had been chosen based on the diplomatic goals of the government rather than the Church's chief criterion, personal compatibility.[61] Married first between 988 and 989 at the direction of his father to Suzanne, the daughter of the king of Italy and widow of the Count of Flanders, Robert repudiated this wife

---

[60] Michel Andrieu, *Les ordines romani du haut moyen âge*, Spicilegium sacrum Lovaniense; Études et documents, fasc. 11, 23–24, 28–29, 5 vols. (Louvain, 1931–1961), IV, 476.

[61] Duby, *The Knight, the Lady and the Priest*, 76–83.

within three years, allegedly because she was barren. His second wife, Berthe, daughter of King Conrad of Burgundy and widow of the Count of Blois, was repudiated apparently for the same reason between 1001 and 1006, after the king had steadfastly refused to leave her for several years when accused by the Church of the crime of incest. His last wife, and the one of longest standing, was Constance, daughter of the Count of Arles. After she had given birth to three sons, Robert tried to repudiate her as well and return to Berthe, but was for the first time stymied when the Church successfully intervened on Constance's behalf. The nuptial blessing in the Cologne Pontifical, composed within the boundaries of France, represents one of the Church's mechanisms to prevent such calamitous events by finally wresting control of marriage away from the royal family and recasting it as a spiritual union.

The *ordo ad benedicendam sponsam* preserved in the Cologne Pontifical, composed contemporary with marriage of Henry and Anne if not for the ceremony itself, was on the cutting edge of marriage ritual. The words of the text encapsulate the developments that had taken place over the previous centuries, both during the Carolingian synods when the Church began to participate more and more actively in the sanctification of marriage, and more recently when reformers pushed to control the legal and contractual negotiation of marriage as well. The prayers and readings incorporated into the wedding mass explained the meaning of marriage and the ideal models for the bride and groom to eleventh-century observers.

Although the development of Christian marriage ritual is still the subject of great debate, from at least the Frankish period onwards the Church had taken tentative steps to intervene in the solemnities surrounding the event. Roman civil marriage custom, which divided the ceremony into two parts (the contractual arrangement called the betrothal, and the nuptials themselves) had been maintained into the medieval period.[62] The Church by the fourth century and perhaps

---

[62] Jean Gaudemet, "Le legs du droit romain en matière matrimoniale," in *Il matrimonio nella società altomedievale*, SSCISAM XXIV (Spoleto, 1977) I, 139–179 and Cyrille Vogel, "Les rites de la célébration du mariage: leur signification dans la formation du lien durant le haut moyen âge," in *Il matrimonio nella società altomedievale*, 426–437. The Christian version of this division is described in detail in Pope Nicholas I's ninth-century letter to the Bulgarian Church on western practice. Kenneth Stevenson, *Nuptial Blessing. A Study of Christian Marriage Rites* (London, 1982), 44 and

earlier had grafted onto these events a blessing, probably inspired by Jewish marriage practice.[63] In the unromanized areas of Gaul and in Spain, the marriage blessing was a *benedictio in thalamo*, or blessing in the bridal chamber.[64] In Rome and romanized areas the nuptial blessing soon seems to have been incorporated into a mass.[65] The Leonine Sacramentary preserves a marriage blessing joined to the mass, as do the Gelasian Sacramentary and the Gregorian Sacramentary.[66] This was the form that came to predominate in the Carolingian realm and later in Capetian France. From the time of Pepin the Short onwards, synods of the Church and the ninth-century Pseudo-Isidorian forgeries had also declared the public nature of marriage, and begun to supervise the publication of the banns and the investigation into any possible familial relationship of those intending to marry.[67] A liturgical ceremony for marriage never became necessary for the majority of the population, but in fact was actually withheld from all but the chosen few, chiefly members of noble and royal families. As the chief beneficiaries of the Church's spiritual advice and the most visible Christian role models for the family, the marriage of the royal couple would have attracted more attention from the clergy than any other union. Thus the marriage ceremonies written for actual royalty are occasionally preserved and we can assume that other preserved wedding liturgies would have been addressed primarily to noble and royal laypeople, the principle targets of the Church's reforms.

In the eleventh-century Cologne Pontifical from Arras, the interests of the reformers came to a head.[68] The redactors of the Cologne

Korbinian Ritzer, *Formen, Riten und religiöses Brauchtum der Eheschliessung in den christlichen Kirchen des ersten Jahrtausends* (Münster-Westfalen, 1962), 344–345.

[63] Stevenson, *Nuptial Blessing*, 13–16.

[64] Korbinian Ritzer, *Le mariage dans les églises chrétiennes du Ier au XIe siècle* (Paris, 1970), 273, and idem, *Formen*, 354–355, 360 and Stevenson, 49. This is preserved in an Irish-influenced prayerbook from the seventh or eighth century now in Bobbio and an eleventh-century sacramentary from Vich (Vich, Museo episcopal, MS 66), where it is followed by another blessing in the Church.

[65] Ritzer, *Le mariage*, 276–278.

[66] Ritzer, *Formen*, 345–349.

[67] Ritzer, *Le mariage*, 334–336, 340–348.

[68] Vogel, 433. Cologne, Erzbishöfliche Diözesan Dombibliothek, Dom MS 141, fols. 175–177. *Les ordines romani* I, 108–114, 113 for the *Ordo ad benedicendum sponsam*.

Pontifical seem to have been at the forefront of changes to marriage policy in the middle of the eleventh century by linking the civil ceremony to the blessing of the couple. Extracted from the marriage mass, a series of prayers are prefaced by a rubric demanding that they only be pronounced *Postquam fuerit mulier viro desponsata et legaliter dotata*.[69] As the priest must confirm that the legal requirements have been met, the public nature of the civil marriage was therefore guaranteed through the intervention of the Church.[70] Furthermore, the nuptial blessing included in the ceremony as preserved in the Pontifical elevated the spiritual nature of the marriage bond by comparing it to that instituted by God between Christ and the Church: "God, you who so consecrated the marriage bond in excellent mystery, that the sacrament of Christ to *Ecclesiae* marked before in contract of marriage . . ."[71] The compiler of the marriage mass borrowed this blessing from its original source, the Gregorian Sacramentary, but for some reason has reversed the usual order of events, putting this blessing and the other prayers at the beginning, in the tradition of older Gallican ritual, rather than imbedding them in the heart of the mass where they were commonly found after the advent of the Gregorian ritual.[72] He also reworked the nuptial prayer to mention both the bride and the groom instead of just the bride, a highly unusual variation, especially since the groom is also mentioned before the bride![73] One is led to wonder, given this new emphasis on the groom, if the explanation for these adjustments might be that the ceremony was composed for King Henry himself.

A contemporary document written for the signature of the Capetian king, Henry, proves that the royal circle was indeed aware of the concept of mystical marriage. Henry, his wife Anne, and their son Philip witnessed a donation to the monastery of Saint-Martin-de-

---

[69] Cologne, Erzbishöfliche Diözesan Dombibliothek, Dom MS 141, fol. 175.

[70] Ritzer, *Le mariage*, 333.

[71] Cologne, Erzbishöfliche Diözesan Dombibliothek, Dom MS 141, fol. 175v and Melchior Hittorp, *De divinis Catholicae ecclesiae officiis et mysteriis* (Paris, 1624), 177, *Deus, qui tam excellenti mysterio coniugalem copulam consecrasti, ut Christi Ecclesiae sacramentum praesignares in foedere nuptiarum.*

[72] Stevenson, 39, on the Gallican ritual and later traditions. For instance, in the early eleventh-century Norman Benedictional of Archbishop Robert (Rouen BM MS 369 [Y.7]), this blessing is found after the readings but before the communion (Ritzer, *Formen*, 366–368).

[73] Cologne, Erzbishöfliche Diözesan Dombibliothek, Dom MS 141, fol. 175v and Stevenson, 42.

Campis in 1060, immediately before the king's death.[74] Before listing the specifics of the gift, the author of the donation described at
great length the mystical marriage between Christ and *Ecclesia*, and
reasoned that in order to please the holy spouse in heaven, one must
venerate his wife, the Church, on earth. The author chose a range
of Biblical quotations designed to establish the continuity of his theme
from the beginning of history to that day. He started with a reference to the marriage of Adam and Eve from Genesis (2:24), and
the Psalter's reference to the heavenly bridegroom leaving his vir-
ginal bride chamber (18:6). From the New Testament he took
Matthew's reference to the age of grace using the analogy of the
presence of the bridegroom in the bridechamber (9:15), and Paul's
injunction from Ephesians that husbands should love their wives as
Christ loves the Church (5:25). Lastly, he called on chapter four of
the Song of Songs, "Come from Libanus, my spouse, come from
Libanus, come: thou shalt be crowned from the top of Amana, from
the top of Sanir and Hermon, from the dens of the lions, from the
mountains of the Leopards (4:8)." The terminology used by the redactor of the Cologne Pontifical's *ordo ad benedicendam sponsam* would have
been quite familiar and understandable to members of the royal family who signed such flowery edicts as this.

The institution of marriage was threatened, in the eyes of the
Church, both by the nobles who constantly mixed and matched
wives based on political expediency, typified by King Robert the
Pious, and by the cries of heretics who sought to banish carnal congress. Gerard, as a princely bishop of the Capetian realm, was called
on to police both of these issues. In the *Acta synodi Atrebatensis* Gerard
defended marriage from the frontal assault of the heretics who visited his diocese in 1025.

The Arras Heretics

The heretics of Arras, while claiming to follow the example set by
the Gospels and the Epistles, professed "legitima connubia exsecrari."[75]

---

[74] *Recueil des historiens des gaules et de la France* XI, 605–606, XXXVI, *Monasterio S. Martini de campis multa concedit.*
[75] Duby, *The Knight, the Lady and the Priest*, 112–114, and *Acta synodi Atrebatensis*, PL 149:1271.

Gerard, in a text littered with biblical quotations, explained that, in fact, marriage was sanctioned in the New Testament as a just and noble outlet for those who had not chosen a religious vocation.[76] While clerics must abstain from marriage, for laymen marriage was suitable as long as they were able to approach their wives with the proper spirit of sanctity rather than lust, and for the love of children.

He reaffirmed at great length the Gospels' and Epistles' pronouncements on the appropriateness of marriage and countered many of the practices that the Church, at that time, found so problematic. Beginning with the recurring issue of divorce, a living concern so soon after King Robert had repudiated two wives and attempted to put away a third, he quoted from both Matthew and the Pauline Epistles injunctions against repudiation, and reaffirmed that one who takes a spouse has not sinned.[77] He repeated Peter's pronouncement that wives should be subject to their husbands,[78] and that an unbelieving man can be won over through conversation with his wife. He pointed out as well the statement from Ephesians, that the man is the head of the wife just as Christ is the head of the Church. Further, men, he said, should love their wives just as Christ loved the Church. Marriage, he reaffirmed, as had many commentators before him, was for the procreation of children and the avoidance of sin.

Gerard of Cambrai was probably already aware of, if not deeply embroiled in, the politics surrounding royal marriage at that time. Add to this the rejection of marriage that he now faced within his own diocese, and suddenly the presence of a series of images addressing Christian marriage and the pious family in a Bible produced in his diocese during his episcopate becomes more than coincidental. If not compiled under his explicit direction, the imagery at least manages to articulate the concerns that must have faced him as the spiritual leader of the area.

---

[76] *Acta synodi Atrebatensis*, PL 149:1299–1300.
[77] Matthew 19:3–9, I Corinthians 7:10–14, 27–28.
[78] II Peter 3:1.

The Iconography of Mystical Marriage

The Saint-Vaast Bible's illustration of the Song of Songs (pl. V), which depicts the mystical union of Christ and the Church joined as *Sponsus* and *Sponsa* before their ideal heavenly home, the city of Jerusalem, thus resonates with the interpretation of marriage then being promoted by the clergy. The ideal heavenly couple of Christ and *Ecclesia* served as the foremost model for Christian earthly couples. Was the image of the heavenly bride and bridegroom intended to reflect the actual marriage ceremony, however?

The iconography of matrimony has been surprisingly consistent over time. Ancient Roman betrothal and marriage ritual had included many steps, including the reading of the auspices of the augurs, a sacrifice, the reading of the marriage contract and giving of a dowry, and the *dextrarum iunctio*, or contractual handshake.[79] Nonetheless, depictions of marriage from Roman antiquity concentrated on two parts of the marriage ceremony, the *dextrarum iunctio* and the nuptial sacrifice. The most popular of these images, the *dextrarum iunctio*, frequently includes the participation of a non-human *pronubus* as officiant, usually a deity such as *Concordia*, who pulls the two spouses together by grasping their shoulders. Thus these artworks (sarcophagi, gold-glass, coins and plates) are not true evocations of the wedding ritual but rather symbols of marital concord or the institution of marriage. This would be true of medieval Christian depictions of marriage as well.

The highly symbolic nature of marriage iconography is most apparent in coins and other artworks that depict the imperial couple, such as in a coin of Antoninus Pius and Faustina.[80] Distributed by the state, such coins emphasized that the unity and concord of the ruling family served to generate cosmic harmony and the stability of the nation.[81] The empress herself was occasionally depicted as *Concordia* or *Homonoia*, although outside the context of marriage iconography.

---

[79] Ernst Kantorowicz, "On the Golden Marriage Belt and the Marriage Rings of the Dumbarton Oaks Collection," *Dumbarton Oaks Papers* XIV (1960), 4.

[80] Harold Mattingly, *Coins of the Roman Empire in the British Museum* (London, 1923–1950), IV, pl. vii, fig. 13.

[81] Kantorowicz, "On the Golden Marriage Belt," 5 and Chiara Frugoni, "L'iconografia del matrimonio e della coppia nel medioevo," *Il matrimonio nella società altomedievale*, SSCISAM XXIV (Spoleto, 1977), II, 904–905, 915.

Empress Livia even served as the patron of marriages in Egypt, although no depictions of the empress as *pronuba* survive.[82] Clearly, then, the writers and artists of the later Middle Ages were not inventing a new concept when they proposed the royal marriage as a model for the realm and a vital aspect of its peace and harmony, and the queen or empress as a special component of that state.

Our knowledge of the physical actions of an eleventh-century Christian wedding is frustratingly slender. We still don't have a clear idea, for instance, of what a marriage ceremony would have looked like, where participants stood, what they wore, or at what point they joined hands. We don't know which parts of the old Roman ceremony were incorporated into the Church ritual in the cases of weddings blessed inside of a church. Because no vows or statements made by couples have been recorded, we don't know if the aspect of consent, essential in the eyes of the Church, had already been integrated into the blessing ceremony or remained a part of the betrothal, as it was in the ninth century when described by Pope Nicholas in his letter to the Bulgarians.[83] On the other hand, the dearth of descriptions of this part of the union may imply that it was so universal that it didn't need to be spelled out. Unfortunately, without clear records of what took place during an eleventh-century church wedding, we must extrapolate either forwards from recorded Roman ritual or backwards from the later Middle Ages when records again become abundant. Neither method can satisfactorily reveal how closely medieval marriage iconography mirrors an actual ceremony. Since the predominant part of the recorded Church marriage ceremony is a blessing appended to a nuptial mass, little of this ritual would have appeared different from a regular mass. Most likely, however, imagery that can be connected with marriage, like its Roman counterpart, was more symbolic than factual in nature.

Because the Early Christians took over almost wholesale the Roman ritual of marriage, they were provided with a ready-made, if rather limited, repertoire of marital iconography. Christian artists concentrated on the legal or contractual bond of marriage while at the same time emphasizing its symbolic spiritual aspect. They simply converted the pagan *dextrarum iunctio* by replacing the Roman deity

---

[82] Kantorowicz, "On the Golden Marriage Belt," 7.
[83] Stevenson, 45 and Ritzer, *Formen*, 344.

who acted as *pronubus* with Christ. He could be shown either full length, drawing the couple together, or bust length, hovering over the bride and groom while crowning them with wreaths.[84] Two early Byzantine wedding rings, one in the Dumbarton Oaks Collection and the other in the British Museum, Christianize the *pronubus* by depicting Christ and his heavenly bride, Mary, crowning the earthly bridal couple.[85] Thus they became the heavenly *exempla* of the concord that the bride and groom aimed to achieve.

In the eleventh and twelfth centuries, the marriage ceremony itself remained the two-stage process described above, with the betrothal, or secular contract, separated from the Christian blessing. Depictions of the betrothal of Joseph and the Virgin nonetheless retained the age-old formula of the contract in preference to inventing a new iconography for the Church ceremony. In a manuscript from the late-eleventh century produced near Arras at the cathedral of Saint-Omer, for instance, Joseph and the Virgin grasp hands, observed by a crowd of witnesses. No religious authority sanctions the union. The only evidence of its holy nature is the hand of God that hovers over the joined hands of the couple.[86] Only in the thirteenth century would a new variant on this iconography develop. In several moralized Bibles, the symbolic marriages of Christ and *Ecclesia*, or *Ecclesia* and a bishop combine the traditional joining of hands with the offering of a chalice, or a chalice placed on an altar between the couple, probably a reference to the nuptial mass that was quickly becoming a standard part of at least noble weddings.[87] As neither of these types of images depict marriage between two contemporary laypeople, however, the information they provide on the appearance of lay marriage is tangential at best.

One image that parallels the composition within the Song of Songs miniature and hints at its message to a royal couple nonetheless does not depict an actual wedding. The San Paolo Bible was probably produced at Reims for Charles the Bald between 869 and 876

---

[84] Frugoni, 901–913, 925–926.

[85] Kantorowicz, "On the Golden Marriage Belt," 13, on Dumbarton Oaks Collection no. 47.15 and O.M. Dalton, *Catalogue of the Finger Rings: Early Christian, Byzantine, Teutonic, Mediaeval and Later* (London, 1912), 8, No. 45.

[86] Saint Omer BM MS 154, fol. 1. *Catalogue général* III, St. Omer, 83–84.

[87] Kantorowicz, "On the Golden Marriage Belt," 12.

(fig. 45).[88] Its dedication image contains, at its core, the same iconography as the Song of Songs illustration in the Saint-Vaast Bible (pl. V). Within a circular canopied enclosure, Charles the Bald sits on a bejeweled throne. In his left hand he holds a golden orb inscribed with a mysterious monogram, while with his right he gestures towards a standing veiled woman, accompanied by a handmaid, who makes a speech gesture with her right hand in return. To his right stand two tunic-clad warriors. Above his head, four female personifications of virtues hover in the arches supporting the gable above his throne, while flanking them two angels brandish cross-staffs.[89] An inscription below the image explains the iconography.

Stripped of all the supporting characters, the core figures in the San Paolo dedication image and their architectural setting strongly recall the Saint-Vaast Bible's image prefacing the Song of Songs of Christ enthroned before a many-gabled city conversing with his heavenly spouse, *Ecclesia*, to his left. Charles' golden orb has been replaced by a book, and Christ gestures upwards with his right hand rather than towards his companion. Nonetheless, the relationship between the two primary figures is identical, as are their relative sizes. Even the layout of the page, with the top three-quarters within a rectangular frame devoted to the image and the bottom one quarter filled with text, mirrors that seen in the San Paolo Bible. Christ now surmounts the gable behind him rather than being crowned by the architecture. As was so frequently pointed out in royal literature, the eternal union of Christ and *Ecclesia* is the heavenly equivalent of the marriage of the king and queen on earth.

Ernst Kantorowicz speculated that the Carolingian dedication miniature reflects a contemporary event. In 866, Charles the Bald asked that his wife of twenty-four years, Ermentrude, be crowned and anointed, seemingly in response to a series of disasters that had robbed them of all but one of their heirs. The text of the blessing ceremony that survives from this event preserves the desires of the king and his clergy, couched in biblical terms. The prayers, written by Hincmar of Reims, were seemingly devised as a request for her

---

[88] Rome, San Paolo fuori le mura, fol. 1r. Ernst H. Kantorowicz, "The Carolingian King in the Bible of San Paolo fuori le mura," in *Late Classical and Mediaeval Studies in Honor of Albert Matthias Friend, Jr.* (Princeton, 1955), 287–300.

[89] Rome, San Paolo fuori le mura, fol. 1r.

fertility, and the coronation mimics a marriage ritual in tone. The
prayers ask that for the good of the realm and especially its Church,
God should bless Charles and Ermentrude with children in their old
age just as he had Abraham and Sarah in the Bible.[90] The prayer
said over the queen emphasizes that from the beginning God instituted the state of marriage in order that man and woman be insep-
arable. Hincmar then compared Ermentrude to the Old Testament
exempla, Rachel, Rebekah and Sarah, commended for their amiabil-
ity, wisdom, length of life and fidelity, respectively, paraphrasing
almost exactly the marriage blessing of the Gregorian Sacramentary.[91]
According to Kantorowicz, Ermentrude's fertility-driven coronation
may be referenced in the inscription under the San Paolo Bible's
dedication image, where one phrase identifies the veiled woman as
the king's consort, "Let her bear rightfully famous offspring into the
kingdom."[92] The San Paolo Bible image is the very earliest image
of an enthroned king accompanied by his wife. Possibly this combination was invented to record Ermintrude's nuptial-tinged coronation, and in that sense it may represent a marriage.[93]

Kantorowicz pointed out that this unique image can also be
explained by another, rather similar, scenario. Ermentrude died in
869, having yet to produce a new heir. Charles the Bald wasted no
time in remarrying, choosing Richildis, sister of the Count of Provence.
Despite two pregnancies she was destined to remain without progeny.[94] Kantorowicz suggests that the creation of the San Paolo Bible
and its dedication image could also have taken place during that
hopeful period around the marriage ceremony itself, in 870. According

[90] Kantorowicz, "The Carolingian King," 292–293. Ordo of Ermentrude, Jackson,
82–86. *Propterea petit benedictionem episcopalem super uxorem suam venire, ut talem sobolem ei
Dominus de illa dignetur donare, unde sancta ecclesia solatium, et regnum necessariam defensiorem,
et fideles illius desiderabile adiutorium, et ista christianitas optabilem tranquillitatem, et legem atque
iustitiam, cum illis quos adhuc habet, annuente et cooperante Domino, possit habere. Et de hoc
in sanctis scripturis habemus auctoritatem, quia sicut Dominus ad Abraham dixit: 'In semine tuo
benedicentur omnes gentes': cui iam centenario de nonagenaria uxore Isaac filium dedit: ita et ipsum
Isaac uxorem sterilem accipere fecit . . .*
[91] Ritzer, *Formen*, 351.
[92] Translation from William J. Diebold, "The Ruler Portrait of Charles the Bald
in the S. Paolo Bible," *Art Bulletin* LXXVI (1994), 9.
[93] Joachim Gaehde also favors this event as the motivation to produce the Bible
and its dedication image. Joachim Gaehde, "The Bible of San Paolo fuori le mura
in Rome: its Date and its Relation to Charles the Bald," *Gesta* V (1966), 10.
[94] Kantorowicz, "The Carolingian King," 295–298.

to Kantorowicz, this may explain the fact that the king's consort is shown wearing an elaborate veil, a frequent part of the marriage ceremony, rather than a crown. Whether the Bible was produced to celebrate the belated coronation and unction of Ermentrude, or the marriage and coronation of Richildis that quickly followed, the addition of the king's wife, who hovers to his left in the image and appears as a prominent character in the dedication inscription, indicates that the king's marriage was one of the themes addressed by the Bible's interlocking text and image program.[95]

The image and its poem echo the writings of other Carolingian royal advisors. William Diebold paralleled both the dedication image and the phrasing of the poem beneath it with Sedulius Scottus' *De rectoribus Christianis*. Scottus had included in that text a direct comparison between the royal marriage and the heavenly marriage of Christ and *Ecclesia*. The composer of the miniature's poem may have alluded to this in its final phrases.

> He [the king] is unbeaten, the eternal defender; may he, warlike,
> Often honor the church of Christ with great triumphs.
> To the left, his noble wife, beautiful as always;
> Let her bear rightfully famous offspring into the kingdom.[96]

The progeny of *Ecclesia*, Christians, were alluded to in the San Paolo Bible poem's call for hoped-for heirs of the royal couple. Diebold claims that the dichotomy of sizes between the king and his companions also indicates that as a virtuous ruler the king is intended to dominate his entire household, including his wife, another one of Sedulius' prescriptions.

Despite the probable connection between the San Paolo Bible dedication image and the marital history of Charles the Bald, however, this image represents the couple in the state of holy matrimony rather than the actual wedding itself. As we have already seen, wedding iconography was specific and confined to a few important motifs: an officiant of some kind near the couple (the *pronubus*), or the joining of the couples' hands. Neither of these is present. The combination of king and queen, and the prominent depiction of the veil on the

---

[95] Diebold, 12–18. He speculates that the Bible was not made on the occasion of a wife's coronation, but rather as a gift to Pope Hadrian or John VIII in anticipation of Charles' imperial coronation in 875.

[96] Diebold's translation, 9.

woman may be details intended to reference matrimony, but they
don't make the image into a depiction of either a betrothal or a
wedding. In the ninth century, as in the eleventh, the marriage ceremonies of royalty probably included, in addition to the negotiation
of a contract (the point that incorporated the handshake), a church
blessing during which both spouses may have been prostrate before
the altar or remained standing. Nothing suggests that the enthroned
king might have been approached by a standing spouse at any point
in the wedding ceremony, as depicted in this miniature. Rather than
representing the wedding itself, the San Paolo Bible image portrays
the marriage of the royal couple, which the Ezra Master mimicked
two hundred years later in the Saint-Vaast Bible's depiction of the
mystical marriage of the heavenly couple.

Another aspect of the marriage ritual that may have found its way
into symbolic depiction in art and may be reflected at least tangentially in the Song of Songs miniature, however, is the kiss. An
essential component of the Roman betrothal ceremony, the kiss was
an important vow of matrimony, and had legal weight in the distribution of property in the case of the death of one of the betrothed
prior to marriage.[97] St. Ambrose mentions the kiss as a pledge of
matrimony in his discussion of the Church as the bride of Christ.[98]
The Life of St. Leonard by Gregory of Tours records that he left
his bride on their wedding day after giving her "anulum, osculum
et calceamentum."[99] Tertullian described that the betrothal of virgins took place with a kiss and by the giving of the right hand.[100]
The kiss was at some point clearly incorporated into Christian marriage ceremonies. It is striking, therefore, that the mystical *Sponsus*
and *Sponsa* of the Saint-Vaast Song of Songs (pl. V), although not
depicted in an embrace, are nonetheless enclosed in a circle that
mimics the initial that starts the word for their unifying action, the
kiss, as the text below opens with the phrase "*Osculetur me osculo oris
sui*—Let him kiss me with the kiss of his mouth." Later images of

[97] Nicolas Perella, *The Kiss Sacred and Profane* (Berkeley, 1969), 40–41.
[98] PL 16:1165.
[99] Frugoni, 940, commenting on Gregory of Tours, *Vitae patrum XX: De sancto
Leobardo reclauso in Majori monasterio prope Turonum*, ed. Bruno Krusch, MGH Scriptores
rerum Merovingicarum I (Hanover, 1885), I, 54–55.
[100] Tertullian, *De oratione* 22:9–10, PL 1:1190. Stevenson, 16.

the *Sponsus-Sponsa* would make this mystical marriage much more explicit by depicting them in the moment of their kiss.[101]

This elaboration of the visual theme developed hand in hand with the writings on the Song of Songs by twelfth-century mystical clerics such as Bernard of Clairvaux and William of Saint-Thierry. Taking as his starting point the kiss that opens the text of the Song of Songs, Bernard in his *Sermones super Cantica Canticorum* explained the kiss at the beginning of the text as the betrothal of the Bride, meaning the Church or the soul, and the Word, or Christ. Through this act, the Bride was infused with the Holy Spirit in a unifying breath.[102] William of Saint-Thierry expanded on this idea and made the real kiss, the union of two bodies, into an exchange of spirits. Through this exchange of spirits the mystical couple, Christ and the Church, became one. The fruit of this union was the Incarnation.[103] Thus with these twelfth-century writers the kiss, as a symbol and mechanism of spiritual union, would come to symbolize the marriage in heaven that ideally was to be imitated on earth. Eleventh-century clerics may not yet have contemplated the meaning of the Song of Song's kiss in exactly those terms. Nonetheless, the rubrics that accompany the text in the eleventh-century Bible and interpret the dialogue as that between a husband and wife suggest that they saw it at least partly as the picture of a mystical marriage. This depiction of the ideal relationship between the King of kings and his heavenly queen that was intended to model the ideal relationship between their earthly prototypes also set the stage for the other miniatures that addressed the roles of royal women sanctioned by the Church.

The Passion of the Maccabees: Family Values

The themes of virtuous motherhood, the devout family and the pious education of children were taken up in the Saint-Vaast Bible's

---

[101] Frugoni, 927, note 96, does not include mystical marriage iconography in her survey because she considers it too late to be within the scope of her investigation.

[102] Perella, 52–56 on *Sermones super Cantica Canticorum* VIII, PL 183:810–814, or in Sources chrétiennes 414, ed. Jean Leclercq, H. Rochais and Ch. H. Talbot, introduction, trans. and notes Paul Verdeyen and Raffaele Fassetta (Paris, 1996), 188–192.

[103] Perella, 57, *Super Cantica Canticorum*, PL 180:483.

miniature before the non-canonical Passion of the Maccabees, volume III, fol. 81v (pl. IX). The full-page illustration shows the trial
of the Jewish priest Eleazar, and the family of seven brothers and
their mother before the Syrian despot Antiochus. Unlike those in
the illustrations for the Song of Songs and in the Esther illustration
that will be explained below, the principle characters of this story
aren't a married couple. Taken together, however, they embody the
ideal of a devout family that put the interests and teachings of the
Church before all other concerns. The mother of the Maccabees
serves as the chief model of religious virtue.

The Old Testament books of the Maccabees were rich sources of
imagery for medieval artists starting in the early Christian period.
In the west, these artists concentrated almost exclusively on the stories of the Jewish wars of Judas Maccabaeus and his companions,
finding in them lively comparisons flattering to the warrior culture
of kings from the Carolingian period onwards.[104] In the east, on the
other hand, artists often chose the stories of the Maccabean protomartyrs, Eleazar the priest, the seven brothers and their mother,
Salomone, as a way to express a devotion to the saints and resistance to threats to religious orthodoxy.

Breaking with western tradition, the Saint-Vaast artist signaled the
first book of Maccabees, which retold the tale of the wars of Judas
Maccabeus, with only decorated initials (vol. III, fol. 52v). The Acts
Master illustrated the second book with a full-page framed initial
showing Judas preaching to the Jews of Egypt (fol. 70v, fig. 17), a
stock scene of a group of seated disputants listening to an enthroned
elder, above. The Acts Master was also responsible for the most
compelling narrative image for Maccabees, showing the confrontation between a sacrilegious conquering king and a group of adamantly
faithful Jews, which appears before the fourth book, a non-canonical
book that survives in only about forty manuscripts. This is the first
illustration of this story to appear in western art. [105]

---

[104] Robert L. McGrath, "The Romance of the Maccabees in Medieval Art and
Literature," Ph.D. Dissertation, Princeton, 1963.
[105] Only one earlier western image of the Maccabees survives, the now frag-
mentary seventh- or eighth-century mural in the nave of Santa Maria Antiqua in
Rome, and that shows only a series of standing, frontal figures. Pietro Romanelli,
Santa Maria Antiqua (Rome, 1964), 53, colorplate II.

Disentangling the sources for imagery of the Passion of the Maccabees is a challenge because the story was retold differently in biblical texts, apocryphal texts, their translations, and commentaries. In all of them, however, the tale of the Maccabee family and its spiritual guide, Eleazar, includes all the elements to make them heroes in any age of religious repression. The events surrounding the martyrdoms were first described in II Maccabees, a work originally written in Greek between 100 B.C. and 70 A.D. Antiochus IV of Syria, after conquering Jerusalem, plundered the Temple and instituted the tradition of blood sacrifice to Olympian Zeus within its precinct. The king decided to make an example of a well-regarded priest, Eleazar, and commanded him to eat the flesh of the pagan sacrifice. When Eleazar refused, bystanders offered to help him eat orthodox Jewish meat as a subterfuge. Eleazar again refused because he feared that younger Jews would emulate his trespass of holy law, and he was martyred.

Once Eleazar had provided this model of righteousness, seven brothers and their mother were apprehended and brought before Antiochus. One by one they were offered the prohibited meat, and one after another they, too, refused it and were tortured and finally martyred. Their mother, far from interfering in the torments of her sons, instead exhorted each of them to resist the temptation to save their own lives by breaking religious law. Her express desire was that they remember their devout upbringing and make her proud by welcoming their martyrdom. After all her sons had been tortured and killed, the mother herself was, in the words of the biblical account, "consumed."[106]

The role of Salomone in the drama of the martyrdoms is most important to our understanding of the meaning of the Maccabees illustration in the Arras Bible. Although in II Maccabees she plays a relatively small part, in another retelling of the martyrdom she becomes the centerpiece of the tale. The Greek Fourth Book of Maccabees, sometimes also called "On the Sovereignty of Reason," was a canonical part of the Eastern Septuagint Bible.[107] It was written in the first century a.d., probably under Caligula, as a defense of Jewish Orthodoxy and an argument in favor of Reason over

---

[106] II Maccabees 6:18–7:42.
[107] Moses Hadas, *The Third and Fourth Books of Maccabees* (New York, 1953), 136.

human passions.[108] The author recounted the story of the martyr-doms taking the version from II Maccabees as his core.[109] He added a lengthy prologue that explains the philosophical meaning of this story and others from the Old Testament as demonstrations that reason can control emotions and desires. He then expanded the narrative dramatically with graphic descriptions of the tortures and murders. He also augmented the accompanying dialogue, particularly that assigned to the mother. The author lauded Salomone's strength and virtue above that of all the other martyrs. "Do not consider it amazing that reason had full command over these men in their tortures, since the mind of a woman despised even more diverse agonies . . . But sympathy for her children did not sway the mother of the young men; she was of the same mind as Abraham."[110] In fact, the book describes Salomone as having the strength of a man, even surpassing Eleazar and her sons. She becomes the ultimate example of the "reason" extolled by the text. "But devout reason, giving her heart a man's courage in the very midst of her emotions, strengthened her to disregard her temporal love for her children . . . O mother of the nation, vindicator of the law and champion of religion, who carried away the prize of the contest in your heart! More noble than males in steadfastness, and more manly than men in endurance! O mother, soldier of God in the cause of religion, elder and woman! By steadfastness you have conquered even a tyrant, and in word and deed you have proved more powerful than a man."[111]

These Old Testament figures received a cult of their own in the fourth century, when once again the story of the Maccabees was called upon to defend religious orthodoxy. Already commentators had pinpointed the value of these martyrs not just as exemplars of religious orthodoxy, but also as a model for the devout family. Gregory of Nazianzen wrote Homily 15 as a protest against the cultural and religious policies of Julian the Apostate.[112] Gregory, like

---

[108] *The Apocrypha and Pseudepigrapha of the Old Testament in English*, ed. Robert H. Charles, 2 vols. (Oxford, 1913), II, 653–654, and Hadas, 96.

[109] IV Maccabees 5–18.

[110] IV Maccabees 14:11–12 and 20.

[111] IV Maccabees 15:23, 29–30 and 16:14.

[112] Martha Vinson, "Gregory Nazianzen's Homily 15 and the genesis of the Christian cult of the Maccabean martyrs," *Byzantion* LXIV (1994), 166–192, especially 166–168.

the original author of the Fourth Book of Maccabees, highlighted the peculiar strength of the mother. "The heart of a man in a woman's body!" he said, paraphrasing II Maccabees 7:21. He also made an important change to the narrative. Although in the two biblical accounts the priest Eleazar never met the seven brothers and their mother, Gregory managed to describe events in such a way that the audiences of the nine martyrs before their killer Antiochus overlap. In addition, through repeated references to Eleazar as the 'father' of the seven brothers, he remade the nine into a biological family whose suffering prefigures that of Gregory and his staunchly orthodox parents under Julian's persecutions.[113] He then suggested the family's value as an *exemplum* for Christian marriage.

> Priests, mothers, children, these let us have as our model: priests, in honor of the spiritual father, Eleazar, who epitomized excellence by his actions as well as his words; mothers, in honor of that noble mother, by showing true devotion to your children and commending them to Christ: such a sacrifice will bring sanctity to the married state as well; children, by revering the holy children and spending your youth not in the gratification of shameful desires but in resistance to the passions and by struggling heroically against the daily Antiochus who assaults us in every limb and subjects us to torments of every description.[114]

Gregory's interpretation of the Maccabee martyrdoms had a profound impact on the Byzantine pictorial tradition. Scenes of the martyrdoms of Eleazar, the seven Maccabaeus brothers, and their mother are not found in surviving western manuscripts before the Arras Bible. They were popular, however, in post-iconoclastic Byzantine manuscript illustration. Such scenes appear in Byzantine marginal Psalters, like the Paleologan Hamilton Psalter, which includes miniatures of Eleazar and the seven Maccabee brothers brought separately before King Antiochus.[115] In three eleventh- and twelfth-century manuscripts of the Homilies of Gregory Nazianzen, Gregory's homily on the martyrdom is accompanied either by scenes of Eleazar and the seven brothers brought serially before Antiochus, or by scenes of the trial of the seven brothers onto which their mother and Eleazar

[113] Oration 15. PG 35:912A–933A, translation *Select Orations*, ed. and trans. Martha P. Vinson, Fathers of the Church CVII (Washington, D.C., 2003), 72–84.
[114] Gregory of Nazienzen, Oration 15:12, p. 84.
[115] Christine Havice, "The Hamilton Psalter in Berlin, Kupferstich-Kabinett 78.A.9," Ph.D. Dissertation, Pennsylvania State University, 1978.

have been grafted.[116] These scenes are not drawn from the text of
the homily they illustrate because it is too general to have provided
the specifics of the martyrdom narrative. Rather, the Psalters probably preserve compositions that were invented for more fully illustrated versions of the four Books of Maccabees.[117] In the illustrated
Gregory manuscripts, the homilist's reference to the martyrs as a
family may have inspired the artist to combine the scenes of the
audiences of Eleazar with the seven brothers and their mother.

This conflation must have been made before the eleventh century, however, for it occurs in the most famous surviving Byzantine
Maccabees illustration, in the tenth-century Bible of Leo Sacellarios
(Rome BAV cod. Vat. Reg. gr. 1, fol. 450v, fig. 46) accompanying
the text that had inspired the original cycle, the fourth Book of
Maccabees. [118] A source very similar to this probably served as the
model for the Saint-Vaast Bible's own illustration for the martyrdom
of the Maccabees (pl. IX).

In the Leo Bible, like in the Gregory manuscripts, Eleazar, the
seven brothers, and their mother are represented as a spiritual and
physical unit.[119] Antiochus sits enthroned to the left in front of a
small crowd of bodyguards, and gestures towards the facing, bearded
figure of the priest Eleazar, who gestures in return. To the right of
Eleazar stand two young men, while behind them hovers a stack of
heads representing the remaining five Maccabee brothers. The head
of their mother Salomone is placed highest, to the right. The figures
are framed by an architectural setting. Much of this composition was
inspired directly by the text of the Fourth Book of Maccabees. IV
Macc. 5 begins, "The tyrant Antiochus, sitting in state with his

---

[116] George Galavaris, *The Illustrations of the Liturgical Homilies of Gregory Nazianzenus*,
Studies in Manuscript Illumination VI (Princeton, 1969), 111–112, and figs. 207,
209, 210, Paris BnF MS Coislin gr. 239, fols. 38, 40, 41v; fig. 126, Florence,
Biblioteca Laurenziana MS Plut. VII.32, fol. 40; and fig. 264, Rome BAV cod.
Vat. gr. 1974, fol. 30.

[117] Galavaris, 111–112 and 117.

[118] *Die Bibel des Patricius Leo: Codex Reginensis graecus 1B*, ed. Suzy Dufrenne and
Paul Canart, 2 vols. (Zurich, 1988).

[119] Dufrenne and Canart, II, 13 and 46, describe the composition of this scene
as belonging to a genre inspired by icon painting, because it is a unified image of
a homogeneous group of people. They also believe that the image was originally
an illustration for the epilogue to the description of the martyrdoms in IV Macc.
17, where Eleazar, the seven brothers and the mother are discussed together as
exempla and an inscription for their tomb is suggested.

counselors on a certain high place, and with his armed soldiers standing about him . . ." while IV Maccabees 8:3–4 describes, "Seven brothers—handsome, modest, noble and accomplished in every way—were brought before him along with their aged mother. When the tyrant saw them, grouped about their mother as if in a chorus, he was pleased with them. And struck by their appearance and nobility, he smiled at them, and summoned them nearer . . ." This almost perfectly describes the Maccabee party held before the enthroned Antiochus. Yet, probably in response to Gregory's homily, the artist of the original composition added Eleazar between Antiochus and the brothers. He has also placed the mother of the Maccabees in the rear of this group, conversing with her youngest son, the final martyr, rather than in the midst of the throng of her sons.

The Arras Bible's copy of this scene is found before the Passion of the Maccabees, or *Passio Machabeorum*, essentially a Christianized Latin paraphrase of the Greek Fourth Book of Maccabees. This Latin translation of the book was produced during the fourth century in the Roman province of Gaul, and survives in around forty manuscripts, the earliest from the eighth century, when it may have been copied as part of the Carolingian textual reform movement.[120] Two versions of the *Passio Machabeorum* were in circulation at the time when the Saint-Vaast Bible was illustrated. In the Arras Bible, as in all surviving biblical manuscripts containing this book, there is a lacuna between the end of chapter one, verse five, and the beginning of chapter five. The text jumps straight from a cursory introduction to the description of the martyrdoms of the main characters. It thus lacks all of the philosophical material found at the beginning of the Greek Fourth Book and in the other version of the *Passio*, which is typically found in legend manuscripts.[121] In the Arras Bible, chapter one, verses one through five are found on folio 81 of volume III, and begin with little fanfare, just a small decorative initial. The text continues on the verso with the beginning of chapter five, which is accompanied by an elaborate frame and figural illustration.[122]

---

[120] Heinrich Dörrie, *Passio SS. Machabaeorum, die antike lateinischen Übersetzung des IV. Makkabäerbuches*, Abhandlungen der Gesellschaft der Wissenschaften zu Göttingen, Philologisch-Historische Klasse, Series 3 n. 33 (Göttingen, 1938), 8–10, 13–14 and 36–39 and Friedrich Stegmüller, *Repertorium Biblicum medii aevi*, 11 vols. (Madrid, 1949), I, no. 102, 1, for a list of relevant manuscripts.

[121] Dörrie, 10.

[122] Unlike any other textual illustrations in the Arras Bible, therefore, the image

In general, the composition of the Arras Bible miniature is strikingly similar to the illustration in the Byzantine Leo Bible for the Greek version of the same text. To the left in the Saint-Vaast Bible image (pl. IX), a crowned king holding a lily scepter in his right hand sits enthroned on a cushioned, backless lion-throne, his feet on a footstool. With his left hand he gestures towards the facing group of nine figures. Foremost among this group, and the only figures shown in their entirety, are Eleazar, depicted with a flowing beard, a skull-cap and diadem, and Salomone, shown with a veil and wide sleeves. From behind these two figures peek one beardless youth and the heads of six others. The Saint-Vaast Bible artists have employed the same combination of moments found in the Leo Bible, once again a combination that is not supported by the text accompanying the illustration. The likelihood of artists in both the East and the West separately inventing the same combination of narrative events to illustrate Greek and Latin versions of the same book is small. Evidence for a tradition of illustrating the Fourth Book of the Maccabees is strong in the East, but nonexistent in the West. This conflation developed over time in Byzantine illustrations of the Fourth Book of Maccabees and the Homilies of Gregory of Nazianzen, and was copied into the Leo Bible.[123] Somehow the conflated image found its way to the West, either illustrating a Greek version of IV Maccabees or another devotional text, or as a free-standing painting, and was adapted by the Arras artist to the Saint-Vaast Bible's program.

The changes made to his model by the Acts Master can be explained, in part, by differences in the text accompanying the miniature. In the Latin *Passio Machabeorum*, much of the textual detail about the cast of characters and their arrangement that inspired the image in the Leo Bible has been lost. "Thus Antiochus sitting in a high place seeing everyone . . . *Igitur Antiochus sedens in excelsiore videndus hominibus loco*," begins the section directly under the image.[124] The Acts Master has simplified the illustration by removing the architectural background and replacing it with a simple color-washed backdrop. He has also removed the bodyguards who crowd behind

---

for the *Passio Machabeorum* interrupts the text so that it is placed close to the passage it pictures, rather than at the beginning of the book.
[123] Galavaris, 111–112 and McGrath, "The Romance of the Maccabees," 124.
[124] Text selections of the Passion of the Maccabees taken from Dörrie. Passio SS. Machabaeorum 5. *Hominibus* is a corruption of the original *omnibus*. Dörrie, 73.

Antiochus in the Leo Bible's miniature, possibly because the Latin version of the text, unlike its Greek source, doesn't mention them. Yet although the Latin text no longer describes the seven brothers grouped as if in a chorus, they are shown as a stacked, overlapping group in almost exactly the same manner as in the Leo Bible illustration.[125]

In adapting this image for his own use the Arras illuminator made a significant change to its appearance and meaning. The mother of the Maccabees has been moved from the back of the group of figures to the front. In the Saint-Vaast Bible illustration, she is one of only three figures shown in their entirety. The new prominence given to Salomone is all the more remarkable because in the Latin version of the Passion of the Maccabees many of the statements from the Greek version that noted her virtues in masculine terms have been elided. For instance, in chapter 15 of the Greek IV Maccabees Salomone was called "mother of the nation, vindicator of the law and champion of religion . . . more noble than males in steadfastness, and more manly than men in endurance."[126] In the Latin *Passio* she is described "O most wise among women, most loving of the people and the law."[127] Nonetheless, the translator of the text added a disclaimer not found in his Greek source: "Thus how useful reason can be, which does not make women the inferiors of men."[128] Although the mother's speeches and the descriptions of her character have been rewritten in less masculine terms, her role in the martyrdom of her sons has not been reduced in the Latin text.

Why did the Saint-Vaast scriptorium include such a striking narrative image before the *Passio Machabaeorum*, a book that perhaps had never before been illustrated in the West? What prompted the Acts Master to adjust his model so that the mother of the Maccabees for the first time gained the same prominence visually that she held in the text? The answers, once again, can be found in the political and religious turmoil surrounding the creation of the Arras Bible. Although

---

[125] Passio SS. Machabaeorum 8:4. *Septem itaque fratres cum matre in senium iam vergente perducti praeclari speciosique corporis notis angelicum quoddam lumen sereni vultus pulchrique radiantes quod humanam formam mortalemque transcenderet.*

[126] Text selections of IV Maccabees taken from *The Apocrypha and Pseudepigrapha of the Old Testament in English.* IV Macc. 15:30.

[127] Passio SS. Machabaeorum 15:21.

[128] Passio SS. Machabaeorum 16:1.

today the Maccabee martyrs do not have a high profile among biblical heroes, to eleventh-century clerics the Maccabean family, with
its spiritually upright father-figure, famously religious mother and sui-
cidally devout sons, provided an ideal model for the Christian ruler
family the Church was then attempting to underwrite.

As Gregory of Nazianzen had already discovered when writing in
the fourth century, the Fourth Book of Maccabees provided won-
derful material for clerics intent on elevating the state of Christian
marriage and the married woman through its description of Salomone.
The last chapter explains that Salomone's ability to educate her children appropriately sprang from her purity even before her marriage
and the correctness of that union. "The spirit of the young men thus
remained constant due to the teachings of the mother, who always
in the privacy of their home expressed those things which are following to raise up her sons. The same woman, moreover, in death
said: I remained maidenly as long as modesty was valued; afterwards
I attached myself in holy matrimony. I did not leave my own home,
I begat no shameful sons, and my husband being struck dead I
nonetheless lost nothing from faith."[129] Strikingly, the translator who
rendered the Greek Fourth Book of Maccabees into Latin transferred
the primary role of educating the Maccabean brothers from their
father to their mother. The Greek text states explicitly that the father
of the martyrs taught them the Law and the prophets.[130] In the Latin
text, the mother overcomes the death of her spouse and succeeds in
leading her children in the reading of the Bible.

Gregory of Nazianzen was certainly not the last commentator to
turn his attention to the Maccabean protomartyrs.[131] The ninth-
century biblical scholar Rabanus Maurus compiled a commentary
on the story of the Maccabees as part of his campaign to gloss almost
the entire Bible. Rabanus commented in detail on the martyrdom
of Eleazar and the seven brothers as part of his exegesis of II

---

[129] Passio SS. Machabaeorum 18:7–8. *Constat tamen talem animum parvulorum doc-
trina matris effectum, quae semper filiis in secreta domus parte sublatis haec quae sunt secuta
narrabat. In ipsa praeterea morte dicebat: Virginalem usque dum licuit pudorem tenui; castis me
postea nuptiis illigavi. Domum propriam non reliqui, procreavi filios non pudendos, et mariti morte
percussa nihil tamen ex fide perdidi.*
[130] IV Maccabees 18:10.
[131] J. Dunbabin, "The Maccabees as Exemplars in the tenth and eleventh centuries," in *The Bible in the Medieval World: Essays in Memory of Beryl Smalley*, Studies
in Church History, Subsidia (1985), 31–32.

Maccabees, giving them a typically Christian allegorical meaning.[132] Antiochus prefigured the coming of the Antichrist in his persecution of the protomartyrs. "Because as the Savior sent in advance Solomon and the rest of the holies as a type of his advent, so the Antichrist correctly is to be believed to have had his type in the most evil King Antiochus who persecuted the saints and violated the Temple."[133] Eleazar, according to Rabanus, should be seen as a type of the faithful Christian people, who will be tempted at the end of time by the snares of the Antichrist. He reserved his most elevating interpretation for the mother of the Maccabees. She was interpreted, not surprisingly, as mirroring *Ecclesia*. "What is depicted through this mother of seven sons unless the fecundity of Mother Church, who through the grace of the sevenfold spirit of God the Father generates adoptive sons?" He explained the eventual suicide of the mother of the Maccabees on the funeral pyre of her sons as an allegory of the triumph of the eternally reigning Church.[134]

In the text of the *Passio Machabeorum*, the mother of the Maccabees is glorified not just for giving birth to such righteous sons, but for encouraging them to resist the temptation to depart from the faith. The text extols her wisdom and fortitude at length, and describes her as "truly an example of patience, not just for all women, but for men."[135] Already in Gregory of Nazianzen's fourth century homily, Salomone had been singled out as a prototype of the ideal wife and mother. By the eleventh century, the stories of the Maccabean martyrs must have been well known.[136] An artist seeking an *exemplum* for married women and especially mothers could easily have called to mind this paradigm of wisdom and virtue. For the queen, whose marriage was, ideally, supposed to be blessed by the Church, she provided an example of chastity before marriage and modesty afterwards, the

---

[132] *Commentaria in libros machabaeorum*, PL 109:1125–1256.

[133] PL 109:1234.

[134] PL 109:1236–7.

[135] Passio SS. Machabaeorum 15–17. 17:3, *O septem triumphorum mater, superatrix tyranni, magistra iustitiae, filios comitata victores, exemplum patientiae non mulieribus solum, sed viris futura, veneranda praesentibus, colenda posteris, admirationi non genti nostrae solum futura sed saeculo.*

[136] Aelfric commented on the martyrdoms of Eleazar, the seven Maccabees and their mother in his book of homilies, although he didn't depart much from the Latin text as offered. Aelfric, Abbot of Eynsham. *Aelfric's Lives of Saints*. Early English Text Society. Original Series XCIV (New York, 1966).

very model then being propounded by the Church for the upper classes. Her chief function after marriage, as the educator of her sons in their duties to the Church and an advocate of the Law, or in Christian terms, doctrine, before secular authority, also makes her a perfect role model for noble women, especially queens.

In the Carolingian period, noble women had been given the task of maintaining Christian education and practice in their households. The Council of Meaux-Paris in 845 and 846 had reinforced that the wife was responsible for teaching the household the Lord's Prayer and the Creed.[137] Pope Nicholas II had picked up the same thread in his 1059 letter to Queen Anne. After charging Anne with the role of intercessor for the Church before her husband, he exhorted her that it was her responsibility alone to make her children into pious Christian rulers. "You, however, most glorious daughter, because you have merited the divine gift of fecundity, so instruct the most illustrious offspring, that among the first lessons to the suckling infant is to be fostered love to his Creator. Therefore, through you they learn to whom most high they are in debt, and that they have been born noble in the royal throne hall, and that far off in the bosom of the church most nobly through the grace of the holy spirit they have been reborn."[138]

Queen Margaret of Scotland was praised in the early-twelfth-century Life of St. Margaret, probably written by her confessor, Turgot, for her Christian education of her sons.[139] "She took great pains, bringing [her sons] very often before her, to teach them, as far as their age could understand, of Christ and of Christ's faith, and to exhort them always to fear him."[140] Although she lived slightly later than the period at hand, a story from the life of Margaret's daughter, Queen Matilda, points out how successful Margaret was at instilling a sense of religious devotion in her children. At Easter in 1105, Matilda not only invited a crowd of lepers into the court in order

---

[137] *Die Konzilien der karolingischen Teilreiche, 843–859*, ed. Wilfried Hartmann, MGH Concilia III, Concilia aevi Karolini DCCCXLIII–DCCCLIX (Hanover, 1984), Act LXXVII, p. 124.

[138] *Recueil des historiens des Gaules et de la France* XI, 653.

[139] Lois L. Huneycutt, "Images of Queenship in the High Middle Ages," *The Haskins Society Journal* I (1989), 70.

[140] Turgot, "Life of Queen Margaret," *Early Sources of Scottish History ad. 500–1286*, trans. Alan Orr Anderson (Stamford, Lincs., 1990, orig. 1922), 66–67.

to wash and kiss their feet, she attempted, unsuccessfully, to compel her younger brother, David, to join her in this ultimate penitential act, one to which he seems to have been less suited than the Maccabean martyrs.[141]

The illustration for the Passion of the Maccabees complements the Song of Songs miniature by highlighting, once again, the responsibilities of royal women, both as wives and mothers. Both illuminations featured Old Testament women, the *Sponsa* of the Song of Songs and the mother of the Maccabees, who were commonly understood as types of *Ecclesia*. Both provided flattering and yet restrictive pictures of the perfect female prototype. The final image in this series brought home the clerical message about the place of women in eleventh-century royal life, for it actually depicts a queen in the midst of political action.

Esther

Only one queen is depicted in the Saint-Vaast Bible, in the miniature accompanying the Book of Esther, vol. III, fol. 44 (pl. VIII). Esther had long embodied the idea of the queen as intercessor in the literary material of Christian court circles; she thus served as one of the prime models for the Christian queen. In fact, illustrations of Esther would become one of the most prominent artistic means of expressing the importance of the Capetian queen's role in the later Middle Ages. The thirteenth-century stained glass program of the Sainte-Chapelle, for instance, directed a series of edifying images at King Louis IX, his wife, and his mother, Blanche of Castile, including a lancet of over 120 scenes dedicated to Esther.[142] Emphasizing the humility and submissiveness of Queen Esther, this may be part of a courtly narrative tailored for a contemporary Capetian queen, Louis IX's wife Margaret of Provence, whose seating niche

---

[141] Lois L. Huneycutt, "Intercession and the High Medieval Queen: The Esther Topos," *Power of the Weak. Studies on Medieval Women*, eds. Jennifer Carpenter and Sally-Beth MacLean (Urbana, IL, 1995), 135 as reported by Aelred, *Genealogia regum Anglorum*, PL 195:736.

[142] Madeline H. Caviness, "Anchoress, Abbess and Queen: Donors and Patrons or Intercessors and Matrons," in *The Cultural Patronage of Medieval Women*, 138.

was directly below the window.[143] The designers of the Ste. Chapelle window may have sought to depict a humble and devout queen in order to combat the seeming threat to the realm represented by Margaret's powerful Provençal relatives. Dan Weiss has shown that the Arsenal Old Testament as well, which he hypothesizes was painted for King Louis IX to underpin his vision of the state, incorporates a program of at least three sets of images of Old Testament female role models: Judith, Esther and Ruth.[144] These three holy women represented three different functions of female leadership: Judith is the soldier who triumphed through her beauty, wisdom, and faith; Esther is the queen who saved her people using courage and good judgment; Ruth is the matriarch of kings. In a five-scene miniature Esther is depicted as a loyal and devoted queen who kneels at the feet of her king, in contrast to her predecessor, Vashti, whose disloyalty is shown in two of the five quatrefoils.[145]

Two centuries before, the programmers of the Saint-Vaast Bible's miniatures also made Esther part of a cycle of images intended to delimit the role of noble and royal women. Despite her centrality to discussions of the function of the queen in literary sources, the Saint-Vaast Bible's miniature was one of the first depictions of the Esther narrative.[146] The miniature takes advantage of the details of the Book of Esther to explicitly address the desires of the clergy for their most powerful advocate at court, the queen. Esther was the ultimate defender of the Old Testament Chosen People. She employed many of the same tools utilized by contemporary queens and noble women when they defended the Christian Church before their spouses.

---

[143] Alyce Jordan, "Narrative Design in the Stained Glass Windows of the Ste. Chapelle in Paris," Ph.D dissertation, Bryn Mawr, 1995, 220–221, 239–246.

[144] Dan Weiss, *Art and Crusade in the Age of St. Louis* (Cambridge, 1998), 166.

[145] Weiss, 168.

[146] Only two earlier illustrations of Esther in the court seem to exist, and one of these is only tentatively identified. At the Late Antique synagogue of Dura Europas, Esther is depicted enthroned behind King Ahasuerus in the scene of Mordecai's triumph. Kurt Weitzmann and Herbert L. Kessler, *The Frescoes of the Dura Synagogue and Christian Art* (Washington, D.C., 1990), 114–119. A now badly damaged late-ninth-century fresco in the lower church of San Clemente in Rome may show Esther kneeling before the king, or may instead show the martyrdom of saint Cyrilla. Josef Wilpert, *Die römischen Mosaiken und Malereien der kirchlichen Bauten vom 4. bis 13. Jahrhundert*, 4 vols. (1917), IV, pl. 217, made the original identification, but John Osborne, *Early Mediaeval Wall-Paintings in the Lower Church of San Clemente, Rome* (New York, 1984), 152–3 has argued convincingly for the Saint Cyrilla iconography.

She formed an alliance with the chief religious leader of the Chosen People in contact with the court, petitioned the king on their behalf taking advantage of her special status in the court and the public aspects of her role, and wrote edicts with the king and his court advisors.[147] The Saint-Vaast Bible illumination depicts her as this kind of intercessor.

The artist, Master A, signaled this special meaning with the choices he made in constructing a new and unique depiction of Esther's court appearance. Inspired by his advisor, Haman, King Ahasuerus condemned the Jews of his realm to death. Esther, his queen, who unbeknownst to the king was Jewish, was persuaded by her uncle, Mordecai, to risk death by visiting the king in his inner court uninvited in order to plead for the lives of her people.

> And on the third day Esther put on her royal apparel, and stood in the inner court of the king's house, over against the king's hall: now he sat upon his throne in the hall of the palace, over against the door of the house. And when he saw Esther the queen standing, she pleased his eyes, and he held out to her the golden scepter (*virgam auream*), which he held in his hand: and she drew near, and kissed the top of his scepter. And the king said to her: What wilt thou, Queen Esther? What is thy request?[148]

The queen then invited Ahasuerus and Haman to a set of banquets in her chambers, where she pleaded with the king for her people.

The illustration in the Arras Bible takes up the top half of a framed text page. The king and queen occupy opposite sides of the miniature, separated from each other by an interlace initial, I, that projects into the picture field. To the viewer's right sits King Ahasuerus. Framed by a canopied throne, he is accompanied by three tiny acolytes who float to his left. The most prominent of these was probably meant to represent his chief advisor, Haman. Opposite the king stand the queen and her supporters. The king's long *virgam auream* crosses this divide, extending from his right hand to touch the lips of the queen, while above and between them are inscribed the words of their conversation.

This is the only case in the entire Bible where first person speech intrudes into the picture area, almost in the form of a speech bubble.

---

[147] Leila L. Bonner, "Reclaiming Esther: From Sex Object to Sage," *The Jewish Bible Quarterly* XXVI (1998), 3–11.

[148] Esther 5:1–3.

The exchange between the king and queen reads: *Quid petis Hester oro o rex si tibi placet dona mihi animam meam pro qua rogo et populum meum pro quo obsecro*, or "What are you asking, Esther? I pray, O King if it pleases you, give me my soul for which I ask, and my people for whom I beg." Again, as in the miniature prefacing the book of Maccabees, the artist has created a conflation of two moments in order to extract a particular message from the text. In the text of the Bible, this dialogue takes place on two quite separate occasions. In the first, Esther visited the court of the king, and he asked her what she wanted from him. It was only later, at the second of two banquets that she hosted for Ahasuerus and Haman, that the queen finally made her request, for the salvation of the Chosen People. By interjecting this text into the framed picture, the artist signaled the most persistent role of the queen within the public sphere. "*Quid petis Hester?*" asks the king. The king here sanctions her actions as an advocate and intercessor before him on behalf of the people.

This is only one example of the choices made by the artist or director who composed this new visualization of the Esther story that was intended to emphasize Esther's public role as her primary duty. Unlike most books of the Old Testament, many different versions of the story of Esther survive in Hebrew, Greek and Latin, either in whole or in part. Even as it is preserved within the Vulgate, the Book of Esther contains traces of two different traditions. The first nine chapters and the first three verses of chapter ten were translated from the Hebrew version, or Masoretic Text, of Esther. The rest of chapter ten and the remaining five chapters of the book are composed of later expansions on the story from the Greek Septuagint version of the book that have been extracted from their original context and placed at the end of the Vulgate version.[149] These 'additions,' as they are frequently called, explain the narrative of some of the incidents in greater detail, and include the texts of letters and prayers to God that were not part of the Hebrew text. Most important for our purposes, the Additions included considerably more information about the role of Esther as protagonist in the struggle between Haman and Mordecai, especially in the moments leading up to her court audience, as well as the audience itself.[150]

---

[149] *The Apocrypha and Pseudepigrapha of the Old Testament in English* I, 665–666.
[150] Linda Day, *Three Faces of a Queen. Characterization in the Books of Esther*. Journal

The Carolingian biblical scholar Rabanus Maurus ended his ninth-century *Expositio in librum Esther*, the most recent commentary on the book and that most likely available to the monks of Saint-Vaast, just before the Additions. He left his educated reader, as he explains in his prologue to Queen Judith, to find the same sense in the Greek material.[151] Jerome, in his prologue to this part of the book of Esther, disparaged the content of the Additions, explaining why he put them at the end of his translation rather than integrating them as they had been in the Septuagint.[152] Jerome's prologue to the additions was included in the Saint-Vaast Bible and even highlighted in orange and green uncials. Nonetheless, the artist of the Esther image, faced with two versions of the court confrontation, one drawn from the Greek tradition and the other from the Hebrew, turned to the more dramatic and descriptive Greek text as his primary source when composing the miniature. This text describes several crucial elements of the miniature. First, just before her audience in the Greek text, Esther prays to God, telling him that she despises the crown she is forced to wear as part of her public role. "Thou knowest my necessity," she prays, "that I abominate the sign of my pride and glory, which is upon my head in the days of my public appearance, and detest it as a menstruous rag, and wear it not in the days of my silence."[153] This sign of her pride and glory, the crown that was awarded to her by Ahasuerus, when "he set the royal crown on her head, and made her queen instead of Vashti," becomes a crucial motif in the depiction of this incident.[154] In the Saint-Vaast Bible's miniature (pl. VIII), she is shown dressed in flowing robes and balancing an out-sized crown, the sign of her office, upon her head, although other royal figures in the Bible wear crowns that are drawn to scale. Master A seems to have underlined that although her modesty led her to avoid public exposure and its accompanying luxury as much as possible, she overcame her objections to enter the court when the

---

for the Study of the Old Testament, Supplement Series CLXXXVI (Sheffield, 1995), 11–18.

[151] Rabanus Maurus, *Expositio in librum Esther*, PL 109:635.

[152] Donatien De Bruyne, "Un nouvelle préface de la traduction hexaplaire de Saint Jérôme," *Revue bénédictine* XXXI (1914–1919), 229–236. Traces of a preface to a lost translation of Esther were attached to the Hieronymian preface found in the Saint-Vaast Bible and most others.

[153] Esther 14:16.

exigencies of her duties required it. At this moment she appears
bearing an exaggerated emblem of her public role, the crown.

Finally, the artist has made a significant change in personnel. The
Hebrew version of the court scene relates simply "And on the third
day Esther put on her royal apparel, and stood in the inner court
of the king's house, over against the king's hall . . ."[155] The version
in the Additions is much more specific about the entrance of Esther
and her retinue.

> And on the third day she laid away the garments she wore, and put
> on her glorious apparel. And glittering in royal robes, after she had
> called upon God the ruler and Savior of all, she took two maids with
> her, and upon one of them she leaned, as if for delicateness and over-
> much tenderness she were not able to bear up her own body. And
> the other maid followed her lady, bearing up her train flowing on the
> ground.[156]

Although the Bible text is quite distinct in its designation of two
women as her companions, Master A has replaced one of these
women with a man who gestures, a mirror image to Haman, who
stands at the far right of the image. This figure must represent
Mordecai. The Hebrew version of the text explained that Mordecai
had garbed himself in the mourning clothes of sackcloth and ashes,
refusing to put them aside even when Esther sent a messenger to
him with other clothes. "And he came lamenting in this manner
even to the gate of the palace: for no one clothed with sackcloth
might enter the king's court."[157] Nonetheless, the artist has inserted
him into this pivotal moment. The two disputing advisors of the king
thus serve as brackets to the narrative, the one representing the chief
Jewish advisor, the other the grand Vizier of the Persians. The fact
that Esther is entering the royal chamber specifically at the request
of the spiritual and institutional leader of the community of the
Chosen People is thus signaled by this departure from the text. Verse
13 of chapter 16, another of the deuterocanonical additions, repeats
the idea that Mordecai, the religious representative, and Esther, the
consort, cooperated in influencing the king to save his people. "For

---

[154] Esther 2:17.
[155] Esther 5:1.
[156] Esther 15:4–7.
[157] Esther 5:1–4.

with certain new and unheard of devices he hath sought the destruction of Mordecai, by whose fidelity and good services our life was saved, and of Esther, the partner of our kingdom, with all their nation."

Furthermore, in choosing the Greek rather than the Hebrew version of the story as his primary source of inspiration, the designer of the Saint-Vaast image has selected the narrative most heavily invested with the idea that the compass of the queen's action by nature included the court. When Esther enters the presence of the king in his court, she swoons for fear that she will be condemned to death for trespassing the law forbidding one to enter without an invitation from the king himself. But when the king sees the queen's reaction he immediately clarifies this dictate: "Thou shalt not die," he says, "for this law is not made for thee, but for all others. Come near then, and touch the scepter."[158]

Esther as a royal role model

Although the origins, original purpose, and the literary genre to which the book of Esther belonged are still enthusiastically debated, by the time the Saint-Vaast illumination was carried out, the purpose of the book in Christian circles, especially those that interacted with the royal court, had been fixed.[159] In fact, Esther was probably the Biblical role model most frequently selected for women of status by clerical writers. Very few medieval commentators bothered to write more than a sentence or two on Esther's history. Nonetheless, in the Carolingian period she became an exemplar for Christian women familiar enough to learned clerics that Hincmar of Reims repeatedly used her as a paradigm for the perfect earthly female intercessor and royal wife. Hincmar also saw her predecessor, Vasthi, as an *exemplum* of the bad wife, who may be repudiated.[160] In the earliest surviving ordo for the coronation of a queen, composed by

---

[158] Esther 15:13–14.

[159] For a summary of recent scholarship on the origins of the book of Esther, see W. Lee Humphreys, "The Story of Esther in its Several Forms: Recent Studies," *Religious Studies Review* XXIV (1998), 335–342.

[160] *De divortio Lotharii et Tetbergae*, PL 125:737 and *Ad regem*, PL 125:1024.

Hincmar for the marriage and coronation of Judith, daughter of
Charles the Bald, Esther is mentioned twice, the only Old Testament
prototype aside from Judith, the princess's namesake, to be accorded
that much attention.[161] Hincmar drafted prayers that compared Judith's
coronation unction to that of Esther, because both were vehicles for
the grace that would allow the wives to move the hearts of their
husbands to mercy, even though no such unction was mentioned in
the biblical text. The Book of Esther was already identified as a
fitting reference work for queens when Rabanus Maurus dedicated
his commentary on the Book of Esther first to Judith, second wife
of Louis the Pious, and later to queen Ermingard, consort of Lothar I,
between 841 and 851.[162] The dedication to Judith makes specific that
the Biblical queen was to serve as a role model for the earthly queen
as protector of her people.[163] Sedulius Scotus referred to her as a
model for the Christian queen in his *De rectoribus christianis*, "Piety,
prudence and sacred authority should adorn her, just as gracious
Esther shone."[164] The most explicit comparison is probably that found
in a letter written by Pope John VII to Queen Richildis, second wife
of Charles the Bald, in 876.

> Whence we rejoice greatly in you, hearing so many commendations
> and we are confident in the Lord, because you will lighten with the
> application of your shoulder the burdens which we bear as much from
> pagans as from the worst Christians, and you will be for the Church
> of Christ to the pious spouse like that holy Esther for the people of
> Israel to the husband. Because truly often we send to your most
> Christian always majestic spouse through various needs either missives
> or letters, of this we ask and beg, be for us mouth, tongue and hands,
> or rather be all for us, performing the offices of advocate, and always
> do all for us in everything . . .[165]

---

[161] Hincmar of Reims, *Coronati Judith Caroli filiae, cum rege Anglorum desponsata est*,
PL 125:811–814.
[162] Huneycutt, "Intercession and the High Medieval Queen," 129. PL 109:635
for the dedication to Judith, and *Epistola XLVI*, ed. E. Dümmler, MGH Epist. V,
Epistolae Karolini aevi III (Berlin, 1899), 500, for the dedication to Ermingard.
[163] Rabanus Maurus, *Expositio in librum Esther*. PL 109:635. *Deus omnipotens, qui illius
reginae mentem ad liberandas populi sui calamitates erexerat, te simili studio laborantem ad aeterna
gaudia perducere dignetur.*
[164] Sedulius Scotus, *On Christian Rulers and the Poems*, trans. Edward G. Doyle,
Medieval and Renaissance Texts and Studies XVII (Binghamton, 1983), 61.
[165] *Epistola XXVII*, MGH Epist. VII, Epistolae Karolini Aevi V, ed. E. Casper
(Berlin, 1928), 25–26.

As is typical of all his Biblical commentaries, Rabanus Christianized the Esther story, finding in it characters who could be allegorized as Christ, *Ecclesia*, and the Christian people. He also managed to lend a profoundly anti-semitic cast to a book originally written as a tale of the salvation of the Jews.[166] Rabanus demonized the villains of the tale, such as Vashti and Haman, by interpreting them as symbols of *Synagoga* and the iniquitous Jews he felt threatened the Christian faithful in the ninth century. In the Saint-Vaast Bible Esther illustration, however, Master A was able to extract a positive message from this Christianization. As in the Song of Songs illustration, when the Ezra Master or his director chose to avoid references to the evil of *Synagoga*, as suggested by the prototype for their marginal inscriptions, and to instead celebrate the union of Christ and the Church, in the Esther illustration the artist has made manifest the success story of this Old Testament royal marriage so that it could serve as a prototype for contemporary rulers.

By the twelfth century, at least a passing comparison between the female subject of a panegyric or ordo and Esther had become commonplace. The author of the Life of St. Margaret of Scotland, written in the early twelfth century, made explicit parallels between events in the life of Margaret, wife of the allegedly difficult king Malcolm III of Scotland, and that of Esther. He depicted Margaret as a queen who, like a second Esther, despised the luxurious garments and jewelry befitting her office, but nonetheless deigned to wear them in pursuit of the higher goals of the Church.[167] Margaret's *vita* was written as a didactic work for her daughter, Matilda, wife of King Henry of England. Matilda was, in turn, assimilated to Esther by chroniclers who praised her peacemaking efforts between England and Scotland.[168] The author of the life of St. Margaret and the chroniclers of Matilda's reign simply built on the *topos* established by ninth-century clerics to encourage the queen's limited intervention in affairs of state at the behest of the Church.

---

[166] Kimberly Vrudny, "Medieval Fascination with the Queen: Esther as the Queen of Heaven and Host of the Messianic Banquet," *Arts: the arts in religious and theological studies* XI (1999), 37–39.

[167] Huneycutt, "Intercession and the High Medieval Queen," 130. "Life of Queen Margaret," 68–69.

[168] Huneycutt, "Intercession and the High Medieval Queen," 130–131. Aelred, *Genealogia regum Anglorum*, PL 195:736.

Although writers consistently suggested Esther as a model for
queenly behavior, it seems she undertook only one of the necessary
roles of the medieval queen, that of defender of the Church.[169] The
biblical text never mentions the details of her life subsequent to her
intervention into royal politics. Esther succeeded in saving the Jews
of the realm, but her career as wife, mother and perhaps widow is
not discussed, and commentators seem to have taken for granted the
lack of a royal heir in the Biblical narrative. Modern scholars have
frequently commented on the seemingly skewed relationship between
the king, the queen, and their advisors in the Book of Esther. King
Ahasuerus is so spineless and indecisive that he is easily manipulated
at least three times in the book. [170] First, he repudiates Vashti at the
suggestion of his princes, then he yields to Haman's desire to slaugh-
ter the Jewish population of his realm. Finally he flip-flops and decides
to spare the Jews but allow a massacre of Haman, his family, and
thousands of other Gentiles at the request of Esther and Mordecai.
Likewise, Esther, the submissive and retiring wife chosen for her
beauty, is seemingly easily led by her uncle Mordecai to conceal her
true identity, and then to unmask it in order to manipulate the
king.[171] It is the power of the advisors in this tale, however, that
may have made it so useful to clerics seeking a picture of court life
where the king and queen bow to the wishes of religious officials.
The Book of Esther, almost ignored before the Carolingian era, came
to the fore in a period when cooperation between Church and State
was at its apogee.

The Book of Esther and the Politics of Royal Divorce

On the other hand, taken at face value, the story of Esther may
seem a surprising choice for clerics who were at that very moment
attempting to reform the attitude of the royal family towards marriage. Esther's arrival at court as the second wife of a king who

[169] Peggy McCracken, *The Romance of Adultery. Queenship and Sexual Transgression in
Old French Literature* (Philadelphia, 1998), 7–8.
[170] Susan Niditch, "Esther: Folklore, Wisdom, Feminism and Authority," in *A
Feminist Companion to Esther, Judith and Susanna*, ed. Athalya Brenner (Sheffield, 1995),
34–35.
[171] Bronner, 3–5, and Niditch, 35.

repudiated his first spouse, Vashti, because of her unsuitability, mirrors the chain of events experienced by many tenth- and eleventh-century queens, and the very situation that caused their clerical advisors so much consternation. Yet again, however, the book provides a useful model for the interaction between the Church and French royalty.

After one hundred and forty days of feasting with his nobles and governors, Ahasuerus ordered the palace eunuchs to bring Queen Vashti into his banquet "with the crown set upon her head." Vashti, who had been hosting her own feast for the women, refused. Vashti was dismissed from the royal household because, according to the Bible, in contravening the command of the king to come to his banquet, she had wronged not only the king himself but all the people of the realm. As an advisor said to the king, "For this deed of the queen will go abroad to all women, so that they will despise their husbands."[172] Carolingian royal clerics who were then debating the issue of divorce were therefore able to rationalize these biblical events by pointing out the role of their Old Testament counterparts. Hincmar of Reims, in parallel passages from *De divortio Lotharii et Tetbergae* and an epistle to the king, refers to the Vashti incident as an example of a publicly mediated, and therefore acceptable, divorce.[173] Vashti offended the sensibilities of the king through her pride and arrogance, but when she was deposed it was not solely by the king in reaction to his rage, but through the public judgment and sentencing of the princes and judges of Media and Persia. The story of Esther thus provided an early example of the necessity of transparency in the negotiation of royal marriages and separations. Once one of the queen's royal duties, in this case to provide an appropriate role model for the good of the kingdom, was compromised, she was deemed expendable, and the king, on the advice of his judges, could legally divorce her. Esther's obvious success at fulfilling a function important to the clerics must have made her seem a worthy replacement for a queen who seems to have valued her private life over her public duties.

---

[172] Esther 1:16–17.

[173] *De divortio Lotharii et Tetbergae*, PL 125:737 (also *De divortio Lotharii regis et Theutbergae reginae*, ed. Letha Böhringer, MGH Concilia IV, suppl. 1 [Hanover, 1992], 225) and *Ad regem*, PL 125:1024. On these epistles, see Stuart Airlie "Private Bodies and the Body Politic in the Divorce Case of Lothar II," *Past and Present* CLXI (1998), 3–38.

Esther and the Eleventh-Century Queen

As described in the biblical text, Esther was chosen more for her compatibility with the king than her suitability to public life. When called on by the chief representative of the Chosen People, her uncle Mordecai, however, she quickly accommodated herself to her new role as their spokesperson. In taking on the role of intercessor, Esther straddled the division between the private and the public realms as medieval queens did daily out of necessity.

As one of the only commentators on the Book of Esther, Rabanus Maurus's interpretation of the book would have formed one of the only glosses available to the scholars and artists of Saint-Vaast. Rabanus's interpretation of Esther's court visit sheds a great deal of light not only on the meaning of this image, but also on its connection to the other components of the Saint-Vaast Bible's queenship program, for he interpreted Esther and Ahasuerus, not surprisingly, as the King and Queen of Heaven, Christ and *Ecclesia*.

> What is it that on the third day Esther was dressed in regal garments, unless that the Church of the people in the third age, that is after the Incarnation, Passion and Resurrection of Christ, dressed herself beautifully in the sacraments of baptism through the confession of the Holy Trinity, and in the faith, hope and charity of the virtues, so that from then she would be made a worthy partner of the king, [and] would burn incessantly with his special love? Who stands in the court of the house of the king which was inside against the king's hall, that is who, in the pious charity of the present life, looks to the future reward in the heavens, where the King of kings himself has been enthroned in the celestial throne, and has promised to those who with pious prayers call to him? Who extends towards this queen the scepter which he holds in his hand, and shows with it the power of his rule, or the cross of his passion, through which he acquired for himself power in heaven and on earth and under the earth . . . The full joy of the holy Church is not bestowed otherwise unless in the gathering of the Kingdom of Heaven, where the happy Queen will rule with Christ the king in eternity.[174]

Thus the two main protagonists of the Esther story, the king and queen, were assimilated to the same two personae who dominate the Song of Songs and its illustration in the Saint-Vaast Bible. The

---

[174] PL 109:655–656.

same themes were echoed by the composer of the ordo for the consecration of a queen found in the mid-eleventh century Cologne
Pontifical, which immediately precedes the *ordo ad benedicendam sponsam* in the same manuscript. Although entitled the *ordo ad benedicendam reginam*, the ceremony in fact provides for both the consecration
unction and coronation of the candidate. Like all coronation ordines
from the time of Hincmar of Reims onwards, this one draws heavily on Old Testament models for contemporary rulership. Not surprisingly, given the expected function of the queen, the themes of
the ordo borrow heavily from those then standard in the marriage
blessing ritual and found in the Cologne Pontifical's marriage ceremony. In the introduction read by the metropolitan during the *adven-
tus*, biblical *exempla* for queenly mothering are conjured: "One with
Sarah and Rebekah, Leah and Rachel, blessed and reverent women,
she may be worthy of being fruitful and give thanks in the fruit of
her womb."[175] Sarah, Rebekah, Leah and Rachel provided models
of women of the Old Testament who glorified the reign of the
Israelites by providing acceptable heirs to the throne, also one of
the principal duties of the Capetian queen. All but Leah were also
mentioned in the nuptial blessing from the ordo for the blessing of
a bride in the same manuscript.[176] These are not the only Old
Testament characters called upon as role models, however. The
author of the ordo has called on two other *exemplae* renowned for
strengths besides childbearing, for the prayer begins with a reference
to Judith, epitome of the self-motivated heroine.

> All powerful and everliving God, source and beginning of all good-
> ness, you who, by no means rejecting, rather choose the fragility of
> the sex of women, and who, choosing the weak of the world you
> diminished the strong confounding each one, and who even wished to
> reveal the triumph of your glory and virtue once in the hand of the
> woman Judith of the Jewish people because of the most terrible enemy,
> consider the prayers of our humility . . .[177]

Esther's actions are highlighted in a second prayer immediately preceding the consecration unction:

---

[175] Jackson, I, 214.
[176] Hittorp, 177.
[177] Jackson, I, 214.

God, who with equitable balance casts down the arrogant from princely rule, and promotes the humble worthily into the heavens, we suppliants entreat your unutterable mercy, that just as, for the sake of the salvation of the Israelites, you freed Queen Esther from the shackle of her captivity, and made her pass through the chamber of King Ahasuerus and to a share in his kingdom, so allow this your servant, N., in service of the welfare of the Christian people, with the blessing of our humility, mercifully to cross to the worthy and elevated bond of our king and of the society of his kingdom.[178]

Here, the composer again framed the duties of the queen in terms of the Old Testament *exemplum*, explaining that as the defender of the Christian people of her husband's realm, the queen must act the part of Esther, bravely facing all obstacles to protect them, even unto the royal chamber itself. This prayer justifies in part the Saint-Vaast artist's conflation of Esther's audience before the king with her later request at the banquet. *Ut sicut Hester reginam Israhelis causa salutis de captivitatis suae compede solutam ad regis Assueri thalamum regnique sui consortium transire fecisti . . .* The illustration shows Esther at the moment where she has crossed the *thalamum regis*, as described in the ordo's prayer, as well as the reason for her boldness, and through the inscription refers to her mission to undertake the duty of the queen and protect the chosen people, in this case the Jews.

In patristic texts describing this sort of event, *thalamus* was generally intended to mean marriage chamber or marriage bed.[179] Although it is not found in the Cologne Pontifical's *ordo ad benedicendam sponsam*, other ordines for the blessing of marriages from the eleventh and twelfth centuries that preserved a blessing of the bridal chamber referred to this as the *thalamus*.[180] The near contemporary charter of Henry I to the monastery of St. Martin quoted above borrows the Psalter's reference to the chamber of the bridegroom as a *thalamus*.[181] At the time the coronation prayer was composed, in the

---

[178] Jackson, I, 215.

[179] Charles Du Fresne Du Cange, *Glossarium ad scriptores mediae et infimae latinitatis*, 10 vols. (Niort, 1883–1887), VIII, 93 and Albert Blaise, *Dictionnaire latin-française des autours chrétiens* (Paris, 1954), 815.

[180] The eleventh-century Sacramentary of Vich, Museo episcopal, MS 66, contains both an *ordo thalami* and a *benedictio thalami* (Ritzer, *Formen*, 360), while a twelfth-century Missal from an abbey in Normandy, Paris BnF Ms lat. 14446, includes a prayer beginning "Benedic domine thalamum hoc et omnes habitantes in eo . . ." (Ritzer, *Formen*, 381).

[181] *Recueil des Historiens des Gaules et de la France* XI, 605–606, XXXVI, *Monasterio S. Martini de Campis multa concedit.*

tenth century, this was probably the meaning implied here, that Esther had achieved her office as queen, and her invitation to the king's marriage bed, in anticipation of her role as the defender of the faith. This is especially likely as coronation ordines for queens traditionally call on many of the tropes of marriage blessing ceremonies. As Mordecai explains in the Masoretic text of the book of Esther, "And who knoweth whether thou art not therefore come to the kingdom, that thou mightest be ready in such a time as this?"[182] The Saint-Vaast image may thus have been intended to resonate with the implication that her marriage to Ahasuerus had been foreordained by God to enable the salvation of the Chosen People. Nonetheless, by the later Middle Ages, in both ecclesiastical and secular writing, *thalamus* more commonly meant simply room or chamber, or a chamber of a more elevated type, such as the chamber where the feast celebrating the coronation of the pope took place. To an observer reading or hearing the text of the ordo, therefore, and attempting to visualize the actions of the queen, the more well-known narrative of her precipitous audience in the king's chamber would have easily sprung to mind.

By the eleventh century, when the direct intervention of queens into the affairs of state was being effectively curtailed, women's more circuitous influence on the management of the realm was fostered by their clerical advisors, if it could be manipulated to further Church interests. Writers from at least the ninth century onwards addressed the power of wives from all walks of life, not just queens, to influence their husbands for the good of the Church.[183] Within the royal family of the Capetians itself, the attention of the queen to the needs of the Church is witnessed by a number of different documents. The letter from Pope Nicholas II to Anne of Kiev, one of the least effective of royal wives in the eleventh century, underlines this polarity. While Anne was excluded from taking the initiative in legislating by her relative isolation within the royal family, especially given that she was a foreigner, Nicholas acknowledged that she could influence her husband for good.[184] As we have already seen above,

---

[182] Esther 4:14.

[183] Farmer, 521.

[184] *Recueil des Historiens des Gaules* XI, 653, letter of 1059. *Hortamur igitur ut eum, quem Deo inspirante semel ingressa es, tramitem teneas: invictissimumque virum tuum, filium nostrum Regem ad pietatis aequitatisque gubernacula moderanda, statumque Ecclesiae retinendum provocare contendas.*

he exhorted her to influence the king and her sons towards just government and protection of the Church.

Nicholas was, at least in part, echoing what had already become the status quo within the Capetian royal family, as well as in the noble families that surrounded them in Northern France.[185] The royal acts of Robert the Pious and his successor, Henry I, list several times when wives witnessed documents that granted ecclesiastical land.[186] As Sharon Farmer points out, in many cases the interested clerics must have sought these signatures as a guarantee that a later inheritance dispute wouldn't rob them of their gift.[187] On other occasions, however, the queen must have been the instigator of the transfer. Surviving donations from the reign of Henry's father, Robert the Pious, show that Robert's second wife, Berthe, his third wife, Constance of Arles, and his mother, Adelaide, were all active intercessors on behalf of churches and monasteries.[188] Both Berthe and Adelaide, for instance, are credited in two acts of Robert the Pious with causing donations through their intervention and at their suggestion, "suggerentibus itaque intervenientibus."[189] Several acts mention that Constance of Arles helped to negotiate a restitution or agreement then enacted by her husband, Robert.[190] The only time that Helgaud of Fleury praised Queen Constance in his otherwise highly critical *Life of Robert the Pious* was when, after Robert's death and early in the reign of their son Henry, she made a donation for the upkeep of the church of St. Anian.[191]

According to chronicles and acts, eleventh-century queens were omnipresent when it came to discussions of the interests of the Church. The presence of Constance at Robert's side at the Council of Orleans in 1022, when a group of clerics that included her confessor were tried for heresy, is taken for granted by contemporary

---

[185] LoPrete, 15–25 and Nicholas, 115–120.
[186] *Recueil des Historiens des Gaules et de la France* XI, 559–600, charters XXXI–XXXIII list her name as one of the witnesses.
[187] This is probably signaled in act 32, with the phrase *annuente mea conjuge Anna, et prole Philippo, Roberto ac Hugone.*
[188] William Mendel Newman, *Catalogue des actes de Robert II, roi de France* (Paris, 1937), acts 9, 13, 19, 78, and 91.
[189] Newman, *Catalogue*, acts 9 and 13.
[190] Newman, *Catalogue*, acts 78 and 91.
[191] Helgaud de Fleury, 108. Friedson, 18–19, surveys the clerical views of Constance, which range from insolent, to avaricious, to cunning, to a horned serpent in conduct.

commentators.[192] Constance also witnessed several acts documenting the foundation of churches and the restitution of goods and lands to religious foundations along with her husband or is described as being present at court when they were negotiated.[193] This is a signal that, at least in royal relations with the Church, she functioned as a co-ruler. All six acts bearing Queen Anne's signature from during the lifetime of her husband, Henry, record the donation or reaffirmation of gifts to churches.[194] In addition to serving as intercessors before their husbands and sons, queens were also able to dispense generosity from their own dower through gifts to religious houses, as both Constance and Anne seem to have done.[195] The message intended by the artists of the Saint-Vaast Bible (pl. VIII), however, was directed at the queen who reigned as the matriarch of the royal household, and thus still fulfilled a public role.

The Kiss

In the Vulgate, the text of the Additions explains, "And as she held her peace, he took the golden scepter, and laid it upon her neck, and kissed her, and said: Why dost thou not speak to me?" This does not describe what we see in the image. At this juncture, the artists turned back to the Vulgate's translation of the Hebrew version of the text. "And he held out toward her the golden scepter, which he held in his hand: and she drew near, and kissed the top of his scepter." In both of these passages, the Latin translator took some liberties with his source texts, for neither the Greek Septuagint version nor the Masoretic text mentioned that Esther kissed either the king or his scepter.[196]

---

[192] Freidson, 23.

[193] Freidson, 22, and Newman, *Catalogue*, acts 14, 66 and 85.

[194] Frederic Soehnée, *Catalogue des actes d'Henri Ier roi de France* (Bibliothèque de l'École des hautes études – CLXI, Paris, 1907), nos. 102, 104, 117, 120, 123, 125 and Freidson, 33, note 1.

[195] Freidson, 6 and 36–37.

[196] Day, 87. The Septuagint text reads "And he raised the golden rod; he laid (it) upon her neck and greeted her affectionately. And he said, 'Speak to me.'" The Masoretic text in its Hebrew version reads "And the king extended to Esther the golden scepter which was in his hand, and Esther drew near and touched the top of the scepter."

Perhaps the artists took this opportunity to establish a connection between this component of their queenship program and the image illustrating the Song of Songs (pl. V). In that case, the first word of the text, "Osculetur," references the physical and mystical union between Christ and *Ecclesia* with a kiss. In the Esther miniature (pl. VIII), the kiss has been made visual, although the artists have still hesitated to depict an actual kiss between the husband and wife, an iconography that would only begin to appear in manuscripts at the end of the eleventh century.

The kiss had important symbolic significance in the text of the Old Testament, where it was often a sign, as in the case of Esther, of reconciliation. In the New Testament, and especially in Early Christian interpretations of the Song of Songs, the kiss came to stand for the uniting of Christians in the body of the Church through the sharing of the soul, and the soul's reception of spiritual grace through the agency of the kiss.[197] This was the rationale for including the "kiss of peace" in the Eucharistic ritual. As already discussed above, in the eleventh and twelfth centuries the kiss could also embody the sealing of a contract between two people at a betrothal or marriage, and in the feudal ceremony of homage.[198] In fact, the contractual kiss, often called in the documents themselves a 'kiss of peace,' could be a kiss delivered to an object. For instance, a late-eleventh-century charter recording donations made by two lords to an abbey in Poitiers noted that the donors confirmed their gift by kissing the crucifix.[199] Examples of women taking part in the ritual kiss confirming a contract are also recorded, although only for donations made to religious institutions.[200] Thus Rabanus's interpretation of Esther's action found a parallel in ceremonial action. Another aspect of this image suggests, however, that again the artists were intending to incorporate marital symbolism into the Esther illustration.

Although the references to the unifying kiss between two people made by these two images are only tangential, they nonetheless could

---

[197] Perella, 12–27.
[198] Perella, 31–50, Yannick Carré, *Le baiser sur la bouche au moyen âge* (Paris, 1992), 153, and J. Russel Major, "'Bastard Feudalism' and the kiss: changing social mores in late medieval and early modern France," *Journal of Interdisciplinary History* XVII (1987), 509–535.
[199] Carré, 156–157 and 160.
[200] Carré, 157–158.

be intended to underline the spiritual and physical unions of these two couples, both of which prefigured that of the contemporary king and queen.[201] The spiritual kiss of the Song of Songs, embodying the mystical marriage of Christ and the Church, served as a proto-type for the earthly marriage of the royal couple. At the same time, as we have seen, the moment of Esther's entrance into the king's court, his *thalamus*, the prelude to her kiss of his rod, was commonly referred to in the marriage and coronation ordines for queens. This underlined her function as an intercessor, but also highlighted their status as a married couple, a union that could be sealed with a kiss.

While these two miniatures highlighted the queen's duties as con-sort and intercessor, the Passion of the Maccabees image (pl. IX) complements them by adding the dimension of Christian mother-hood to the queen's responsibilities. Taken together, they summa-rize the contemporary clerical view that a queen could be a useful arm of the Church and a powerful tool for good, if her actions were properly limited.

---

[201] Rabanus Maurus, in his commentary on the Book of Esther, refers to the kiss as a sign of veneration, rather than an opportunity for the sharing of spiritual grace, or a reenactment of any nuptial bond (PL 109:655–656).

CHAPTER SIX

CONTINUITY AND CHANGE IN THE
SAINT-VAAST SCRIPTORIUM

Several narrative miniatures in the Saint-Vaast Bible have not been discussed as part of the Bible's program of secular and ecclesiastical leadership in this study. They are the miniatures prefacing IV Kings, Ezekiel, II Maccabees, I Peter and I John. For the most part these are relatively straightforward images of the transmission of the text itself. In the miniature for Ezekiel (vol. II, fol. 42v, fig. 9), God transmits the content of the text to Ezekiel through divine inspiration. In the images prefacing II Maccabees (vol. III, fol. 70v, fig. 17) and I Peter (vol. III, fol. 133v, fig. 21), the text is transmitted by the respective authors to the recipients, the brothers in Egypt and the elect in Pontus, Galatia, Cappodocia, Asia, and Bithynia. Within the initial beginning I John (vol. III, fol. 136v, fig. 23), a bowing scribe presents a volume to the enthroned Christ. While these images underline the divine origin of the text of the Bible, and the authority of its transmission, they don't appear to directly contribute to the Bible's pictorial themes of royal and episcopal supremacy. Only the drawing added to the remainder of a mostly blank folio before the incipit page of IV Kings presents a historical narrative (vol. I, fol. 144v, fig. 6). Here, one sees a combination of moments from IV Kings, including the often depicted Prophecy and Ascension of Elijah, and the more unusual Battle of the Kings of Israel, Judah and Edom against the King of Moab. It is not immediately apparent what role this combination of scenes was intended to play in the larger program of the Bible, and because it has not been integrated within the initial and its framework, but was apparently added as an afterthought to a nearly empty folio, it may not have been foreseen as part of the Bible's original program.

Between twenty and fifty years after the artists of Saint-Vaast planned and executed their exploration of the biblical origins of ecclesiastical and secular governance in the Arras Bible, they revisited the manuscript to insert several illuminations into spaces left on the original early-eleventh-century folios and surrounded by script of the

original scribes. A total of five figural illuminations and many decorative details were added to all three volumes of the Bible in a style that is clearly different from the style employed by the artists of Saint-Vaast earlier in the century. As discussed above, the figural illuminations added in this campaign, namely those prefacing the Old Testament prologue *Frater Ambrosius* in volume I, the two minor prophets Nahum and Habakkuk in volume II, and the Wisdom book of Ecclesiasticus, and Paul's Epistle to the Colossians in volume III, were carried out in opaque paints by an artist, the Colossian Master, interested in lending his figures and objects an aura of three-dimensionality.[1]

Four of the illuminations added to the Bible in this final campaign are very straightforward. The illustration for the preface *Frater Ambrosius* (vol. I, fol. 2, pl. I) mimicked a framed initial page in a much older Saint-Vaast manuscript, the Saint-Vaast Lectionary (Arras BM MS 1045 [233], fig. 29) by copying the seated evangelists in frame medallions. Although the preface does not address the Gospels alone, it does survey the typological relevancy of the Bible as a whole, and thus the Evangelists, as biblical authors, were an appropriate illustration of the text. The historiated initials for Nahum and Habakkuk (vol. II, fols. 106v and 108, figs. 10 and 11) each contain a single figure. The historiated initial prefacing Nahum illustrates the first few words of the Book of Nahum, which predict the destruction of the city of Nineveh, "The Lord is a jealous God, and a revenger." Appropriately, the artist has depicted a standing Christ-logos brandishing a sword in his right hand. The Book of Habakkuk is instead illustrated with an author portrait. A haloed Habakkuk stands against a swirling backdrop of green and yellow waves with a furled scroll in his left hand. In the illustration for Paul's Epistle to the Colossians (vol. III, fol. 1, fig. 19), one can surmise that at one point the cluster of figures crowded into the top lobe of the frame would have been listening to the Apostle, who once stood to the left of the initial, before the miniature was defaced. Thus this was, again, a form of author portrait. Although each illumination illustrates the book it prefaces well, none significantly adds to the thematic program constructed for the Bible several decades earlier.

---

[1] See also above, chapter one.

Ecclesiasticus

The illumination prefacing the Wisdom book of Ecclesiasticus is, however, of an entirely different character (now vol. III, fol. 1, fig. 14). Once again, there is no evidence that this illumination replaced an earlier image. The artists of the first campaign left at least three-quarters of folio 1v of volume III blank. In this space the artist of the second campaign added a very colorful foliate-filled initial O for the beginning of the text, and the most complex figural illumination in the Saint-Vaast Bible. Despite the fact that he worked between twenty and fifty years after the first artists, his illustration can be tied to the earlier program on several levels. First, like the early-eleventh-century Ezra and Acts Masters, he borrowed extensively from the Carolingian visual and exegetical traditions, imbuing the Ecclesiasticus illustration with the same kinds of educated references found in the miniatures making up the programs addressing royal and episcopal leadership. Second, the theme of the Ecclesiasticus illumination, the supremacy of Divine Wisdom as it is embodied in earthly and heavenly rulers, overlaps with the theme that tied together so many of the earlier illustrations. In the middle of the eleventh century when artists returned to the Saint-Vaast Bible to complete its pictorial cycle they not only understood the earlier messages encoded in the Bible's miniatures, this theme was still so important to them that they chose to add a new and elaborate miniature in the same vein. This second campaign of illustration also coincided with the redaction in the same scriptorium of the Cologne Pontifical, Cologne, Erzbischöfliche Diözesan Dombibliothek, Dom MS 141, the service book containing so many ordines that reflected the same concerns as the Saint-Vaast Bible's pictorial program. The Ecclesiasticus illumination has inspired more discussion than any other part of the Bible's pictorial program but its place in the Saint-Vaast Bible has never before been satisfactorily explained.[2]

The book of Ecclesiasticus must have been just as challenging as the Song of Songs to illustrate because, like that book, it is not a narrative. Instead, it is comprised of a series of moral exhortations on wisdom and good conduct, many of them first person statements

---

[2] Most recently, Henry Mayr-Harting, *Ottonian Book Illumination; an Historical Study*, 2 vols. (New York, 1991), II, 176–178.

delivered by Wisdom itself.[3] Earlier illuminators therefore drew on this aspect of the text and illustrated the initial prefacing the book with either a female personification of Wisdom, or a depiction of wisdom incarnate, Christ.[4] For instance, the historiated initial prefacing the Book of Ecclesiasticus in the Carolingian Grandval Bible holds a hand gripping a cross-staff with Alpha and Omega pendants, and a chalice, symbol of the Incarnation.[5] This iconography refers to the first words of the text, "All wisdom comes from God." In chapter nine of the Book of Proverbs, Wisdom herself says "And to the unwise she said: Come, eat my bread, and drink the wine which I have mingled for you. Forsake childishness and live." Using this statement, Wisdom was often interpreted by commentators eucharistically as God incarnate in Christ.[6] In the Carolingian Bamberg Bible, the initial O beginning the text of Ecclesiasticus instead houses an enthroned female personification labeled *Sophia Sancta*, holding an open codex and palm.[7] The mid-eleventh-century artist of the Saint-Vaast Bible Ecclesiasticus, perhaps inspired by some Carolingian pictorial model, drew on both of these ideas by depicting Wisdom incarnate, Christ, enthroned as Holy Wisdom within a circle.[8] He stressed Christ's identity with Holy Wisdom by placing him in front of the house of Wisdom, the Temple, with pillars topped with female

---

[3] B. Botte, "La Sagesse dans les livres sapientiaux," *Revue des sciences philosophiques et théologiques* XIX (1930), 85.

[4] *Lexikon der christlichen Ikonographie*, ed. Engelbert Kirschbaum, 8 vols. (Basel, 1968–1976), IV, 39–43. The literature on various depictions of Wisdom is vast. See, for instance, André Grabar, "Iconographie de la Sagesse divine," *Cahiers archéologiques* VIII (1956), 254–261, and W. Hormann, "Probleme einer Aldersbacher Handschrift, Clm 2599," in *Buch und Welt. Festschrift für G. Hofmann* (Weisbaden, 1965), 335–389, F. Ronig, "Der thronende Christus mit Kelch und Hostie zwischen Ecclesia und Synagoge," *Archiv für mittelrheinische Kirchengeschichte* XV (1963), 391–403, and for the east, J. Meyersdorff, "L'iconographie de la Sagesse divine dans la tradition byzantine," *Cahiers archéologiques* X (1959), 259–277.

[5] London BL MS Add 10546, fol. 269.

[6] Marie Thérèse D'Alverny, "Le symbolisme de la Sagesse et le Christ de Saint Dunstan," *Bodleian Library Record* V (1956), 234, on the interpretations of St. Cyprian.

[7] Bamberg, Staatsbibliothek Bibl. 1, fol. 260v.

[8] Once again, the Saint-Vaast Bible's image is echoed in part by that in the near contemporary Catalan Ripoll Bible, Rome BAV cod. Vat. lat. 5729, fol. 299. Here, the Book of Ecclesiasticus is prefaced by an image of an enthroned Christ-logos in conversation with two companions bearing books and wearing Phrygian caps, or according to Neuß, monks' cowls. Wilhelm Neuß, *Die katalanische Bibelillustration um die Wende des ersten Jahrtausends und die altspanische Buchmalerei* (Bonn, 1922), 83 and fig. 193.

heads probably meant to represent the Liberal Arts, inspired by the beginning of chapter nine of the Book of Proverbs, "Wisdom hath built herself a house, she hath hewn her out seven pillars."[9]

The artist may have been consciously referring to the Bible's earlier program when he echoed the composition of one of its miniatures. As in the Song of Songs, the Ecclesiasticus illustration is organized around a jeweled circle in the top half of the folio that, like the zodiac-inhabited circle before the Song of Songs in the second volume, echoes the shape of the first letter of the text. Once again, Christ-logos sits enthroned in the middle of the circle, although he is shown not as the *Sponsus* in conversation with his heavenly bride, but rather as the avenging world ruler. The artist surrounded Christ-logos with the attributes of rule, such as the orb, spear, and diadem as well as flanking Cardinal Virtues found in Carolingian ruler portraits, especially the portrait of a ruler in a ninth-century Gospel book then found in nearby Cambrai, Cambrai BM MS 327, fol. 16v, where the ruler and the Cardinal virtues all hold the same attributes.[10] The artists of Saint-Vaast may already have mined this manuscript for motifs when illustrating the Saint-Vaast Gospel Book, Boulogne BM MS 9, but this echoing of the Cambrai Gospels' dedication page points to an even more specific message on the part of the later artist, who integrated the Ecclesiasticus illumination into the rest of the Bible's program by assimilating it to a ruler portrait.[11]

Just like the earlier artists, the artist of the Ecclesiasticus page seems to have relied heavily on the commentaries of the Carolingian

[9] Marie Thérèse D'Alverny, "La Sagesse et ses sept filles," in *Mélanges dédiés à la mémoire de Félix Grat* I (Paris, 1946), 245, and Walter Cahn, *Romanesque Bible Illustration* (Ithaca, 1982), 114. Visual sources for this motif abound, particularly in Carolingian and Anglo-Saxon manuscripts of Prudentius' *Psychomachia*. See, for instance, Leiden, Bibliothek der Universiteit, MS Burm Q.3, fol. 148v, or London BL MS Cotton Cleopatra C. VIII, fol. 33, H. Woodruff, "The Illustrated Manuscripts of Prudentius," *Art Studies: Medieval, Renaissance and Modern* VII (1929), 33–79.

[10] On the Cardinal Virtues, *Lexikon der christlichen Ikonographie* IV, 364–380, and Adolph Katzenellenbogen, *Allegories of the Virtues and Vices in Medieval Art* (London, 1939).

[11] Katzenellenbogen, *Allegories*, 31. Fol. 17 of the Cambrai Gospels, with its bust-length evangelist symbol for Matthew springing from a cloudy base and surrounded by a circular frame, seems to have been copied wholesale into the Saint-Vaast Gospel book, Boulogne BM MS 9, fol. 15. The Cambrai Gospels ruler portrait was, of course, not the only example to include such iconography. The ruler portrait in the San Paolo Bible also included virtues. William J. Diebold, "The Ruler Portrait of Charles the Bald in the San Paolo Bible," *Art Bulletin* LXXVI (1994), 6–18.

scholar Rabanus Maurus in interpreting the book he sought to illustrate. Rabanus glossed chapter 24:35–37, "Who filleth up wisdom as the Phison, and as the Tigris in the days of the new fruits. Who maketh understanding to abound as the Euphrates, who multiplieth it as the Jordan in the time of harvest. Who sendeth knowledge as the light, and riseth up as Gehon in the time of the vintage," with this interpretation: "The four rivers of Paradise flowing from one source imitate the wisdom of the King, who descended from David, meaning, the four Gospels flow out from our Lord Jesus Christ, the true son of God, also the true son of Man, that is, David, because from his seed he was born into flesh."[12] The evangelists in the Saint-Vaast image are arrayed in the arcades below Christ's feet like the four rivers of paradise flowing from their source, supporting the superstructure of Holy Wisdom above, but at the same time the product of its inspiration.

Commenting on Ecclesiasticus 10:4, "The power of the earth is in the hand of God, and in his time he will raise up a profitable ruler over it," Rabanus recalled the statement of Psalm 73, "God is our King before the ages: he hath wrought salvation in the midst of the earth . . ." He then elaborated, "All the power in heaven and earth has been given to him, and there is no one who is able to resist his will. It is fitting that he reigns while he may subjugate all his enemies under his feet."[13] This passage casts light on the designer's addition of the crossed-orb and diadem to Christ, as well as his enthronement over the cowering figures whose heads serve as the Lord's footstool.

The visual motif of figures crushed under Christ's feet was probably originally inspired by the text of Psalm 109:1, "The Lord said to my Lord, sit thou at my right hand, until I make thy enemies thy footstool." In the Carolingian Utrecht Psalter illustration for Psalm 109, God the Father and God the Son are shown sitting enthroned over crushed figures.[14] This composition was echoed in

---

[12] PL 109:942. *Quod autem quatuor flumina paradisi ex uno fonte procedentia assimilat sapientia regi, qui ex David ortus est, significat ex Domino nostro Jesu Christo vero Filio Dei, nec non et vero filio hominis, hoc est David, quia ex eius semine secundum carnem natus est, quatuor Evangelia procedere . . .*

[13] PL 109:826. *. . . data est illi omnis potestas in coelo et in terra, et non est qui possit resistere voluntati eius. Oportet enim eum regnare donec subjiciat omnes inimicos eius sub pedibus suis.*

[14] Utrecht, Universiteitsbibliotheek MS 32, fol. 64v.

the early-eleventh century by the artist of the New Minster prayer-book.[15] Here, in addition to a number of other changes, the artist labeled the figures flanking the hellmouth under Christ's feet as Arius and Judas, inspired by Jerome's glosses on Psalm 109, where he refutes the Arian heresy.[16] The equating of the "enemies" of Christ specifically with heretics may shed some light on how the Saint-Vaast Bible's version of this motif should be interpreted.

In his commentary, Rabanus set up a dichotomy between the heterodox and the orthodox, between those who disregard the doctrines of the holy fathers and misinterpret the sense of Holy Scripture, and those who wisely follow the teachings of the Gospels and the doctrines of the Church, who commend virtue while persecuting vice, and who follow the sacraments. In many cases, he interpreted the admonitions of Ecclesiasticus as directed specifically against heretics. Most tellingly, Rabanus emphasized the gulf between heretics as those who, because of their actions, are denied the insights of Divine Wisdom, and the true faithful, who alone may benefit from the understanding of wisdom.

Commenting on Ecclesiasticus 14:10, "An evil eye is towards evil things: and he shall not have his fill of bread, but shall be needy and pensive at his own table," Rabanus stated, "The eye of heretics, because it is always intent on following errors, does not merit the heavenly bread, that is, the understanding of Divine Wisdom."[17] Glossing Ecclesiasticus 15:7, "But foolish men shall not obtain her [Wisdom], and wise men shall meet her, foolish men shall not see her: for she is far from pride and deceit," he defined the errors of heretics as the misinterpretation of the scriptures.

> Heretics are those who corrupt the integrity of the Holy Scriptures through their errors, and men who deceive men with false doctrine. They all, therefore, do not take hold of wisdom, because the Holy Spirit flees from falsehood, and wisdom will not enter into a malicious spirit. To the contrary, however, intelligent men, that is, religious and orthodox men, resist them, because in thinking, discourse and likewise in works, they resolve to obey the wishes of the divine.[18]

---

[15] London BL MS Cotton Titus D. XXVI and XXVII, fol. 75v.

[16] Ernst Kantorowicz, "The Quinity of Winchester," *Art Bulletin* XXIX (1947), 80–81.

[17] PL 109:857. *Mystice autem haereticorum oculus, quia semper ad errores sequendos intentus est, panem coelestem, hoc est intellectum divinae sapientiae non meretur . . .*

[18] PL 109:861. *Sunt etiam et haeretici, qui sinceritatem sacrarum Scripturarum suis erroribus*

Peter Brieger saw the inclusion of the evangelists and the curtain, which he interpreted as a reference to the Temple of the Old Testament, as an expression of the desire of contemporary clerics to defend the unity of the scriptures against the attacks of *Sapientia*'s enemies, the heretics.[19] Although Brieger derived his hypothesis from the visual evidence alone, his interpretation is reinforced by a reading of Rabanus's commentary. Glossing Ecclesiasticus 11:10, Rabanus said, "It is the custom to say one book of the scriptures, however many books, if among themselves they do not disagree, and they are written about the same thing."[20] The unity of the Old and New Testaments is further reinforced by their common origin. Commenting on chapter 24:38–39, Rabanus said, "Truly in fact our Lord is author of spiritual knowledge and beneficial doctrine, because he established the first law through Moses, he inspired the prophets, he taught the apostles, he appointed the evangelists and the eulogists of the New Testament . . ."[21] The artist of the Ecclesiasticus illustration has visualized the unity of the two testaments by joining the veil of the temple of the Old Covenant with the four evangelists of the New in the bottom arcade of the miniature.

The combination of the Liberal Arts with the Cardinal Virtues as an expression of Wisdom and a means towards the understanding of the divine was a common topos in Carolingian literature. The Ecclesiasticus illustration of the Saint-Vaast Bible is the first surviving illustration of this system.[22] In his own discussion of the Ecclesiasticus

---

corrumpunt, et homines falsis doctrinis decipiunt. Hi ergo omnes non apprehendent sapientiam, quia Spiritus sanctus disciplinae effugiet fictum; et in malevolam animam non introibit sapientia. E contrario autem homines sensati, hoc est, homines catholici et religiosi, hi obviant illi, quia cogitatione, sermone, simul et opere divinae decernunt obtemperare voluntati.

[19] Brieger, 158–159.

[20] PL 109:841. *Moris est Scripturarum, quamvis plures libros, si inter se non discrepent, et de eadem re scribant, unum volumen dicere.*

[21] PL 109:943. *Vere enim Dominus noster auctor est scientiae spiritalis et salubris doctrinae, quia ipse per Moysen primum condidit legem, ipse inspiravit prophetas, ipse docuit apostolos, ipse ordinavit evangelistas, et praedictores Novi Testamenti . . .*

[22] Peter Brieger, "Bible Illustration and Gregorian Reform," in *Studies in Church History* II (1965), 158–159, compared this composition with the seventeenth-century description of the now destroyed floor mosaic of Saint-Remi at Reims. Unfortunately, there is no firm evidence for the date of the mosaic, which may have been created as late as 1170. Henri Stern, *Recueil général des mosaiques de la Gaule*, I. Province de Belgique, 1. Partie ouest (Paris, 1957), 91 and Émile Mâle, *Art religieux du XIIe siècle en France: étude sur les origines de l'iconographie du moyen âge* (Paris, 1922), 318–319. Later encyclopedic schemes like this abound. See, for instance, Francis Wormald,

illumination, Peter Brieger pointed out that the precedent for combining many of the elements found in this miniature had already
been set in the writings of Alcuin on the study of the Liberal Arts.[23]
In his *De grammatica*, Alcuin described the seven columns of the
Temple of Wisdom as symbolizing the seven Gifts of the Holy Spirit,
but also the seven Liberal Arts.[24] The seven heads surmounting the
columns of the Temple in the Saint-Vaast image are thus interpreted
as personifying the Liberal Arts.[25] Furthermore, in *De rhetorica et virtutibus*, Alcuin promoted the four Cardinal Virtues as a means to
understand the divine by making them part of *Philosophia*, the love
of wisdom, under *Ethica*, one of the three divisions containing the
Liberal Arts.[26] Nonetheless, Rabanus Maurus's commentary on
Ecclesiasticus may have proved a more compelling sourcebook for
the artist than the more tangentially related writings on wisdom by
Alcuin specifically because of its concentration on the dangers of
heresy and the sins of heretics.[27] Throughout the commentary, Rabanus
repeatedly returns to the theme of the threat posed by heretics and

---

"The Throne of Wisdom and St. Edward's Chair," *De artibus opuscula XL* (1961), I, 532–539.

[23] Brieger, 158.

[24] Alcuin, *De grammatica*, PL 101:853. *Legimus, Salomone dicente, per quem ipsa se cecinit [Sapientia]: Sapientia aedificavit sibi domum, excidit columas septem* (Prov. IX:1). *Quae sen- tentia licet ad divinam pertineat sapientiam, quae sibi in utero virginali domum, id est corpus, aedificavit, hanc et septem donis sancti spiritus confirmavit; vel Ecclesiam, quae est domus Dei, eisdem donis illuminavit; tamen sapientia liberalium litterarum septem columnis confirmatur; nec aliter ad perfectam quem libet deducit scientiam, nisi his septem columnis vel etiam gradibus exaltetur.*

[25] D'Alverny, "Le symbolisme de la Sagesse," 243, and Brieger, 158. On the rep- resentations of the seven Liberal Arts, see *Lexikon der christlichen Ikonographie* II, 703–713, Jutta Tezmen-Siegel, *Die Darstellung der septem artes liberales in der bildenen Kunst als rezeption der Lehrplangeschichte*, (Munich, 1985), especially 144 on the Arras miniature, Adolph Katzenellenbogen, "The Representation of the Seven Liberal Arts," in *Twelfth-Century Europe and the Foundations of Modern Society* (Madison, Wisconson, 1961), 39–58, M. Masi, "Boethius and the Iconography of the Liberal Arts," *Latomus* XXXIII (1974), 57–75 and Elisabeth Klemm, "Artes Liberales und antike Autoren in der Aldersbacher Sammelhandschrift, Clm 2599," *Zeitschrift für Kunstgeschichte* XLI (1978), 1–15.

[26] Alcuin, *Dialogus de rhetorica et virtutibus*, PL 101:945–950. In connecting the lib- eral arts with the four Cardinal Virtues in his scheme, Alcuin echoed the system described by Isidore of Seville in his *Etymologiarum*, PL 83:141. *Philosophia est rerum humanarum divinarumque cognitio . . . Ethicam socrates primus ad corrigendos componendosque mores instituit, atque mone studium eius ad bene vivendi disputationem perduxit, dividens eam in quatuor virtutes animae, id est, prudentiam, justitiam, fortitudinem, et temperentiam.* Rabanus Maurus also picked up on this, and included it in his *De universo*, PL 111:414–148.

[27] Rabanus Maurus, *Commentariorum in Ecclesiasticum*, PL 109:763–1126.

schismatics to both Church and individual. Thus Rabanus's work provides an explanation for the combination of motifs found in the Saint-Vaast Bible's Ecclesiasticus illumination, for the first time connecting them specifically with the Book of Ecclesiasticus.

As we saw in chapter three, the monks of Arras were no strangers to heresy. Although the Synod of Arras had been held decades before in 1025, the record, the *Acta synodi Atrebatensis*, had been composed with more than one goal in mind. According to the *Acta*, not only did Gerard attempt to counter the imputed vices of the heretics, he also sought to shore up the secular and ecclesiastical hierarchies on which he relied. It seems obvious from the iconography of the Ecclesiasticus miniature that his concerns were still vivid years later when the Saint-Vaast Bible was renovated and that the monks of Saint-Vaast had access to the *Acta synodi*.

In listing the transgressions of the defendants, Gerard reported first that the Italian heretic Gundulf had taught his followers to reject the entire Bible with the exception of the Gospels and the writings of the Apostles.[28] Throughout the *Acts*, Gerard defended the unity of the scriptures by pointing out repeatedly the origins of Church practices and beliefs in the Old Testament. He defended the study of the Old Testament by pointing out the references to it in the same scriptures that were considered acceptable by the heretics. Gerard stated, for instance, "But also Paul, who always teaches us to pass over from the old to the new, writes over much from Moses, the prophets and the psalms in his own writings, as it is in Genesis, 'The first man Adam was made into a living spirit (I Cor. 15:45).'"[29]

In illustrating the Book of Ecclesiasticus in the Saint-Vaast Bible with this pictorial expression of the unity of the two testaments, the artist could not have chosen a better setting to express his beliefs.

---

[28] PL 151:1271. *At illi referunt se esse auditores Gundulfi, cuiusdam ab Italiae partibus viri, et ab eo evangelicis mandatis et apostolicis informatos, nullamque praeter hanc scripturam se recipere, sed hanc verbo et opere tenere.*

[29] PL 151:1288–1289. *Sed et Paulus, qui semper a veteribus nos docet transire ad nova, multa de Moyse et prophetis et psalmis, suis scriptis inscrit, ut est illud in Genesi: Factus est primus homo Adam in animam viventem.* Gerard continues with a further example, *Quid igitur? Nunquid Vetus Testamentum reprobasse dicendus est, qui in Epistola ad Hebraeos ita scribit: Tabernaculum factum est primum, in quo erant candelabra, et mensa, et propositio panum, quod dicitur sancta; post velamentum autem secundum tabernaculum, quo dicitur Sancta sanctorum, aureum habens thuribulum, et arcam testamenti circumtectam omni ex parte auro (Hebr. 9), et caetera, quae in eadem Epistola de Veteri Testamento prosequitur.*

As one of the first illustrated Giant Bibles of the Romanesque era, the manuscript in itself represented how important the Old Testament remained for monastic practice.[30] In addition, the portrayal of Christ as the conquering ruler uses the format and attributes of a Carolingian ruler portrait to complete the Bible's pictorial cycle of ruler images.[31] Christ-logos is shown as the heavenly ruler, of which all earthly rulers were types, enthroned before the Temple of Wisdom, the very virtue which was God's gift to worthy rulers such as David and Solomon, enabling them to rule justly. The Ecclesiasticus illumination therefore forms a fitting culmination of the Bible's earlier program, although it was added as much as fifty years later and by a different artist.

It is not surprising that the artists in the Saint-Vaast scriptorium would have returned to the Bible to complete the unfinished pictorial program so long after it was begun. The Bible was clearly heavily used throughout its history, as is obvious from the numerous sets of chapter markings in both Roman and Arabic numerals, the replacement of lost folios in later Gothic script, and the network of lection marks and neums written throughout the text. As the Bible was intended for day-to-day use in the choir and the refectory, the monks would have been constantly reminded of the Bible's unfinished state, as well as the content of its original figurative decoration. Furthermore, the same political issues faced Bishop Gerard of Cambrai's immediate successor, who most likely held the seat at the very time when these additions to the program were carried out.[32] He would have understood and sympathized with the political theology expressed in the Bible's miniature program, and echoed in many of the ordines found in the Cologne Pontifical, executed at nearly the same time as the Bible additions.

Lietbertus of Lessines, Gerard's nephew, held the position of bishop of Arras-Cambrai from 1051 through 1076. Educated under his uncle's guidance at the cathedral of Cambrai, he was quickly elevated

---

[30] See chapter two on the intended use of the Saint-Vaast Bible and other North French Giant Bibles.

[31] See chapter four on the kingship cycle in the Saint-Vaast Bible.

[32] On Lietbertus and his political context, see the insightful essay by John Ott, "Both Mary and Martha: Bishop Lietbertus of Cambrai and the Construction of Episcopal Sanctity in a Border Diocese around 1100," in *The Bishop Reformed: Studies in Episcopal Power and Culture in the Central Middle Ages*, ed. John S. Ott and Anna E. Trumbore (New York: Ashgate, forthcoming). I am very grateful to the author for allowing me to read the essay in advance of its publication.

to the post of archdeacon of the cathedral chapter. Like Gerard, his election was confirmed by the reigning emperor, the Salian Henry III, yet he was consecrated to his office by the Archbishop of Reims. Like his uncle, Lietbertus from early in his episcopacy deftly managed the high-wire act necessary for those whose diocese crossed national boundaries. Like Gerard, he had been invested with his office through the power of the Imperial court, and returned there periodically, particularly when issues such as the increasing threat posed by the counts of Flanders were discussed.[33] According to Lietbertus' *vita*, the French king, Henry I, upon hearing of the impending consecration, insisted that his marriage and the consecration of his new queen, Anne of Kiev, be celebrated at the same time, a sure sign of his respect for the new bishop.[34] Lietbertus' participation in the marriage of the French monarch was a harbinger that his ties to the French court would be closer than those of his predecessor and uncle, Gerard I, and he attended the French court of Henry's son Philippe I at least twice more.[35] As John Ott has recently observed, "[Lietbertus was] politically amphibious, equally at ease amidst his Frankish brother-bishops or the bustling throngs of the German court."

Yet Bishop Lietbertus faced the same harassment from the castellans of Cambrai and their backers, the counts of Flanders, that had dogged Gerard, making any strong, divinely consecrated ruler a potential defender. In a chain of events that mirrored almost exactly those of Gerard's episcopacy, immediately after his consecration in 1051 Lietbert was prevented from entering the city of Cambrai by the local castellan, John, who had seized the episcopal palace.[36] This castellan was soon replaced by Lietbertus's favored candidate, Hugh d'Oisy, who later sacked the palace when the bishop was on pilgrimage to Jerusalem. In response to this and other assaults, Lietbertus led the townsmen in a campaign against one of Hugh's palaces.[37]

---

[33] Ott, "Both Mary and Martha," and *Gesta pontificum Cameracensium: Continuatio— Gesta Lietberti episcopi*, PL 149:177–192.

[34] See above, chapter 5. Rudolfus, *Vita sancti Lietberti*, chapter 19, PL 146:1459.

[35] Ott, "Both Mary and Martha," and Maurice Prou, ed. *Recueil des actes de Philippe Ier, roi de France (1059–1108)* (Paris, 1908), 60–61, no. 22, 79, no. 26.

[36] *Gesta pontificum Cameracensium: Continuatio* 4.2–14 PL 149:182–186, and *Vita sancti Lietberti*, chapters 8, 14–15 and 28, PL 146:1453, 1457 and 1464.

[37] *Vita sancti Lietberti* chapters 28, 42 and 44, PL 146:1464, 1471–1473, and *Gesta pontificum* chapter 4, verses 15 and 19, PL 149:182–183.

In 1054 Lietbertus participated in a military campaign led by Henry III against Count Baldwin V of Flanders and over twenty years later he was transported from his death-bed into the siege tents of Count Robert of Flanders outside the walls of Cambrai so that he could excommunicate him in person.[38]

The Legacy of the Saint-Vaast Bible

Although the complexity of the Saint-Vaast Bible's Ecclesiasticus illustration was never replicated, twelfth-century Romanesque Bibles took up many of the iconographic motifs used first at Arras. The unfinished Winchester Bible illustration for this Wisdom book, for instance, pictures a crowned female personification of Wisdom holding a cross-orb, emphasizing the royal nature of Divine Wisdom as described in Rabanus's commentary on Ecclesiasticus.[39] The Sawalo Bible illustration for Ecclesiasticus shows Christ enthroned as Wisdom incarnate.[40] The artists of the Bible of Saint-Thierry depicted *Philosophia* surrounded by the three divisions of the Liberal Arts and virtues outlined by Alcuin in *De rhetorica et virtutibus*.[41] The most striking example must be the illustration for Ecclesiasticus in a Bible from Western England, which includes the crowned female personification enthroned in front of a seven columned temple of Wisdom, crushing a lion and a serpent beneath her feet.[42]

The illustration for Ecclesiasticus was not the only image from the Saint-Vaast Bible that is echoed in later Romanesque Bibles. In fact, the Arras Bible contains the first surviving examples of many subjects that would later become part of the standard repertoire of Romanesque Bible imagery. The Saint-Vaast Bible's illustration of God's charge to Joshua is echoed in several later Bibles, including two twelfth-century French Bibles,[43] the Mosan Stavelot Bible, and

---

[38] Ott, "Both Mary and Martha." and *Vita sancti Lietberti*, chapter 60, PL 146:1480.
[39] Winchester, Cathedral Library, vol. III, fol. 278v.
[40] Valenciennes BM MS 4, fol. 131v.
[41] Reims BM MS 22–23, vol. II, fol. 25.
[42] Oxford, Bodleian Library MS Laud. Misc. 752, fol. 265v.
[43] The Second Bible of St. Martial of Limoges, Paris BnF MS lat. 8, vol. I, fol. 82, and a Bible from Languedoc, London BL MS Harley 4772, fol. 99.

an Italian Bible now in Parma.[44] Images of David and Abishag also appear before III Kings in several later Bibles. In both the Pantheon Bible and the Lyon Bible, David is shown actually being warmed by Abishag,[45] while in the Saint-Yrieix Bible, as in the Saint-Vaast Bible, the moment of introduction is shown.[46] The artists of the Winchester Bible even combined this with an image of David's last charge to Solomon.[47] As noted in chapter three, the Saint-Vaast illustration of the Book of Ezra showing both Ezra and King Artaxerxes is also paralleled in the Winchester Bible.[48] There are similar illustrations in a Bible from Marchiennes now in Douai, in a Bible from Champagne or Northern Burgundy, and in the Parisian Manerius Bible.[49]

The image of Esther's audience with Ahasuerus became one of the most popular illustrations for the Book of Esther. Examples can be found in the Bible of Souvigny, the Bible of Saint-Thierry, the Lyons Bible, and a twelfth-century Bible from the Chartres region.[50] The image with the greatest number of parallels, however, is undeniably that for the Song of Songs. Representations of Christ and Ecclesia abound in Romanesque manuscripts, though their relationship was depicted with various degrees of explicitness.[51]

In spite of these individual similarities to other Bibles, however, the pictorial program of the Saint-Vaast Bible was never copied in its entirety, or even strongly echoed in a later Bible. Many of the scenes in the Bible that are essential to understanding its message about kings, queens and bishops are almost unique in Romanesque

[44] London BL MS Add 28106, fol. 75v, and Parma, Bibliotheca Palatina, Palat. MS 386, fol. 58v.
[45] Rome BAV cod. Vat. lat. 12958, vol. I, fol. 98, and Lyon BM MS 410–411, fol. 132v.
[46] Saint-Yrieix BM Bible, fol. 93v.
[47] Winchester, Cathedral Library, vol. I, fol. 109.
[48] Winchester, Cathedral Library, vol. III, fol. 342.
[49] Douai BM MS 3a, fol. 93v, Paris, Bibliothèque Sainte-Geneviève, MSS 8–10, vol. III, fol. 47, and Paris BnF MSS lat. 11534–11535, vol. II, fol. 138.
[50] Moulins BM, fol. 284, Reims BM MS 22–23, vol. II, fol. 69v, Lyon BM MS 410–411, vol. II, fol. 23, and Paris BnF MS lat. 116, fol. 65.
[51] A few of these are the twelfth-century Chambre des Députés Bible, Paris, Bibliothèque de la Chambre des Députés, MS 2, fol. 195v, a Bible from Western England now in Oxford, Oxford, Bodleian Library, MS Laud. Misc. 752, fol. 258v, the Bible of Souvigny, Moulins BM, fol. 235, the Frowinus Bible, Engelberg, Stiftsbibliothek MS 3–5, vol. II, fol. 69v, the Sawalo Bible, Valenciennes BM MS 1–5, vol. III, fol. 137v, and the Bible of Saint-Remi, Reims BM MS 16–18, vol. III, fol. 149r.

Bible illumination, including the images prefacing Jeremiah, II Maccabees, the *Passio Machabeorum* and the Book of Acts. Also, while many later Bibles have images of Moses communicating with God illustrating the Pentateuch, in no case is the scene found before Deuteronomy.[52] In addition, although later artists tended to concentrate a great deal of biblical decoration at the beginning of the Bible illustrating the Book of Genesis, the Saint-Vaast Bible's Genesis page has no figural illustration and very little decoration of any sort.

One is led inevitably towards the conclusion that the choice of which books to illustrate, along with the way in which they were illustrated, was guided by programmatic imperatives specific to early-eleventh-century Arras. The historical circumstances surrounding the creation of the Bible, the political uncertainties besetting Flanders, and the reform movement with its threat to the traditional ecclesiastical hierarchy all contributed to mold the Bible's pictorial program. At the same time, the monastic reform movement itself, with its emphasis on the importance of the reading of scripture and its rejuvenation of local monasteries and their scriptoria, provided the opportunity for these ideas to be expressed in this lavish format. While later Romanesque artists expanded the system of Bible illustration to include many more books, and seemingly more consistent cycles of imagery, the Saint-Vaast Bible serves as an invaluable record of the genesis of Romanesque Bible illustration because it documents the concerns that gave rise to one of the most important artistic movements of the eleventh and twelfth centuries.

The Saint-Vaast Bible also provides an interesting example of the method of work of a scriptorium just rebuilding itself after at least a century's lapse in manuscript production. The monastery of Saint-Vaast, recovering from the Norse raids that had swept the region during the tenth century, and flowering anew under the leadership of the reforming abbot Richard of Saint-Vanne, set itself the task of creating a monumental three-volume Bible as one of its very first artistic projects of the eleventh century. The monks' desire to create such a mammoth work probably reflects the renewed monastic practice

---

[52] In several cases one does find Moses speaking with the Israelites before Deuteronomy, including Oxford, Bodleian Library, MS Laud. Misc. 752, fol. 64v, and Florence, Biblioteca Laurenziana, MS S. Cr. Plut. V, dex. 1, fol. 61, and the Stavelot Bible, London BL MS Add. 28106, fol. 62v.

of daily choir and refectory reading from the Bible instituted by Richard of Saint-Vanne after he reformed the monastery in 1018, for the Saint-Vaast Bible was, as discussed above, only the first of a series of Giant Bibles associated with monasteries reformed by Richard or his followers.

Faced with this marathon task, the artists turned to a number of different sources, both visual and written, as resources for their pictorial program. Although the scriptorium still had examples of manuscripts from its own Franco-Saxon tradition in its collection, the monks did not feel compelled to employ only this decorative vocabulary. Instead, they mined earlier and contemporary manuscripts from England and the Continent for decorative and figurative motifs in order to construct their pictorial cycle. Drawing on their Carolingian heritage, the artists adopted Franco-Saxon interlace frames and initials as the framework for their miniatures. They then added to this the restless tendrils, acanthus and animal interlace of contemporary Anglo-Saxon manuscripts. Earlier Saint-Vaast manuscripts, however, apparently provided very few models for figural illustration. As has become clear from a survey of the illuminations in the Arras Bible, the Saint-Vaast monks drew their inspiration from a variety of pictorial sources, nonetheless rarely copying any model outright. While they may have had an illustrated Carolingian Tours Bible in their possession, it is likely that such a manuscript was sparingly illustrated with a few narrative or symbolic scenes, as is, for instance, the Bamberg Bible,[53] because there seem to be few instances when the illustration of the Tours Bibles and the Saint-Vaast Bible coincide. Generally, the same books were not chosen for illustration. Only one subject found in the Touronian Bible narrative miniatures is even vaguely paralleled in the Saint-Vaast Bible, where the setting, the moment and the text illustrated are all different.[54]

The artists at Saint-Vaast may still have had access to some Carolingian pictorial models, such as those accompanying the writings

---

[53] Bamberg, Staatsbibliothek MS Misc. class. Bibl. 1.
[54] This is the scene of Moses receiving the Law and passing it on to the Israelites. Although the Saint-Vaast illustrations for Deuteronomy, introduced in chapter four, present the same type of subject matter, the transmission of the dictates of God, the setting is now not Mt. Sinai but the plains of Moab, the moment is now immediately before Moses' death, and the text illustrated is now Deuteronomy instead of Exodus or Leviticus.

of Rabanus Maurus.[55] That they did not rely exclusively on Carolingian sources, however, is made clear by the illuminations seemingly copied from or inspired by Byzantine models.[56] In addition, after mining Anglo-saxon manuscripts for decorative motifs, they may have returned to them for narrative material.[57] The Arras Bible's illuminations offer no strong parallels with Ottonian narrative imagery, probably because Ottonian artists concentrated their efforts on creating cycles of images for the New Testament rather than the Old Testament. In fact, for the majority of images in the Saint-Vaast Bible no clear visual source can be found. Some appear to be ad hoc creations, combining a variety of different motifs into compositions invented for this occasion by the artists.[58] Others find parallels in either the extensive miniature cycles of the Catalonian Bibles,[59] or in a series of later Romanesque Bibles, indicating that all may mirror early miniature cycles which have now been lost.[60]

Although the artists or programmers of the Saint-Vaast Bible appear to have relied on a wide variety of pictorial sources when creating the illustrative cycle, in choosing their written sources they were much more consistent. The monks of Saint-Vaast were obviously steeped in the ideas of Richard of Saint-Vanne and Gerard of

---

[55] For instance, as discussed in chapter five, one of the only illustrations in the Bible which closely mirrors an identifiable prototype, the illustration for the Song of Solomon with Christ and Ecclesia seated within a zodiac circle, may have been inspired by an illustrated Carolingian manuscript of Rabanus Maurus.

[56] The other illumination in the Saint-Vaast Bible with a close parallel is the illustration of Eleazar, the seven Maccabean brothers and their mother for the Passion of the Maccabees, discussed in chapter five. This miniature was clearly inspired by either a Byzantine illustration from IV Maccabees, or some work copied from a Byzantine source. Two other miniatures may also be more loosely related to Byzantine sources. The illustration prefacing Acts, discussed in chapter four, may be based on a Byzantine model which provided an image of Luke preaching to Theophilus in combination with Christ preaching to the Apostles, while the scene of David and Abishag and David's charge to Solomon in the upper register of III Kings, also discussed in chapter four, may combine two separate moments from a Byzantine cycle of images.

[57] The illustration of Moses Preaching to the Israelites prefacing Deuteronomy may have been inspired by an image of Moses Blessing the Israelites such as that in the Aelfric Hexateuch, London BL MS Cotton Claudius B.IV, fol. 139v.

[58] The illustrations for Jeremiah, Wisdom, and possibly II Chronicles fall into this category.

[59] The Roda Bible, Paris BnF MS lat. 6, and the Ripoll Bible, Rome BAV MS Vat. lat. 5729.

[60] This may be true of the illustrations for the lower register of III Kings, as well as the Books of Joshua, Ezra, and Esther.

Cambrai, either from the series of writings connected with the best known events of early-eleventh-century Arras, including the Peace of God and the heretical incident of 1025, or from hearing the same issues debated in sermons or in the chapter during the visits of these two popular leaders.[61] The writings and chronicle associated with the episcopate of Gerard of Cambrai provided interpretations of many biblical stories which found their way into the Saint-Vaast Bible's program. The artists fleshed out these interpretations with references to Carolingian commentators on the Bible. In particular, the Arras Bible's pictorial cycle appears to be a veritable encyclopedia of the biblical commentaries of Rabanus Maurus. This is hardly surprising, as the library of Saint-Vaast owned several biblical commentaries by Rabanus in the eleventh century, and more have probably been lost.[62] Finally, the artists also must have been familiar with contemporary liturgy for the consecration of rulers and bishops and the blessing of marriages. Although the surviving written versions of these liturgies in the Cologne Pontifical were composed at Saint-Vaast only in the middle of the eleventh century, the main sources used by the composer, and perhaps the composer himself, were probably at Saint-Vaast a few years earlier when the project of illustrating the Bible was begun.[63]

From these disparate written and pictorial sources, the artists and programmers constructed a complex program that simultaneously reinforced a traditional interpretation of the rights and responsibilities of kings, queens and bishops, and located the origin of their rule in the divine law of the Old and New Testaments. Using biblical

---

[61] The *Gesta episcoporum Cameracensium* and the *Acta synodi Atrebatensis* were probably first written down in the scriptorium of the Cathedral of Cambrai, instead of the Cathedral of Arras, but undoubtedly copies of both works found their way to Arras. Arras BM MS 398 (666) is a fifteenth-century copy of a now lost original of the *Gesta* from the Cathedral of Arras.

[62] Philip Grierson, "La bibliothèque de Saint-Vaast d'Arras au XIIᵉ siècle," *Revue bénédictine* LII (1940), 132.

[63] The king's ordo in Cologne, Erzbishöfliche Diözesan Dombibliothek, Dom MS 141 is a combination of the Ratold ordo and the Mainz ordo. An eleventh-century copy of the Ratold ordo originally from Trier, now Paris BnF MS lat. 13313, was adapted to the use of Cambrai perhaps as early as the eleventh century. Victor Leroquais, *Les pontificaux manuscrits des bibliothèques publiques de France*, 3 vols. (Paris, 1937), II, 175–179. The ordo for the consecration of an abbot shares the same pledge of loyalty to the church of Cambrai as the two ordines connected with Arras (see chapter two).

prototypes of these officeholders, the artists sketched a description of Christological kingship, and the ideal union of the king and queen, which was to mirror that of Christ and *Ecclesia* in heaven. The artists supported the role of the ecclesiastical hierarchy, headed by the bishop, and the biblical precedents for cooperation between Church and State based on the Augustinian political principles learned by both Richard and Gerard at Reims at the close of the tenth century. By pairing imagery of Christological kingship with a depiction of the divinely-inspired nature of the office of bishop, they underlined the cooperation they believed was necessary between the king and bishop for a just and stable society.

CATALOGUE OF THE SAINT-VAAST BIBLE

Size

All three volumes are roughly equal in overall dimensions. Vol. I is slightly smaller than the other two, with measurements of 48 × 35 cm. Vols. II and III measure 50–51 cm × 33.5–35 cm. All three volumes were trimmed when rebound, which could account for minor variations in size.

Ruling

Ruling is consistent throughout the three volumes. Pricking is usually not visible except on a few outside edges, where it appears that efforts to trim it off were unsuccessful, although it is somewhat more visible in vol. II. The ruling itself was carried out in dry-point, with three vertical lines in each outer margin and four lines in the central gutter, leaving two columns for text. There are two horizontal lines in each of the upper and lower margins. The text block encloses 45 lines ruled for text in vol. I, and 43 lines for text in vols. II and III, averaging between 0.8 and 0.9 cm apart. The writing area on each of these folios is therefore 38 × 25.5 in vol. I, and 35.5 × 24–24.5 cm in vols. II and III. A section of vol. II (fols. 110–132) has been ruled for only 35 lines, with lines 1.1 cm apart, and a writing area of 35 × 25 cm.

Binding

The Bible was rebound with undyed leather over pasteboard held together with raised cords in the seventeenth century. This modern binding is so tight that it is virtually impossible to examine the quire structure of the manuscript. In addition, the endbands at the head and tail of the backbone of the book obscure the spine.

Stubs visible throughout the manuscript provide evidence of the considerable loss of folios that took place, according to the records of the period, at the beginning of the nineteenth century. It is easy to identify stubs that are the remnants of cut out folios, instead of signs of tipped in folios, because cut marks often carry over onto flanking folios. The damage to so many of the manuscripts preserved in the Bibliothèque municipale at Arras is believed to have taken place under the librarian P. J. Caron between 1814 and 1816. According to Philip Grierson, the succeeding librarian documented that in his survey of 779 manuscripts, 734 had parts removed.[1] By his estimate, at least 40,000 folios were cut out and sold. André Boutemy surmised that between a quarter and a third of the original folios in the Bible had been removed.[2] He observed that the quire marks in the Bible are placed at the end of each quire, and run consecutively through all three volumes, for a total of 78. Assuming that each quire held eight folios, he suggested that originally the marked part of the manuscript contained 624 folios. Of this hypothetical total, only 451 folios survive. One must add to this the 32 folios at the end of volume three that had no quire marks, but show ample evidence of having been pillaged for parchment like the rest of the manuscript, with lacunae detectable after fifteen folios. The parchment thief seems to have systematically worked through the manuscript, removing folios one at a time or in small groups, not in entire books. Remarkably, most of the illustrations seem to have survived this assault.

Vol. I has 181 surviving folios, vol. II has 149 (numbered to 150 folios, of which three are later additions, and fol. 121 was lost after numeration), and vol. III has surviving 156 folios.

Volume I

fol. 1   Twelfth-century calendar

---

[1] "La bibliothèque de St. Vaast d'Arras au XIIe siècle," *Revue bénédictine* LII (1940), 120.
[2] "Une Bible enluminée de Saint-Vaast à Arras (Ms. 559)" *Scriptorium* IV (1950), 68–69.

Genesis

fol. 1v   Prol., *Quidquid ab hebraeo stilus atticus atque latinus*[3]
               Theodulph of Orleans' preface to Genesis
               (*Préfaces* 9–14,[4] B. #9,[5] Steg. #298)[6]
               An initial F in a full-page rectangular frame, with both
               foliate and interlace decoration.

fol. 2   Ownership inscription in bottom margin: *Bibliothecae
               Monasterii Sancti Vedasti Atrebatensis 1628 A*
               Prol., *Frater ambrosius tua mihi munuscula perferens*
               Jerome's epistle 53 to Paulinus
               (*Préfaces* 1–7, B. #1, Steg. #284)
               An initial F in a full-page rectangular frame, with both
               foliate and interlace decoration, and medallion portraits
               of evangelists in the corners.

fol. 3   Prol., *Desiderii mei desideratas accepi epistulas*
               Jerome's preface to Desiderius for the Pentateuch
               (*Préfaces* 7–8, B. #2, Steg. #285)
               An initial D in a full-page rectangular frame, and inter-
               lace decoration with foliate infill in the corners of the
               frame.

fols. 4–4v   Chapter list for Genesis
               (BSi Series L, forma a or b,[7] *Sommaires* group A)[8]

fols. 5v–6   A double-framed opening, with an initial I in a full-page
               rectangular frame on fol. 5v, predominantly of interlace
               with some foliate infill, and a matching framed text page
               on fol. 6.

---

[3] Orthography of all prologues has been standardized according to Donatien De Bruyne, *Préfaces de la Bible latine* (Namur, 1920).

[4] *Préfaces* = De Bruyne, *Préfaces de la Bible latine*.

[5] B. = Samuel Berger, "Les préfaces jointes aux livres de la Bible dans les manuscrits de la Vulgate," *Mémoires présentés par divers savants à l'Académie des inscriptions et belles-lettres*, 1st ser., XI/2 (Paris, 1902), 1–78.

[6] Steg. = Friedrich Stegmüller, *Repertorium Biblicum Medii Aevi*, 11 vols. (Madrid, 1950–1961), I.

[7] BSi = *Biblia Sacra iuxta Latinam Vulgatam Versionem ad codicum fidem . . .*, ed. Henri Quentin et al., 18 vols. (Rome, 1926–1995).

[8] *Sommaires* = Donatien De Bruyne, *Sommaires, divisions et rubriques de la Bible latine* (Namur, 1914).

fols. 16–16v   After 2 stubs of cut out pages between fols. 15 and 16, the text starts in the middle of the chapter list for Exodus.
(BSi Series L, forma a, *Sommaires* group A)

Exodus

fol. 17   An initial H in a full-page rectangular frame, with both interlace and foliate decoration.

Leviticus

fols. 29–29v   Chapter list for Leviticus
(BSi Series L, forma a, *Sommaires* group A)
An initial V, of interlace and foliate decoration.

Numbers

fol. 39   The preceding folios are lost. Numbers begins here in the midst of chapter 1.

Deuteronomy

fols. 52–53   Chapter list for Deuteronomy
(BSi Series L, forma a, *Sommaires* group A)
fols. 53v–54   A double-framed opening showing, on fol. 53v above a rectangular foliate and interlace frame, Moses in discussion with the Lord, with the inscription *Dominus ad Moysen loquitur*. On fol. 54, a matching frame is surmounted by Moses addressing a group of standing Israelites, labeled *Moyses ad filios israel loquitur*.
fol. 54v   A text page in a rectangular frame with quarter-circles excised in the corners.

Joshua

fol. 71	Prol., *Tandem finita pentateucho moysi velut grandi* Jerome's preface to Joshua, Judges and Ruth (*Préfaces* 22–23, B. #22, Steg. #311)
fol. 71v	Chapter list for Joshua (BSi Series L, forma a, *Sommaires* group A)
fol. 72	An initial F with a full-page rectangular frame of both foliate and interlace decoration, with the Lord transferring his mission to Joshua in the two upper roundels, explained by the inscription *Dominus Josue monet ut confortetur ad docendum filios israel.*

Judges

fol. 81v	An eleventh- or early-twelfth-century replacement folio with an unframed initial P beginning Judges.

Ruth

fol. 93v	Prol., *Ruth moabitis isaiae explet vaticinum dicentis* Jerome's preface to Ruth (B. #27, Steg. #315)
fol. 94v	An eleventh- or early-twelfth-century replacement folio. An unframed initial R in a column, an initial for repetition of the same prologue as above. An unframed initial I in a column.

I Kings

fols. 96–97	Prol., *Viginti et duas esse litteras apud hebreos* Jerome's preface to Kings (*Préfaces* 24–26, B. #30, Steg. #323)
fol. 97v	An initial F with a full-page rectangular interlace and foliate frame, supported by two crouching nude atlas figures in the lower corners whose genitals have been defaced.

II Kings

fol. 113v   An initial F in a column.

III Kings

fols. 128v–129   A double framed opening. 128v has a rectangular
                    frame of interlace with foliate tendril corners and
                    center half-rosettes. In the upper register, David is
                    introduced to Abishag and admonishes Solomon,
                    inscribed, *Hic David calefit ab adolescentula et salomon
                    ante eum quem monet ut confortetur in mandatis et in . . . viis
                    domini.* In the lower register, Solomon has a vision
                    of the Lord described with the titulus *Post mortem
                    David apparuit dominus salomoni per somnium dicens pos-
                    tula quod uis ut dem tibi. . . .* The facing folio has a
                    matching frame with initials ET of interlace and
                    foliate decoration.

fol. 129v   A framed text page.

IV Kings

fol. 144v   The end of the text for the third book of Kings,
                    upper left hand column. The rest of page, unframed
                    narrative scenes of, the Sharing of the Double Spirit,
                    the Ascension of Elijah, and the Battle of the Kings
                    of Israel, Juda and Edom against the King of Moab.

fol. 145   An initial P with a quadrilobed full-page frame of
                    interlace and foliate decoration.

I Chronicles

fols. 157–157v   Prol., *Si septuaginta interpretum pura et, ut ab eis*
                    Jerome's preface to the two books of Chronicles.
                    (*Préfaces* 30–31, B. #36, Steg. #328)

fol. 158   An initial A framed by an arch on two columns,
                    with interlace and foliate decoration.

II Chronicles

fol. 170   An initial C inside a quatrefoil frame, interlace decoration, and a depiction of the Dream of Solomon
at Gibeon

Volume II

Isaiah

fols. 1–2   Thirteenth-century additions begin the manuscript,
including a prologue and Chapter lists.
An inscription of ownership in top margin of fol. 1:
Bibliothecae monasterii sancti vedasti atrebaten. 1628 A
In the right margin, a list of contents added at that
time:
*In hoc volumino Isaias Jeremias Ezechiel Daniel Osee Joel
amos abdias Jonas Micheas nahum abadiah sophanias aggeus
sacharias malachias job parabolae solomonis ecclesiastes cantica canticorum sapientiae*

fol. 3   After several stubs of missing folios, the book of Isaiah
picks up in mid-text.

Jeremiah

fols. 13–13v   Prol., *Hieremias propheta, cui hic prologus scribitur*
Jerome's preface to Jeremiah
(*Préfaces* 124, B. #155, Steg. #487)

fols. 13v–14v   Chapter lists for Jeremiah
(BSi Series A, forma a, *Sommaires* group A)

fol. 15   An initial U in a full-page frame with straight sides
separated from semi-circular tops and bottoms by
griffon bases and capitals and interlace decoration is
surrounded by a depiction of Jeremiah robed as a
bishop, and his vision of the Lord.

Ezekiel

fols. 40v–41   Prol., *Hiezechiel propheta cum ioachim rege iudae*
                Jerome's preface to Ezekiel
                (*Préfaces* 124–125, B. #162, Steg. #492)
fols. 41–42   Chapter lists for Ezekiel
                (*Sommaires* group A)
fol. 42v   An initial E with a full-page rectangular frame and
                interlace decoration. In the top of this frame a depic-
                tion of Ezekiel inspired by the Lord.

Daniel

fols. 75–76   Prol., *Danihelem prophetam iuxta septuaginta interpretes*
                Jerome's preface to Daniel
                (*Préfaces* 125, B. #166, Steg. #494)
fol. 76   Chapter lists for Daniel
                (*Sommaires* group A)
fol. 77   Initial A in full-page rectangular frame, interlace and
                tendril decoration.

Hosea

fol. 90v   Prol., *Non idem ordo est duodecim prophetarum apud*
                Jerome's preface to the Minor Prophets
                (*Préfaces* 135, B. #170, Steg. #500)
fol. 91   Folio missing between fols. 90 and 91 may have held
                other prefatory matter. Next prologue begins mid-text.
                Prol., *Temporibus oziae et ioathae, achaz et ezechiae*
                Pseudo-Jerome
                (*Préfaces* 136–137, B. #174, Steg. #507)
fol. 91v   Initial V

Joel

fols. 95v–96   Prol., *Sanctus iohel apud hebreos post osee ponitur*
                Pseudo-Jerome
                (*Préfaces* 137, B. #180, Steg. #511)
fol. 96   Initial V

Amos

fols. 98–98v   Prol., *Ozias rex cum dei religionem sollicite*
                   Pseudo-Jerome
                   (*Préfaces* 137–8, B. #184, Steg. #515)
fol. 98v   Initial V

Obadiah

fols. 100v–101   Prol., *Iacob patriarcha fratrem habuit esau*
                   Pseudo-Jerome
                   (*Préfaces* 138, Steg. #519)
fol. 101   Initial V

Jonah

fols. 101v–102   Prol., *Ionam sanctum hebrei adfirmant filium mulieris*
                   Pseudo-Jerome
                   (*Préfaces* 138–9, Steg. #524)
fol. 102   Initial E

Micah

fol. 103v   Prol., *Temporibus ioatham achaz et ezechiae regum iuda*
                   Pseudo-Jerome
                   (*Préfaces* 139, Steg. #526)
fol. 104   Initial V

Nahum

fols. 106–106v   Prol., *Naum prophetam ante adventum regis assyriorum*
                   Pseudo-Jerome
                   (*Préfaces* 139, Steg. #528)
fol. 106v   Initials DS

                   The Vengeful Lord
                   The initial contains one standing figure, a cross-
                   nimbed, bearded Christ-Logos holding an upturned
                   sword, against a dark background.

Habakkuk

fols. 107–108   Prol., *Quattuor prophetae in duodecim prophetarum*
                 Pseudo-Jerome
                 (*Préfaces* 140–141, Steg. #531)
fol. 108   Initial O on purple ground.

                 Author Portrait
                 The initial contains an author portrait of a bearded
                 man holding a furled scroll standing against a back-
                 ground of swirling stars and clouds.

Zephaniah

fols. 109v–110   Prol., *Tradunt hebrei cuiuscunque porphe pater aut avus*
                 Pseudo-Jerome
                 (*Préfaces* 141–142, Steg. #534)
fol. 110v   Initial V

Zechariah

fol. 112   Many folios missing between fols. 111–112, includ-
                 ing the book of Haggai. Only the explicit for Haggai
                 survives on fol. 112.
                 Prol., *Zacharias, memor domini sui, multiplex*
                 Jerome's epistle 53 to Paulinus
                 (*Préfaces* 5, Steg. #540)
                 Initial I

Malachi

fols. 117v–118   Prol., *Deus per moysen populo israhel praeceperat*
                 Pseudo-Jerome
                 (*Préfaces* 143–144, Steg. #543)
fol. 118   Initial O

Job

fols. 119v–120	Chapter lists for Job (BSi Series A, *Sommaires* group A)
fol. 120v	Prol., *Cogor per singulos scripturae divinae libros* Jerome's preface to Job (*Préfaces* 38, B. #55, Steg. #344)
fol. 121	Missing, along with any introductory decoration for book.

Proverbs

fol. 132v	Prol., *Iungat epistula quos iungit sacerdotium, immo* Jerome's preface to the Wisdom books *Chromatio et Heliodoro episcopus* (*Préfaces* 118, B. #129, Steg. #457) Prol., *Tres libros salomonis id est proverbia,* Jerome's preface to the Wisdom books from the Septuagint (*Préfaces* 118–119, B. #131, Steg. #455)
fol. 133	Folio missing between fols. 132 and 133, so have lost end of *Tres libros* prologue and beginning of Chapter list. End of Chapter list. (BSi Series A, forma b, *Sommaires* group A) Initial P
fol. 135	Initial F, Proverbs 10:1
fol. 137	Initial G, Proverbs 25:1

Ecclesiastes

fol. 138v	Chapter list for Ecclesiastes (BSi Series A, forma b, *Sommaires* group A)
fol. 139	Initial V in full-page frame. Combination of interlace, foliate and tendril decoration. Surviving corner medallions hold birds and beasts.

Song of Solomon

fol. 141v   3/4-page illustration inside rectangular full-page frame

> *Sponsus and Sponsa*
> The O initial of the beginning of the text seems to have
> inspired the shape of the illustration above. A continu-
> ous looping white band encloses the twelve symbols of
> the zodiac in circles, with the bull at the top, and the
> scorpion at the bottom. In between the circles white ten-
> drils sprout outwards to wrap around an outside, darker
> circle.
> Inside the zodiac circle is a cityscape constructed of roofs,
> towers and doorways. The Christ-Logos with a cross nim-
> bus is seated in front of this background. His right hand
> is raised and his left holds an open book, while his feet
> are placed on a small footstool within a white band form-
> ing a circle. To his left stands a veiled woman who gazes
> at the Christ-Logos with her left hand raised.

Wisdom

fol. 143v   Chapter list for Wisdom
             (BSi Series A, forma a, *Sommaires* group A)
fol. 144   Initial D in rectangular full-page frame. Predominantly
             interlace decoration, with foliate infill in bow of letter.

> *Author Portrait*
> The corner medallions of the frame hold tunic-wearing
> horn blowers, the two on left side accompanied by busts
> of dogs, the two on right each grasping the hilt of the
> sword at his waist. Inside the initial a bearded King
> Solomon sits on a bench-throne. He wears a lily crown
> with dangling *infulae* and carries a delicate foliate scepter
> in his left hand, while his right is raised. Behind him is
> a two-part mandorla, with an oval behind his body and
> a circle behind his head.

Volume III

Ecclesiasticus

fol. 1   Folio has decayed completely around all edges, meaning
          that it has probably lost at least a quarter of its original
          area. It has been removed from volume at some point and
          glued to a piece of paper of the same type pasted to the
          inside of the binding. The paper has been cut so that the
          illumination of recto side shows through, and edges appear
          on verso side. Verso holds the chapter lists, and recto has
          illumination, including beginning of text. To follow the pro-
          gram of the rest of the book, recto with illumination was
          probably originally the verso.
          Half page illumination above.
          Initial O below, interlace and foliate with busts of four winds
          in outside corners.

          Allegory of the Wisdom of the Lord Punishing Heretics
          This illumination is the most complex in the manuscript.
          At the centre, a beardless, diademed Christ-Logos is enthroned
          before a seven-columned temple front with a head above
          each column on the entablature. The Christ-Logos holds a
          cross-orb and a long spear that reaches down to touch two
          men who crouch beneath his feet. These elements of the
          scene are contained within a jeweled circle which sets them
          off from the rest of the image. Above the circle are the
          rooftops of a cityscape. Around the circle are grouped two
          sets of figures. In the two arches found on either side of
          the circle, four personifications of the cardinal virtues sit,
          each holding an attribute and labeled with white ink: *Justitia,*
          Fortitudo, Prudentia and *Temperantia.* Below the circle are five
          more arches. In the four to the right, four figures, proba-
          bly the evangelists, busily write in books. At the far left, the
          one remaining arch is closed with a dangling white curtain.
          The entire composition is unframed.
fol. 1v   Chapter list for Ecclesiasticus
          (BSi Series A, forma a, *Sommaires* group A)

fol. 2   Inscription of ownership of 1628 *Bibliothecae monasterii sancti vedastii atrebatensis 1628 A,* added here, implying that the first folio was loose already in seventeenth century. Also list of contents added at that time:
in hoc volumino primus Ecclesiasticus Tobias Judith Esdras Esther Machabeorum libri II Passio Machabeorum Epistoli Pauli ad Romanos corinthios ii galatios ephesios philippiensos coloss. Laoudicensis thessalonicensos Timothy Johann Philemonen hebreus Jacobi Petri . . . dna Johannis Judae Actus Apostolorum Apocalypsin

Tobit

fols. 16v–17   Prol., *Mirari non desino exactionis vestrae instantiam*
                  Jerome's preface to Tobit
                  (*Préfaces* 35, B. #45, Steg. #332)
fol. 17   Chapter list for Tobit
                  (*Sommaires* group Am[Fr])
fol. 17v   Initial T in rectangular frame with interlace and tendril decoration.

                  Author Portrait
                  Entangled within the tendril decoration at the bottom of the initial are birds, animals, and a bearded, nude man. A medallion embedded in the bottom horizontal bar of the frame holds a bust portrait of the author, shown as a short-haired, beardless man.

Judith

fol. 22   Prol., *Apud hebraeos liber iudith inter apocrypha*
                  Jerome's preface to Judith
                  (*Préfaces* 35, B. #48, Steg. #335)
fols. 22–22v   Chapter list for Judith
                  (*Sommaires* series Am[Fr])
fol. 23   Initial A in full-page rectangular frame, interlace and tendril decoration.
                  Five of the six original frame medallions survive. The two in the bottom corners hold tendril decoration. The

two at the mid-point of the vertical bars hold bust portraits of beardless men, each with a scale balanced on his head. The one surviving medallion at the top of the folio shows a crouching man holding a shield and spear.

Ezra

fols. 28–28v   Prol., *Utrum difficilius sit, facere quod poscitis*
               Jerome's preface to Ezra
               (*Préfaces* 33, B. #42, Steg. #330)

fol. 29   Initial I in full page frame with straight sides and semi-circular top and bottom. Interlace and foliate decoration.

               Artaxerxes Sends Ezra to Preach the Law (7:14, 25)
               Two medallions embedded into either side of the frame within the vertical bars combine to create a two-part scene. In the left-side medallion, a bearded nimbed man in a long robe stands in profile on a small hillock and gazes heavenward. He holds an open book in outstretched hands draped with a maniple. Opposite him stands a bearded man in a tunic.
               In the right-side medallion a king wearing a lily crown and holding a scepter sits on an animal throne with his feet on a *suppedaneum* in a draped enclosure. He is regarding the scene to the left and gesturing towards it with his open right hand.

Esther

fols. 43–43v   Prol., *Librum esther variis translatoribus constat esse*
               Jerome's preface to Esther
               (*Préfaces* 36, B. #51, Steg. #341)

fol. 43v   Chapter lists for Esther
               (*Sommaires* group Am[Fr])

fol. 44   Initial I in full-page rectangular frame, with scenes in top third.

Ahasuerus Receives the Petition of Esther
To the right, a bearded king wearing a lily crown sits
enthroned in a draped enclosure, his feet on a footstool. To his right are three tiny floating courtiers. In
his left hand, the king holds a short rod. In his right,
he holds a longs staff which he stretches out towards
the left. Opposite him, a queen, wearing her own out-
sized lily crown, stands in front of a male and a female
attendant. She raises draped hands to grasp the staff
which is held up to her mouth. Between them, an
inscription can barely be distinguished against the dark
background of the scene: *Quid petis Hester oro o rex si
tibi placet dona mihi animam meam pro qua rogo et populum
meum pro quo obsecro.*

I Maccabees

fol. 52   Chapter list for I Maccabees
               (*Sommaires* group A)
fol. 52v   Initials ET in full-page rectangular frame, interlace
               and tendril decoration.

II Maccabees

fols. 69v–70   Chapter list for II Maccabees
               (*Sommaires* group A)
fol. 70v   Initial F in full page frame with small lobes on top and
               bottom horizontal bars. Tendril and foliate decoration.
               Inside the frame is a two-layer illustration. On the
               top, a bearded man with a diademed cap sits on a
               folding camp stool to the left, and gestures towards
               two men seated on a bench to the right, who gesture
               in return. In the level below, eight men and two women
               sit on an architectural bench scattered with cushions,
               and gaze and gesture towards the scene above.

Passion of the Maccabees

fol. 81   Beginning of Passion of the Maccabees marked by red
               initial P.
fol. 81v   Initial I in complex full-page frame of rectangle with
               corner lobes intertwined with diamond-shaped frame
               with upper and lower lobes. All in interlace and ten-
               dril decoration.

               The Trial of Eleazar, the Seven Maccabean Brothers and their
               Mother before Antiochus
               To the left, a king in a solid, pill-box style crown with
               three foliate projections, holding a foliate scepter, sits
               enthroned on a cushioned lion throne, and gestures
               toward the crowd to the right. There, a bearded man
               with a diademed cap gestures in return. Beside him,
               a veiled woman in a flamboyantly sleeved dalmatic
               stands before a grape-cluster of one man and seven
               other beardless male heads.

Paul's Epistle to the Romans

fols. 85v–86   Prol., *Epistolae pauli ad romanos causa haec est.*
               Pelagius
               (*Préfaces* 217–218, B. #254, Steg. #651)
fols. 86–87   Prol., *Primum quaeritur quare post evangelia*
               Pelagian preface to the Epistles
               (*Préfaces* 213–215, B. #253, Steg. #670)
fols. 87–87v   Prol., *Romani sunt qui ex iudeis gentibus crediderunt*
               Pelagian preface to Romans
               (*Préfaces* 215–217, B. #255, Steg. #674)
fols. 87v–88   Prol., *Iam dudum saulus procerum praecepta secutus*
               Poem by Pope Damasus
               (*Préfaces* 234, B. #273, Steg. #654)
fol. 88   Chapter list for Paul's Epistle to the Romans
               (*Sommaires* group M)
               Prol., *Paulus apostolus quattuordecim epistolis*
               Isidore
               (*Préfaces* 219–220, Steg. #661)

Prol., *In primis romanae plebis fidem collaudat*
Isidore
(B. #260, Steg. #655)
Prol., *Romani sunt in partibus italiae*
(*Préfaces* 235, B. #280A, Steg. #677)
Marcion

fol. 88v   Initial P in full-page rectangular frame, interlace and
                  tendril decoration.

Paul's First Epistle to the Corinthians

fol. 95v   Prol., *Corinthii sunt achaei. Et hi similiter*
                  Marcion
                  (*Préfaces* 235, B. #280B, Steg. #684)
fols. 95v–96   Chapter list for Paul's epistle to the Corinthians
                  (*Sommaires* group A)
fol. 96v   Initial P in full-page rectangular frame

Paul's Second Epistle to the Corinthians

fol. 103v   Prol., *Post actam paenitentiam consolatoriam scribit*
                  Marcion
                  (*Préfaces* 235–6, B. #280C, Steg. #700)
                  Prol., *(Secundam epistolam apostolus scribit corinthiis) Cum
                  haec principalis est causa, quoniam in prima pro*
                  Pelagius
                  (*Préfaces* 236, B. #281, Steg. #704)
                  Chapter list for II Corinthians
                  (*Sommaires* group A)
fol. 104   Initial P, interlace and tendril decoration

Paul's Epistle to the Galatians

fol. 108v   Prol., *Galatae sunt graeci. Hi verbum veritatis*
                  Marcion
                  (*Préfaces* 236, B. #280D, Steg. #707)
                  Chapter lists for Paul's Epistle to the Galatians

(*Sommaires* group A)
Initial P
At least one folio missing between 108–109.
End of Galatians, beginning of Ephesians missing.

Paul's Epistle to the Philippians

fol. 111   Prol., *Philippenses sunt machedones. Hi accepto*
             Marcion
             (*Préfaces* 236, Steg. #728)
             Prol., *In Actibus apostolorum legimus, quod ipso*
             Pelagius
             (*Préfaces* 237, Steg. #726)
             Chapter lists for Paul's Epistle to the Philippians
             (*Sommaires* group A)
fol. 111v   Initial P, bottomless house-shaped frame over three-quarters
             of page encloses initial.

Paul's Epistle to the Colossians

fol. 113v   Prol., *Colosenses et hi sicut laudicenses sunt asiam.*
             Marcion
             (*Préfaces* 236, Steg. #736)
             Prol., *Colosenses quorum auditam fidem in principiis*
             Pelagius
             (*Préfaces* 237, Steg. #737)
             Chapter lists for Paul's Epistle to the Colossians
             (*Sommaires* group A)
fol. 114   Initial P, tri-lobed bottomless frame on vertical column-
             like bars encloses initial and top two-thirds of page.
             Predominantly interlace and tendril decoration.
             The top lobe of the frame holds bust-length images of a
             group of five men and one woman, all of whom look to
             the space to the left of the initial below. This area has
             been excised, along with the descender of the initial P.
             It may once have held an image of Paul, making this a
             depiction of Paul preaching or writing to the Colossians.

Paul's Epistle to the Laudicians

fol. 116   Initial P

Paul's First Epistle to the Thessalonians

fol. 116v   Initial T, tendril and interlace decoration
                        Prol., *Thessalonicenses sunt machedones, qui accepto*
                        Marcion
                        (*Préfaces* 237, Steg. #747)
                        Prol., *Non solum ipsi in omnibus perfectu erant*
                        Pelagius
                        (*Préfaces* 237, Steg. #746)
                        Chapter list for I Thessalonians
                        (*Sommaires* group A)
                        Chapter list for II Thessalonians
                        (*Sommaires* group A)
fol. 117   Initial P in bottomless full page frame with column-
                        like vertical bars with lion capitals and semicircular
                        top. Interlace and tendril decoration.

Paul's Second Epistle to the Thessalonians

fol. 119   Prol., *Ad Thessalonicenses secundam scribit*
                        Marcion
                        (*Préfaces* 237, Steg. #752)
                        Chapter list for II Thessalonians
                        (*Sommaires* group A)
                        Initial P

Paul's First Epistle to Timothy

fol. 120   Prol., *Timotheum instruit et docet de ordinatione*
                        Marcion
                        (*Préfaces* 237, Steg. #765)
fols. 120–120v   Prol., *Hic episcopus fuit, discipulus pauli apostoli*
                        Pelagius
                        (*Préfaces* 238, Steg. #760)

fol. 120v   Chapter list for Paul's First Epistle to Timothy
             (*Sommaires* group A)
             Initial P, interlace and tendril.

Paul's Second Epistle to Timothy

fol. 123   Prol., *Item timotheo scribit de exhortatione martyrii*
             Marcion
             (*Préfaces* 238, Steg. #772)
             Prol., *Cum esset romae in vinculis constitutus scribit*
             Pelagius
             (*Préfaces* 238, Steg. #770)
             Chapter lists for Paul's Second Epistle to Timothy
             (*Sommaires* group A)
fol. 123v   Initial P in three-quarter page bottomless frame with ver-
             ticals, and horse-shoe lobe on top horizontal. Interlace,
             foliate and tendril decoration.

Paul's Epistle to Titus

fol. 125   Prol., *Titum commonefacit et instruit de constitutione*
             Marcion
             (*Préfaces* 238, Steg. #780)
fol. 125v   Prol., *Ad titam, discipulum suum, episcopum, quem*
             Pelagius
             (*Préfaces* 238, Steg. #6366)
             Chapter list for Paul's Epistle to Titus
             (*Sommaires* group A)
             Initial P

Paul's Epistle to Philemon

fol. 126   Folios missing between fols. 125 and 126. Therefore, end
             of II Timothy, introductory material for Philemon lost.
             Initial P, interlace and tendril decoration

Paul Composing the Epistle
Inside the bow of the initial P, a bearded balding
man sits on a cushioned bench throne, holds an
unfurled scroll with his left and writes on it with
his right.

Paul's Epistle to the Hebrews

fol. 126v	Prol., *In primis dicendum est, cur apostolus paulus* Pelagius (*Préfaces* 253–4, B. #283, Steg. #793) Prol., *Argumentum epistolae praefertur ad hebreos quid non eiusdem apostoli creditur propter stili* (B. #287, Steg. #787)
fols. 126v–127	Chapter lists for Paul's Epistle to the Hebrews (*Sommaires* group H)
fol. 127	Initial M

Epistle of St. James the Apostle (Jacob)

fol. 131	Folios lost between fols. 130 and 131, means text jumps from Hebrews to James 1:5

First Epistle of Peter

fol. 133	Prol., *(Symon petrus, iohannis filius provinciae galilieae a vico bethsaida, frater andreae apostoli) discipulos salvatoris invicti toto orbe diffusos* (*Préfaces* 256, B. #301, Steg. #816) Chapter list for Peter's first epistle. (*Sommaires* group A)
fol. 133v	Initial P in full-page bottomless frame with column-like verticals and a semi-circular top. Interlace and tendril decoration.

Peter Preaching to the Elect
The elements of a scene are squeezed around the
initial. On top of the bow of the P, Peter himself

appears, beardless and bust length, with his arms stretched out like an orant. Below the bow of the P and to the right of the descender, a crowd of three women and six men stand in the midst of a debate, some observing and some making hand gestures.

The Second Epistle of Peter

fol. 135   Prol., *Symon petrus per fidem huic mundo sapientes*
            (*Préfaces* 256, B. #303, Steg. #818)
            Chapter list for Second Epistle of Peter
            (*Sommaires* group A)
fol. 135v   Initial S of white tendril inside full-page rectangular frame.

            Author Portrait
            In the bottom left-hand column of the folio, a nimbed, tonsured Peter stands holding a pair of keys in his right hand and a book in his draped left hand.

First Epistle of John

fol. 136v   Chapter list for First Epistle of John
            (*Sommaires* group A)
            Initial Q, right-hand column, interlace, foliate and tendril. Inside the bow of the Q is a scene resembling a dedication. A centre column divides the scene. To the left, Christ is seated on a bench-throne, and gestures with his left hand towards the man approaching him from the right. This nimbed man bows and proffers a book across the column towards Christ.

Second Epistle of John

fol. 138   Chapter list for Second Epistle of John
            (*Sommaires* group A)
            Initial S

Third Epistle of John

fol. 138v   Chapter list for Third Epistle of John
            (*Sommaires* group A)
            Initial S

Epistle of Jude

fol. 139   Folios missing between 138 and 139 include Third Epistle
            of John.
            Chapter list for Epistle of Jude
            (*Sommaires* group A)
            Initial I

Acts of the Apostles

fol. 141   Folios cut out between fols. 140 and 141 included end
            of Epistle of Jude and all prefatory material for Acts.
            Initial P in full-page rectangular frame.

            Luke Preaching to Theophilus and Christ Preaching to the Apostles
            Once again, this is a two-layered image worked into the
            space around and within the initial. In the bow of the
            P, a nimbed beardless Luke to the left gestures towards
            a tunic-wearing, bearded, bust-length man to the right.
            Below them is the substance of the scene he is describ-
            ing. A cross-nimbed, bearded Christ sits on a bench with
            his feet on a *suppedaneum*. He gestures with both hands.
            On benches to either side are the twelve apostles, who
            strain forward with eager gestures to hear what he preaches.

Revelations

fol. 153v   Prol., *Johannes apostolus et evangelista a domino*
            Pseudo-Isidore
            (*Préfaces* 261, B. #310, Steg. #835)
            Chapter list for Revelations
            (*Sommaires* group A)

BIBLIOGRAPHY

Primary Sources

Achéry, Luc D'. *Veterum aliquot scriptorum quo in Galliae bibliothecis, maxime benedictinorum latuerant, Spicilegium* XIII (Paris, 1677).
———, and De La Barre, Louis. *"Synodus attrebatensis a Gerardo . . .", Spicilegium, sive collectio veterum aliquot scriptorum qui in Galliae bibliothecis delituerant* I (Paris, 1723), 606–624.
Adalbéron de Laon. *Poème au roi Robert*, ed. Claude Carozzi, Les classiques de l'histoire de France au moyen âge XXXII (Paris, 1979).
Aelfric, Abbot of Eynsham. *Aelfric's Lives of Saints*. Early English Text Society. Original Series XCIV (New York, 1966).
———. *Epistula ad monachos Egneshamnenes directa*, ed. Hadrian Nocent, CCM VII/3 (Siegburg, 1984), 155–185.
Aelred of Rievaulx, *Genealogia regum Anglorum*, PL 195:711–737.
Aimon and André de Fleury. *Miracula sancti Benedicti*, ed. E. de Certain, Société de l'histoire de France (Paris, 1858) repr. 1968.
Alcuin of York. *Epistola* 195, MGH Epist. IV, Epistolae Karolini aevi II, ed. Ernst Dümmler (Berlin, 1895), 322–323.
———. *Carmina*, MGH Poetarum Latinorum medii aevi I, Poetae Latini aevi Karolini I, ed. Ernst Dümmler (Berlin, 1881), 160–351.
———. *De Grammatica*, PL 101:849–902.
———. *Dialogus de rhetorica et virtutibus*, PL 101:919–950.
Amalarius of Metz. *De ecclesiasticus officiis libri IV*, PL 105:985–1242.
———. *Amalarii episcopi opera liturgica omnia*, ed. Jean-Michel Hanssens (Vatican City, 1970).
———. *Liber de ordine antiphonarii, Prologus*, PL 105:1245–1246.
Andrieu, Michel. *Les ordines romani du haut moyen âge*, Spicilegium sacrum Lovaniense; Études et documents, fasc. 11, 23–24, 28–29, 5 vols. (Louvain, 1931–1961).
———. *Le pontifical romain au moyen-âge*, Studi e Testi LXXXVI–LXXXVIII and IC (Vatican City, 1964–1965).
Angelomus of Luxeuil. *Enarrationes in libros Regum*, PL 115:243–552.
———. *Enarrationes in Cantica Canticorum*, PL 115:551–628.
Annales Marchianensis, ed. Louis Bethmann, MGH SS XVI, ed. Georg Heinrich Pertz (Hanover, 1859), 609–617.
Annales Vedastini, MGH SS II, ed. Georg Heinrich Pertz (Hanover, 1828), 196–209.
The Annals of Fulda, trans. Timothy Reuter (Manchester, 1992).
The Annals of St-Bertin, trans. Janet L. Nelson (Manchester, 1991).
The Apocrypha and Pseudepigrapha of the Old Testament in English, ed. Robert H. Charles, 2 vols. (Oxford, 1913).
Arno of Salzburg, *Concilium Rispacense* (798), MGH Leges sectio III, Concilia II, Concilia aevi Karolini I, ed. Albert Werminghoff (Hanover, 1906), 196–201.
Augustine of Hippo. *The City of God against the Pagans*, trans R. W. Dyson, (Cambridge, 1998).
———. *Contra Faustum Manichaeum*, ed. Josephus Zycha, CSEL XXV (Vienna, 1891–1892).
———. *Epistulae*, ed. A. Goldbacher, CSEL XXXIV/1–2, XLIV, LVII–LVIII (Vienna, 1895–1923).

———. *The Rule of Saint Augustine. Masculine and Feminine Versions*, Cistercian Studies CXXXVIII, trans. Raymond Canning, commentary Tarsicius J. Bavel (Kalamazoo, 1996).

———. *Sermones*, PL 38.

Bede. *In Cantica Canticorum allegorica expositio*, PL 91:1065–1236.

Benedict of Aniane. *Benedicti Anianensis concordia regularum*, ed. Pierre Bonnerue (Turnhout, 1999).

Benedict of Nursia. *Regula monasteriorum*, CSEL LXXV, ed. Rudolphus Hanslik (Vienna, 1960).

———. *The Rule of St. Benedict*, trans. Anthony C. Meisel and M. L. del Mastro (Garden City, N.Y., 1975).

Bernard of Clairvaux. *Sermones super Cantica Canticorum*, PL 183:785–1198 and *Sermones super Cantica Canticorum*, Sources chrétiennes 414, ed. Jean Leclercq, H. Rochais and Ch. H. Talbot, introduction, trans. and notes Paul Verdeyen and Raffaele Fassetta (Paris, 1996).

Bernard of Cluny. *Ordo Cluniacensis* in Marquard Herrgott, *Vetus disciplina monastica: seu collectis auctorum ordinis s. Benedicti maximam partem ineditorum . . .* (Paris, 1726), 133–364.

Biblia sacra iuxta Latinam vulgatam versionem ad codicum fidem . . ., ed. Henri Quentin et al., 18 vols. (Rome, 1926–1995).

Biblia sacra iuxta vulgatam Clementinam nova editio, 7th edition (Madrid, 1985).

The Canons of Hippolytus, ed. Paul F. Bradshaw, trans. Carol Bebawi (Bramcote, 1987).

Cesarius of Arles. *Oeuvres monastiques* II: Oeuvres pour les moines, Sources chrétiennes CCCXCVIII, eds. Joël Courreau and Adalbert de Vogüé (Paris, 1994).

Catalogus abbatum sancti Amandi Elnonensis, MGH SS XIII, ed. Georg Waitz (Hanover, 1881), 386–388.

Charlemagne. *Admonitio generalis*, MGH Leges II, Capitularia regum Francorum I, ed. Alfredus Boretius (Hanover, 1883), 52–62.

———. *Epistola generalis*, MGH Leges II, Capitularia regum Francorum I, ed. Alfredus Boretius (Hanover, 1883), 80–81.

Chrodegang of Metz. *Sancti Chrodegangi Metensis episcopi regula canonicorum secundum Dacarii recensionem* (Aachen Version), PL 89:1057–1097.

Chronicon Cameracense et Atrebatense, sive historia utriusque ecclesiae III libris . . . ed. Georges Colveneere (Douai, 1615).

Chronicon Vedastinum, MGH SS XIII, ed. Georg Waitz (Hanover, 1881), 674–709.

Chronicon sancti Laurentii Leodinensis, ed. Wilhelm Wattenbach, MGH SS VIII, ed. Georg Heinrich Pertz (Hanover, 1848), 262–279.

Chronique ou livre de fondation du monastère de Mouzon, ed. Michel Bur (Paris, 1989).

Claudius of Turin. *Commentarii in libros Regum*, PL 50:1047–1208.

Clement of Alexandria. *Excerpta ex Theodoto*, ed. Robert P. Casey (London, 1934).

Columban. *Sancti Columbani opera*, Scriptores Latini Hiberniae II, ed. G. S. M. Walker (Dublin, 1957).

Concilium Aquisgranense (816), MGH Leges sectio III, Concilia II, Concilia aevi Karolini I, ed. Albert Werminghoff (Hanover, 1906), 307–421.

Concilium Francofurtense (794), MGH Leges sectio III, Concilia II, Concilia aevi Karolini I, ed. Albert Werminghoff (Hanover, 1906), 110–171.

Consuetudines Cluniacensium antiquiores cum redactionibus derivatis, ed. Kassius Hallinger, CCM VII/2 (Siegburg, 1983).

Consuetudines monasticae, ed. Bruno Albers, 5 vols. (Monte Cassino, 1900–1912).

Consuetudinum saeculi X/XI/XII monumenta non-Cluniacensia, ed. Kassius Hallinger, CCM VII/3, (Siegburg, 1984).

Council of Meaux-Paris, *Die Konzilien der karolingischen Teilreiche, 843–859*, ed. Wilfried

Hartmann, MGH Concilia III, Concilia aevi Karolini DCCCXLIII–DCCCLIX (Hanover, 1984), 81–131.

De Bréquigny, Louis, La Porte du Theil, François and Pardessus, Jean-Marie. *Diplomata, chartae, epistolae, leges, aliaque instrumenta res Gallo-Francicas spectantia* (Paris, 1849).

DeBruyne, Donatien. *Préfaces de la Bible latine* (Namur, 1920).

——. *Sommaires, divisions et rubriques de la Bible latine* (Namur, 1914).

Dehaisnes, Chrétien. *Les annales de Saint-Bertin et de Saint-Vaast* (Paris, 1871).

Deshusses, Jean. *Le sacramentaire Gregorien* (Fribourg, 1971).

Diplomata Henrici I Francorum Regis, *Recueil des historiens des Gaules et de la France* XI, Congrégation de Saint-Maur (Paris, 1767).

Elze, Reinhard. *Ordines coronationis imperialis: Die Ordines für die Weihe und Krönung des Kaisers und der Kaiserin*, MGH Fontes iuris Germanici antiqui in usum scholarum separatim editi IX (Hanover, 1960).

Everhelmo of Hautmont. *Vita Popponis abbatis Stabulensis*, ed. Wilhelm Wattenbach, MGH SS XI (Hanover, 1854), 293–316.

Faverot et Petit. *Chronique d'Arras et de Cambrai, par Balderic, chantre de Thérouanne au XIᵉ siècle* (Valenciennes, 1836).

Flodoard of Reims. *Historia ecclesiae Remensis*, PL 135:27–328.

Gelasius I. *Epistolae et decreta*, PL 59:13–140.

Gerard of Cambrai. *Acta synodi Atrebatensis*, PL 142:1269–1312.

Gerbert of Reims. *Die Briefsammlung Gerberts von Reims*, ed. Fritz Weigle, MGH Die Briefe der deutschen Kaiserzeit II (Weimar, 1966).

Gesta pontificum Cameracensium, PL 149:21–176, also *Gesta episcoporum Cameracensium*, ed. C. L. C. Bethmann, MGH SS VII, ed. Georg Heinrich Pertz (Hanover, 1846), 393–489.

Gesta pontificum Cameracensium: Continuatio—Gesta Lietberti episcopi, PL 149:177–192, also *Gesta episcoporum Cameracensium: Comtinuatio*, ed. C. L. C. Bethmann, MGH SS VII, ed. Georg Heinrich Pertz (Hanover, 1846), 489–500.

Gestis episcoporum Virdunensium continuatis, MGH SS IV, ed. Georg Heinrich Pertz (Hanover, 1841), 39–51.

Giacchero, Marta. *Edictum Diocletiani et collegarum de pretiis rerum venalium* (Genoa, 1974).

Glaber, Radolfus. *Historiarum libri quinque*, ed. Neithard Bulst, trans. John France and Paul Reynolds (Oxford, 1989).

Gonzo of Florennes. *Ex miraculis s. Gengulfi*, ed. Oswald Holder-Egger, MGH SS XV (Hanover, 1888), 791–796.

Gregory of Nazienzen. *Select Orations*, ed. and trans. Martha P. Vinson, Fathers of the Church CVII (Washington, D.C., 2003).

Gregory of Tours. *Liber miraculorum*, PL 71:705–828.

——. *Vitae patrum*, ed. Bruno Krusch, MGH Scriptores rerum Merovingicarum I (Hanover, 1885), 663–744, or PL 71:1009–1096.

Guimanus of Arras. *Libro de possessionibus sancti Vedasti*, MGH SS XIII, ed. Georg Waitz (Hanover, 1881), 710–715.

Helgaud de Fleury. *Vie de Robert le pieux. Epitoma vitae regis Rotberti pii*, ed. Robert H. Bautier and Gillette Labory, Sources d'Histoire Médiévale I (Paris, 1965).

Herimannus. *Liber de restauratione s. Martini Tornacensis*, MGH SS XIV, ed. Georg Waitz (Hanover, 1883), 274–327.

Hincmar of Reims. *Coronati Judith Caroli filiae, cum rege Anglorum desponsata est*, PL 125:811–814.

——. *De divortio Lotharii et Tetbergae*, PL 125:619–772.

——. *De divortio Lotharii regis et Theutbergae reginae*, ed. Letha Böhringer, MGH Concilia, IV, suppl. 1 (Hanover, 1992).

——. *Ad regem*, PL 125:1017–1036.

———. *De ordine palatii*, editio Altera, ed. Thomas Gross and Rudolf Schieffer, MGH Fontes iuris Germanici antiqui III (Hanover, 1980).

Hittorp, Melchior, ed. *De divinis catholicae ecclesiae officiis et mysteriis* (Paris, 1624).

The Holy Bible, Douay-Rheims Version (Baltimore, 1899).

The Holy Bible, Revised Standard Version (New York, 1962).

Hugh of Flavigny, *Chronicon*, PL 154:21–400.

Initia consuetudines Benedictinae: Consuetudines saeculi octavi et noni, ed. Kassius Hallinger, CCM I (Siegburg, 1963).

Innocent I. *Epistolae et decretae*, PL 20:463–612.

John VII. *Epistola XXVII*, MGH Epist. VII, Epistolae Karolini aevi V, ed. E. Caspar (Berlin, 1928), 25–26.

Jonas of Orleans. *De istitutione laicali*, PL 106:121–278.

Julius Caesar. *De bello Gallico*, ed. Renatus du Pontet (Oxford, 1900).

Lanfranc of Bec. *Decreta Lanfranci monachis Cantuariensibus transmissa*, ed. David Knowles, CCM III (Siegburg, 1967).

Le Glay, André Joseph Ghislain. *Chronique d'Arras et de Cambrai, par Balderic, chantre de Thérouane au XIᵉ siècle* (Paris, 1834).

Martène, Edmond. *De antiquis ecclesiae ritibus libri*, 2nd ed., 4 vols. (Antwerp, 1737–1738).

The Monastic Constitutions of Lanfranc, trans. David Knowles (London, 1951).

The Monastic Ordinale of St. Vedast's Abbey Arras, Henry Bradshaw Society LXXXVI–LXXXVII, ed. Louis Brou, 2 vols. (Bedford, 1957).

Newman, William M. *Catalogue des actes de Robert II, roi de France* (Paris, 1937).

Norman Anonymous. *De consecratione pontificum et regnum*, ed. H. Boehmer, MGH Libelli de lite III, imperatorum et pontificum saeculis XI et XII (Hanover, 1897), 662–679.

Odilo of Cluny. *Liber tramitis aevi Odilonis abbatis*, ed. Peter Dinter, CCM X (Siegburg, 1980), 47–188.

Ordines coronationis Franciae. Texts and Ordines for the Coronation of Frankish and French Kings and Queens in the Middle Ages, 2 vols., ed. Richard A. Jackson (Philadelphia, 1995–2000).

Paul I. *Epistolae*, MGH Epist. III, Epistolae Merovingici et Karolini aevi I, ed. W. Gundlach (Berlin, 1842), 507–558.

Prou, Maurice, ed. *Recueil des actes de Philippe Ier, roi de France (1059–1108)* (Paris, 1908), 60–61, no. 22, 79, no. 26.

Prudentius. *Cathemerinon*, PL 59:775–914.

Rabanus Maurus. *Commentaria in libros Machabaeorum*, PL 109:1125–1256.

———. *Commentaria in Paralipomena*, PL 109:281–540.

———. *Commentariorum in Ecclesiasticum*, PL 109:763–1126.

———. *Epistola XLVI*, ed. E. Dümmler, MGH Epist. V, Epistolae Karolini aevi III (Berlin, 1899), 500–501.

———. *Expositio in librum Esther*, PL 109:635–670.

———. *De laudibus sancti crucis*, PL 107:133–294.

———. *De universo libri XXII*, PL 111:13–614.

———. *In honorem sanctae crucis*, ed. Michel Perrin, Corpus christianorum, Continuatio mediaevalis C (Turnhout, 1997).

Radulfus Glaber. *Historiarum libri quinque*, ed. Neithard Bulst, trans. John France and Paul Reynolds (Oxford, 1989).

Rathier of Verona. *Praeloquiorum libri sex*, PL 136:145–344.

Recueil des historiens des Gaules et de la France, 24 vols. (Paris, 1738–1904).

Rehle, Sieghild. *Sacramentarium Gelasianum mixtum von Saint-Amand* (Regensburg, 1973).

Richer. *Histoire de son temps*, ed. Georg Heinrich Pertz (Paris, 1845).

Rudolph of Saint-Trond. *Gesta abbatum Trudonensis*, ed. Rudolf Köpke, MGH SS X, ed. Georg Heinrich Pertz (Hanover, 1852), 227–317.

——. *Vita sancti Lietberti*, PL 146:1449–1484.

San Leandro, san Isidoro, san Fructuoso. Reglas monásticas de la España visigoda. Los res libros de las 'Sentencias'. Santos padres Españoles II (Madrid, 1971).

Sedulius Scottus. *On Christian Rulers and the Poems*, trans. Edward G. Doyle, Medieval and Renaissance Texts and Studies XVII (Binghamton, 1983).

Soehnée, Frédéric. *Catalogue des actes d'Henri Ier, roi de France (1031–1060)*, Bibliothèque de l'École des hautes études . . . CLXI (Paris, 1907).

Stegmüller, Friedrich. *Repertorium biblicum medii aevi*, 11 vols. (Madrid, 1950–1961).

Tertullian. *De oratione*, PL 1:1143–1196.

Theodomar. *Epistula ad Karolum regem*, ed. Kassius Hallinger and M. Wegener, Initia consuetudinis Benedictinae, Consuetudines saeculi octavi et noni, CCM I, (Siegburg, 1963), 157–175.

——. *Epistula ad Theodoricum gloriosum*, ed. J. Winandy and Kassius Hallinger, Initia consuetudinis Benedictinae, Consuetudines saeculi octavi et noni, CCM I, (Siegburg, 1963), 129–136.

Theodulph of Orléans? *Libri Carolini, sive, Caroli Magni capitulare de imaginibus*, ed. Beda Bastgen, MGH Leges III, Concilia II, suppl. (Hanover, 1924).

——. *Opus Caroli regis contra synodum (Libri Carolini)*, ed. Ann Freeman, MGH Concilia II, supp. I (Hanover, 1998).

Turgot. "Life of Queen Margaret," *Early Sources of Scottish History A.D. 500–1286*, trans. Alan Orr Anderson (Stamford, Lincs., 1922, repr. 1990).

Udalric of Cluny. *Antiquiores consuetudines Cluniacensis monasterii*, PL 149:643–778.

Van Drival, E. *Cartulaire de l'abbaye de Saint-Vaast rédigé au XIIIᵉ siècle par le moine Guiman* (Arras, 1875).

Vetus Latina; die Reste der altlateinischen Bibel, ed. Bonifatius Fischer et al. (Freiburg, 1949–)

Vita Richardi abbatis S. Vitoni Virdunensis, ed. Wilhelm Wattenbach, MGH SS XI, ed. Georg Pertz (Hanover, 1854), 281–290.

Vogel, Cyrille and Elze, Reinhard. *Le pontifical Romano-Germanique du dixième siècle*, 3 vols., Studi e Testi CCXXVI–CCXXVII, CCLVIX (Vatican City, 1963–1972).

Walahfrid Strabo, *Libellus de exordiis et incrementis quarundam in observationibus ecclesiasticus rerum*, ed. Alice L. Harting-Correa (Leiden, 1996).

William of Hirsau. *Constitutiones Hirsaugienses seu Gengenbacenses*, PL 150:927–1146.

William of Saint-Thierry. *Super Cantica Canticorum*, PL 180:441–545.

Zeno of Verona. *Tractatus*, PL 11:253–528.

Secondary Sources

Airlie, Stuart. "Private Bodies and the Body Politic in the Divorce Case of Lothar II," *Past and Present* CLXI (1998), 3–38.

Alexander, J. J. G. *Norman Illumination at Mont St Michel 966–1100* (Oxford, 1970).

Andrieu, Michel. "Le sacre épiscopal d'après Hincmar de Reims," *Revue d'histoire ecclésiastique* XLVIII (1953), 22–73.

Angenendt, Arnold. *"Rex et sacerdos.* Zur Genese der Königssalbung," in *Tradition als historische Kraft*, ed. N. Kamp and J. Wollasch (Berlin, 1982), 100–118.

L'art du moyen âge en Artois (Arras, 1951).

Ayres, Larry. "Le Bibbie atlantiche. Dalla riforma alla diffusione in Europa," in *Le Bibbie atlantiche. Il libro delle scritture tra monumentalità e rappresentazione*, ed. Marilena Maniaci and Giulia Orofino (Rome, 2000), 27–37.

——. "The Italian Giant Bibles: aspects of their Touronian ancestry and early history," in *The Early Medieval Bible: Its production, decoration and use*, ed. Richard Gameson (Cambridge, 1994), 125–154.

Batiffol, Pierre. *History of the Roman Breviary* (London, 1912).
——. "La liturgie du sacre des évêques," *Revue d'histoire ecclésiastique* XXIII (1923), 732–63.
Bautier, Robert-Henri. "Anne de Kiev, reine de France, et la politique royale au XIᵉ siècle," *Revue des études slaves* LVII/4 (1985), 539–564.
——. "L'avènement de Hugues Capet et le sacre de Robert le Pieux," *Le roi de France et son royaume autour de l'an mil*. Actes du colloque Hugues Capet 987–1987. La France de l'an mil, Paris-Senlis, 22–25 juin 1987, ed. Michel Parisse and Xavier Barral i Altet (Paris, 1992), 27–37.
——. "Sacres et couronnements sous les Carolingiens et les premiers Capétiens: Recherches sur la genèse du sacre royal français," *Annuaire-bulletin de la Société de l'histoire de France, 1987* (1989), 7–56.
Belting, Hans. "Die Einhardsbogen," *Zeitschrift für Kunstgeschichte* XXXVI (1973), 93–121.
Berg, Knut. *Studies in Tuscan Twelfth-Century Illumination* (Oslo-Bergen-Tromsö, 1968).
Berger, Samuel. *Histoire de la Vulgate pendant les premiers siècles du moyen âge* (Paris, 1893 reprinted New York, 1958).
——. "Les préfaces jointes aux livres de la Bible dans les manuscrits de la Vulgate," *Mémoires présentés par divers savants à l'Académie des inscriptions et belles-lettres*, 1st ser., XI/2 (Paris, 1902), 1–78.
Besnier, G. "Le Cartulaire de Guiman d'Arras, ses transcriptions. Les autres cartulaires de Saint-Vaast," *Moyen-âge* LXII (1956), 453–478.
Die Bibel des Patricius Leo: Codex Reginensis Graecus 1B, ed. Suzy Dufrenne and Paul Canart, 2 vols. (Zurich, 1988).
Die Bibel von Moutier-Grandval, British Museum ADD. MS. 10546 (Bern, 1971).
Binski, Paul. *Westminster Abbey and the Plantagenets. Kingship and the Representation of Power 1200–1400* (New Haven, 1995).
Biographie nationale, 44 vols. (Brussels, 1866–1986).
Black, Jonathan. "The Divine Office and Private Devotion in the Latin West," in *The Liturgy of the Medieval Church*, eds. Thomas J. Heffernan and E. Ann Matter (Kalamazoo, M.I., 2001), 45–71.
Blaise, Albert. *Dictionnaire Latin-Français des auteurs chrétiens* (Paris, 1954).
Bloch, Marc. *Feudal Society* (London, 1961).
Boinet, Amédée. *La miniature carolingienne* (Paris, 1913).
Bonnaud-Delamare, Roger. "Les institutions de paix dans la province ecclésiastique de Reims au XIᵉ siècle," *Bulletin philologique et historique du Comité des travaux historiques et scientifiques* (Paris, 1957), 165–200.
Bonner, Leila L. "Reclaiming Esther: From Sex Object to Sage," *The Jewish Bible Quarterly* XXVI (1998), 3–11.
Botte, B. "La Sagesse dans les livres Sapientiaux," *Revue des sciences philosophiques et théologiques* XIX (1930), 83–94.
Bouman, Cornelius A. *Sacring and Crowning* (Groningen, 1957).
Boutemy, André. "La Bible enluminée de Saint-Vaast à Arras (Ms. 559)" *Scriptorium* IV (1950), 67–81.
——. "La miniature," in *Histoire de l'église en Belgique des origines aux débuts du XIIᵉ siècle*, ed. Edouard de Moreau (1940), 311–361.
——. "Le style franco-saxon, style de Saint-Amand," *Scriptorium* III (1949), 260–264.
——. "Les enluminures de l'abbaye de Saint-Amand," *Revue belge d'archéologie et d'histoire de l'art* XII (1942), 135–145.
——. "Un trésor injustement oublié: les manuscrits enluminés du nord de la France (période pré-gothique)," *Scriptorium* III (1949), 110–122.
Bradshaw, Paul. *Daily Prayer in the Early Church. A Study of the Origin and Development of the Divine Office* (New York, 1982).
Braun, Joseph. *Die liturgische Gewandung im Occident und Orient* (Darmstadt, 1964).

Brieger, Peter. "Bible Illustration and Gregorian Reform," *Studies in Church History* II (1965), 154–164.

Brown, Peter. "Saint Augustine," in *Trends in Medieval Political Thought*, ed. Beryl Smalley (Oxford, 1965), 1–21.

Brown, Virginia. "Contenuti, funzione e origine della 'Bibbia di San Vincenzo al Volturno' (Roma, Biblioteca Vallicelliana, D 8)," *Nuovi annali della Scuola speciale per archivisti e bibliotecari* XVIII (2004), 37–60.

Bruce-Mitford, R. L. S. "The Art of the Codex Amiatinus," *Journal of the British Archaeological Association* XXXII (1969), 1–25.

——. "The Cassiodorus-Ezra Miniature in the Codex Amiatinus," in Thomas D. Kendrick et al., *Evangeliorum quattuor codex Lindisfarnensis; Musei Britannici codex Cottonianus Nero D. IV permissione Musei Britannici totius codicis similitudo expressa.* 2 vols. (Lausanne, 1956–1960), II.

Buc, Philippe. "Ritual and interpretation: the Early Medieval Case," *Early Medieval Europe* IX (2000), 183–210.

Buchthal, Hugo. *Miniature Painting in the Latin Kingdom of Jerusalem* (Oxford, 1957).

Bur, Michel. "Saint-Thierry et le renouveau monastique dans le diocese de Reims au Xe siècle," in *Saint-Thierry, une abbaye du VIe au XXe siècle. Actes du colloque international d'histoire monastique Reims-Saint-Thierry*, 11 au 14 octobre 1976, ed. Michel Bur (Saint-Thierry, 1979), 39–49.

Burke, Peter. *The Fabrication of Louis XIV* (New Haven, 1992).

Cahn, Walter. "A defense of the Trinity in the Citeaux Bible," *Marsyas* XI (1962), 58–59.

——. *Romanesque Bible Illustration* (Ithaca, 1982).

——. *Romanesque Manuscripts: The Twelfth Century*, 2 vols. (London, 1996).

Callura, P. *La precarolina e la carolina a Bobbio* (Florence, 1965).

Cantor, Norman. *Inventing the Middle Ages* (New York, 1991).

Carré, Yannick. *Le baiser sur la bouche au moyen âge* (Paris, 1992).

Caron, Zephir François Cicéron. *Catalogue des manuscrits de la bibliothèque de la ville d'Arras* (Arras, 1860).

Catalogue général des manuscrits des bibliothèques publiques des départements, in 4° (Paris, 1849–1885), 7 vols., continued as *Catalogue général des manuscrits des bibliothèques publiques de France*, Départements, in 8° (Paris, 1885–1904), 62 vols.

Catalogue of Additions to the Manuscripts in the British Museum in the Years MDCCCXLI–MDCCCXLV (London, 1850).

Cauchie, Alfred. "Richard de Saint-Vannes," in *Biographie nationale* (Brussels, 1907), XIX, 251–267.

——. *La querelle des investitures dans les diocèses de Liège et de Cambrai* (Louvain, 1890).

Cavallo, Guglielmo. *Exultet. Rotoli liturgici del medioevo meridionale* (Rome, 1994).

Caviness, Madeline H. "Anchoress, Abbess and Queen: Donors and Patrons or Intercessors and Matrons," in *The Cultural Patronage of Medieval Women*, ed. June Hall McCash (Athens, Ga., 1996), 105–154.

Ceruti, Antonio. *Inventorio Ceruti dei manoscritti della Biblioteca Ambrosiana* (Milan, 1973).

Cipriani, Renata. *Codici miniati dell'Ambrosiana*, Fontes Ambrosiani XL (Milan, 1968).

Claussen, Martin A. *The Reform of the Frankish Church: Chrodegang of Metz and the Regula Canonicorum in the Eighth Century* (Cambridge, 2004).

Cohen, Adam S. *The Uta Codex: Art, Philosophy and Reform in Eleventh-Century Germany* (Penn State Press, 2000).

Cologne, Schnütigen Museum. *Ornamenta Ecclesiae: Kunst und Künstler der Romanik. Katalog zur Ausstellung des Schnütigen-Museums in der Josef-Haubrich Kunsthalle*, ed. Anton Legner, 3 vols. (Cologne, 1985).

Constable, Giles. "The Orders of Society," in *Three Studies in Medieval Religious and Social Thought* (Cambridge, 1995), 251–341.

Consuetudinum saeculi X/XI/XII monumenta: Introductiones, ed. Kassius Hallinger, CCM VII/1 (Siegburg, 1984).

Contreni, John. "Carolingian Biblical Studies," in *Carolingian Essays: Patristics and Early Medieval Thought*. Andrew W. Mellon Lectures in Early Christian Studies, ed. Uta-Renate Blumenthal (Washington, D.C., 1983), 71–98.

Coolidge, Robert T. "Adalbero, Bishop of Laon," *Studies in Medieval and Renaissance History* II (1965), 1–114.

Cowdrey, E. J. *The Cluniacs and the Gregorian Reform* (Oxford, 1970).

Les cultes à Arras au bas empire, ed. Eric Belot, Exhibition 26 April–17 September, 1990, Musée des Beaux Arts (Arras, 1990).

Dalton, O. M. *Catalogue of the Finger Rings: Early Christian, Byzantine, Teutonic, Mediaeval and Later* (London, 1912).

D'Alverny, Marie Thérèse. "La Sagesse et ses sept filles," in *Mélanges dédiés à la mémoire de Félix Grat* I (Paris, 1946), 245–278.

——. "Le symbolisme de la Sagesse et le Christ de Saint Dunstan," *Bodleian Library Record* V (1956), 232–244.

Dauphin, Hubert. *Le bienheureux Richard, abbé de Saint-Vanne de Verdun, 1046* (Louvain, 1946).

——. "Monastic Reforms from the Tenth Century to the Twelfth," *The Downside Review* LXX (1952–1953), 62–74.

Day, Linda. *Three Faces of a Queen. Characterization in the Books of Esther*. Journal for the Study of the Old Testament, Supplement Series CLXXXVI (Sheffield, 1995).

DeBruyne, Donatien. *Les anciennes traductions latines des Machabées*, Anecdota Maredsolana IV (Maredsous, 1932).

——. "Les anciennes versions latines du Cantique des Cantiques," *Revue bénédictine* XXXVIII (1926), 97–122.

——. "Un nouvelle préface de la traduction hexaplairede Saint Jérôme," *Revue bénédictine* XXXI (1914–1919), 229–236.

de Hamel, Christopher. *Western Manuscripts and Miniatures*, Sotheby's Auction Catalogue, June 23, 1987 (London, 1987).

——. *The Book. A History of the Bible* (New York, 2001).

Delisle, Léopold. *Le cabinet des manuscrits de la Bibliothèque nationale*, 3 vols. (Paris, 1868–1881).

——. *L'evangéliaire de Saint-Vaast d'Arras et la calligraphie franco-saxonne du IXᵉ siècle* (Paris, 1888).

Denny, Don. "The Historiated Initials of the Lobbes Bible," *Revue belge d'archéologie et d'histoire de l'art* XIV–XV (1976), 3–26.

Deshman, Robert. *The Benedictional of Aethelwold*, Studies in Manuscript Illumination IX (Princeton, 1995).

——. "*Benedictus monarcha et monachus*. Early Medieval Ruler Theology and the Anglo-Saxon Reform," *Frühmittelalterliche Studien* XXII (1988), 204–240.

——. "*Christus rex et magi reges*: Kingship and Christology in Ottonian and Anglo-Saxon Art," *Frühmittelalterliche Studien* X (1976), 367–405.

——. "The Exalted Servant: the Ruler Theology of the Prayerbook of Charles the Bald," *Viator* XI (1980), 385–417.

——. "The Leofric Missal and tenth-century English art," *Anglo-Saxon England* VI (1977), 145–176.

——. "Otto III and the Warmund Sacramentary: A Study in Political Theology," *Zeitschrift für Kunstgeschichte* XXXIV (1971), 1–20.

Desmulliez, Janine and Milis, Ludo. *Histoire des provinces françaises du Nord; 1. De la préhistoire à l'an mil* (Dunkerque, 1988).

Dictionary of the Bible, ed. J. Hastings (New York, 1954).

Diebold, William J. "The Ruler Portrait of Charles the Bald in the San Paolo Bible," *Art Bulletin* LXXVI (1994), 6–18.

Dodwell, C. R. *The Pictorial Arts of the West 800–1200* (New Haven, 1993).

Dodwell, C. R. and Clemoes, P. *The Old English Illustrated Hexateuch*, Early English Manuscripts in Facsimile XVIII (London, 1974).

Donovan, Claire. *The Winchester Bible* (London, 1993).

Dörrie, Heinrich. *Passio SS. Machabaeorum, die antike lateinische Übersetzung des IV. Makkabäerbuches*, Abhandlungen der Gesellschaft der Wissenschaften zu Gottingen, Philologisch-Historische Klasse, Series 3 n. 33 (Göttingen, 1938).

Du Cange, Charles Du Fresne. *Glossarium ad scriptores mediae et infimae Latinitatis*, 10 vols. (Niort, 1883–1887).

Duby, Georges. "Gérard de Cambrai, la paix et les trois fonctions sociales, 1024," *Compte rendu des séances de l'Academie des inscriptions et belles-lettres* (1976), 136–146.

——. *History Continues*, trans. Arthur Goldhammer (Chicago, 1994).

——. "L'image du prince en France au début du XIe siècle," *Cahiers d'histoire* XVII (1972), 211–216.

——. *Medieval Marriage. Two Models from Twelfth-Century France* (Baltimore, 1978).

——. *The Knight, the Lady and the Priest: The Making of Modern Marriage in Medieval France* (New York, 1983).

——. *The Three Orders: Feudal Society Imagined*, trans. Arthur Goldhammer (Chicago, 1980).

Dufrenne, Suzy. *Les illustrations du psautier d'Utrecht. Sources et apport carolingien* (Paris, 1978).

Dunbabin, J. "The Maccabees as Exemplars in the tenth and eleventh centuries," in *The Bible in the Medieval World: Essays in Memory of Beryl Smalley*, Studies in Church History, Subsidia (1985), 31–41.

Dutschke, C. W. *Guide to Medieval and Renaissance Manuscripts in the Huntington Library* (San Marino, CA, 1989).

Dutton, Paul E. *The Politics of Dreaming in the Carolingian Empire* (Lincoln, NE, 1994).

——. and Kessler, Herbert L. *The Poetry and Painting of the First Bible of Charles the Bald* (Ann Arbor, 1997).

Dynes, Wayne. *The Illuminations of the Stavelot Bible* (New York, 1978).

Dyson, R. W. *The Pilgrim City. Social and Political Ideas in the Writings of St. Augustine of Hippo* (Rochester, N.Y., 2001).

Eggenberger, Christoph. *Psalterium aureum Sancti Galli; Mittelalterliche Psalterillustration im Kloster St. Gallen* (Sigmaringen, 1987).

Das Einhardkreuz: Vorträge und Studien der Münsteraner Diskussion zum arcus Einhardi, ed. Karl Hauck (Göttingen, 1974).

English Romanesque Art 1066–1200 (London, 1984).

Enright, Michael J. *Iona, Tara and Soissons: The Origin of the Royal Anointing Ritual* (Berlin, 1985).

Erkens, Franz-Reiner. "*Sicut Esther regina*. Die westfränkische Königin als *consors regni*," *Francia* XX (1993), 26–36.

Escudier, Denis. "Le scriptorium de Saint-Vaast d'Arras des origines au XIIe siècle: contribution à l'étude des notations neumatiques du Nord de la France," 3 vols., Thèse, Paris, École nat. Chartes (1970).

——. "Le scriptorium de Saint-Vaast d'Arras des origines au XIIe siècle," *Positions des thèses de l'École des Chartes* (1970), 75–82.

Evergates, Theodore. "The Feudal Imaginary of Georges Duby," *Journal of Medieval and Early Modern Studies* XXVII (Fall, 1997), 641–660.

Facinger, Marion. "A Study of Medieval Queenship: Capetian France 987–1237," *Studies in Medieval and Renaissance History* V (1968), 3–48.

Farmer, Sharon. "Persuasive Voices: Clerical Images of Medieval Wives," *Speculum* LXI (1986), 517–526.

Ferrari, Guy. *Early Roman Monasteries. Notes for the History of the Monasteries and Convents at Rome from the V through the X Century*, Studi di antichità Cristiana XXIII (Vatican City, 1957).

Fichtenau, Heinrich. "Neues zum Problem der italienischen 'Riesenbibeln'," *Institut für Österreichische Geschichtsforschung: Mitteilungen* LVIII (1950), 50–67.

Fischer, Bonifatius. "Bibelausgaben des frühen Mittelalters," *La Bibbia nell'alto medioevo*, SSCISAM X (Spoleto, 1963), 519–600.

——. "Bibeltext und Bibelreform unter Karl dem Grossen," in *Karl der Grosse. Lebenswerk und Nachleben II: Das geistige Leben*, ed. Bernard Bischoff (Dusseldorf, 1965), 156–216.

——. *Die Alkuin-Bibel* (Freiburg, 1949).

Frassetto, Michael. "Reaction and Reform: Reception of Heresy in Arras and Aquitaine in the Early Eleventh Century," *Catholic Historical Review* LXXXIII (1997), 385–400.

Freeman, Ann. "Theodulf of Orléans and the *Libri Carolini*," *Speculum* XXXII (1957), 663–705.

Freidson (Facinger), Marion F. "A Study of Medieval Queenship. Capetian France 987–1237," Ph.D Dissertation, University of Chicago, 1964.

Fried, Johannes. "Ernst Kantorowicz and Postwar Historiography. German and European Perspectives," in *Ernst Kantorowicz: Erträge der Doppeltagung, Institute for Advanced Study, Princeton, Johann Wolfgang Goethe-Universität, Frankfurt*, ed. Robert L. Benson and Johannes Fried, Frankfurter Historische Abhandlungen XXXIX (Stuttgart, 1997), 180–201.

Frugoni, Chiara. "L'iconografia del matrimonio e della coppia nel medioevo," *Il matrimonio nella società altomedievale*, SSCISAM XXIV (Spoleto, 1977), II, 901–963.

Gaehde, Joachim. "The Bible of San Paolo fuori le mura in Rome: its Date and its Relation to Charles the Bald," *Gesta* V (1966), 9–21.

——. "The Touronian Sources of the San Paolo Bible," *Frühmittelalterliche Studien* V (1971), 359–400.

Galavaris, George. *The Illustrations of the Liturgical Homilies of Gregory Nazianzenus*, Studies in Manuscript Illumination VI (Princeton, 1969).

——. *The Illustrations of the Prefaces in Byzantine Gospels* (Vienna, 1979).

Gameson, Richard. "La Bible de Saint-Vaast d'Arras et un manuscrit Anglo-Saxon de Boèce," *Scriptorium* LII (1998), 316–321.

——. *The Role of Art in the Late Anglo-Saxon Church* (Oxford, 1995).

Ganshof, François Louis. *Feudalism* (New York, 1964).

Ganz, David. "Mass Production of Early Medieval Manuscripts: The Carolingian Bibles from Tours," in *The Early Medieval Bible: Its production, decoration and use*, ed. Richard Gameson (Cambridge, 1994), 53–62.

Garrison, Edward B. *Studies in the History of Medieval Italian Painting*, 4 vols. (Florence, 1953–1962).

Gatch, M. McC. "The Office in Late Anglo-Saxon Monasticism," in *Learning and Literature in Late Anglo-Saxon England*, eds. Michael Lapidge and Helmut Gneuss (Cambridge, 1985), 341–362.

Gaudemet, Jean. "Le legs du droit romain en matière matrimoniale," in *Il matrimonio nella società altomedievale*, SSCISAM XXIV (Spoleto, 1977) I, 139–179.

——. "Note sur le symbolisme médiéval: le mariage de l'évêque," in *La société ecclésiastique dans l'occident médiéval* (London, 1980), 71–80.

Genet, Jean-Philippe. "Kantorowicz and the *King's Two Bodies*: A non Contextual History," in *Ernst Kantorowicz: Erträge der Doppeltagung, Institute for Advanced Study, Princeton, Johann Wolfgang Goethe-Universität, Frankfurt*, ed. Robert L. Benson and Johannes Fried, Frankfurter Historische Abhandlungen XXXIX (Stuttgart, 1997), 265–273.

Gheyn, Joseph van den. *Catalogue des manuscrits de la Bibliothèque royale de Belgique*, 13 vols. (Brussels, 1901–1948).

Gibson, Margaret T. *The Bible in the Latin West*. The Medieval Book, I (Notre Dame, 1993).

The Golden Age of Anglo-Saxon Art 966–1066, ed. Janet Backhouse, D. H. Turner, and Leslie Webster (London, 1984).

Grabar, André. "Iconography de la Sagesse divine," *Cahiers archéologiques* VIII (1956), 254–261.

Grierson, Philip. "La bibliothèque de Saint-Vaast d'Arras au XIIe siècle," *Revue bénédictine* LII (1940), 117–140.

——. "Les livres de l'abbé Seiwold de Bath," *Revue bénédictine* LII (1940), 96–116.

——. "The Relations between England and France before the Norman Conquest," *Transactions of the Royal Historical Society*, Ser. 4, XXIII (1941), 71–112.

Grimme, Ernst. *Das Evangeliar Kaiser Ottos III im Domschatz zu Aachen* (Freiburg, 1984).

Grossman, Grace C. *Jewish Art* (New York, 1995).

Gruy, Henry. *Histoire d'Arras* (Arras, 1967).

Guyotjeannin, Olivier. "Les évêques dans l'entourage royal sous les premiers Capétiens," in *Le roi de France et son royaume autour de l'an mil*. Actes du colloque Hugues Capet 987–1987. La France de l'an mil, Paris-Senlis, 22–25 juin 1987, ed. Michel Parisse and Xavier Barral i Altet (Paris, 1992), 91–98.

Hadas, Moses. *The Third and Fourth Books of Maccabees* (New York, 1953).

Hallinger, Kassius, ed. *Corpus consuetudinum monasticarum*, 14 vols. (Siegburg, 1963–1996).

——. *Gorze-Kluny. Studien zu den monastischen Lebensformen und Gegensätzen im Hochmittelalter*, Studia Anselmiana XXII–XXIII (Rome, 1950).

Handschriftcensus Rheinland, ed. Günter Guttermann (Wiesbaden, 1993).

Hannemann, Otto. *Die Kanonikerregeln Chrodegangs von Metz und der Aachener Synode von 816, und das Verhältnis Gregors VII dazu* (Greifswald, 1914).

Havice, Christine. "The Hamilton Psalter in Berlin, Kupferstich-Kabinett 78.A.9," Ph.D. Dissertation, Pennsylvania State University, 1978.

Heitz, Gerhard et al. "Vorwort," in *Mittelalter und demokratische Geschichtsschreibung: Ausgewählte Abhandlungen*, ed. Manfred Unger (Berlin, 1971), vii–x.

"Heinrich Sproemberg," *Wer is Wer? Das Deutsche Who's Who* XII (1955), 1138.

Heresies of the High Middle Ages, eds. Walter L. Wakefield and Austin P. Evans (New York, 1969).

Hermann, Hermann Julius. *Die illuminierten Handschriften und Inkunabeln der Nationalbibliothek in Wien*, I: *Die frühmittelalterlichen Handschriften des Abendlandes* (Leipzig, 1923).

Hocquard, Gaston. "La règle de Saint Chrodegang. État de quelques questions," in *Saint Chrodegang. Communications présentées au colloque tenu à Metz à l'occasion du douzième centenaire de sa mort* (Metz, 1967), 55–89.

Hormann, W. "Probleme einer Aldersbacher Handschrift, Clm 2599," in *Buch und Welt. Festschrift für G. Hofmann* (Weisbaden, 1965), 335–389.

Huber, Paul. *Apokalypse. Bilderzyklen zur Johannes-Offenbarung in Trier, auf dem Athos und von Caillaud d'Angers* (Düsseldorf, 1989).

Hubert, J., Porcher J., and Volbach, W. F. *L'empire carolingien* (Paris, 1968).

Hübner, Wolfgang. *Zodiacus Christianus. Jüdische-christliche Adaptionen des Tierkreises von der Antike bis zur Gegenwart*, Beiträge zur klassischen Philologie CXLIV (Hain, 1983).

Humphreys, W. Lee. "The Story of Esther in its Several Forms: Recent Studies," *Religious Studies Review* XXIV (1998), 335–342.

Huneycutt, Lois L. "Images of Queenship in the High Middle Ages," *The Haskins Society Journal* I (1989), 61–71.

——. "Intercession and the High Medieval Queen: The Esther Topos," in *Power of the Weak. Studies on Medieval Women*, eds. Jennifer Carpenter and Sally-Beth MacLean (Urbana, IL, 1995), 126–146.

——. "'Proclaiming her dignity abroad:' The Literary and Artistic Network of

Matilda of Scotland, Queen of England 1100–1118," in *The Cultural Patronage of Medieval Women*, ed. June Hall McCash (Athens, GA, 1996), 155–174.

Hyam, J. "Ermentrude and Richildis," in *Charles the Bald. Court and Kingdom*, eds. Margaret T. Gibson and Janet L. Nelson, 2nd revised edition (Aldershot, Hampshire, 1990), 154–168.

Ihm, Christa. *Die Programme der christlichen Apsismalerei vom vierten Jahrhundert bis zur Mitte des achten Jahrhunderts* (Wiesbaden, 1960).

Innes, Matthew. *State and Society in the Early Middle Ages: The Middle Rhine Valley, 400–1000* (Cambridge, 2001).

Jacques, Alain. "Arras gallo-romaine," *Archeologia* CCXIII (1986), 58–63.

Jacques, Alain et al. *Histoire d'Arras*, ed. Pierre Bougard, Yves-Marie Hilaire and Alain Nolibos (Arras, 1988).

Jégou, Laurent. "L'évêque entre autorité sacrée et exercice du pouvoir. L'exemple de Gérard de Cambrai (1012–1051)," *Cahiers de civilisation médiévale, X^e–XIIe siècles* XLVII (2004), 37–55.

Jones, Christopher A. *Aelfric's Letter to the Monks of Eynsham* (Cambridge, 1998).

Jordan, Alyce. "Narrative Design in the Stained Glass Windows of the Ste. Chapelle in Paris," Ph.D. dissertation, Bryn Mawr, 1995.

Kahsnitz, Rainer. "Der christologische Zyklus im Odbert-Psalter," *Zeitschrift für Kunstgeschichte* LI (1988), 33–125.

——. "'*Matheus ex ore Christi scripsit*:' Zum Bild der Berufung und Inspiration der Evangelisten," in *Byzantine East, Latin West. Art Historical Studies in Honor of Kurt Weitzmann*, eds. Christopher Moss and Katherine Kiefer (Princeton, 1995), 169–176.

Kantorowicz, Ernst H. "The Carolingian King in the Bible of San Paulo fuori le mura," *Selected Studies* (Locust Valley, New York, 1965), 82–95.

——. "*Deus per naturam, Deus per gratiam*: a Note on Mediaeval Political Theology," in *Selected Studies* (Locust Valley, New York, 1965), 121–137.

——. *The King's Two Bodies: a Study in Medieval Political Theology* (Princeton, 1957).

——. *Laudes regiae: A Study in Liturgical Acclamations and Mediaeval Ruler Worship*, University of California Publications in History XXXIII (Berkeley, 1946).

——. "On the Golden Marriage Belt and the Marriage Rings of the Dumbarton Oaks Collection," *Dumbarton Oaks Papers* XIV (1960), 3–16.

——. "The Quinity of Winchester," *Art Bulletin* XXIX (1947), 73–85.

Kaspersen, Søren. "Cotton-Genesis, die Toursbibeln und die Bronzetüren—Vorlage und Aktualität," in *Bernwardinische Kunst: Bericht über ein wissenschaftliches Symposium in Hildesheim vom 10.10 bis 13.10.1984*, ed. Martin Gosebruch and F. Neidhart Steigerwald, Schriftenreihe der Kommission für Niedersächsische Bau- und Kunstgeschichte bei der Braunschweigischen Wissenschaftlichen Gesellschaft III (Göttingen, 1988), 79–103.

Katzenellenbogen, Adolph. *Allegories of the Virtues and Vices in Medieval Art* (London, 1939).

——. "The Representation of the Seven Liberal Arts," in *Twelfth-Century Europe and the Foundations of Modern Society* (Madison, Wisconson, 1961), 39–58.

Kelleher, Claire. "Illumination at Saint-Bertin at Saint-Omer under the Abbacy of Odbert," Ph.D. Dissertation, University of London, 1968.

Keller, Hagen. "Herrscherbild und Herrschaftslegitimation. Zur Deutung der ottonischen Denkmäler," *Frühmittelalterliche Studien* XIX (1985), 290–311.

Kessler, Herbert L. "An Apostle in Armor and the Mission of Carolingian Art," *Arte medievale*, Ser. 2, IV/1 (1990), 17–39.

——. *The Illustrated Bibles from Tours* (Princeton, 1977).

——. "A Lay Abbot as Patron: Count Vivian and the First Bible of Charles the Bald," *Committenti e produzione artistico-letteraria nell'alto medioevo occidentale*, SSCISAM XXXIX (1992), 647–675.

———. "Traces of an Early Illustrated Pentateuch," *Journal of Jewish Art* VIII (1981), 20–27.

Klauck, Hans-Josef. *4 Makkabäerbuch*. Jüdische Schriften aus hellenistisch-römischer Zeit III/6 (Gütersloh, 1989).

Klein, Peter. "The Romanesque in Catalonia," in *The Art of Medieval Spain, A.D. 500–1200* (New York, 1993), 306–309.

Klemm, Elisabeth. "Artes Liberales und antike Autoren in der Aldersbacher Sammelhandschrift, Clm 2599," *Zeitschrift für Kunstgeschichte* XLI (1978), 1–15.

Köhler, Wilhelm. *Die karolingischen Miniaturen*, 7 vols. (Berlin, 1930–1971).

Körntgen, Ludger. *Königsherrschaft und Gottes Gnade. Zu Kontext und Funktion sakraler Vorstellungen in Historiographie und Bildzeugnissen der ottonisch-frühsalischen Zeit* (Berlin, 2001).

Koziol, Geoffrey. *Begging Pardon and Favor. Ritual and Political Order in Early Medieval France* (Ithaca, 1992).

———. "Monks, Feuds, and the Making of Peace in Eleventh-Century Flanders," in *The Peace of God: Social Violence and Religious Response in France around the Year 1000*, ed. Thomas Head and Richard Landes (Ithaca, 1992), 239–258.

Laborde, A. de. *La Bibles moralisée illustrée conservée à Oxford, Paris et Londres: Reproduction intégrale du manuscrit du XIIIe siècle accompagnée de planches tirées de Bibles similaires et d'une notice* (Paris, 1911–1927).

Lambot, C. "L'homilie du Pseudo-Jérome sur l'Assomption et l'évangile de la Nativité de Marie d'après une lettre inédite d'Hincmar," *Revue bénédictine* XLIV (1934), 265–282.

Lassus, Jean. *L'illustration byzantine du livre des Rois, Vaticanus Graecus 333*, Bibliothèque des cahiers archéologiques IX (Paris, 1973).

Lauer, Philippe. *Bibliothèque nationale. Catalogue général des manuscrits latins*, 6 vols. (Paris, 1939).

Le Berrurier, Diane O. *The Pictorial Sources of Mythological and Scientific Illustrations in Hrabanus Maurus' De rerum naturis*, (New York, 1978).

Leesti, Elizabeth. "New Testament Illustrations in the Drogo Sacramentary," Ph.D. Dissertation, University of Toronto, 1984.

Lemarignier, Jean F. "L'exemption monastique et les origines de la réforme grégorienne," in *À Cluny. Congrès scientifique* (Dijon, 1950), 288–340, reprinted in *Recueil d'articles rassemblés par ses disciples* (Paris, 1995).

———. *Le gouvernement royal aux premiers temps Capétiens (987–1108)* (Paris, 1965).

———. "Paix et réforme monastique en Flandre et en Normandie autour l'année 1023," in *Droit privé et institutions régionales: Études historiques offertes à Jean Yver* (Paris, 1976), 443–468.

Leclercq, Jean. "Rôle et pouvoir des épouses au moyen âge," in *La femme au moyen âge*, eds. Michel Rouche and Jean Heuclin (Maugeuge, 1988), 87–97.

Leroquais, Victor. *Les pontificaux manuscrits des bibliothèques publiques de France*, 3 vols. (Paris, 1937).

Lestocquoy, Jean. "Les étapes du développement urbain d'Arras," *Revue belge de philologie et d'histoire* XXIII (1944), reprinted in *Études d'histoire urbaine: Villes et abbayes Arras au moyen-âge* (Arras, 1966), 122–137.

Lexikon der christlichen Ikonographie, ed. Engelbert Kirschbaum, 8 vols. (Basel, 1968–1976).

Lewis, Andrew W. "Anticipatory Association of the Heir in Early Capetian France," *American Historical Review* LXXXIII (1978), 906–927.

Leyser, Karl J. *Rule and Conflict in an Early Medieval Society. Ottonian Saxony* (Bloomington, 1979).

Light, Laura. "French Bibles c. 1200–1230: a new look at the origin of the Paris Bible," in *The Early Medieval Bible: Its production, decoration and use*, ed. Richard Gameson (Cambridge, 1994), 155–176.

——. "Versions et révisions du texte biblique," in *Le moyen âge et la Bible*, ed. Pierre Riché and Guy Lobrichon, Bible de tous les temps IV (Paris, 1984), 55–93.

Lobrichon, Guy. "Riforma ecclesiastica e testo della Bibbia," in *Le Bibbie atlantiche. Il libro delle scritture tra monumentalità e rappresentazione* (Rome, 2000), 15–26.

LoPrete, Kimberly. "Adela of Blois: Familial Alliances and Female Lordship," in *Aristocratic Women in Medieval France*, ed. Theodore Evergates (Philadelphia, 1999), 7–43.

LoPrete, Kimberly and Evergates, Theodore. "Introduction," in *Aristocratic Women in Medieval France*, ed. Theodore Evergates (Philadelphia, 1999), 1–5.

Lowden, John. *The Making of the Bibles Moralisées*, 2 vols. (University Park, 2000).

Lowry, Susan. "New York, Pierpont Morgan Library M. 333 and Manuscript Illumination at the Monastery of Saint Bertin under Abbot Odbert (986–ca. 1007)," Ph.D. Dissertation, Columbia University, 1996.

Luchaire, Achille. *Histoire des institutions monarchiques de la France sous les premiers capétiens (987–1180)* (Paris, 1891).

Magnani, Luigi. *Le miniature del sacramentario d'Ivrea e di altri codici Warmondiani*, Codices ex ecclesiasticis Italiae bybliothecis delecti phototypice expressi VI (Vatican City, 1934).

Major, J. Russell. "'Bastard Feudalism' and the kiss: changing social mores in late medieval and early modern France," *Journal of Interdisciplinary History* XVII (1987), 509–535.

Mâle, Émile. *Art religieux du XIIᵉ siècle en France: étude sur les origines de l'iconographie du moyen âge* (Paris, 1922).

Mango, Cyril. "The date of Cod. Vat. Regin. Gr. 1 and the Macedonian Renaissance," *Acta ad archaeologiam et artium* IV (1969), 121–126.

Mattingly, Harold. *Coins of the Roman Empire in the British Museum*, 6 vols. (London, 1923–1950).

Mariaux, Pierre Alain. *Warmund d'Ivrée et ses images: Politique et création iconographique autour de l'an mil*, Publications universitaires Européennes, Série XXVIII, Histoire de l'art CCCLXXXVIII (Bern, 2002).

Marsden, Richard. "Job in his place: the Ezra miniature in the Codex Amiatinus," *Scriptorium* IL (1995), 3–15.

Martimort, Aimé-Georges. *La documentation liturgique de Dom Edmond Martène: Étude codicologique*, Studi e Testi CCLXXIX (Vatican City, 1978).

——. *Les lectures liturgiques et leurs livres*, Typologie des sources du moyen âge occidental LXIV (Turnhout, 1992).

Masai, François. "Bulletin codicologique," *Scriptorium* XXI (1968), 102–103.

Masi, M. "Boethius and the Iconography of the Liberal Arts," *Latomus* XXXIII (1974), 57–75.

Mayer-Thurman, Christa C. *Raiment for the Lord's Service: A Thousand Years of Western Vestments* (Chicago, 1975).

Mayr-Harting, Henry. *Ottonian Book Illumination; an Historical Study*, 2 vols. (New York, 1991).

McCracken, Peggy. *The Romance of Adultery. Queenship and Sexual Transgression in Old French Literature* (Philadelphia, 1998).

McGrath, Robert L. "The Martyrdom of the Maccabees on the Brescia Casket," *Art Bulletin* XLVII (1965), 257–261.

——. "The Romance of the Maccabees in Medieval Art and Literature," Ph.D. Dissertation, Princeton University, 1963.

McKitterick, Rosamund. "Carolingian Bible Production: the Tours Anomaly," in *The Early Medieval Bible: Its production, decoration and use*, ed. Richard Gameson (Cambridge, 1994), 63–77.

——. *The Frankish Church and the Carolingian Reforms, 789–895* (London, 1977).

McNamara, Joanne and Wemple, Suzanne F. "The Power of Women through the

Family in Medieval Europe, 500–1100," in *Women and Power in the Middle Ages*, ed. Mary Erler and Maryanne Kowaleski (Athens, Ga., 1988), 83–101.

Meyersdorff, J. "L'iconographie de la Sagesse divine dans la tradition Byzantine," *Cahiers archéologiques* X (1959), 259–277.

Meyvaert, Paul. "Bede, Cassiodorus and the Codex Amiatinus," *Speculum* LXXI (1996), 827–883.

Die mittelalterlichen Handschriften der Universitätsbibliothek Basel. Abteilung B Theologische Pergamenthandschriften, 3 vols. (Basel, 1960–1975).

Molinier, Auguste. *Catalogue des manuscrits de la Bibliothèque Mazarine*, 4 vols. (Paris, 1885–1892).

Moore, Robert I. *The Birth of Popular Heresy* (London, 1975).

———. *The Formation of a Persecuting Society: Power and Deviance in Western Europe, 950–1250* (New York, 1987).

———. "Literacy and the Making of Heresy, c. 1000–1150," in *Heresy and Literacy, 1000–1530* (Cambridge, 1994), 19–37.

———. *The Origins of European Dissent* (Toronto, 1994, orig. 1977).

Morin, G. "Le catalogue des manuscrits de l'abbaye de Gorze au XIᵉ siècle," *Revue bénédictine* XXII (1905), 3–11.

Mostert, Marco. *The Political Theology of Abbo of Fleury: A Study of the Ideas about Society and Law of the Tenth Century Monastic Reform Movement*, Middeleeuwse Studies en Bronnen II (Hilversum, 1987).

Moyse, Gérard. "Monachisme et réglementation monastique en Gaule avant Benoît d'Aniane," in *Sous la règle de saint Benoit. Structures monastiques et sociétés en France du moyen âge à l'époque moderne*. Centre de recherches d'histoire et de philologie V, Hautes études médiévales et modernes XLVII (Geneva, 1982), 3–19.

Müller, Heribert. "Theodor Schieffer. Leben und Werk," in *Theodor Schieffer, 1910–1992* (Munich, 1992), 3–20.

Muller, Jerry Z. *The Other God that Failed. Hans Freyre and the Deradicalization of German Conservatism* (Princeton, 1987).

Mütherich, Florentine and Gaehde, Joachim. *Carolingian Painting* (New York, 1976).

Nees, Lawrence. *The Gundohinus Gospels* (Cambridge, Mass., 1987).

———. "Problems of Form and Function in Early Medieval Illustrated Bibles from Northwest Europe," in *Imaging the Early Medieval Bible*, ed. John Williams (University Park, P.A., 1999), 121–177.

Nelson, Janet L. "The Earliest Surviving Royal Ordo: Some Liturgical and Historical Aspects," in *Authority and Power: Studies on Medieval Law and Government Presented to Walter Ullman on his Seventieth Birthday* (Cambridge, 1980), 29–48.

———. "Early Medieval Rites of Queen-making and the Shaping of Medieval Queenship," in *Queens and Queenship in Medieval Europe*, ed. Anne Duggan (London, 1997), 301–315.

———. "England and the Continent in the Ninth Century: II, the Vikings and Others," *Transactions of the Royal Historical Society* XIII (2003), 1–28.

———. "Inauguration rituals," in *Early Medieval Kingship*, ed. P. H. Sawyer and Ian N. Wood (Leeds, 1977), 50–71.

———. "Kingship and Empire in the Carolingian World," in *Carolingian Culture: Emulation and Innovation*, ed. Rosamund McKitterick (Cambridge, 1994), 52–87.

———. "Kingship, law and liturgy in the political thought of Hincmar of Reims," *English Historical Review* XCII (1977), 241–279.

———. "National Synods, Kingship as Office, and Royal Anointing," *Studies in Church History* VII (1971), 41–59, reprinted in *Politics and Ritual in Early Medieval Europe* (London, 1986), 239–258.

———. "Queens as Jezebels: the Careers of Brunhild and Balthild in Merovingian History," in *Medieval Women*, ed. Derek Baker (Oxford, 1978), 31–77.

Der Nersessian, Sirarpie. "A Psalter and New Testament Manuscript at Dumbarton Oaks," *Dumbarton Oaks Papers* XIX (1965), 153–183.

——. "Recherches sur les miniatures du Parisinus Graecus 74," *Jährbuch der Österreichischen Byzantinistik* XXI (1972), 109–117.

Neuß, Wilhelm. *Die katalanische Bibelillustration um die Wende des ersten Jahrtausends und die altspanische Buchmalerei* (Bonn, 1922).

Nicholas, Karen. "Countesses as Rulers in Flanders," in *Aristocratic Women in Medieval France*, ed. Theodore Evergates (Philadelphia, 1999), 111–128.

Niditch, Susan. "Esther: Folklore, Wisdom, Feminism and Authority," in *A Feminist Companion to Esther, Judith and Susanna*, ed. Athalya Brenner (Sheffield, 1995), 26–46.

Nightengale, John. *Monasteries and Patrons in the Gorze Reform. Lotharingia c. 850–1000* (Oxford, 2001).

Noiroux, J. M. "Les deux premiers documents concernant l'hérésie aux Pays Bas," *Revue d'histoire ecclésiastique* IL (1954), 842–855.

Nordenfalk, Carl. "Ein karolingisches Sakramentar aus Echternach und seine Vorläufer," *Acta archaeologica* II (1931), 207–244.

——. *Early Medieval Book Illumination* (Geneva, 1988).

——. "Miniature ottonienne et ateliers capétiens," *Art de France* IV (1964), 49–54.

Norris, Herbert. *Church Vestments: Their Origin and Development* (London, 1949).

Ohly, Friedrich. *Hohelied-Studien. Grundzüge einer Geschichte der Hoheliedauslegung des Abendlandes bis um 1200* (Wiesbaden, 1958).

O'Meara, Carra Ferguson. *Monarchy and Consent. The Coronation Book of Charles V of France* (London, 2001).

Omont, Henri. *Evangiles avec peintures byzantines*, 2 vols. (Paris, 1908).

——. *Les plus anciens manuscrits grecs de la Bibliothèque nationale* (Paris, 1926).

Orchard, Nicholas, ed. *The Leofric Missal*, Henry Bradshaw Society CXIII–CXIV (London, 2002).

Ortenberg, V. "Archbishop Sigeric's Journey to Rome," *Anglo-Saxon England* XIX (1990), 197–246.

Osborne, John. *Early Mediaeval Wall-Paintings in the Lower Church of San Clemente, Rome* (New York, 1984).

Ott, John. "Both Mary and Martha: Bishop Lietbertus of Cambrai and the Construction of Episcopal Sanctity in a Border Diocese around 1100," in *The Bishop Reformed: Studies in Episcopal Power and Culture in the Central Middle Ages*, ed. John S. Ott and Anna E. Trumbore (London: Ashgate, forthcoming).

Oursel, Hervé, Deramble-Moubès, Colette, and Thiébaut, Jacques. *Nord roman*, La nuit de temps LXXXII (Saint-Léger-Vauban, 1994).

Palazzo, Eric. *A History of Liturgical Books from the Beginning to the Thirteenth Century*, trans. Madeleine Beaumont (Collegeville, MN, 1973).

Parisse, Michel. "Princes laiques et/ou moines, les évêques du Xᵉ siècle," in *Il secolo di ferro: mito e realtà del secolo X*, SSCISAM XXXVIII, 2 vols. (Spoleto, 1991), I, 449–516.

Parker, Elizabeth C. and Little, Charles T. *The Cloisters Cross; its Art and Meaning* (New York, 1994).

Parsons, John Carmi. "Family, Sex and Power: the Rhythms of Medieval Queenship," in *Medieval Queenship*, ed. John Carmi Parsons (New York, 1993), 1–12.

Patzold, Steffan. "*Omnis anima potestatibus sublimioribus subdita sit.* Zum Herrscherbild im Aachener Otto-Evangeliar," *Frühmittelalterliche Studien* XXXV (2001), 243–272.

Perella, Nicholas. *The Kiss Sacred and Profane* (Los Angelos, 1969).

Peroni, Adriano. "Il ruolo della committenza vescovile alle soglie del mille: il caso di Warmundo di Ivrea," in *Il secolo di ferro: mito e realtà del secolo X*, SSCISAM XXXVIII, 2 vols. (Spoleto, 1991), I, 243–270.

Alain Peyrefitte, "Réponse," in *Discours de réception de Georges Duby à l'Académie française et réponse d'Alain Peyrefitte* (Paris, 1988), 41–86.

Pierrard, Pierre. *Histoire du nord: Flandre-Artois-Hainaut-Picardie* (Paris, 1978).
Pippal, Martina. "Distanzierung und Aktualisierung in der Vivianbibel: Zur Struktur der touronischen Miniaturen in den 40er Jahren des 9. Jahrhunderts," *Aachener Kunstblätter* LX (1994), 61–78.
Platelle, Henri. "La violence et ses remèdes en Flandre au XIe siècle," *Sacris erudiri* XX (1971), 101–173.
Poly, Jean-Pierre and Bournazel, Eric. *The Feudal Transformation, 900–1200* (New York, 1991).
Poulet, Andre. "Capetian Women and the Regency: the Genesis of a Vocation," in *Medieval Queenship*, ed. John Carmi Parsons (New York, 1993), 93–116.
Reilly, Diane. "The Cluniac Giant Bible and the *Ordo librorum ad legendum*: a reassessment of monastic Bible reading and Cluniac customary instructions," in *From Dead of Night to End of Day: The Medieval Cluniac Customs/Du cour de la nuit à la fin du jour: les coutumes clunisiennes au Moyen Age*, eds. Susan Boynton and Isabelle Cochelin, Disciplina Monastica I (Turnhout: Brepols, 2005), 163–189.
———. "French Romanesque Giant Bibles and their English Relatives: Blood Relatives or Adopted Children?" *Scriptorium* LVI (2002), 294–311.
———. "Picturing the monastic drama: Romanesque Bible illustrations of the Song of Songs," *Word & Image* XVII (2001), 389–400.
Reuter, Timothy. "The Making of England and Germany, 850–1050: Points of Comparison and Difference," in *Medieval Europeans. Studies in Ethnic Identity and National Perspectives in Medieval Europe*, ed. Alfred P. Smyth (New York, 1998), 53–70.
———. "Pre-Gregorian Mentalities," *Journal of Ecclesiastical History* XLV (1994), 465–474.
Reynolds, Roger E. "Image and Text: the Liturgy of Clerical Ordination in Early Medieval Art," *Gesta* XXII (1983), 27–38.
Richards, Mary P. "A Decorated Vulgate Set from 12th-Century Rochester, England," *The Journal of the Walters Art Gallery* XXXIX (1981), 59–67.
———. *Texts and Their Traditions in the Medieval Library of Rochester Cathedral Priory* (Philadelphia, 1988).
Riedlinger, Helmut. *Die Makellosigkeit der Kirche in den lateinischen Hohelied Kommentaren des Mittelalters*, Beiträge zur Geschichte der Philosophie und Theologie des Mittelalters: Text und Untersuchungen XXXVIII/3 (Münster Westfalen, 1958).
Ritzer, Korbinian. *Le Mariage dans les églises chrétiennes du Ier au XIe siècle* (Paris, 1970).
———. *Formen, Riten und religiöses Brauchtum der Eheschliessung in den christlichen Kirchen des ersten Jahrtausends* (Münster-Westfalen, 1962).
Roman, J. *Manuel de sigillographie française* (Paris, 1912).
Romanelli, Pietro. *Santa Maria Antiqua* (Rome, 1964).
Ronig, F. "Der thronende Christus mit Kelch und Hostie zwischen Ecclesia und Synagoge," *Archiv für mittelrheinische Kirchengeschichte* XV (1963), 391–403.
Rosenwein, Barbara H. *Rhinoceros Bound: Cluny in the Tenth Century* (Philadelphia, 1982).
Russel, Jeffrey Burton. *Dissent and Order in the Middle Ages: The Search for Legitimate Authority* (New York, 1992).
———. *Dissent and Reform in the Early Middle Ages* (Los Angeles, 1965).
———. "À propos du synode d'Arras en 1025," *Revue d'histoire ecclésiastique* LVII (1962), 66–87.
Ruthven, Malise. *Torture: the Grand Conspiracy* (London, 1978).
Sabbe, Etienne. "Notes sur la réforme de Richard de Saint-Vannes dans les Pays Bas," *Revue belge de philologie et d'histoire* VII (1928), 551–570.
Sackur, Ernst. *Die Cluniacenser in ihrer kirchlichen und allgemeingeschichtlichen Wirksamkeit bis zur Mitte des elften Jahrhunderts*, 2 vols. (Halle A.S., 1892–1894).
———. "Richard, Abt von St. Vannes," Ph.D. Dissertation, Breslau, 1886.
St. Clair, Archer. "The Basilewsky pyxis: typology and topography in the exodus tradition," *Cahiers archéologiques* XXXII (1984), 15–30.

———. "A New Moses: Typological Iconography in the Moutier-Grandval Bible Illustrations of Exodus," *Gesta* XXVI (1987), 19–28.

Sanderson, Warren. *Monastic Reform in Lorraine and the Architecture of the Outer Crypt, 950–1100*, Transactions of the American Philosophical Society, NS, LXI, (Philadelphia, 1971).

Schapiro, Meyer. *Words and Pictures. On the literal and the symbolic in the illustration of a text* (The Hague, 1973).

Schieffer, Rudolf. "Bischofserhebungen im westfränkisch-französischen Bereich im späten 9. und im 10. Jahrhundert," in *Die früh- und hochmittelalterliche Bischofserhebung im europäischen Vergleich*, ed. Franz-Reiner Erkens (Cologne, 1998), 59–82.

Schieffer, Theodor. "Cluniazensische oder gorzische Reformbewegung," *Archiv für mittelrheinische Kirchengeschichte* IV (1952), 22–44.

———. "Ein deutscher Bischof des elfen Jahrhunderts: Gerhard I. von Cambrai (1012–1051)," *Deutsches Archiv für Erforschung des Mittelalters* I (1937), 323–260.

———. "In Memoriam Wilhelm Levison," *Rheinische Vierteljahrsblätter* XL (1976), 225–242.

Schiller, Gertrud. *Ikonographie der christlichen Kunst*, 5 vols. (Gütersloh, 1966–1991).

Schipke, Renate. *Die Maugérard-Handschriften der Forschungsbibliothek Gotha*, Veröffentlichungen der Forschungsbibliothek Gotha XV (Gotha, 1972).

Schramm, Percy Ernst. *Die deutschen Kaiser und Könige in Bilder ihrer Zeit; 751–1190*, ed. Florentine Mütherich (Munich, 1983).

———. "Die Kronen des frühen Mittelalters," *Herrschaftszeichen und Staatssymbolik*, MHG Schriften XIII/2 (Stuttgart, 1955), II, 377–417.

———. "Ordines-Studien II. Die Krönung bei den Westfranken und des Franzosen," *Archiv für Urkundenforschung* XV (1938), 3–55.

Schulten, Sigrid. "Die Buchmalerei im Kloster St. Vaast in Arras im 11 Jahrhundert," Ph.D. Dissertation, Ludwig-Maximilians-Universität, Munich, 1954.

———. "Die Buchmalerei im Kloster St. Vaast in Arras," *Münchner Jahrbuch der bildenden Kunst* VII (1956), 49–90.

Scriptoria medii aevi Helvetica. Denkmäler schweizerischer Schriebkunst des Mittelalters V. Schriebschulen der Diözese Konstanz. Stift Einsiedeln, ed. A. Bruckner (Geneva, 1943).

Sears, Elizabeth. "Louis the Pious as *Miles Christi*; the Dedicatory Image in Hrabanus Maurus's *De laudibus sanctae crucis*," *Charlemagne's Heir; New Perspectives on the Reign of Louis the Pious (814–840)*, eds. Peter Godman and Roger Collins (Oxford, 1990), 605–628.

Semmler, Josef. "Das Erbe der karolingischen Klosterreform im 10 Jahrhundert," in *Monastische Reformen im 9. und 10. Jahrhundert*, ed. Raymond Kottje and Helmut Maurer (Sigmaringen, 1989).

Senebier, Jean. *Catalogue raisonné des manuscrits* (Geneva, 1779).

Sproemberg, Heinrich. "Gérard Ier, évêque de Cambrai," *Biographie nationale*, Supplément VII/1 (Brussels, 1969), 286–299.

———. "Gerhard I, Bischof von Cambrai," in *Mittelalter und demokratische Geschichtsschreibung: Ausgewählte Abhandlungen*, ed. Manfred Unger (Berlin, 1971), 103–118.

Stafford, Pauline. *Queens, Concubines and Dowagers: The King's Wife in the Early Middle Ages* (Athens, Georgia, 1983).

Stähli, Marlis. *Die Handschriften im Domschatz zu Hildesheim*, Mittelalterliche Handschriften in Niedersachsen VII (Wiesbaden, 1984).

Stern, Henri. *Recueil général des mosaïques de la Gaule*, I. Province de Belgique, 1. Partie ouest (Paris, 1957).

Stevenson, Kenneth. *Nuptial Blessing. A Study of Christian Marriage Rites* (London, 1982).

Stock, Brian. *The Implications of Literacy: Written Language and Models of Interpretation in the Eleventh and Twelfth Centuries* (Princeton, 1983).

Stout, Ann M. "Jewelry as a Symbol of Status in the Roman Empire," in *The World*

of Roman Costume, eds. Judith Lynn Sebesta and Larissa Bonfante (Madison, 2001), 77–100.

Strayer, Joseph. "France: the Holy Land, the Chosen People, and the most Christian King," in *Medieval Statecraft and the Perspectives of History* (Princeton, 1971), 300–314.

Strubbe, Egied I. "La paix de Dieu dans le Nord de la France," *Recueil de la Société Jean Bodin* XIV, no. 1 (1961), 489–501.

Stuard, Susan Mosher. "Fashion's Captives: Medieval Women in French Historiography," in *Women in Medieval History & Historiography*, ed. Susan Mosher Stuard (Philadelphia, 1987), 59–80.

Swarzenski, Hans. "The Anhalt Morgan Gospels," *Art Bulletin* XXXI (1949), 77–83.

Tailliar, Eugène F. J. "Recherches pour servir à l'histoire de l'abbaye de St. Vaast d'Arras, jusqu'à la fin du XIIᵉ siècle," *Mémoires de l'académie des sciences, lettres et arts d'Arras* XXXI (1859), 171–501.

Temple, El˙zbieta. *Anglo-Saxon Manuscripts 900–1066* (London, 1976).

Testini, Pasquale. *Le catacombe e gli antichi cimiteri cristiani in Roma* (Bologna, 1966).

Tezmen-Siegel, Jutta. *Die Darstellung der septem artes liberales in der bildenen Kunst als rezeption der Lehrplangeschichte* (Munich, 1985).

Trésors de la Bibliothèque municipale de Reims (Reims, 1978).

Trierer Apokalypse: vollständige Faksimile-Ausgabe im Originalformat des Codex 31 der Staatsbibliothek Trier, Codices selecti phototypice impressi XLVIII (Graz, 1974–1975).

Ullmann, Walter. *The Carolingian Renaissance and the Idea of Kingship* (London, 1969).

van Dijk, Stephen Joseph Peter. "The Bible in Liturgical Use," in *The Cambridge History of the Bible* II: *The West from the Fathers to the Reformation*, ed. Geoffrey William Hugo Lampe (Cambridge, 1969), 220–251.

Van Meter, David C. "Apocalyptic Moments and Eschatological Rhetoric of Reform in the Early Eleventh Century: the Case of the Visionary of Saint Vaast," in *The Apocalyptic Year 1000: religious expectation and social change 950–1050* (Oxford, 2003), 311–325.

——. "Count Baldwin IV, Richard of Saint-Vanne and the Inception of Monastic Reform in Eleventh-Century Flanders," *Revue bénédictine* CVII (1997), 130–148.

——. "Eschatological Order and the Moral Arguments for Clerical Celibacy in Francia Around the Year 1000," in *Medieval Purity and Piety: essays on medieval clerical celibacy and religious reform*, ed. Michael Frassetto (New York, 1998), 149–175.

——. "The Peace of Amiens-Corbie and Gerard of Cambrai's Oration on the Three Functional Orders: the Date, the Context, the Rhetoric," *Revue belge de philologie et d'histoire* LXXIV (1996), 633–657.

Van Mingroot, Erik. "*Acta synodi Attrebatensis* (1025): problèmes de critique de provenance," in *Mélanges G. Fransen*, ed. Stephan Kuttner, 2 vols. (Rome, 1976), II, 203–229.

——. "Kritisch underzoek omtrent de datering van de *Gesta episcoporum Cameracensium*," *Revue belge de philologie et d'histoire* LIII (1975), 281–332.

Velmans, Tania. *Le tétraévangile de la Laurentienne, Florence, Laur. IV.23* (Paris, 1971).

Vinson, Martha. "Gregory Nazianzen's Homily 15 and the genesis of the Christian cult of the Maccabean martyrs," *Byzantion* LXIV (1994), 166–192.

Vogel, Cyrille. "La réforme liturgique sous Charlemagne," in *Karl der Grosse. Lebenswerk und Nachleben II: Das geistige Leben*, ed. Bernard Bischoff (Dusseldorf, 1965), 217–232.

——. "Les échanges liturgiques entre Rome et les pays francs jusqu'à l'epoque de Charlemagne," in *Le chiese nei regni dell'Europa occidentale e i loro rapporti con Roma sino all'800*, SSCISAM VII (Spoleto, 1960), 218–257.

——. "Les rites de la célébration du mariage: leur signification dans la formation du lien durant le haut moyen âge," in *Il matrimonio nella società altomedievale*, SSCISAM XXIV (Spoleto, 1977), 426–437.

Volbach, Wolfgang. *Elfenbeinarbeiten der Spätantike und frühen Mittelalters*, 2nd ed. (Mainz, 1952).

Vrudny, Kimberly. "Medieval Fascination with the Queen: Esther as the Queen of Heaven and Host of the Messianic Banquet," *Arts: the arts in religious and theological studies* XI (1999), 36–43.

Waddell, Chrysogonus. "The Song of Songs in the Stephen Harding Bible," *Liturgy* XVIII/2 (1984), 27–67.

Wagner, Anne. "Les manuscrits de la bibliothèque de Gorze. Remarques à propos du catalogue," in *Religion et culture autour de l'an mil. Royaume capétien et Lotharingie*. Actes du colloque Hugues Capet 987–1987. La France de l'an mil, Auxerre, 26 et 27 juin 1987– Metz, 11 et 12 septembre 1987 (Paris, 1990), 111–116.

Wanscher, Ole. *Sella Curulis: the Folding Stool, an Ancient Symbol of Dignity* (Copenhagen, 1980).

Weicherding-Goergen, Blanche. *Les manuscrits à peintures de la Bibliothèque nationale de Luxembourg* (Luxembourg, 1968).

Weiss, Daniel. *Art and Crusade in the Age of Saint Louis* (Cambridge, 1998).

——. "Biblical History and Medieval Historiography: Rationalizing Strategies in Crusader Art," *MLN* CVIII (1993), 710–737.

——. "The Three Solomon Portraits in the Arsenal Old Testament and the Construction of Meaning in Crusader Painting," *Arte medievale*, Ser. II, VI/2 (1992), 15–38.

Weithman, Paul. "Augustine's Political Philosophy," in *The Cambridge Companion to Augustine*, eds. Eleonore Stump and Norman Kretzmann (Cambridge, 2001), 234–252.

Weitzmann, Kurt. "Die Illustration der Septuaginta," *Münchner Jahrbuch der bildenden Kunst* III/IV (1952–1953), 96–120, translated in "The Illustration of the Septuagint," *Studies in Classical and Byzantine Manuscript Illumination*, ed. Herbert Kessler (Chicago, 1971), 45–75.

——. *Late Antique and Early Christian Book Illumination* (New York, 1977).

——. *The Miniatures of the Sacra Parallela, Parisinus graecus 923*, Studies in Manuscript Illumination VIII (Princeton, 1979).

Wemple, Suzanne Fonay. "Le pouvoirs des femmes en Europe occidentale au Xe siècle," in *La Femme au moyen âge*, eds. Michel Rouche and Jean Heuclin (Maugeuge, 1988), 343–351.

Williams, George H. *The Norman Anonymous of ca. 1100 A.D.; Towards the identification and evaluation of the so-called Anonymous of York* (Cambridge, MA, 1951).

Williams, John. "A Castilian Tradition of Bible Illustration: the Romanesque Bible from San Millán," *Journal of the Warburg and Courtauld Institutes* XXVIII (1965), 66–85.

——. *Early Spanish Manuscript Illumination* (New York, 1977).

Wilpert, Josef. *Die Malerei der Katakomben Roms* (Freiburg, 1903).

——. *Die römischen Mosaiken und Malereien der kirchlichen Bauten vom 4. bis 13. Jahrhundert*, 4 vols. (1917).

——. *I sarcofagi cristiani antichi* I (Rome, 1929).

Wolf, Gunther. "Königinnen-Krönungen des frühen Mittelalters bis zum Beginn des Investiturstreits," *Zeitschrift der Savigny-Stiftung für Rechtsgeschichte* CVII, Kanonistische Abteilung LXXVI (1990), 62–88.

Wollasch, Joachim. "Zur Datierung des *Liber tramitis* aus Farfa anhand von Personen und Personengruppen," *Person und Gemeinschaft im Mittelalter* (Sigmaringen, 1988), 237–255.

——. "Zur Verschriftlichung der klösterlichen Lebensgewohnheiten unter Abt Hugo von Cluny," *Frühmittelalterliche Studien* XXVII (1993), 317–324.

Woodruff, H. "The Illustrated Manuscripts of Prudentius," *Art Studies: Medieval, Renaissance and Modern* VII (1929), 33–79.

Wormald, Francis. "The Development of English Illumination in the Twelfth Century," *Journal of the British Archaeological Association*, 3rd ser. VIII (1943), 31–49, reprinted in *Collected Writings*, 2 vols., ed. J. J. G. Alexander, T. J. Brown and Joan Gibbs (London, 1988), II, 21–42.

———. "The Throne of Wisdom and St. Edward's Chair," *De Artibus Opuscula XL: Essays in Honour of Erwin Panofsky*, ed. Millard Meiss (1961), I, 532–539.

Zaluska, Yolanta. *Manuscrits enluminés de Dijon*, Corpus des manuscrits enluminés des collections publiques des départements (Paris, 1991).

GENERAL INDEX

Aachen Gospel Book: *See* Index of
   Manuscripts Cited *s.v.* Aachen,
   Cathedral Treasury
Aaron (biblical priest)   128, 188, 191,
   211, 213–14, 224
Abbo of Fleury (abbot)   153–54
Abigail (biblical)   239
Abishag (biblical)   196–200, 299, 310,
Abraham (biblical)   190, 208, 252
Acre, Scriptorium of Saint-Jean d'Acre
   5, 197
Acta synodi Atrebatensis   119, 121–29,
   154, 162, 165, 185, 217, 224, 226,
   242, 246, 295
Adalbero of Reims (archbishop)   85,
   89, 91, 100, 135–36, 145–46,
   148–49, 152–53, 166, 185, 192–93,
   199
Adalbero of Laon   118, 156, 194–5
Adelaide (fourth wife of Robert the
   Pious)   282
Admonitio generalis   48–49
Aelfric   70–72
Aethelwold of Winchester (bishop)   7,
   31, 172, 183
Ahasuerus (biblical king)   269–70,
   276–77, 279, 284–85, 299, 320
Alardus Bible: *See* Index of
   Manuscripts Cited *s.v.* Valenciennes,
   Bibliothèque municipale, MS 9–11
Alcuin   10, 47–49, 51–52, 67, 294,
   298
Alexander II (pope)   89
Amalarius of Metz   57, 59–60, 63
Angelom of Luxeuil   199
Angilramm of Metz (bishop)   63
Anhalt Morgan Gospels   20–21, 27,
   30
Anne of Kiev (second wife of Henry I
   of France)   233, 238–40, 242, 245,
   266, 281, 283
Antiochus IV (biblical king)   257–63,
   265, 321
Arduin of Ivrea (king of Italy)   180
Arianism   90, 292
Arn (bishop)   64

Arnulf of Orléans (bishop)   154
Arras, Abbey of Saint-Vaast   2–3, 7,
   13, 17, 18, 21–23, 30, 35, 38,
   165–6
Arras, Cathedral of Notre Dame
   117
Arras, Heresy of 1025   10, 111,
   121–125, 242, 295, 303
Arsenal Old Testament: *See* Index of
   Manuscripts Cited *s.v.* Paris,
   Bibliothèque de l'Arsenal MS 5211
Artaxerxes (biblical king)   34, 139–41,
   147, 168–69, 299, 319
Augustine of Hippo   120–21, 145–46
Audradus Modicus   4

Baldwin IV, Count (Flanders)   6, 20,
   94, 97, 157, 160, 164–65
Baldwin V, Count (Flanders)   155,
   157, 298
Bamberg Bible: *See* Index of
   Manuscripts Cited *s.v.* Bamberg,
   Staatsbibliothek Bibl. 1
Bathsheba (biblical)   197 n. 110,
   198
Beauvais   19
Benedict VIII (pope)   158
Benedict of Aniane   61
Benedict of Nursia   172–73
Benedictine Rule   57, 61, 85, 98,
   98 n. 192, 116–118, 172
Benedictional of Aethelwold   7, 131,
   141
Bernard of Clairvaux   255
Bernard of Cluny   70
Beraldus of Soissons (bishop)   159
Berthe of Burgundy (second wife of
   Robert the Pious)   243, 282
Biasca Bible: *See* Index of Manuscripts
   Cited *s.v.* Milan, Bibliotheca
   Ambrosiana MS E.53 inf.
Bible
   Arrangement of   51–52, 62, 73–80,
      84–87, 209
   "Atlantic" (Italian)   67–68, 73,
      88–89

INDEX OF MANUSCRIPTS CITED

REFERENCES TO BOOKS OF THE BIBLE

PLATES

I. Arras BM MS 559 (435), vol. I, fol. 2, Saint-Vaast Bible, Frater Ambrosius

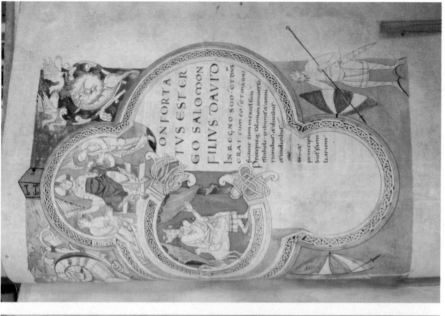

III. Arras BM MS 559 (435), vol. I, fol. 170, Saint-Vaast
Bible, II Chronicles

II. Arras BM MS 559 (435), vol. I, fol. 144v, Saint-Vaast
Bible, III Kings

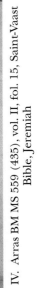

V. Arras BM MS 559 (435), vol. II, fol. 141v, Saint-Vaast
Bible, Song of Solomon

IV. Arras BM MS 559 (435), vol. II, fol. 15, Saint-Vaast
Bible, Jeremiah

VI. Arras BM MS 559 (435), vol. II, fol. 144, Saint-Vaast Bible, Wisdom

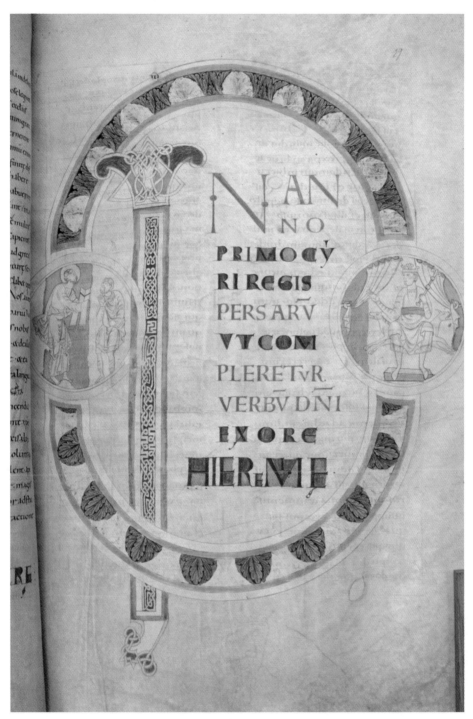

VII. Arras BM MS 559 (435), vol. III, fol. 29, Saint-Vaast Bible, Ezra

CAP·I·

INCIPIT
LIBER
HESTER:

P

uN DIE BUS
ASSUERI

qui regnauit Abindia usq;
æthiopiam super centum ui
ginti septem puintas; quando
sedit insolio regnisui· susa ciui
tas regni ei exordiu fuit· Tertio
igit anno impn sui fecit grande
coniuiu cunctis princib; & pu
eris suis fortissimis psaru & me
doru inclytis· & pfectis; puin
tiaru coris se· ut ostende gloriu
tis gloe regnisui ac magnitu
dine atq; iactantiu potentie
suze multo tepore centu uide
lice & octoginta diebus

VIII. Arras BM MS 559 (435), vol. III, fol. 44, Saint-Vaast Bible, Esther

IX. Arras BM MS 559 (435), vol. III, fol. 81v, Saint-Vaast Bible, Passion of the Maccabees

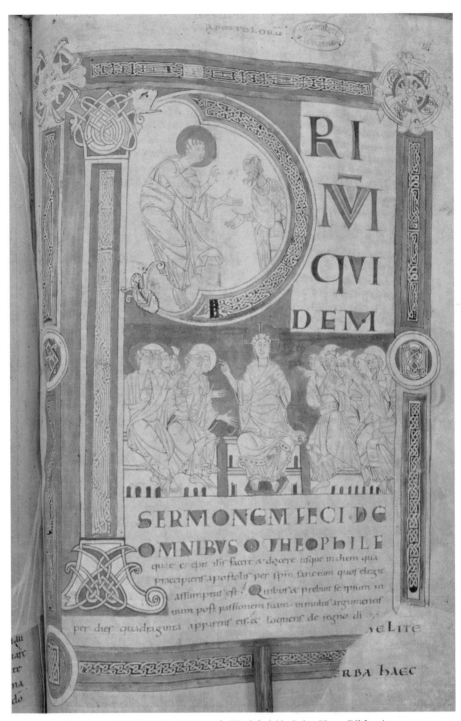

X. Arras BM MS 559 (435), vol. III, fol. 141, Saint-Vaast Bible, Acts

FIGURES

Fig. 1. Arras BM MS 559 (435), vol. I, fol. 2, Saint-Vaast Bible, Frater Ambrosius.

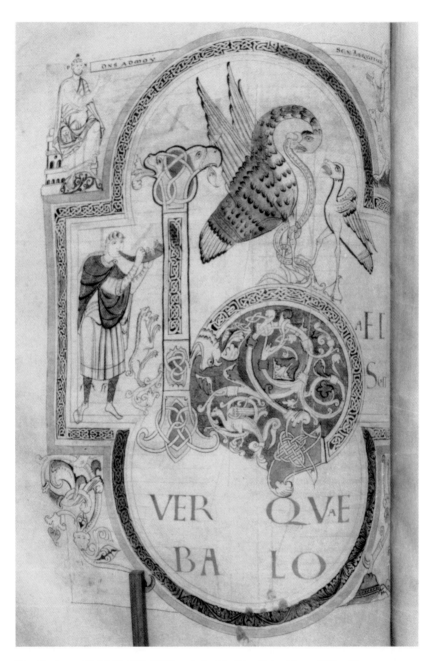

Fig. 2. Arras BM MS 559 (435), vol. I, fol. 53v, Saint-Vaast Bible, Deuteronomy.

Fig. 3. Arras BM MS 559 (435), vol. I, fol. 54, Saint-Vaast Bible, Deuteronomy.

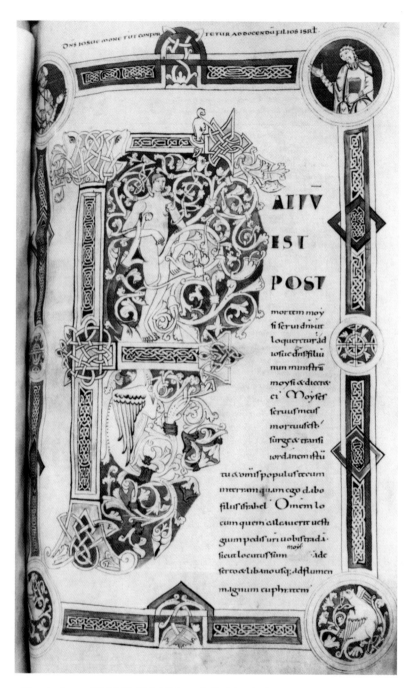

Fig. 4. Arras, BM MS 559 (435), vol. I, fol. 72, Saint-Vaast Bible, Joshua.

Fig. 5. Arras BM MS 559 (435), vol. I, fol. 128v, Saint-Vaast Bible, III Kings.

Fig. 6. Arras BM MS 559 (435), vol. I, fol. 144v, Saint-Vaast Bible, IV Kings.

ONFORTA
TVS EST ER
GO SALOMON
FILIVS DAVID
IN REGNO SUO·ET DNS
ERAT CUM EO·ET MAGNI
ficauit eum in excelsum·
Precepitq; salomon uniuerso
israheli· tribunis et centu
rionibus· et ducibus·
et iudicibus·

et
principi
bus fami
liarum·

Fig. 7. Arras BM MS 559 (435), vol. I, fol. 170, Saint-Vaast Bible, II Chronicles.

Fig. 8. Arras BM MS 559 (435), vol. II, fol. 15, Saint-Vaast Bible, Jeremiah.

Fig. 9. Arras BM MS 559 (435), vol. II, fol. 42v, Saint-Vaast Bible, Ezekiel.

Fig. 10. Arras BM MS 559 (435), vol. II, fol. 106v, Saint-Vaast Bible, Nahum.

Fig. 11. Arras BM MS 559 (435), vol. II, fol. 108, Saint-Vaast Bible, Habakkuk.

Fig. 12. Arras BM MS 559 (435), vol. II, fol. 141v, Saint-Vaast Bible,
Song of Solomon.

Fig. 13. Arras BM MS 559 (435), vol. II, fol. 144, Saint-Vaast Bible, Wisdom.

Fig. 14. Arras BM MS 559 (435), vol. III, fol. 1, Saint-Vaast Bible, Ecclesiasticus.

Fig. 15. Arras BM MS 559 (435), vol. III, fol. 29, Saint-Vaast Bible, Ezra.

Fig. 16. Arras BM MS 559 (435), vol. III, fol. 44, Saint-Vaast Bible, Esther.

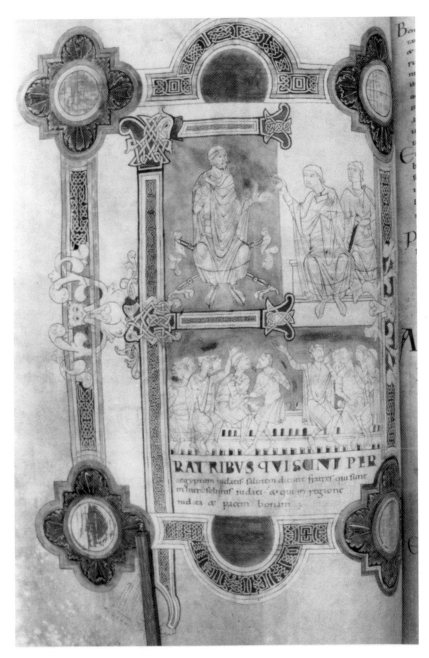

Fig. 17. Arras BM MS 559 (435), vol. III, fol. 70v, Saint-Vaast Bible, II Maccabees.

Fig. 18. Arras BM MS 559 (435), vol. III, fol. 81v, Saint-Vaast Bible,
Passion of the Maccabees.

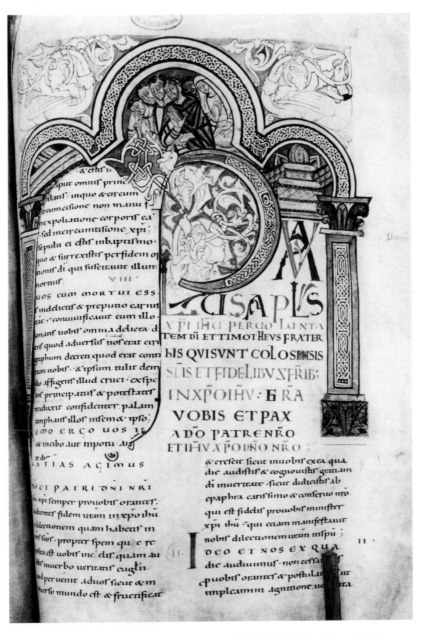

Fig. 19. Arras BM MS 559 (435), vol. III, fol. 114, Saint-Vaast Bible,
Paul's Epistle to the Colossians.

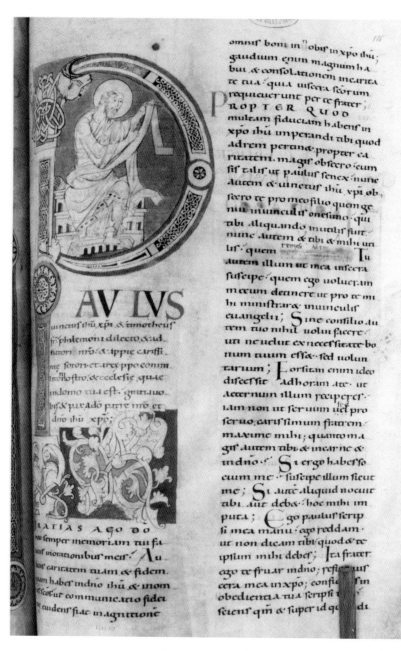

Fig. 20. Arras BM MS 559 (435), vol. III, fol. 126, Saint-Vaast Bible,
Paul's Epistle to Philemon.

Fig. 21. Arras BM MS 559 (435), vol. III, fol. 133v, Saint-Vaast Bible, I Peter.

Fig. 22. Arras BM MS 559 (435), vol. III, fol. 135v, Saint-Vaast Bible, II Peter.

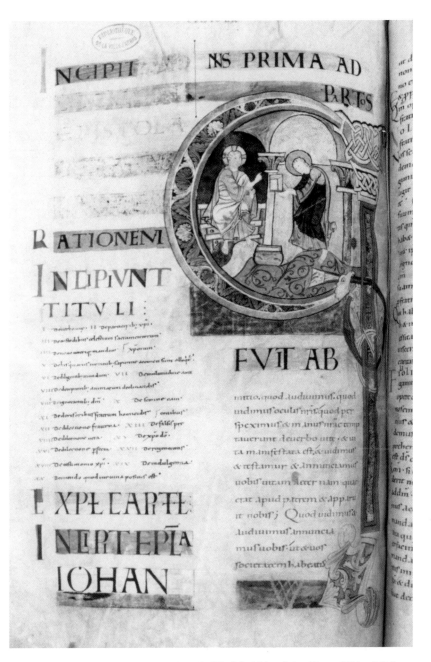

INCIPIT ⟨EPISTOLA IOHANNI⟩S PRIMA AD PARTOS

EDISTOLA

RATIONEM

INCIPIVNT

TITVLI :

FVIT AB

...ratio, quod audiuimus. quod
uidimus oculis nris. quod per
speximus. & manus nrae temp
tauerunt de uerbo uite. & ui
ta manifestata est. & uidimus
& testamur. & annunciamus
uobis uitam aeter nam. quae
erat apud patrem & appar
it nobis j Quod uidimus
audiuimus. annuncia
mus uobis. ut & uos
societatem habeatis

EXPL CARTL

INERT EPLA

IOHAN

Fig. 23. Arras BM MS 559 (435), vol. III, fol. 136v, Saint-Vaast Bible, I John.

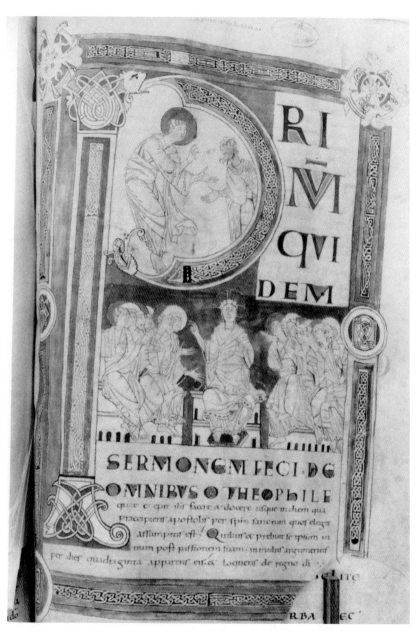

Fig. 24. Arras BM MS 559 (435), vol. III, fol. 141, Saint-Vaast Bible, Acts.

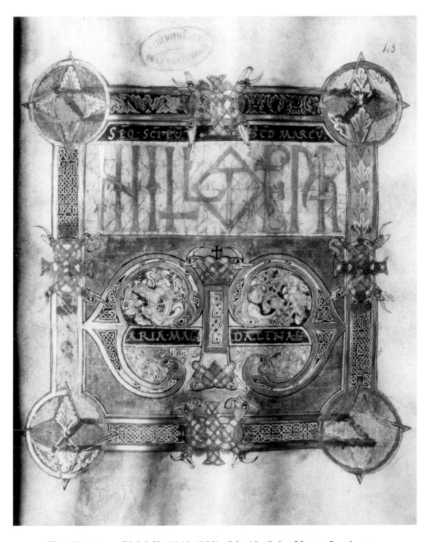

Fig. 25. Arras BM MS 1045 (233), fol. 43, Saint-Vaast, Lectionary.

Fig. 26. Boulogne BM MS 9, fol. 1, Saint-Vaast, Gospels.

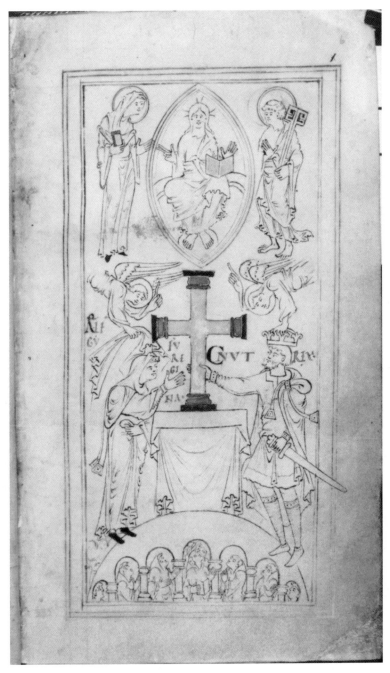

Fig. 27. London BL Stowe MS 944, fol. 6, Winchester, New Minster *Liber Vitae*.

Fig. 28. Paris BnF MS lat. 943, fol. 5b, Sherborne Pontifical.

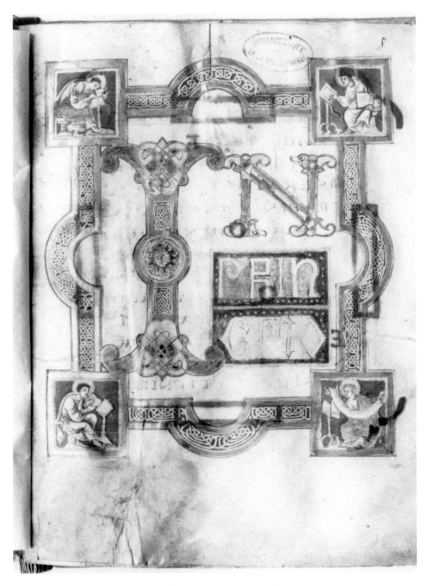

Fig. 29. Arras BM MS 1045 (233), fol. 8, Saint-Vaast, Lectionary.

Fig. 30. Boulogne BM MS 11, fol. 56, Saint-Bertin, Gospels.

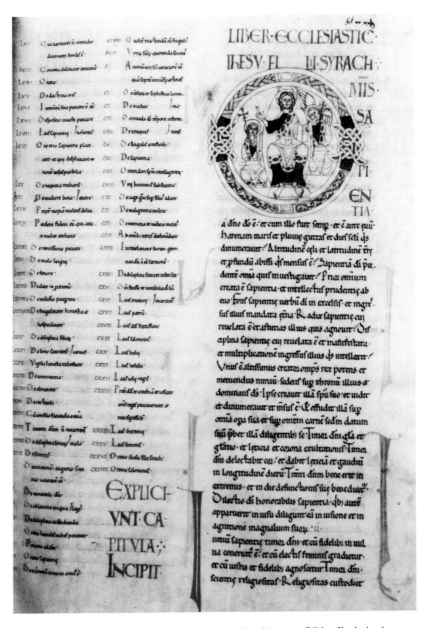

Fig. 31. Douai BM MS 1, fol. CCXXV, Marchiennes, Bible, Ecclesiasticus.

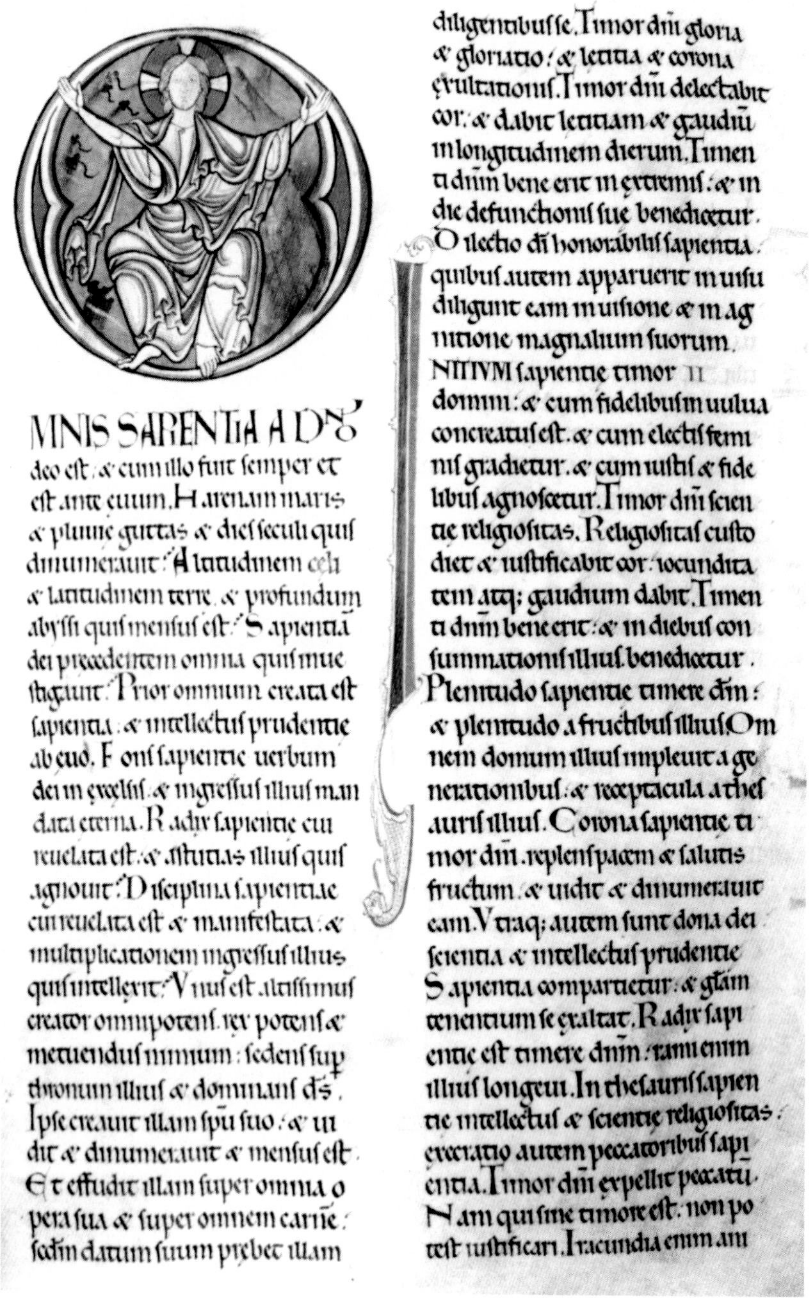

OMNIS SAPIENTIA A DNO
deo est. & cum illo fuit semper et
est ante euum. Harenam maris
& pluuie guttas & dies seculi quis
dinumerauit? Altitudinem celi
& latitudinem terre. & profundum
abyssi quis mensus est? Sapientia
dei precedentem omnia quis inue
stigauit? Prior omnium creata est
sapientia. & intellectus prudentie
ab euo. Fons sapientie uerbum
dei in excelsis. & ingressus illius man
data eterna. Radix sapientie cui
reuelata est. & astutias illius quis
agnouit? Disciplina sapientiae
cui reuelata est & manifestata. &
multiplicationem ingressus illius
quis intellexit? Unus est altissimus
creator omnipotens. rex potens &
metuendus nimium. sedens sup
thronum illius & dominans ds.
Ipse creauit illam spu sco. & ui
dit & dinumerauit & mensus est.
Et effudit illam super omnia o
pera sua & super omnem carnē.
secdm datum suum prebet illam
diligentibus se. Timor dni gloria
& gloriatio. & letitia & corona
exultationis. Timor dni delectabit
cor. & dabit letitiam & gaudiū
in longitudinem dierum. Timen
ti dnm bene erit in extremis. & in
die defunctionis sue benedicetur.
Dilectio di honorabilis sapientia.
quibus autem apparuerit in uisu
diligunt eam in uisione & in ag
nitione magnalium suorum.
INITIUM sapientie timor II
domini. & cum fidelibus in uulua
concreatus est. & cum electis femi
nis gradietur. & cum iustis & fide
libus agnoscetur. Timor dni scien
tie religiositas. Religiositas custo
diet & iustificabit cor. iocundita
tem atq; gaudium dabit. Timen
ti dnm bene erit. & in diebus con
summationis illius. benedicetur.
Plenitudo sapientie timere dnm.
& plenitudo a fructibus illius. Om
nem domum illius implebit a ge
nerationibus. & receptacula a thes
auris illius. Corona sapientie ti
mor dni. replens pacem & salutis
fructum. & uidit & dinumerauit
eam. Utraq; autem sunt dona dei
scientia & intellectus prudentie
Sapientia compartietur. & glam
tenentium se exaltat. Radix sapi
entie est timere dnm. rami enim
illius longeui. In thesauris sapien
tie intellectus & scientie religiositas.
execratio autem peccatoribus sapi
entia. Timor dni expellit peccatū.
Nam qui sine timore est. non po
test iustificari. Iracundia enim ani

Fig. 32. Douai BM MS 3a, fol. 50v, Marchiennes, Bible, Ecclesiasticus.

Fig. 33. Boulogne BM MS 107, fol. 6v, Saint-Bertin, *Vitae Sanctorum*, Dedication.

Fig. 34. Boulogne BM MS 107, fol. 7, Saint-Bertin, *Vitae Sanctorum*, Dedication.

Fig. 35. Arras BM MS 616 (548), fol. 1v, Saint-Vaast, Augustine,
Confessiones, Dedication.

Fig. 36. Arras BM MS 732 (684), fol. 2v, Saint-Vaast, Compilation,
Assumption of the Virgin.

Fig. 37. Paris BnF MS lat. 1, fol. 215v, Tours, First Bible of Charles the Bald,
Psalter.

Fig. 38. Paris BnF MS lat. 1, fol. 329v, Tours, First Bible of Charles the Bald, Maiestas Domini.

Fig. 39. Paris BnF MS lat. 1, fol. 423, Tours, First Bible of Charles the Bald,
Dedication.

Fig. 40. Aachen, Cathedral Treasury, fol. 16, Gospel Book, Otto III.

Fig. 41. Ivrea, Biblioteca Capitolare MS LXXXVI, fol. 2, Warmund
Sacramentary, Consecration of a King.

Fig. 42. Paris, Bibliothèque de l'Arsenal 5211, fol. 183v, Bible, Kings III.

Fig. 43. London BL MS Add. 10546, fol. 25v, Tours, Moutier-Grandval Bible,
Exodus.

Fig. 44. Paris BnF MS lat. 1, fol. 27v, First Bible of Charles the Bald, Exodus.

Fig. 45. Rome, San Paolo fuori le mura, fol. 1, San Paolo Bible, Dedication.

Fig. 46. Rome BAV cod. Vat. Reg. gr. 1, fol. 450v, Bible of Leo Sacellarios,
IV Maccabees.